LEARNING, KEEPING AND USING LANGUAGE I

LEARNING
KEEPING
AND
USING
LANGUAGE

VOLUME I

SELECTED PAPERS FROM THE 8TH WORLD CONGRESS
OF APPLIED LINGUISTICS, SYDNEY, 16-21 AUGUST 1987.

EDITED BY
M.A.K. HALLIDAY
JOHN GIBBONS
HOWARD NICHOLAS

JOHN BENJAMINS PUBLISHING COMPANY
AMSTERDAM/PHILADELPHIA 1990

Library of Congress Cataloging in Publication Data

International Congress of Applied Linguistics (8th : 1987 : Sydney, N.S.W.)
Learning, keeping, and using language : selected papers from the Eight World Congress
of Applied Linguistics, Sydney, 16-21 August 1987 / edited by M.A.K. Halliday, John
Gibbons, and Howard Nicholas.
    p.   cm.
Includes bibliographical references.
1. Applied linguistics -- Congresses. I. Halliday, M.A.K. (Michael Alexander
Kirkwood), 1925-   . II. Gibbons, John, 1946-   . III. Nicholas, Howard. IV. Title.
P129.I5   1987
418 -- dc20   90-335
                                                                                        CIP
ISBN 1-55619-100-6 (set)/1-55619-104-9 (vol.I)/1-55619-105-7 (vol. II) (U.S.; alk. paper)
ISBN 90 272 2071 9 (set)/90 272 2073 5 (vol.I)/90 272 2074 3 (vol. II) (Eur.; alk. paper)

Contents

Contents volume II

PART III: USING LANGUAGE

Contributors

DIANA E. ADAMS-SMITH
P.O. Box 87 Waitara
Taranaki
New Zealand

JILL ANDERSON
Department of French
University of Melbourne
Parkville Vic 3052
Australia

PETER AUER
FG Sprachwissenschaft
University of Konstanz
P.O. Box 5560
D 7750 Konstanz 1
Federal Republic of Germany

DAVID BENDOR-SAMUEL
Summer Institute of Linguistics
7500 W. Camp
Wisdom Rd
Dallas TX 75236
U.S.A.

CAMILLA BETTONI
Department of Italian
University of Sydney
Sydney NSW 2006
Australia

HELGA BISTER
Department of Germanic Languages
University of North Carolina
438 Dey Hall 014 A
Chapel Hill NC 27514
U.S.A.

JEAN-GUY BLAIS
Department of French
Boul de Forges
CP 500
Trois-Rivières QC
Canada G9A 5H7

MARIA BOLANDER
Department of Scandinavian Languages
University of Stockholm
S10691 Stockholm
Sweden

HELEN BORLAND
School of Humanities
Western Institute
McKechnie St
P.O. Box 315
St Albans Vic 3021
Australia

TOVE BULL
School of Languages and Literature
University of Tromsø
Breivika
N 9000 Tromsø
Norway

CHRISTOPHER N. CANDLIN
School of English and Linguistics
Macquarie University
NSW 2109
Australia

RONALD A. CARTER
Department of English Studies
University of Nottingham
University Park
Nottingham NG7 2RD
U.K.

ANNA CILIBERTI
Dipartimento di Economia
Università degli Studi
Via Verdi 26
I 38100 Trento
Italy

CARMEL CLORAN
School of English and Linguistics
Macquarie University
NSW 2109
Australia

MICHAEL CLYNE
Department of Linguistics
Monash University
Clayton Vic 3168
Australia

JUDITH COMEAU
Department of Psychology
University of Montreal
C.P. 6128, Succ. A
Montreal QC
Canada H3C 3J7

ELIZABETH COUPER-KÜHLEN
FG Sprachwissenschaft
University of Konstanz
P.O. Box 5560
D 7750 Konstanz
Federal Rupublic of Germany

SUSANNE DÖPKE
Department of Linguistics
& Language Studies
University of Melbourne
Parkville Vic 3051
Australia

ALDO DI LUZIO
FG Sprachwissenschaft
University of Konstanz
P.O. Box 5560
D 7750 Konstanz 1
Federal Republic of Germany

ROBERT DI PIETRO
Department of Linguistics
University of Delaware
Newark, DE 19716
U.S.A.

MARIETTA ELLIOTT
54 Michael St.
North Fitzroy Vic 3068
Australia

LEOPOLD K. ENGELS
Language Institute
KU Leuven
Vesaliusstraat 21
B 3000 Leuven
Belgium

LOIS FOSTER
School of Education
La Trobe University
Bundoora Vic 3083
Australia

PETER H. FRIES
English Department
Central Michigan University
Mount Pleasant MI 48859
U.S.A.

GILLES GAGNÉ
2 Elmview
Dollard-des-Ormeaux QUE
Canada H8A 2M9

JUNE GASSIN
Horwood Language Centre
University of Melbourne
Parkville Vic 3052
Australia

JOHN GIBBONS (Editor)
Department of Linguistics
University of Sydney
NSW 2006
Australia

MICHAËL GOETHALS
Applied Linguistics
KU Leuven
Blijde-Inkomststraat 21
B 3000 Leuven
Belgium

ANDREW GONZALEZ
De La Salle University
2401 Taft Avenue
Manila
Philippines

HARRY L. GRADMAN
Department of Linguistics
Indiana University
Bloomington IN 47405
U.S.A.

BRITT-LOUISE GUNNARSSON
FUMS, Department of Scandinavian
   Languages
Uppsala University
Box 1834
S 75148 Uppsala
Sweden

M.A.K. HALLIDAY (*Editor*)
5 Laing Avenue
Killara NSW 2071
Australia

JENNIFER HAMMOND
National Centre for English Language
   Teaching & Research
Macquarie University
NSW 2109
Australia

RUQAIYA HASAN
School of English & Linguistics
Macquarie University
NSW 2109
Australia

HELEN JENKINS
Department of Linguistics
La Trobe University
Bundoora Vic 3083
Australia

BRAJ B. KACHRU
Department of Linguistics
University of Illinois
707 S. Mathews Avenue
Urbana IL 61801
U.S.A.

ANNA KWAN-TERRY
English Department
National University of Singapore
Kent Ridge
Singapore 0511
Singapore

THEO LEENDERS
Programmer
Muizendijkstraat 67
B 3690 Bree
Belgium

JAY L. LEMKE
Brooklyn College
School of Education
City University of New York
Brooklyn NY 11210
U.S.A.

PHILIP A. LUELSDORFF
Institut für Anglistik
D 8400 Regensburg 1
Federal Republic of Germany

JEAN-FRANÇOIS MAIRE
Ecole de Français Moderne
University of Lausanne
Faculty of Humanities 2
CH 1015 Lausanne
Switzerland

WILLIAM B. MCGREGOR
School of Humanities
Bond University
Gold Coast Qld 4229
Australia

GORDON B. MCKELLAR
Matrix Heuristics
147 Yale Avenue
Claremont CA 91711
U.S.A.

HELEN MOORE
School of Education
La Trobe University
Bundoora Vic 3083
Australia

DENISE E. MURRAY
Linguistics Program
San Jose State University
San Jose CA 95192
U.S.A.

HOWARD R. NICHOLAS (*Editor*)
School of Education
La Trobe University
Bundoora Vic 3083
Australia

JANE OLDENBURG
School of English and Linguistics
Macquarie University
NSW 2109
Australia

LUC OSTIGUY
Department of French
Boul de Forges
CP 500
Trois-Rivières QC
Canada G9A 5H7

CHRISTINE C. PAPPAS
College of Education
University of Illinois
P.O. Box 4348 M/C 147
Chicago IL 60680
U.S.A.

JOHN PLATT †

ANNARITA PUGLIELLI
Viale Trastevere 231
I 00153 Roma
Italy

MARTA RADO
School of Education
La Trobe University
Bundoora Vic 3083
Australia

WILGA M. RIVERS
Department of French
Harvard University
Cambridge MA 02138
U.S.A.

GEORGE SAUNDERS
School of Education &
    Language Studies
University of Western Sydney
    (Mac Arthur)
P.O. Box 555
Campbelltown NSW 2560
Australia

ALMA SIMOUNET DE GÉIGEL
Box 3039
Christiansted, St. Croix
U.S. Virgin Islands 00820
U.S.A.

ANNA SHNUKAL
Department of English
University of Queensland
St Lucia Qld 4067
Australia

JEFF SIEGEL
Linguistics Department
University of New England
Armidale NSW 2351
Australia

MARC SPOELDERS
Pedagogical Laboratory
State University
Henri Dunantlaan 1
B 9000 Gent
Belgium

PETER VAN STAPELE
Department of Literature
State University Leiden
2311 BD Leiden
The Netherlands

MARIE-CLAUDE THERRIEN
Department of Psychology
University of Montreal
C.P. 6128, Succ. A
Montreal QC
Canada H3C 3J7

LEE THOMAS
Office of Internationl Programs
   & Services
130 Mackay Science Building
University of Nevada-Reno
Reno, NV 89557
U.S.A.

MAKHAN LAL TICKOO
RELC
30 Orange Grove Rd
Singapore 1025
Singapore

SONJA TIRKKONEN-CONDIT
Savonlinna School of Translation Studies
University of Joensuu
P.O. Box 48
SF 57101 Savonlinna
Finland

G. RICHARD TUCKER
Center for Applied Linguistics
118 22nd Street N.W.
Washington DC 20037
U.S.A.

EIJA VENTOLA
Language Centre
University of Helsinki
Fabianinkatu 26
SF 00100 Helsinki
Finland

ROLAND W. WALKER
Summer Institute of Linguistics
7500 W. Camp Wisdom Road
Dallas TX 75236
U.S.A.

CATHERINE WALLACE
Ealing College of Higher Education
Grove House
1 The Grove, Ealing
London W5 5DX
U.K.

LYDIA WHITE
Department of Linguistics
McGill University
1001 Sherbrooke St W
Montreal QUE
Canada H3A 1G5

ROLAND WILLEMYNS
Department of Dutch Linguistics
Free University
Pleinlaan 2
B 1050 Brussels
Belgium

PHILIP YDE
Pedagogical Laboratory
State University
Henri Dunantlaan 1
B 9000 Gent
Belgium

Foreword

The Eighth World Congress of Applied Linguistics was held in Sydney, Australia, at Sydney University, on 16-21 August 1987. The number of those attending was just over 800 — 801, to be exact. It was the first time the World Congress had been held outside the circuit of Europe and North America; and we in the Applied Linguistics Association of Australia, as the host organization, were highly gratified both by the number of people participating and by the richness and variety of the papers presented.

Papers from the Congress are appearing in various publications. First, there are the special publications arising from the Symposia, most of which were organized by AILA Scientific Commissions. Secondly, there are the special issues of publications of the Applied Linguistics Association of Australia: (i) Occasional Paper no. 10, *Asian-Pacific Papers*, edited by Brian McCarthy, which contains sixteen papers of particular interest to readers in the Asian-Pacific region; and (ii) the *Australian Review of Applied Linguistics*, Vol. 11 no. 1, which is devoted entirely to contributions from the Congress. And thirdly, there is the present collection.

In selecting the papers to be included here, we have not tried to cover all the topics dealt with in the section meetings (parallel sessions) of the Congress. In the event, there were 23 such sections; it may be of interest to list them here:

1	First language development and child language
2	Language education: mother tongue
3-A	Second language development: comprehension; aspects of interlanguage
3-B	Second language development: pragmatics/semantics; grammar/lexis; reading and writing
3-C	Second language development: orthography, phonology; learning conditions
4-A	Language education, second language: contexts and curriculum

As the numbering shows, our original list had had twenty topics; we then modified these in response to the distribution of the papers that were offered. In preparing the present collection, we decided to concentrate on those topics which had proved to be the dominant motifs of the Congress. These had emerged as three broad areas of concern: (1) the learning and teaching of languages, both the mother tongue and second or foreign languages; (2) language as institution, including ethnography, language maintenance and loss, and language policy and planning; (3) the nature and analysis of text, including register variation and the social construction of discourse. Our title *Learning, Keeping, and Using Language* is meant to suggest these three general motifs.

Within these areas, we have tried to select papers that collectively would give a sense of present achievements and future directions. We wanted to show what issues were currently on the agenda and where new insights and new applications were beginning to appear. But we have also tried, as far as possible, to remain at a fairly non-technical level. In other words, our aim has been not so much to make a specialist contribution to the field of applied linguistics — the breadth of topics covered would in any case militate against this — as to present and open up the field to those who are not specialists, so that they can see what goes on under the heading of applied linguistics and discover what is in it for them. Obviously we hope that some readers, at least, will be lured — and challenged — to explore these issues further. For those who are already active in applied linguistic work, including those who contributed by their presence at the Congress, we hope that there will be enough of interest both in their own specialist domain and in other domains where they might not, perhaps, regularly browse.

We had originally intended this to be a bilingual edition. But since only two of the papers were submitted to us in French, we felt that the result would appear rather unbalanced; so the two papers in question have been translated and appear here in English. We are grateful to the authors for allowing us to publish their contributions in English and for vetting and improving the translations before they appeared.

In every other respect we have tried to interfere as little as possible with the authors' manuscripts as received. In just a few instances we asked for the text to be shortened; but the publishers have been generous with space, and where we have reduced the length of a contribution this has been more from the point of view of the overall balance of the content than because we wanted to impose a uniform limit on length. Similarly we have not attempted to homogenize the style of writing or the manner of presentation, believing that the value and interest of a publication of this kind is enhanced, rather than reduced, by the variety of its textual practices.

The Congress opened with Richard Tucker's overview of applied linguistics, and this forms a natural introduction to the book. The four papers presented to plenary sessions of the Congress, by Wilga Rivers, Michael Clyne, Braj Kachru and Christopher Candlin, appear at the major boundaries: at the beginning, at the end, and between the different parts. These plenary addresses offer a wide-angle perspective, and hence allow the reader to step back from the more specific topics of the section papers and survey the field with a broader sweep of vision. Following these we have inserted a short editorial introduction to each Part, in which we refer to the various contributions separately and give a quick summary of the topics covered. At the end is a very brief 'Afterword' in which we raise certain questions for applied linguistics in the future.

Our thanks to Ross Steele, Terry Threadgold and Robert Eagleson, all of A.L.A.A., for the help they have given us, in many different ways, in preparing these two volumes and steering them through. To Judy Faulkner for her not merely careful but also extremely thoughtful work in producing the entire manuscript on disk. And to Yola de Lusenet, of Benjamins, for her moral support, practical guidance, and unfailingly positive approach.

M.A.K. Halliday
John Gibbons
Howard Nicholas

An Overview of Applied Linguistics

G. Richard Tucker

Work in the field of applied linguistics during the past three years has been exciting, socially rewarding, and expanding. It is obviously not possible in a short introduction to provide a comprehensive or even adequate summary of the state of our art; rather, let me identify four exemplary foci which for me characterize important strands of our work. These strands comprise (1) activities in the area of innovative language education; (2) work within the area of language planning or language (education) policy; (3) the utilization of newer technologies in the service of language teaching; and (4) the expanding roles of the linguist in nontraditional settings. Let me say a few words about each of these four areas.

Innovative Language Education

In many parts of the world, renewed attention has been directed toward providing the soundest possible education for language minority and for language majority individuals. Increasingly, applied linguists concerned about language pedagogy have been working with their counterparts who are subject-matter specialists to develop innovative programs which seek to integrate, to the fullest degree possible, the teaching of language and content. We find such programs now in industrialized and in non-industrialized countries; we find such programs being implemented to improve the teaching of second or foreign languages for language majority individuals; and we find such programs to enhance the teaching of the national, or official language where it is not spoken as the mother tongue by language minority youngsters. In some places, the logical extension of the integration of language and content instruction involves the development and implementation of two-way bilingual (or of so-called interlocking) programs. From my perspective, the work of Michael Clyne (1986) has been extremely important. Likewise Bernard Mohan (1986) and Gina Cantoni-Harvey (1987) have provided valuable summaries from both theoretical and practical perspectives of this work. It is likely that researchers and practitioners will continue to explore diverse facets of the integration of language and content instruction over the next several years. I have been particularly struck by work in Kenya (Cleghorn, Merritt and Abagi 1987) — so obviously influenced by that of M.A.K. Halliday which examines the acquisition of the special science and mathematics register of English, as well of course as by work here in Sydney by Lloyd Dawe (1984) on the development of cognitive academic mathematics proficiency by bilingual youngsters. This "movement" has profound implications for syllabus design, materials production, teacher preparation, student grouping, and ultimately, of course, for student achievement.

Language (Education) Policy

This topic has received renewed attention during the past three years. I believe that the single most important recent study in this domain has been the summative evaluation of bilingual education policy conducted by the Linguistic Society of the Philippines (1986). In 1974, the Philippines introduced a bilingual policy which required the use of Pilipino and English to teach specific subjects in elementary and secondary schools throughout the country. This policy — intended to encourage the diffusion of Pilipino (the national language) and to ensure the development of proficiency in English (the language of primary access to science and technology) — was implemented after discussion and input from the Filipino language education community.

In 1985 and 1986 the Linguistic Society of the Philippines conducted an evaluation of diverse aspects of policy implementation. Their evaluation involved an empirical study of the English and Pilipino proficiency of representative students and teachers from grades four, six and ten, together with an assessment of their science, mathematics, and social studies achievement. Additionally, the evaluation examined the contributions of scholarly societies to the implementation of the bilingual policy and the awareness and attitudes of representatives from government and non-government organizations toward the policy. This study culminated in a symposium involving language educators and Filipino government decision makers to study, discuss and formulate recommendations for policy modifications. This activity followed more than 20 years of careful attention to language education policy matters by Filipino educators and hence — I believe — serves as the basis for an interesting case study. (See Gonzalez' paper in the present volume.)

In the United States, attempts by a number of individuals and groups to sponsor an amendment to the Constitution to declare English to be the official language of the United States has prompted vigorous debate. After a somewhat languid beginning, the language education community has mobilized its resources and is now actively involved in information dissemination and in discussion intended to inform U.S. residents about the diverse roles of language in public life, and — hopefully — to encourage widespread acceptance not for a policy of English Only, but rather for a policy of English Plus — namely, active societal encouragement of what Wallace Lambert (1986) has described as "additive bilingualism."

Newer Technologies and Language Teaching

In the last few years, we have witnessed continual developments in the area of computer-assisted language instruction and computerized-adaptive testing (Gillespie 1986). The emergence of a strong scientific commission on this topic at AILA marks this important development. The potential power of computer-assisted instruction utilizing interactive videodisc has only begun to be realized. From my perspective, work in the earlier part of this decade was characterized by groups who comprised two solitudes — those trained in computer technology who knew little about language, language learning and language teaching; and experienced applied linguists who had little knowledge of the technologies. Gradually, emerging partnerships are developing and, of course, as the newer technologies become less expensive linguists are gaining increasing familiarity and first-hand experience with the newer technologies. It seems likely that work in this area will have a major impact on the nature of language inquiry, the shaping of research strategies to examine (second) language acquisition, the delivery of instruction, the monitoring of proficiency development, the nature of programs to prevent language attrition or loss over time, etc. The implications should be particularly profound for· the teaching of the so-called 'less commonly taught languages' where the low volume of demand typically does not permit the hiring of teachers, the development of materials, the development of testing instruments, etc.

Applied Linguists in Non-Traditional Settings

As the most recent issue of the *Annual Review of Applied Linguistics* (Kaplan 1987) demonstrates, increasingly applied linguists have come to play an important and prominent role in the fields of business, law, the media and the sciences. It is evident from the bibliographies included in ARAL VII that the interest has, in the very recent past, expanded enormously both in scope and in variety. As Robert Kaplan noted in his introduction:

> It has been the purpose of this volume to examine these more recent trends in the development of applied linguistics, to examine the languages *of* and the language usage *in* a number of professional disciplines, to survey various pedagogical implications deriving from changes in the conceptualization of the role and function of applied linguistics in its relation to the various professions, and to mark the emergence of a paradigm which seems to be moving the object of analysis from the sentence to the discourse, whether written or spoken.

This expanding of the roles of the applied linguist seems likely to continue for the foreseeable future.

Conclusion

The selection of these particular perhaps atypical but yet prominent strands of our work is intended to be merely illustrative of the dynamism characterizing our field. Certainly the tradition of developmental psycholinguistic studies continues; work within the domain that has come to be known as classroom-centered research expands; the dialogue among researchers in Europe and North America has blossomed; and attention has been focused on issues related to second language acquisition for adults (immigrants, refugees, guest workers) as well as for youngsters who are newcomers to an educational setting. The energy, the commitment and the acceptance by theorists, practitioners and policy makers of our profession is gratifying. I believe we can look forward to even more growth and expansion during the coming three years than we have seen during the past.

References

Cantoni-Harvey, G. 1987. *Content-Area Language Instruction: Approaches and strategies*. Reading, MA: Addison-Wesley.

Cleghorn, A., M. Merritt & J.O. Abagi. 1987. *Language Use in the Teaching of Science in Kenyan Privacy Schools*. McGill University, Montreal.

Clyne, M. ed. 1986. *An Early Start: Second language at primary school*. Melbourne: River Seine Publications.

Dawe, L. 1984. "A Theoretical Framework for the Study of the Effects of Bilingualism on Mathematics Teaching and Learning". Sydney, Australia, Sydney Institute of Education. Paper presented at the Fifth International Congress on Mathematical Education, Adelaide, Australia, August.

Gillespie, J. 1986. "Effective Use of New Technology in Language Learning Centers". *Application of Technology: Planning and using Language Learning Centers* (CALICO Monograph Series) ed. by J.W. Larson. Provo, UT: Brigham Young University.

Kaplan, R.B. ed. 1987. *Annual Review of Applied Linguistics*. New York: Cambridge University Press.

Lambert, W.E. 1980. "The Two Faces of Bilingual Education". *NCBE Forum* 3.

Linguistic Society of the Philippines. 1986. "Eleven Years of Bilingual Schooling in the Philippines (1974-1985): A summative evaluation". Mimeographed Report.

Mohan, B.A. 1986. *Language and Content*. Reading, MA: Addison-Wesley.

Interaction: The Key to Communication

Wilga M. Rivers

I remember my first AILA Congress in Cambridge. It was the second one in the series, and there have been five more since then — Copenhagen, Stuttgart, Montreal, Lund, and Brussels. I came to Cambridge in 1969 from Monash University, which funded my venture, at the invitation of Paul Pimsleur of the Ohio State University, with whom I had developed a collegial correspondence. That first time, I came to England from Australia at the invitation of an American. Now it is a great pleasure for me to be at the 8th AILA World Congress, the first in the Southern Hemisphere and the Pacific region, coming this time from the United States to my native land, at the invitation of the Applied Linguistics Association of Australia (whose forerunner association I established) and of a British linguist whom we all admire. As a dinkum Aussie, it is a great pleasure for me to help celebrate my country's Bicentennial in this way.

Looking back to the Cambridge Congress, I reflected on the highlights of the psycholinguistics section, in which I participated, contributing my first serious application of cognitive psychology (Rivers 1971). Much quoted at that conference was Simon Belasco's question as to whether even 50,000 structure-dependent operations internalized by a foreign language student could be considered "a fair sample of the 'real' world" (Belasco 1971:5). John Oller concluded that "there is fairly general agreement that the basic goal for foreign language teaching is to enable the student to successfully send and receive messages in the foreign language; that the necessary and sufficient means for achieving this objective is to involve the student in active communication in the target language. The sooner, the better," he said (Oller 1971:177). Eighteen years and six AILAs later, we say "Amen".

Our old friend, Otto Jespersen, had already asserted in 1904 that:

> The first condition for good instruction in foreign languages would seem to be to give the pupil as much as possible to do with and in the foreign language; he must be steeped in it, not only get a sprinkling of it now and then; he must be ducked down in it and get to feel as if he were in his own element, so that he may at last disport himself in it as an able swimmer. (Jespersen 1904:48)

In 1916, Thomas Cummings summed it up this way: "We must learn to talk by talking. We cannot learn to swim before we go into the water" (Cummings 1916:22). Now we would include in Cummings's statement: "And we learn to listen by listening," which was the theme of my 1969 Cambridge paper.

Certainly, much water has flowed under the bridges of the Cam since then; much ink has flowed from the pens of AILA members; much information has come to us from linguistics (we now talk familiarly of discourse attributes, pragmatic functions, and Gricean implicatives); from cognitive psychology (particularly in areas of listening, retention and recall, and scripts, plans, and schemas); and from the burgeoning fields of first- and second-language acquisition, with ongoing research on interim grammars, interlanguage, and the creative role of errors. Pedagogy too has become focused on the learner's needs, on motivation, individual capacities, and on the autonomous role of the learner. But, we may ask, are we any nearer than in 1969 to helping learners send and receive messages in a foreign language, that is, to communicate with each other in some real sense of that term?

The title of this paper is "Interaction: The Key to Communication." Why am I focusing on interaction, when communication is the "in" word? I would like to suggest that interaction is the process by which students can be motivated and encouraged to communicate. Communication springs from within: one individual may have something to convey to another, in speech or writing — information, an emotional reaction, a personal viewpoint, a request to do something — but this personal intent is realized or inhibited in an interactional setting. We may feel the urge to tell the woman in the red hat on the bus something of importance, but "the moment doesn't arise": we don't know her well enough or we are afraid of a rebuff. "I couldn't. tell her; it didn't seem the right time," we say. There was no interaction at that point and, therefore, the opportunity for communicating did not arise. If we were both strap-hanging and there was a sudden lurch, then a moment of interaction might have been forced on us, thus providing an opportunity for some communication, although probably not to any great depth. What ensued would most likely be (to use Brown and Yule's terms) *interactional* use of language (social chitchat to make the participants feel comfortable), rather than *transactional* use of language (where information of any importance to the participants is exchanged) (Brown and Yule 1983:10-14). The sudden opportunity for interaction may have precipitated a communicative interlude. Just throwing people together, however, will not necessarily result in communication, as many an inexperienced "conversation instructor" has soon discovered. For communication of genuine messages, we need interactive situations which arouse communicative intentions that reflect deeper involvement of the participants. How to bring such situations into being in a formal setting is a considerable challenge to the language teacher.

Recently, I had a serious accident in Japan. Falling down a flight of stairs in a railway station, I broke some vital bones and consequently was confined to a hospital bed. In the Japanese system of family care, I needed a practical nurse, so Sano-san from Fuji City came into my life — a jolly, rosy-cheeked lady, with black curly (curled) hair — and we spent two and a half weeks together, in constant company. There was inevitably interaction — things had to be done — and this interaction grew, as we came to know and like each other, and had many hours to fill. It was inevitable that we would want to share meanings. To use the felicitous description of Wells and his colleagues in the Bristol study, "linguistic interaction is a collaborative activity" (Wells *et al.* 1981:29, 46-47).

There was much communication of meaning between myself and Sano-san during those eighteen days. Was this through language? No, only very minimally. It was in this interactive situation, with much motivation to communicate, that I learned how much of communication is non-linguistic — 80%? 90%? in my case. How does one calculate? How then were meanings shared? And they were shared in a happy, laughing relationship, with never a dull moment.

First of all, there was a shared context, with clear expectations as to the matters to be communicated and with few surprises. Objects and pictures (on television or in the newspaper, for instance) and the hospital routine — all of these helped. Next in importance came gestures, facial expressions, head movements, and then intonation, tone of voice, degree of emphasis, and persistence on both our parts. With a few content words in Japanese closely related to the context, communication was ample: "Breakfast ... you (pointing) ... now"; "Tomorrow 3 p.m. Temma sensai or Koike sensai"; "Dozo akete kudasai", when the room became too hot. There was a desire to communicate; we were mutually at ease; there was no feeling of criticism, no embarrassment, and no need to impress, so there was no anxiety in the interaction. (Laughter is always relaxing.)

There was plenty of communication, but to a small degree through language. This linguistic interaction was beginning but I did not have the necessary knowledge of the Japanese language. Every day, I sought more from my Berlitz and Instant Japanese books, and through questions. As soon as I acquired some linguistic knowledge, the communication of meaning increased and became communication through language. The linguistic interaction then grew (as a two-way process) because Sano-san presumed I knew more than I did. Then she really talked; I tried to latch on to clues (words, context, expectations), but despite her enthusiasm, communication ceased at times, when I did not have the knowledge to inform my guesses, unless it was revived again by non-linguistic means (objects, pictures, or mime).

One day, on Coming-of-Age Day, a special day for young women who are twenty years old, there was a picture in the English-language newspaper of a female gorilla in the zoo who was twenty years old and who was fed a special feast of bananas and fresh fruit for her festival day. I tried to share this amusing incident with Sano-san, who could see only the picture of a gorilla. With persistence and words in Japanese like "young woman", "feast", "20 years old", "fruit", and "today", and with a little pointing at the television where we had seen young women sauntering around in beautiful kimonos, light dawned for Sano-san and communication finally took place, with great hilarity on her part.

We have all had these experiences, you may say. What of it? We certainly have, and they are worth reflecting on. It is well for us to remember that, in these situations, most of the communication comes from shared context, cultural knowledge, and expectations, rather than from the conveying and receiving of a linguistic message of any sophistication.

Interaction provides a process by which communication via language may take place, but it does not ensure that this will be so. Nor does the use of words in itself constitute "communication via language". Words, as we know, fill in embarrassing pauses; they act as a social cushion; we talk for the sake of talking. Who of us has not said in a moment of conversational desperation, "Lovely day today, isn't it?" then looked out of the window to see the rain pouring down? Goffman observes that "the discovery that

communication could be used broadly to refer to what happens when individuals come together has been almost disastrous: Communication between
persons in each other's presence," he continues, "is indeed a form of face-
to-face interaction or conduct, but face-to-face conduct itself is never
merely and not always a form of communication" (Goffman 1969:ix). There
must be involvement and communicative intent. It is the task of the
teacher, in cooperation with the learners, to develop opportunities for
involved interaction. To quote Goffman again, when "this moment of talk
in a communion of reciprocally sustained involvement" takes place, it is the
"spark that lights up the world" (Goffman 1969:116-117).

Talk we do have in the classroom — communicative drills, communicative activities, Total Physical Response (Asher 1966), lots of comprehensible input, communication over texts, but unless we have involved students
who care about what is being communicated and wish to communicate
reciprocally, all this activity remains sterile and unproductive. Halliday sees
"an 'act' of speaking" as "something that might more appropriately be called an 'interact' ... an exchange, in which giving implies receiving and
demanding implies giving in response" (Halliday 1985:68). "In the act of
speaking," he says, "the speaker adopts for himself a particular speech role,
and in so doing assigns to the listener a complementary role which he
wishes him to adopt in his turn" (Halliday 1985:68). Allwright speaks of
interaction as a "coproduction of all the participants" (Allwright 1984:159).
How rarely do episodes of talk in the classroom seem to reflect this com-
plementarity and reciprocity! We teach "openers" and "closers", ways of
taking the floor and holding it, even how to take "turns at talk" (Kramsch
1987:21); then, the practice over, the teacher moves on in a continuing
unilateral pattern. In Kramsch's words, "the teacher selects the next
speaker and automatically selects him or herself for the succeeding turn.
There is little motivation for students to listen to one another and the only
motivation to listen to the teacher is the fear of being caught short on an
answer" (Kramsch 1987:22). There is an old adage worth remembering: "A
good teacher is one whose ears get as much exercise as his mouth" (or hers,
of course).

To achieve interactive communication via a foreign or second language, we need more than something to share, gorillas notwithstanding.
We need both *knowledge of language* and *control of language* (see Rivers
1981:356-357 for a discussion of these terms). We need, in Leontiev's
terms, to be able to say not only what we have to say, but also to say it "as

it needs to be said in order to influence or to promote interaction" (Leontiev 1981:23). This is a point some seem to have lost sight of in the last few years. As we speak, we have a mental representation of the lexicogrammatical structure of the language we are using (call it competence, if you will); the more highly developed this linguistic and sociological competence, the more precisely and effectively we will convey and receive meanings. "What are communicated in language are the semantic content and the pragmatic intent, but the vehicle of their transmission remains the lexicogrammatical structure of the utterance" (Waryas and Stremel-Campbell 1983:101). In recent years, we have become caught up with the former (the semantic content and pragmatic intent) in the hopes that the latter (the lexicogrammatical structure) will take care of itself. A book worth rereading is T.F. Cummings's slender 1916 volume, *How to Learn a Language* (a very contemporary-sounding title). In this book, Cummings gives helpful ideas to language learners, who, in far-off lands, may be receiving instruction in a language from a native informant who knows very little of how languages are learned or should be taught. It is Cummings's intention that the reader of his book be able to push his or her instructor gently in the right direction. The book is full of common sense and wise counsel. "Every art and science," Cummings observes, "has its fundamentals. He who would be a master of any art must gain an automatic control of its basic principles" (Cummings 1916:22).

When Cummings insists on "automatic control" of basic principles, he is not promoting a traditional, grammar-steeped rule-learning approach. "We must, of course, learn grammar," he says, "but concretely, and after it is so learned we shall be able to appreciate it when stated abstractly." Beginning with the abstract "does not make speakers of a language," he continues, and he quotes a grammar-bedevilled student who maintained that "Arabic grammars ought to be well bound, so as to stand being thrown violently about the room" (Cummings 1916:15). Unpopular as it is to speak of a grasp of grammatical structure, it is through lexicogrammatical control that we achieve precision and nuance of meaning, and it is by lexicogrammatical control that we will be judged, because this is basic to our ability to use the language appropriately in social situations. Through lexicogrammatical control we are liberated to choose among the many available ways of expressing our meaning. In "Notional Syllabuses Revisited," published in 1981, Wilkins says: "The notion that an individual can develop anything other than a rudimentary communicative ability without an extensive mastery of the grammatical system is absurd" (Wilkins 1981:85), but the way we acquire this ability is fundamental to its future use.

How, then, do we reconcile this emphasis on language knowledge as basic to language control with our theme of promoting communication through interaction? The approach we take to the internalization of language structure forms the bridge. "Learning grammar ... is not listening to expositions of rules, but rather inductively developing rules from living language material and then *performing rules*" (Rivers 1987:13). But the way we acquire this ability is fundamental to its future use.

We learn rules concretely, in Cummings's sense, through use — through experimentation in expressing meanings. What better way to internalize rules than to perform them in genuine interaction from the beginning?

To round off our discussion of Cummings, we find that he was not hung up on accuracy in grammatical use; in fact, he was well aware of the interrelationships of fluency and accuracy. "Some will argue," he says, "that accuracy should come first and not fluency. Taking the cue from nature, however, we find that children attain fluency first, and that sometimes many years elapse before all their inaccuracies clear away." He makes an exception, however, for pronunciation and rhythm. In these areas, he finds, "the only way to learn accuracy is by being fluent, for fluency is an integral part of accuracy" (Cummings 1916:23). Would-be speakers of a language, he maintains, must learn to communicate at a natural speed of speech, with acceptable and comprehensible stress and intonation. This will carry the flow of not necessarily accurate speech, enabling them to convey their meaning comprehensibly while they are learning to express meanings through communicative interaction.

To return to *performing rules*: rules in the Chomskyan sense are not consciously studied, but subconsciously determine our performance. They may be acquired in equally indirect ways, but the mental representation will be there — approximating more or less to the native model, depending on the care with which it has been developed and the time and motivation the student has given it. As teachers, we must recognize the limitations of the formal classroom and arrive at a rough approximation, which can be polished and perfected when opportunities arise for real communicative use. Leontiev develops the concept of an "absolute minimum" — a core — "of language knowledge without which the teaching of any speech activity would be impossible." He speaks of three floors of language development of increasing complexity — ground floor, first floor, and second floor. "In practice", he says, "we always put finishing touches to the lower floors while work on the upper floors is already under way" (Leontiev 1981:25).

On the basis of information-processing research, McLaughlin *et al.* have hypothesized that active use of language utilizes both controlled and automatic processes. The automatic processes, they maintain, become routinized through constant use, but are available for scrutiny as controlled processes when our more sophisticated knowledge of the language requires us to increase their complexity. Conversely, controlled processes of which we are consciously aware can become routinized and automatic with frequent use and familiarity (McLaughlin, Rossman and McLeod 1983). Both of these processes constitute active knowledge of language, in the sense in which I am using it. By control of language, I mean ability to use the forms and structures of the language (linguistic, kinesic, and pragmatic) to express personal meanings comprehensibly and acceptably, and to do this with ease and confidence in social settings while the speaker is concentrating on communicative interaction. Control of language necessarily implies also the ability to understand messages and their full implications in the context, interpreting tone of voice, stress, intonation, and other paralinguistic features, as well as actual words and structures.

Knowledge of language is what many teachers concentrate on; control of language in this rich sense is supposed somehow to take care of itself. Long and Sato (1983) found that, in the ESL classrooms they studied, display questions like "Is this a book?" with its anticipated response: "Yes, it's a book", which encourage manipulation of structure, constituted 51% of classroom questions, but were "virtually unknown" in native speaker-nonnative speaker conversation, where, conversely, information-seeking questions occurred 76% of the time, although they were heard only 14% of the time in class. Long and Sato concluded that "contrary to the recommendations of many writers on second-language teaching methodology, communicative use of the target language makes up only a minor part of typical classroom activities." "Is the clock on the wall?" and "Are you a student?" they say, "are still the staple diet, at least for beginners" (Long and Sato 1983: 280). Mueller found that in foreign-language classes she studied: "In class after class purporting to teach students to understand, read, write and speak a foreign language, the language is spoken only in bone-dry grammar exercises, never in an authentic exchange of ideas or information" (Mueller 1983).

Where are imagination, innovation, and dynamism in so many of our classrooms? Where there is no interest on the part of the students, there may be a perfunctory exchange of words, but communication of personal messages does not take place. We need to stimulate interactive situations and activities, if communication, authentic even if elementary, is to take place among our students, or even between teacher and students or students and teacher.

To promote interaction in another language, we must stimulate and maintain a lively attention and active participation among our students. Do we ourselves lack imagination? Then we draw on the imagination and inventiveness of our students. This is the essence of the participatory classroom. Students are too often treated as blocks of wood (or sponges) — identical ones at that — whereas, encouraged and stimulated to take responsibility for what is going on, they are full of ideas. We need to recognize and encourage Seliger's High Input Generators, who seek opportunities to communicate, to stimulate their less confident fellows and support and encourage the Low Input Generators to take risks and launch out (Seliger 1983).

To use language communicatively, any content, any activity will do, so long as the students' interest is caught and held. Morgenstern at MIT uses simulations a great deal. In one lesson I saw he divided the class into two neighboring countries, providing them with maps and demographic, economic, and cultural information. These countries had a border dispute and one had invaded the other. Morgenstern acted as a radio broadcaster announcing the fast-moving events, while the students hastily decided on their course of action and mobilized their fellow citizens (Morgenstern 1986). Here was an interactive situation with an urgency for communication. Simulations like this have enormous possibilities, which are realized only through student decisions and elaboration (all in the language being learned, of course).

Perhaps this sounds too easy? It needs, however, a very skilled teacher for it to work well within the time limits of an ordinary class. We can acquire the skill of developing communication in interactive situations through careful preparation and openness to learn from experience and from our students. As Seneca once said, "While we teach, we learn" (*Ad Lucilum*, V, vii), and Aristotle before him observed: "What we have to learn to do, we learn by doing" (*Nicomschean Ethics*, II, i). Active, interactive teaching has a long and honorable history.

For interactive teaching, the teacher needs to know the students well, being quick to note the stirring of emotions that militate against or for com-

fortable participation: the impulse to guard oneself from hurt; fear of the
reactions of peers or authority figures; desire to excel, to please, to be successful; or anxieties based on factors of which the teacher is unaware (be they
peer relationships, fear of failure, perfectionism, or discouragement caused
by previous unpleasant classroom experiences). Teacher and students need
to cultivate open relationships that encourage initiation of activities from
either side, because interaction is not just a matter of words. (Words, we
may note, may express or camouflage the interactive intent.) The caring
teacher "tempers the wind to the shorn lamb."

With care and thought, interactive activities can be made to appear
natural and to develop naturally. Then interaction becomes desirable, even
inevitable, and words (in communication) slip out, or pour out, to accompany the developing interest. As the whole is greater than the sum of its
parts, the interactive, participatory activity brings more experience and
develops more confidence than the isolated utterances of the individuals
involved.

Are these interactive experiences just "pie in the sky" for the average
teacher? Not at all. Interactive techniques are available to all because they
are invented by all, but each of us must begin one day soon. The sooner,
the better.

To quote Montaigne:

> Voicy mes lecons: Celui-là y a mieux
> proffité qui les fait, que qui les sçait!

References

Allwright, A.L. 1984. "The Importance of Interaction in Classroom Language Learn-
    ing". *Applied Linguistics* 5(2). 156-171.
Aristotle. *Nicomschean Ethics*, II, i.
Asher, J.J. 1966. "The Learning Strategy of the Total Physical Response: A review".
    MLJ 50. 79-84.
Belasco, S. 1971. "The Feasibility of Learning a Second Language in an Artificial
    Unicultural Situation". *The Psychology of Second Language Learning* ed. by P.
    Pimsleur & T. Quinn. Cambridge: Cambridge University Press.
Brown, G. & G. Yule. 1983. *Teaching the Spoken Language: An approach based on the
    analysis of conversational English*. Cambridge: Cambridge University Press.
Cummings, T.W. 1916. *How to Learn a Language. An exposition of the phonetic induc-
    tive method for foreign resident language students. A direct, practical, scientific way of
    mastering any foreign tongue*. New York: privately printed.

Goffman, E. 1967. *Interaction Ritual: Essays on face-to-face behavior*. Garden City, N.Y.: Doubleday.

———. 1969. *Strategic Interaction*. Philadelphia: University of Pennsylvania Press.

Halliday, M.A.K. 1985. *An Introduction to Functional Grammar*. London: Edward Arnold.

Jespersen, O. 1904. *How to Teach a Foreign Language*. London: George Allen and Unwin.

Kramsch, C.J. 1987. "Interactive Discourse in Small and Large Groups". *Interactive Language Teaching* ed. by W.M. Rivers. Cambridge: Cambridge University Press.

Leontiev, A.A. 1981. *Psychology and the Language Learning Process*. Oxford: Pergamon Press.

Long, M.H. & C.J. Sato. 1983. "Classroom Foreigner Talk Discourse: Forms and functions of teachers' questions". *Classroom Oriented Research in Second Language Acquisition* ed. by H.W. Seliger & M.H. Long. Rowley, Mass.: Newbury House.

McLaughlin, B., T. Rossman & B. McLeod. 1983. "Second Language Learning: An information-processing perspective". *Language Learning* 33(2). 135-158.

Morgenstern, D. 1986. "Simulation, Interactive Fiction and Language Learning: Aspects of the MIT Project". *Bulletin of the CAAL* 8(2). 23-33.

Mueller, M. 1983. "The Tower of Babel in Libertyville". *Daedulus* 112(3). 229-247.

Oller, J.W. Jr. 1971. "Language Communication and Second Language Learning". *The Psychology of Second Language Learning* ed. by P. Pimsleur & T. Quinn. Cambridge: Cambridge University Press.

Rivers, W.M. 1971. "Linguistic and Psychological Factors in Speech Perception and their Implications for Teaching Materials". *The Psychology of Second Language Learning* ed. by P. Pimsleur & T. Quinn. Cambridge: Cambridge University Press.

———. 1981. *Teaching Foreign-Language Skills*. 2nd ed. Chicago: University of Chicago Press.

———. 1987. "Interaction as the Key to Teaching Language for Communication". *Interactive Language Teaching* ed. by W.M. Rivers. Cambridge: Cambridge University Press.

Seliger, H.W. 1983. "Learner Interaction in the Classroom and its Effect on Language Acquisition". *Classroom Oriented Research in Second Language Acquisition* ed. by H.W. Seliger & M.H. Long. Rowley, Mass.: Newbury House.

Seneca, H. *Ad Lucilum*, V, vii.

Waryas, C.L. & K. Stremel-Campbell. 1978. "Grammatical Training for the Language-Delayed Child". *Language Intervention Strategies* ed. by R. Schiefelbusch. Baltimore: University Park Press. Quoted in F.J. Newmeyer. 1983. "On the Applicability of Transformational Generative Grammar". *Applied Linguistics* 3(2). 101.

Wells, G. *et al.* 1981. *Learning Through Interaction: The study of language development*. Cambridge: Cambridge University Press.

Wilkins, D.A. 1981. "Notional Syllabuses Revisited". *Applied Linguistics* II(1). 83-90.

Part I: Learning Language

Introduction

The first two areas that Richard Tucker identified in his 'Overview' were those of innovative language education and language education policy. The papers in this section could be seen as leading off from there.

Their overall focus is that of the individual language learner, and how that individual, in given contexts or in interaction with specific others, develops a command of a first language, of two or more first languages, or of a second language, in home and classroom settings. At the same time, cutting across these variables, there is a gradual shifting of attention, throughout this Part, from investigations of the language learning process to proposals for language teaching curricula and syllabuses.

Some of the papers examine the implementation of various approaches to language teaching in the classroom. But those with a clear classroom focus are in a minority. Many are concerned as much with issues of applied linguistic research as with the audience to whom such research is addressed or the uses to which it might be put. Here the tone is set by the final paper in Volume II, that by Christopher Candlin, who challenges applied linguists to reflect on what they perceive themselves as doing, and to explore the boundaries between themselves and other socially conscious researchers and disciplines. Given this orientation, it is clear that there is much to be gained in the area of language learning from exploring the relationship between applied linguistic research and research in various branches of education. The papers in this first section suggest very strongly that the theme of "learning language" could be an effective domain within which the activities of applied linguists and those of other researchers might hope to reinforce each other.

The first paper in this section begins in early infancy. Jane Oldenburg discusses some features of a child's construction of experience, and of personal relationships, by means of language; and she considers what may have been the effects on this process of her being the second child in the family. The paper by Judith Comeau and Marie-Claude Therrien is a study of linguistic interaction between mothers and five-year-olds in situations of play, in which the authors analyse the speech of both parties in terms of conversational acts and show to what extent the mothers take on a guiding and instructional role.

Ruqaiya Hasan and Carmel Cloran report on a portion of a large-scale study of natural interaction between mothers and 3½-4 year old children, based on a semantic analysis of over 20,000 messages. In this paper they focus on one area, that of explanation-seeking questions asked by the children and the answers the mothers give to them. Their findings are interpreted statistically, by means of principal components analysis; and significant differences appear according to the sex of the child and the social class background of the family.

Anna Kwan-Terry's paper moves the focus from monolingual to bilingual language development, and provides an insight into the manner in which a young boy draws on both of the languages available to him to create a systematic personal variety. Since the two language involved (English and Cantonese) are typologically dissimilar, the paper raises interesting issues for models of language learning which seek to explain developmental features by reference to the setting of parameters (cf. Hyams 1986). Susanne Döpke makes use of detailed observations of firstborn children in six bilingual families (English and German) to examine the influence of mothers and fathers on children's language development. In her data the fathers seem to be more child-centred than the mothers, and this has had implications for the extent to which the children have opted for one or other of the two languages available to them. The paper suggests that interpersonal factors might outweigh the effects of other aspects of the social context in bilingual language development, at least in the pre-school years. George Saunders' paper continues the discussion of bilingual development into the school years, and documents how children in a consistently bilingual family can achieve remarkable results even in a social setting where there is little exposure to the minority language. The author makes the point very strongly that a bilingual family need not necessarily depend on the parents having different mother tongues.

In contrast to Saunders' perspective, Marta Rado and Lois Foster are concerned with the effects on bilingual language development where the parents are limited in their ability to communicate with the children in one of the languages used. They compare the written narratives of children of English-speaking and of non-English-speaking background, and conclude that, while the two groups show many features in common, so that the language of the NESB children is more similar to that of their ESB peers than to that of their parents, nevertheless the stories written by the NESB children tend to be shorter, less elaborated in their structure and less enriched with relevant detail.

Christine Pappas has made a detailed study of how preliterate children develop their sense of the register of written narrative. Analysing the way in which they retell a story they have had read to them, aided by pictures, she shows how they construct the semantic "problem space" which defines the first two elements of a narrative, the Placement and Initiating Event; and draws out a clear relationship between this learning process and their general conceptual development. The paper by Philip Yde and Marc Spoelders examines the development of cohesive ties in the written Dutch of children under twelve years of age. Concentrating on intersentential cohesion, the authors recorded significant differences in the devices used on similar writing tasks between pupils in the third year and those in the fifth year of school; and they suggest that, while this might seem fairly late especially in the context of narrative, it should be seen as a move towards the construction of a distinct written form of the language. Luc Ostiguy, Gilles Gagné and Jean-Guy Blais have investigated the teaching of formal varieties of French at upper primary level in Canada, specifically examining the role of metalinguistic knowledge in bringing about changes in language use. They are cautious in interpreting their findings, which might however suggest that there is a place for explicit knowledge about language in the primary school curriculum.

In the next paper Catherine Wallace moves to the consideration of second language literacy, and specifically the case of adults becoming literate in their second language. There is a strong suggestion that, in certain types of context such as this, learning to read can have a major impact on the development of the spoken language. The paper provides a model for research in this area, which could be significant for older people, still illiterate, who are returning to second language studies once they no longer have family responsibilities, as often happens in Australia. Marietta Elliott's paper examines the development of second language writing among Arabic-speaking students of English. She find that certain generic patterns develop in a non-random fashion and suggests that learners may employ one of two distinct strategies when learning to write in a second language. Jennifer Hammond looks at writing activities in a Year 3 (age 7-8) primary classroom, comparing a text written by one child who is an accomplished writer in English (as his second language) with that same child's spoken language in discussion. The written text appears childish and unstructured by comparison, and Hammond suggests the reason may lie partly in the way the teacher has led up to the writing task: the child has not been able to identify any clearly distinct function for a written narrative of experience.

The three papers by Lydia White, Maria Bolander and Helen Borland form a segment dealing with oral second language acquisition. Bolander considers word order development in Swedish, specifically the development of inversion and the influence of particular grammatical and communicative contexts. Extending from previous work done on German, she suggests how grammatical and functional contexts interact in promoting the use of complex structures. White's paper adopts a different theoretical standpoint. She considers recent work within a generative framework in an attempt to define when explicit grammatical teaching can assist the learning of a second language, and develops a number of hypotheses susceptible to easy testing. Borland describes adolescents' learning of English predicate complements. In a detailed application of various analytic techniques, she demonstrates how, regardless of first language, learners initially favour *that* complements but subsequently move to favour *to* complements. Like White, Borland suggests the influence of markedness and target language typology in her interpretation of the data; and she shows a complex inter-relationship between first language type and second language performance, which raises interesting issues for the perspective developed by White.

The next three papers are linked by their common interest in neurolinguistics and language processing, although their authors' perspectives are significantly divergent. Lee Thomas and Harry L. Gradman examine theories of the localization of speech functions in the brain, and argue that in research in this area not enough attention has been devoted to the particular attributes of the language being learnt. Using dichotic listening tasks with advanced learners of English whose mother tongue is Mandarin Chinese, they suggest that Mandarin and English are processed differently because of the different role of intonation in the two languages — Mandarin having lexical tone. McKellar's paper discusses the theoretical background of neurolinguistics and argues that there is a need for a general framework within which to relate theories of neurology and linguistics. He considers to what extent Halliday's linguistic theories, as encapsulated in his notion of "social man", might be expected to provide such a general conceptual foundation. At the other end of the scale, Luelsdorff's paper focusses on a highly specific problem, errors made by German students in the spelling of English words. He adopts a language processing view of spelling complexity, suggesting that it needs to be viewed within a bidimensional framework; this framework can then be used to predict the sequence in which certain written forms will be mastered.

The papers by Helen Moore and Makhan Lal Tickoo move into a new area of concern, that of proposals for syllabus development. Both of these writers take issue with the notions of process and of procedural syllabuses — Tickoo because of the educational needs of what he calls "acquisition-poor learning contexts", such as those of India and many other countries, Moore because of what she sees as a false dichotomy between "process" and "product". Taken together, these two papers, by raising a number of specifically educational issues, lead from complementary perspectives to a reopening of debates about syllabus and curriculum development within the scope of applied linguistics.

The next three papers consider various classroom or other teaching techniques. Robert di Pietro provides an analysis of the kinds of language production that are likely to be occasioned by the use of techniques of "strategic interaction". In a study based on classroom observations, he suggests ways in which different aspects of learning can be identified in different phases of instruction. June Gassin's paper raises the issue of synchrony (the rhythmic co-ordination of speech and body movements) in the learning of a second language. She provides some evidence that this aspect of language can be taught and that the learning of it can interact with grammatical and communicative performance. Ronald Carter presents a view of the role of vocabulary in discourse which has significant implications for language teaching, and suggests how by using "discourse-sensitive cloze procedures" one can help the learner to develop an awareness not merely of patterns of lexical cohesion but also of the deeper knowledge structures and socio-cultural schemata which underlie an effective control of the language.

The last two papers in Part I provide a bridge to the next section, where the motif is that of "keeping language". Both set out to analyse how language is used and then employ the results of the analysis as a basis for pedagogical innovation. Alma Simounet de Géigel gives a comprehensive ethnographic account of the distinctive features of sales encounters in the United States Virgin Islands, while Eija Ventola describes the different behaviours of native English speakers and (Finnish) speakers of English as a second language in their dealings with English-speaking travel agents. Although they are using different models of discourse, both these papers bring out very clearly how the results of a theory-based analysis of carefully observed data have great potential value in meeting the needs of language learners.

Reference

Hyams, N. 1986. *Language Acquisition and the Theory of Parameters*. Dordrecht: D. Reidel Publishing Company.

Learning the Language and Learning through Language in Early Childhood

Jane Oldenburg

0. Introduction

In this paper, I shall discuss some of the results of a long-term case study of my daughter Anna's early linguistic development. I recorded Anna's language from the age of 8 months to 2 and a half years, and I analysed her emerging grammar using functional-systemic theory. The actual data were analysed at 6-weekly intervals, using the same general methodology employed by Halliday in his (1975) description of the emergence of his son Nigel's early grammar. More recently, Painter (1984) described her son Hal's linguistic development, and compared it with Nigel's development. I tried to make my descriptions of Anna's language directly comparable with these other two studies, in order to determine which features of the children's development were simply individual strategies, and which features constituted general developmental milestones. I was particularly keen to make comparisons between the three children, as Anna has a sister Carla, who is 20 months her senior, whereas Hal and Nigel had no siblings during the early years of their linguistic development. Very little has been written about the influence of siblings on early language development, yet my study suggests that the influence may be considerable.

In this paper, I shall focus on three aspects of the developmental process. Firstly, I shall discuss the ways in which Anna learnt through language from the age of 2 to 2 and a half years — in other words, how she used her language to learn about the world, to interpret reality, to observe and classify experience. It is possible to discern in her conversations during this time a number of semantic strategies, which will be discussed in the following pages.

Secondly, I shall briefly discuss the way in which Anna learnt the language; in other words, her grammatical development prior to 2 years, before she reached the mother tongue stage. I shall compare her development with that of Hal and Nigel, pointing out some of the differences between the children.

Finally, I shall focus on the relationship between learning the language and learning through language (that is, the above two points). The way in which Anna learnt her language is closely related to the way in which she learnt about the world through language. In both processes, the interpersonal function appeared to be the dominant one, suggesting that the child's construal of the linguistic system is part of a more general construal of all experience.

It is, of course, difficult to separate the language learning process from the more general process of learning about the world. The two are inextricably related. One thing which has emerged strikingly from my research is that the context in which learning occurs is conversation. It is through conversation that the child verbally represents perceived phenomena, assessing present experience in the light of past experience and resolving tension between her own interpretation of the world and that of her addressee. My aim in this paper is, then, to provide some insight into the way in which a very young child used her language as a vehicle for learning about the world. The emphasis throughout is on the child's own construal of her experience.

When looking at texts in which Anna could be seen to be using language as a tool for learning, it is possible to discern a number of general semantic strategies being employed by her to classify and interpret phenomena. The strategies appeared to be of two kinds; they were either interpersonal, in the sense that they involved the relationship between the self and other in the exchange of meanings, often including the exercise of control over the addressee, or they were ideational, in the sense that they were concerned with aspects of external reality observed by Anna.

1. Learning through Language — Semantic Strategies

1.1 *Interpersonal Semantic Strategies*

1.1.1 *Question/Answer adjacency pairs*

Perhaps the most obvious situation in which the child can be seen to be using language as a tool for learning is her use of the resources of the adult mood system (in particular question/answer adjacency pairs) to explore reality as well as to categorize it. Anna's questions were almost invariably addressed to an adult rather than to her sister Carla, although Anna would use questions to request confirmation from Carla that she was correctly carrying out some task, such as pasting or making pictures, etc.

This interpersonal semantic strategy is illustrated in the following example:

25(27)   (A finds a wooden puzzle piece which previously had a picture of a duck in profile on it. The face of the duck has been torn off, and M. attempts to draw a new face on the piece).
   M: It'll need a beak, won't it? And its head. ... we'll do an eye ... its coat. There we are ... it's all fixed up now.
   A: *Thêre beak. Where êye two?*
   M: What, darling?
   A: *Where('s) òther eye?*
   M: Another eye? Oh no, it only needs ... the other eye's over on the other side of its head and we can't see its other side.
   A: *Òther eye ... hèad.*
   M: Mm. Look, I'll show you with ... what can I show you with? Here, see this duck (holding up a plastic model of a duck and turning it sideways) see, you can only see one eye when you hold it like that. If you turn it round you see its other eye.
   A: *Other èye. Seè other eye. <   > Seè other side ... other èye... seè other eye.*

(Note: The number preceding each example indicates the child's age in months and days, the latter enclosed in brackets. Tone marks show falling, rising, rising-falling and falling-rising tone.)

In the above example, the child is attempting to resolve an apparent disparity between her interpretation of reality based on past experience (i.e. that ducks have two eyes), and that suggested by the mother's pictorial depiction of a duck's head in profile with only one eye, which appears to contradict Anna's interpretation of reality.

Here we can see the child struggling to understand a concept which the mother had taken so much for granted that she was initially puzzled by the child's question. The relationship between the object and its symbolic representation is not a direct one, and the child is here being encouraged to share the adult perspective. The semantic strategy employed by Anna involves firstly the statement of accepted and undisputed knowledge about the facial features of ducks (*There beak*), followed by a question (*where eye two*), which is employed as a means of resolving the conflict between Anna's interpretation and the mother's. Anna then uses her language to assimilate the explanation she has received (*see other eye*).

Inherent in most of the questions asked by Anna were presuppositions about the nature of reality, and by asking questions Anna was expanding on the knowledge on which her presuppositions were based.

1.1.2 *Modelling*

This consisted of the repetition by Anna of questions and comments which Carla had just addressed to the mother. Typically Anna would listen to Carla's utterance, then immediately turn to her mother and utter a very similar comment or question. Anna rarely modelled from adult utterances: it appears that Carla provided particular contexts in which learning could occur, which were in some ways more accessible to Anna than those provided by adults, perhaps because they were closer to her own conceptual level. Here are some examples of typical contexts in which this modelling occurred:

26(4)   C: Did Uncle break a bone?
          M: Yes, Uncle Glen broke a bone.
          A: *Uncle Glen broke a bóne?*
          M: Yes, on his motor bike.

25(21) F: (asking children about an outing to a farm)
          C: Yeah, I holded a little chickie.
          A: *I hold chickie.*
          C: And it had a little house with holes for the mouses.
          F: Really! And what did you see, Anna?

> A: *I hold chick.*
> C: And I gave it a little tickle.
> F: (laughs)
> A: *I tickle.*
> F: And you tickled it too!

The function of these modelled utterances was not to learn the language itself — Anna had already reached the mother tongue stage of development and was quite capable of spontaneously producing such utterances. The function was rather a learning one — Anna was using these modelled utterances as a resource for learning, not only about the social world, but about the discourse skills necessary to participate in interactions with others.

1.2 *Ideational Semantic Strategies*

I shall now briefly discuss the ideational semantic strategies which I noted in Anna's use of language to learn about the world at this time. All Anna's ideational semantic strategies involved the observation of points of similarity and difference between objects, processes and qualities. Many such observations related presently observed events with past ones, drawing comparisons or contrasts between familiar and unfamiliar aspects of experience (cf. Phillips in press). Five ideational strategies were identifiable in Anna's use of language to learn; these were analogy, antonymy, paradigmatic contrast of items, generalisation and inference.

1.2.1 *Analogy*
Example:

> 25(21)   (A. falls off chair, and draws a comparison between her
>   action and a character in a book, who fell off a wall)
>   A: (I) *fell down wall like Tom Kitten.*

In the case of analogy, a partial likeness between two or more entities forms the basis for comparison. The word "like" was sometimes explicitly stated, and sometimes conveyed implicitly through cohesive links (Given/New).

1.2.2 *Antonymy*
Example:

> 26(0)   A: *Yellow one tórn, blue one tòrn* (the latter clause said while shaking her head to mean "blue one not torn").

Here Anna is using her lexicogrammatical resources to represent observed contrasts between phenomena, either by using an antonym or by expressing the opposition of entities through negation of one of the items being contrasted, as in the above example.

1.2.3 *Paradigmatic contrast of items*
This involved the listing of objects or entities in books or in the real world, which were alike in all respects but one, the contrasting quality almost always being colour or number, for example:

> 25(23)   A: (to herself, as she looks at pictures in a ᴅᴏᴏᴋ) *Rèd flower, yèllow flower, òne … twò flowers(s)*.

1.2.4 *Generalisation*
Here Anna was making generalisations on the strength of her observations about typical behaviours of people, or using the system of modality to express ways in which people should behave, as in this example:

> 27(27)   A: (after seeing two clowns in a play knock a hole in a wall) *People … people … people not allòwed knock down walls. People shòuld* (accompanied by head shaking to signify negative) *knock down wàlls*.

In all cases, Anna presented her generalisations to her mother as hypotheses, on the basis of her perception of how things are at the present time.

1.2.5 *Inference*
Here Anna is using language to make inferences about the possible relationship between one aspect of experience and another. In the following example, Anna's observation of the current situation is expressed first (*Knife sharp*), then the implications in terms of subsequent behaviour are expressed (i.e. that because of this her mother will not let her use the knife):

> 25(15)   A: (watching M. chop vegetables) *Knife sharp. Lèt me* (said with head shaking) *Mùmmy* (= Mummy won't let me use the sharp knife).

1.3 *Interpersonal/Ideational Strategies Combined — the Imaginative Function*

In some of Anna's texts it is possible to see both ideational and interpersonal strategies combined, and these texts invariably involved the use of language in its imaginative function. In this sort of language, Anna was engaging in imaginary conversations when she was alone, using clause complexes, prosodic features and distinctive voice quality to distinguish between the various "people" engaged in the conversation. Here is a typical example of such a text:

25(7)   M. is trying to get ready to collect C. from kindergarten. A. demands two small books, which M. has put out of reach. M. offers one, refusing the other.

M: Here it is.
A: *Thànks. Twò book(s) mè* (= I want 2 books).
M: No, you ... half and half.
A: *Nò.*
M: Share? Shall we share?
A: *Nò.*
M: (attempts to change subject, in order to get ready to go out, A. ignores this)
A: (crying) *Twò nów.*
(M. leaves room to get ready for outing. A remains in room alone)
A: *Lòt book(s), twò book(s).*
Six ... six boòk(s).
Mummy sóme, mè some.
Thère. Shàre.
(M. re-enters room briefly to get something, unaware of the content of A's discussion)
M: Good girl. Sharing (M. leaves room).
A: *Shàre. Shàre.* (loudly) *Lot Múmmy, yès, shàre. Yès, or Mummy crý:* (adopts "crying" voice) *"Nŏ mòre book(s). Hey, I wănt book(s)".* Oh, oh Múmmy. (normal voice) *(I) gìve Mummy book(s). Be kìnd.*

Both ideational and interpersonal strategies can be seen in a text such as this. The ideational interpretation of experience in terms of comparison and contrast of past and present events and the drawing of inferences on the strength of the currently observed situation is embedded in the interpersonal mode of interpreting experience through a self-created and self-sustained dialogue.

In this example, Anna is both learning language (i.e. the meaning of the linguistic sign "share") and learning about the world through language, and she does this interpersonally through the construction of an imaginary dialogue in which she examines the implications of the concept "share" in terms of the functional consequences for each participant (i.e. her mother and herself).

The mother's refusal to give both books to the child was due to the fact that at the age of two, the child would inadvertently damage them. In order not to say this directly to Anna, the mother provided a reason for her refusal in terms of a more general principle which she felt would be within the child's understanding — the distribution of objects called "sharing". Left alone, Anna attempts to analyse the meaning of this concept.

As in the ideational strategies described above, she begins by establishing the known situation — the books must be divided so that *Mummy some, me some*. The child's expression of the paratactic relations (*or*) facilitates an exploration of the consequences which would ensue if sharing did not happen, and in order to do this Anna assumes the role and interprets the likely response of the mother by literally assuming the voice and perspective of the other person. The whole notion of sharing is concerned with the fact that a finite number of objects exist which are equally desired — both participants want the books. The resumption of normal voice at the end is Anna's solution *give Mummy books*. It will be remembered, however, that the mother already has a book, having given one to Anna and retained one herself. Yet the child has linguistically construed the situation in such a way that she is the Actor and sharing is defined as a type of doing, indicated by the material process *give*. The self-directed imperative at the end, *Be kind*, suggests that the child has analysed the purpose behind an externally imposed constraint in social and personal terms, defining sharing as the volitional giving of objects. We can clearly see in this example the way in which a young child, barely on the threshold of adult language, uses her language as a tool to analyse her experience, both linguistic and non-linguistic.

I have just described the sorts of semiotic strategies employed by Anna in the early mother tongue period, in order to provide some insight into the very young child's use of language for exploration and observation. In general terms there appeared to be a tendency for Anna to analyse the relevance of her experience in interpersonal terms. I say this because although both interpersonal and ideational strategies were used by Anna, interpersonal strategies appeared far more frequently than ideational ones. Even when ideational strategies *were* used, they were invariably in conversational contexts. Sustained narrative-type texts rarely occurred in Anna's language at this time. Rather, Anna's exploration of external reality was frequently embedded in self-created dialogues, where she would supply both sides of the conversation herself.

This reflected a consciousness of the fact that her perspective as a participant in the discourse was not necessarily shared by other participants in the interaction. This awareness provided Anna with a resource for interpreting experience in terms of the perspectives of the crucially involved participants, particularly for understanding the motivations behind externally-imposed constraints on her behaviour. Not only did Anna make more frequent use of interpersonal strategies, but the *areas* of concern (that is, the topics of her texts) tended to be concerned with human relationships, rather than external physical phenomena, suggesting that the social world is foregrounded in Anna's use of language to learn.

2. Learning the Language

I now wish to discuss the second aspect of the development process mentioned in the introduction to the paper — learning the language. It seems that the interpersonal orientation in Anna's use of language as a tool for learning may be related to lexicogrammatical developments during the *transition* period (the period of transition from protolanguage to mother tongue), a stage which typically occurs in the second half of the second year.

It is during this period that the child begins to produce adult-type lexical items, and the child's utterances tend to occur in one of two general functional contexts, the *pragmatic* function or the *mathetic* function (see Halliday 1975). The pragmatic function is the use of language to obtain goods and services from an addressee, and the mathetic function is the use of language as a vehicle for learning about and commenting on the world. At first all items are assigned by the child to one or other function, and each function receives a distinct phonological coding. In the case of Hal and

Nigel, pragmatic (demanding) utterances were all said on non-falling tones, while mathetic (commenting) utterances were all said on falling tones. Anna did not use tone to make this distinction — rather, she said all pragmatic utterances with tense voice quality, and all mathetic ones without tense voice quality. Gradually, during the transition, the children began to combine words structurally, and finally began to use the adult mood and transitivity systems to encode their meanings.

When I compared the transitions of Anna on the one hand, and Hal and Nigel on the other, I found that although in general grammatical terms the developmental process was remarkably similar, some interesting differences did emerge (see Oldenburg 1986 for a more detailed discussion of similarities and differences between the children during this period).

One difference lay in the development of adult-like mood forms, which are the grammatical realisation of the interpersonal function of language. These appeared earlier in Anna's language than they did in the boys' language.

Another difference concerned the types of structures which developed and the functions in which they first appeared. For Anna, almost all structures appeared first in the pragmatic function (which is the one which evolves into the non-declarative moods in the mother tongue), and these structures were clause-like and action-oriented in that they involved the words *want*, *have* or *need* plus the object or service desired e.g. *want see*, *want juice*, *have that*, *have one*. By 21 months, these pragmatic structures were becoming more elaborate, with expressions such as *want see star*, *have bath*, *I want that on*, *balloon up there*, *open up lid* and *Mum draw*.

The mathetic function remained very unelaborated in comparison. Structures were very rare, consisting only of deictic expressions like *There scissors*, and comments on actions like *I do this*. Even at 24 months, the nominal groups in both functions were very unelaborated, consisting mostly of unmodified nouns.

For comparative purposes, it is interesting to compare this process with Painter's son Hal's development. For Hal, the picture was, in a sense, reversed. The first structures appeared at 21 months in the mathetic function. These structures consisted almost entirely of modified nominal groups and clause-like structures, e.g. *nice book*, *hot porridge*, *blue shirt* and *make tower* (Painter 1984).

Differences also occurred between Anna, Hal and Nigel in the sizes of their lexicons and the type of vocabulary items used. All developed lexical taxonomies in the mathetic function; however, Hal placed a greater emphasis on naming and classifying than did Anna. Hal's mathetic vocabulary greatly exceeded Anna's.

One possible explanation for the differences observed between Hal and Nigel on the one hand, and Anna on the other, may lie in Anna's status as a second-born child. Indisputably, the environment of a second-born or subsequent child is vastly different from that of an only child, and this may influence the developmental process in a number of ways. Anna's sister Carla played an overtly pedagogical role in her interactions with Anna on some occasions, but less directly Carla appeared to provide particular contexts in which learning could occur, which were unlike those provided by an adult. At the lexicogrammatical level, for example, Carla was the source of many of Anna's expressions (for example *dummy*, *yuck*). At the discourse level, Carla provided Anna with a model of interactional behaviour, enabling Anna to develop concepts of relationships and of how to interpret experience (as can be seen in the examples in Section 1.2 above).

The apparent dominance of the pragmatic (demanding) function in Anna's language during her second year may reflect the fact that such utterances (encompassing as they do areas such as the acquisition of objects, control of behaviour, territory and possession) are perhaps more salient to a child sharing her environment with one or more young siblings. In other words, Anna's language (in common with that of all speakers) was shaped by the needs it had to serve in everyday social encounters. Her family structure meant that certain types of meanings were more frequently called forth in comparison with Hal and Nigel and their respective family members (see Oldenburg 1987 for a more detailed discussion).

3. The Relationship between Learning the Language and Learning through Language

The above differences between the children's language development suggested to me that, as Anna moved from child tongue to mother tongue, it was possible to see a sort of interpersonal orientation in her strategies for learning the language.

When one then looks at the way in which Anna used language as a tool for learning in the months after she gained mastery of the adult language, as I did in the first section of this paper, a similar interpersonal orientation can be observed in the more general learning process.

This suggests that a very close relationship exists between learning the language and learning through language about the world. A study of Anna's language in the early years of linguistic development suggests that the young child's strategies for construing the linguistic system reflect more general strategies for construing all experience. Such a hypothesis must remain tentative at this stage. Only when we have more long-term case studies of children learning to talk in the natural environment in which learning occurs — the home — will we be able to expand on the developmental picture and progress further towards a language-based theory of learning.

References

Halliday, M.A.K. 1975. *Learning How to Mean: Explorations in the development of language*. London: Edward Arnold. (Explorations in Language Study).

Oldenburg, Jane. 1986. "The Transitional Stage of a Second Child: 18 months to 2 years". *Australian Review of Applied Linguistics* 9(1).

————. 1987. *From Child Tongue to Mother Tongue: A case study of language development in the first two and a half years*. Ph.D. thesis, University of Sydney.

Painter, Clare. 1984. *Into the Mother Tongue: A case study in early language development*. London: Frances Pinter. (Open Linguistics Series).

Phillips, Joy. in press. "The Development of Comparisons and Contrasts in First and Second Language". *Australian Review of Applied Linguistics* 11.

Conversational Exchange between a 5- to 6-Year-Old and the Mother in a Playroom Situation

Judith Comeau and Marie-Claude Therrien

This study looks at the verbal interaction between mother and child from the point of view of the language acts that are produced during a conversation. It is an exploratory study which comes within the framework of a larger project on the evolution of the pragmatic skill repertoire of preschool children and their parents.

A Functional Approach to Language Acts

When it is devoted to the analysis of behaviour expressing the subjective, intersubjective and social reality of the child, the study of language development looks at this behaviour from a pragmatic point of view.

In this perspective, it is considered that when children speak, they not only formulate an utterance with a morpho-syntactic structure, they also produce and perform a language act which can fulfill various other functions. The interpretation of these requires not only that we examine the utterance itself, but also that we consider its context (Ochs 1979).

Today, research in language psychology increasingly takes into account the following parameters: language act, context, function, intention and skill. These cannot be conceptualized within the traditional framework of lingusitics.

This research is based on a conception of language as a communicative instrument used to send and receive messages, and it considers language development as a process of adaptation to the environment. This process relies on the progressive acquisition of communicative skills by individuals who actively organise their dynamic interaction with others.

The aim of pragmatics is thus to give an account of the various aspects of the functional relationship between the language act, its users and its context (Bates 1976; Recanati 1981); then analysing as an interpersonal and social exchange what occurs between speakers who are face to face in a particular context (Beaudichon 1982). More particularly, pragmatics deals with the relationship to context in, and by, the analysis of discursive sequences and their production by speakers (Parret 1980).

Van Dijk (1977) stresses the essentially dynamic relationship between the context, the speakers and the acts performed by these speakers when they resort to language. The notion of conversation defines this dynamism, since it is a privileged communicative context from the point of view of the actualisation of significant intentions. Conversation is more than a simple succession of functional and independent utterances; it is an interactive structure with its own rules and techniques, i.e. successive turntakings, theme, role negotiation etc., as explained by Wells (1981).

Pragmatic Approach and Mother-Child Conversation

The study of child-mother conversation dates back, for the most part, to the socio-linguistic works circulated at the beginning of the seventies which focused on the child's linguistic environment, which they described in terms of social class and mother's language type. These studies not only identified a relationship between such variables and the child's linguistic development; they also brought to light the fact that specific processes take place in conversation between the mother and her child (Tough 1977).

Studies have clearly shown that the language used by the mother and the adult when speaking to the child is different in several aspects from the one used between adults (Dale and Ingram 1981). A lot of research has demonstrated that the mother's language develops with the child's age and, more recently, more detailed studies have pointed out that such changes are closely related to the ones occurring in the child (Cross 1981).

When studying the structure of the mother's linguistic input and when comparing her exchanges with her child and her conversation with adults, one notices that the mother's language is greatly simplified and has a limited vocabulary when she speaks to the child; the mother uses a vocabulary which is more concrete and less diversified than when she speaks to an adult (Phillips 1973). Moreover, her language contains more repetitions (Rondal 1978) and her voice has a higher pitch.

In addition to using shorter sentences, her language is syntactically simpler and more regular. Her pauses are clearly marked between each utterance (Broen 1972) and she asks a great number of questions to the child (Cross 1977). It is also noted that the syntactic complexity and the length of the sentences contained in the mother's discourse increase with the child's age (Broen 1972; Phillips 1973; Remick 1976; Snow 1972).

Newport et al. (1977) have described this adjustment with the term "motherese". The mother's discourse would seem to adjust to the level of the child's linguistic skill development. This language would even take on such a stereotyped form that the age of the child could be predicted by analysing the mother's linguistic style (Bellinger 1980). As the child grows older, the parent's discourse would become more and more similar to the one used when talking to an adult (Cross 1977).

It would seem that the mother's adjustments are associated with the changes occurring at the level of the child's comprehension and language production. Indeed, the mother's language adjustment would constitute an answer to the feedback given by the child (Newport et al. 1977).

Other studies (Bohannon and Marquis 1977) have brought to light that in demonstrating different levels of comprehension the young child can control the quantity of repetitions that are addressed to him and the degree of simplicity of the language used by the adult. As soon as children are old enough to answer to the content and linguistic form of utterances, they are able to give some indications of their language skill — that is, their comprehension and production ability. These are instrumental in the mother's language modification and adjustment. Similarly, Cross (1977, 1981) also suggests that most aspects of the mother's discourse are adjusted according to the child's communicative and receptive skills. The adjustment would be, as it were, a reaction to the child's linguistic level. Rondal (1980) has called this phenomenon "hypothesis of linguistic feedback"; Snow (1977) used the term "conversational hypothesis".

It thus appears to be an exchange between the mother and the child that acts as a mechanism enabling the mother to adjust her discourse according to the child's level of development.

Objectives

This work aims at exploring how the mother adjusts to the 5- to 6-year-old child in a conversational exchange by looking at the use of language acts during that interaction.

Firstly, we will consider the distribution of each speaker's language acts.

We will then compare the distribution of the language acts of the mother and the child, respectively.

Methodology

The sample consists of 6 mother-child pairs. The age of the three girls and three boys ranges from 5.3 to 6.1 years. The children come from a middle-class socio-economic background.

Situation and Material

The interactions between mother and child are collected in a playroom situation. The material consists of a small table and two chairs, a shelf on which various games are accessible to the child: a teddy bear, small farm animals, matchbox cars, a Fisher-Price farm with animals and tractors, two Little Red Riding Hood and Wolf puppets, building blocks, a jack-in-the-box, a Perfection game, a "slinky", some paper and coloured pencils, some Smurfs, etc.

The layout of the rooms and the games are the same for all, but the situation is as close as possible to an interaction context in a natural environment; the situation aims to recreate a frame in which the conversational exchange can take place.

The 30 minute interaction for each mother-child pair is videotaped.

Results

Method of Analysis

Dore's (1979) classification of conversational acts has been used to analyse the children's corpus. As far as the analysis of the mothers' language corpus is concerned, we have used Folger and Chapman's (1978) taxonomy of language acts. The analysis focused on a corpus of about 3,500 utterances. The agreement between judges is 97%.

Results

A. *Children*

As Table 1 shows, children use a language that mainly consists of statements (34%), answers (27%), and requests (23%). Eight percent of utterances aim at regulating the conversation; expressions (exclamations, supports, repetitions) make up 3%, and performatives 1% only. These rates are approximately the same from one child to another.

If we look at the categories that are the most commonly observed in children, what are the main sub-categories in each of them?

If we refer to Table 2, we notice that, among the statements, children often use descriptions: 43% of statements are of a descriptive nature. What do we mean by descriptions? They are utterances used to describe objects, events, places, their properties.

Table 1: Frequency and percentage of conversational acts (Dore 1979) in the children's speech

Conversational acts	N	% of total
Request	374	23%
Statement	547	34%
Performative	19	1%
Answer	446	27%
Regulation	129	8%
Expression	48	3%
Uncategorized utterances	62	4%
Total	1625	100%

Table 2: Frequency and percentage of the subcategories of statements, requests and answers in the children's speech

Conversational act	Subcategory	N	%
Statement	Description	233	43%
	Identification	144	26%
	Explanation	61	11%
Answer	Yes-no answer	142	32%
	Answer relating to the result	88	20%
	Answer to a request	85	19%
	Appreciation	84	19%
Request	Question requiring a choice or a decision	100	27%
	Request for action	89	24%
	Suggestion for action	87	23%
	Question relating to the result	67	18%

e.g. (1) Annie: *Hey Maman, il s'arrête jamais de tourner.*
     Annie: Hey Mum, it never stops turning.
     (Annie is examining the dial on the Perfection game)

We also find 26% of identifications. These utterances identify objects, events or characters.

e.g. (2) Martin: *Ça, c'est les clôtures.*
     Martin: Look, these are fences.
     (while playing with the small animals and the Fisher-Price farm)

Lastly, explanations (representing 11% of the statements) express reasons, causes, justifications.

e.g. (3) Martin: *Quand il va tourner, là ça va marcher tout seul.*
     Martin: Once it starts turning, it keeps on going by itself.
     (Martin is explaining to his mother the starting mechanism of the Perfection game)

As far as answers go, these utterances include 32% of yes-no answers. They occur after the mother has asked a question requiring a choice or a decision.

e.g. (4) Mother: *Alors, tiens, tu connais déjà le jeu?*
     Charlie: *Oui.*

> Mother: Well then, do you already know this game?
> Charlie: Yes.

We find in 20% of the cases answers to questions referring to the result.

e.g. (5) Mother: *Qu'est-ce qu'il te reste à faire?*
Véronique: *Rien, j'ai fini.*
Mother: What have you still got to do?
Véronique: Nothing, I've finished.

19% of the answers come after a request; answers to a request consist in the acceptance or the refusal of requests and suggestions for action coming from the mother.

e.g. (6) Mother: *Je pense qu'on va être obligées d'agrandir notre parc.*
Dominique: *Non, non, on a pas besoin de faire ça.*
Mother: I think we'll have to make our park bigger.
Dominique: No, we don't need to do that.

19% of the answers are appreciations. These utterances express agreement or disagreement with a previous non-interrogative utterance.

e.g. (7) Mother: *Ah! la femme de ménage va venir.*
Véronique: *Oui, c'est ça, tu as raison.*
Mother: Well, the cleaning lady will soon be here.
Véronique: Yes, you're right.
(Interaction observed during a roleplay where the mother-child pair are playing "mother")

Lastly, as far as the third and most important category of conversational act — the request — is concerned, we find four main types:
27% of requests or questions call for a choice or a decision.

e.g. (8) Olivier: *Est-ce qu'il y en a des papiers?*
Mother: *Oui.*
Olivier: Is there any paper?
Mother: Yes, there is.
(In this situation the child wants to draw)

There are 24% of requests for action; these utterances require of the partner that he carries out or does not carry out an action.

e.g. (9) Véronique: *Ah! Viens voir ici.*
Véronique: Hey, come and see this.
(Véronique wants to show her mother an object on the shelf)

Suggestions for action make up 23% of the requests: they aim at soliciting an action from the partner, or a joint action.

e.g. (10) Olivier: *On va jouer ensemble avec les autos.*
     Olivier: Let's play together with the cars.

Lastly, 18% of the requests are formulated in the form of questions referring to the result. These questions call for simple answers and are formulated using interrogative pronouns such as *where?*, *what?*, *who?*, etc. (i.e. wh- questions).

e.g. (11) Martin: *Où est-ce que tu penses que ça va?*
     Martin: Where do you think this goes?
     (Martin holds a geometric piece and looks in turn at his mother and the Perfection game)

To sum up, during an interaction with their mother in a playroom situation, the 5- to 6-year-old children use language to identify and describe objects and events, and also, but in a lesser proportion, to provide explanations. Their utterances are used to make requests and suggestions for action, to ask precise questions and to also answer those types of questions; children also interact with their mothers to refuse or to accept requests or suggestions for action formulated by the mothers.

B. *Mothers*

As Table 3 indicates, mothers use mainly statements (27%), requests for information (21%), descriptions (21%) and requests for action (17%). If we add up the sum of the two types of requests, we notice that 38% of the mothers' utterances are of the request type. Mothers use 7% of utterances with a conversational turn of phrase; repetitions represent only 3% of the mothers' utterances; only one mother resorts to the Performative game (1%) and another to the elicited imitation (0.2%).

By examining the main categories of the mothers' typical language acts, we can get a precise idea of their content (see Table 4).

As far as statements are concerned, 69% of the mothers' utterances are assessments. What is meant by "assessment" in Folger and Chapman's taxonomy?

This type of utterances express impressions, attitudes and judgements.

e.g. (12) Martin's mother: *Je ne me souviens pas que c'était comme ça que ça se jouait.*

Table 3: Frequency and percentage of language acts (Folger and Chapman 1978) in the mothers' speech

Language act	N	% of total
Description	415	21%
Statement	548	27%
Request for information	429	21%
Request for action	351	17%
Conversational turn of phrase	149	7%
Performative game	23	1%
Elicited imitation	5	0.2%
Repetition	61	3%
Uncategorized utterances	38	2.8%
Total	2019	100%

Table 4: Frequency and percentage of the subcategories of statement, description and request for information and for action in the mothers' speech

Language act	Subcategory	N	%
Statement	Assessment	367	69%
	Explanation	65	12%
Request for information	Request requiring a yes-no answer	238	55%
	Request requiring an answer to interrogative pronouns	191	45%
Description	Event	193	33%
	Property	125	30%
	Identification	117	28%
Request for action	Order	202	58%
	Suggestion for joint action	129	37%
	Indirect request for action	16	5%

> Martin's mother: I didn't remember this was the way you were
> supposed to play it.

The assessment also consists in yes-no answers to questions requesting a choice or a decision. Answers such as "I don't know" are also assessments.

e.g. (13) Martin: *Tu ne te souviens pas?*
         Mother: *Non.*
         Martin: Don't you remember?
         Mother: No.

Utterances indicating agreement or disagreement with regard to a previous non-interrogative utterance also belong to the subcategory of assessment.

e.g. (14) Martin: *Il y a plein d'affaires pareilles.*
         Mother: *Oui.*
         Martin: All of these are the same.
         Mother: Yes.

Moreover, only 12% of statements are of an explanatory nature.

Requests for information, which represent 21% of the mothers' utterance corpus, include:
– requests (55%) calling for a yes-no answer prompting the child to assert, confirm or deny one of the mother's utterances,

e.g. (15) Annie's mother: *Voyons, ça n'a pas l'air de vouloir marcher, hein?*
         Annie's mother: Well, this doesn't seem to be working, does it?
         (utterance noted down as they were playing with the Smurfs)

– and requests that are more strictly informative (45%) and are structured around wh- questions (what, who, where, when).

e.g. (16) Martin's mother: *Quand est-ce qu'on avait joué avec ça?*
         Martin's mother: When did we last play with this?

As far as descriptions are concerned, descriptions of events, actions and processes represent 33% of the descriptive utterances.

e.g. (17) Martin's mother: *Cette fois-ci, les blocs n'ont pas sauté.*
         Martin's mother: Well, this time the blocks did not jump.
         (utterance produced while playing with the Perfection game)

Utterances indicating properties of objects, actions and events represent 30% of the descriptions.

e.g. (18) Véronique's mother: *Ah! Grand-mère comme vous avez une grande bouche.*
         Véronique's mother: Oh Grandma, what a big mouth you have.

(during a roleplay using the puppets of Little Red Riding Hood and the Wolf)

The identifications of objects, events or situations are worth 28%.

e.g. (19) Olivier's mother: *Ce jeu-là, ça s'appelle Perfection.*
     Olivier's mother: That game is called Perfection.

Lastly, requests for action include 58% of orders,

e.g. (20) Olivier's mother: *Assieds-toi.*
     Olivier's mother: Sit down.

and 37% of suggestions for joint action; "we" is used in the formulation of the action proposed.

e.g. (21) Martin's mother: *Après ça, on va mettre la minuterie pour jouer ensemble.*
     Martin's mother: After that we'll put the timer on so we can play together.

The corpus includes very few indirect requests for action or suggestions (5%).

It emerges from this study of utterances produced by mothers in an interactive playroom situation with their children that they frequently use utterances with an evaluating content, that they ask a lot of questions, and that they often prompt their children to act, either by orders or by suggestions for joint action. They identify and also describe objects, events and situations for their children.

Comparison of the Mother-Child Results

To compare results, we have taken into account categories or subcategories that are the most comparable with Doré's and Folger and Chapman's taxonomy (see Table 5).

Mothers use many more requests than children, with a ratio of nearly two to one; we also observe that the two types of requests (for action and information) are more frequent in the mothers' speech.

Mothers use a slightly higher percentage of statements.

By grouping comparable utterances under the category assessment, we notice a difference of 2% between mothers and children as far as evaluating utterances are concerned.

Table 5: Comparison of frequencies and percentages of the mothers' and children's various types of utterances

Taxonomy and Type of Subject		Average number per subject	% in the set of utterances
Dore (children)	Folger & Chapman (mothers)		
Request		62	23%
	Request for information and for action	129	38%
Question requiring a choice or a decision		33	12%
Question relating to the result (where, what, who …) Question relating to the development or the origin (why, how)			
	Request for information	71	21%
Request and suggestion for action		30	11%
	Request for action	58	17%
Assessment, self-expression, attribution, utterance about rules, processes and definitions, explanation, yes-no answer, appreciation		67	24%
	Statement	91	27%
Assessment, yes-no answer, appreciation		45	16%
	Assessment	61	18%
Regulation		22	8%
	Conversational turn of phrase	25	7%
Identification and description		63	23%
	Description	69	21%

The children's conversation regulations and the corresponding mothers' utterances called conversational turns of phrase are in relatively equal number between both groups.

As far as descriptions are concerned, there is no notable difference between the children's and mothers' speech.

Interpretation

How can we interpret these results?

The equal proportion of regulations and conversational turns of phrase can lead us to think, at least in the type of exchanges taking place in a playroom situation, that mothers and children participate in more or less the same way in the regulation of conversation.

Both speakers seem to cooperate in an exchange where they not only mutually control the conversation, but also exchange an equal quantity of information between themselves; the frequencies and rates of descriptive utterances are approximately the same in the mothers' and children's speech.

However, when we examine the statements there is less similarity; in the mothers' speech we find a few more assessments expressing impressions, attitudes and judgements, a few more appreciations, attributes of internal states to others, utterances about rules, processes and definitions. It appears that the mother more frequently takes the initiative in the conversation.

The leading and stimulating role of the mother becomes decidedly obvious when we consider the percentages of requests for information and for action expressed by both speakers. Nearly half of the mothers' language takes the form of incitement to action and requests for information. The mother definitely leads and controls the conversational exchange.

The mothers' linguistic competence, as shown in this study, goes beyond the process of adaptation to the interlocutor which is characteristic of the interaction between a mother and a younger child. As Snow points out (1985),

> ... after the first stages of language development, it is possible that the child's linguistic and cognitive development is facilitated by parental behaviour patterns that go beyond a simple answer to the children's intentions, their acceptance, and the expansion of their words. When children are able to deal with a more complex language, they should be exposed to new information, be encouraged to develop their imagination, to be faced with fanciful and humorous situations. In other words, the style of interaction that is optimum for the young child is not any more for the older one.

It can still be added that the mother's language undergoes an evolution with the age of the child and that the mother adjusts to the child's level of linguistic development. However, the adjustment that takes place in the conversational exchange between the mother and a pre-school child is different and depends on other principles. It is the mother who plays the leadership role and takes the initiative in the conversation. She guides the child knowing that he is now cognitively and linguistically equipped to actively face a new interactive pattern offering more challenges, more demands and a greater openness to the world.

References

Bates, E. 1976. *Language and Context: The acquisition of pragmatics*. New York: Academic Press.

Beaudichon, J. 1982. *La communication sociale chez l'enfant*. Paris: Presses Universitaires de France.

Bellinger, D. 1980. "Consistency in Pattern of Change in Mother's Speech: Some discriminant analyses". *Journal of Child Language* 7. 469-487.

Bohannon, J. & A. Marquis. 1977. "Children's Control of Adult Speech". *Child Development* 48. 1002-1008.

Broen, P.A. 1972. "The Verbal Environment of Language Learning Child". *ASHA Monographs* no.17.

Cross, T.G. 1977. "Mother's Speech Adjustments: The contribution of selected child listener variables". *Talking to Children: Language input and acquisition* ed. by C.E. Snow & C.A. Ferguson, 151-188. Cambridge: Cambridge University Press.

———. 1981. "Parental Speech as Primary Linguistic Data: Some complexities in the study of the effect of the input in language acquisition". *Child Language: An international perspective* ed. by P.S. Dale & D. Ingram, 215-228. Baltimore: University Park Press.

Dale, P.S. & D. Ingram. 1981. *Child Language: An international perspective*. Baltimore: University Park Press.

Dore, J. 1979. "Conversational Acts and the Acquisition of Language". *Developmental Pragmatics* ed. by E. Ochs & B. Schiefflin, 339-361. New York: Academic Press.

Folger, J.P. & L. Chapman. 1978. "A Pragmatic Analysis of Spontaneous Imitations". *Journal of Child Language* 5. 25-38.

Newport, E., L. Gleitman & H. Gleitman. 1977. "Mother, I'd Rather do it Myself: Some effects and non-effects of maternal speech style". *Talking to Children: Language input and acquisition* ed. by C.E. Snow & C.A. Ferguson, 109-149. Cambridge: Cambridge University Press.

Ochs, E. 1979. "What Child Language can Contribute to Pragmatics". *Developmental Pragmatics* ed. by E. Ochs & B. Schiefflin, 1-17. New York: Academic Press.

Parret, H. 1980. "Le statut théoretique de la pragmatique". *Le langage en contexte: études philosophiques et linguistiques de pragmatique* ed. by H. Parret. Amsterdam: Benjamins.

Phillips, J. 1973. "Syntax and Vocabulary of Mothers' Speech to Young Children: Age and sex comparisons". *Child Development* 44. 182-185.

Recanati, F. 1981. *Les énoncés performatifs*. Paris: Les Editions de Minuit.

Remick, H. 1976. "Maternal Speech to Children During Language Acquisition". *Baby Talk and Infant Speech* ed. by W. Von Raffler-Engel & Y. Lebrun, 223-233. Amsterdam: Swets and Zeitlinger.

Rondal, J.A. 1978. *Langage et éducation*. Bruxelles: Mardaga.

———. 1980. "Fathers' and Mothers' Speech in Early Language Development". *Journal of Child Language* 7. 353-369.

Snow, C.E. 1972. "Mother's Speech to Children Learning Language". *Child Development* 43. 549-565.

———. 1977. "The Development of Conversation between Mothers and Babies". *Journal of Child Language* 4. 1-22.

———. 1985. "Parent-Child Interaction and the Development of Communication Ability". *The Acquisition of Communicative Competence* ed. by R.L. Schiefelbusch & J. Pikar, 69-107. Baltimore: University Park Press.

Tough, J. 1977. *The Development of Meaning*. New York: Wiley.

Van Dijk, T.A. 1977. "Context and Cognition: Knowledge frames and speech act comprehension". *Journal of Pragmatics* 1. 211-232.

Wells, G. 1981. *Learning through Interaction: The study of language development*. Cambridge: Cambridge University Press.

The Role of Transfer in Simultaneous Language Acquisition

Anna Kwan-Terry

Introduction

This paper is based on a longitudinal study of the simultaneous acquisition of English and Cantonese by a pre-school child in Singapore. English is one of the four official languages in Singapore and the main medium of instruction in schools. Cantonese, on the other hand, is one of several Chinese dialects spoken by Chinese Singaporeans as a first language, mostly in the home but also in some work and social situations outside the home. The subject of this study is Elvoo who was 3;6 when the study began. He is the younger of two children from a middle-class family of Chinese ethnicity and learned to speak Cantonese from his parents who spoke predominantly Cantonese in the home, although their Cantonese was mixed with many words from English. It was this no doubt which accounted for the highly mixed nature of Elvoo's Cantonese utterances. Elvoo also learned Cantonese from his grandparents who lived in the same household and who spoke a "purer" form of Cantonese unadulterated by English words. English was the main medium of communication in the kindergarten where the child spent five mornings a week. English was also used in the home among Elvoo, his older sister and the maid who took care of the child when his parents were away at work.

In investigating the role of transfer in simultaneous language acquisition, attention in this paper will be focused on Elvoo's development in expressing certain concepts of phase, in positioning the wh- word and its Cantonese equivalent in asking interrogative word questions and in the use of the relative clause in the two languages he was learning.

Specification of Event Completed at a Prior Time

At 3;6, Elvoo had already acquired the concept of event completed at a prior time and had been using the Cantonese perfect aspect marker *dʒɔ* with dynamic verbs to indicate that the event specified by the verb is performed at a prior time, as in:

> *nei   sik   dʒɔ̱   jæk   na?*
>
> you   eat   ⎛perfect⎞   medicine ⎛interrogative⎞
>   ⎜aspect ⎟   ⎜cum aspect ⎟
>   ⎝marker⎠   ⎝marker   ⎠
>
> "You have taken your medicine?"   (3;6)

where the verb *sik* "eat" is marked by *dʒɔ* to indicate the completion of eating at a prior time. Another example is:

> *kæy hæy dʒɔ̱*   *ma ma room*
> he   go   ⎛perfect   ⎞ Mama room
>   ⎝aspect marker⎠
>
> "He has gone to Mama's room."   (3;6)

where the verb *hæy* "go" is marked similarly by *dʒɔ* to denote the completion of the action of going at a prior time.

How did Elvoo express in English the same notion of event completed at a prior time? At 3;6 and even as late as 5;0, Elvoo was not able to use the English perfect aspect marker, instead he would use the English adverb "already" to denote this notion. Some examples are:

> You eat your cream *already*?   (3;6)
> You finish the *tɔŋ tɔŋ* ("sweets") *already*?   (3;6)
> The red car go *already*.   (4;0)

The use of "already" for event completed at a prior time is a feature of Colloquial Singapore English and Elvoo no doubt learned it from the English spoken around him. What is interesting is that in using *dʒɔ* in Cantonese and "already" in English to denote this notion, Elvoo came to see a parallel between the two items, so that the position of one was affected by the position of the other. How was this so? The Cantonese perfect aspect marker *dʒɔ* is a verbal suffix in adult Cantonese, yet in Elvoo's Cantonese, it was often placed after the object or an adverbial, positions characteristic of the adverb "already" in colloquial Singapore English, as in the following examples:

sɐi   sɐu   d̲ʒ̲ɔ̲

wash   hand $\left(\begin{array}{l}\text{perfect}\\\text{aspect marker}\end{array}\right)$

"(I) have washed my hands."   (3;6)

nei   dʒœk   ŋɔ   gɛ   fu   d̲ʒ̲ɔ̲

you   put   on   I $\left(\begin{array}{l}\text{possessive}\\\text{marker}\end{array}\right)$ pants $\left(\begin{array}{l}\text{perfect}\\\text{aspect marker}\end{array}\right)$

"You have put on my pants."   (3;7)

kœy · dʒɐi hɐi nei   gɛ   room d̲ʒ̲ɔ̲

he   put   in   you $\left(\begin{array}{l}\text{possessive}\\\text{marker}\end{array}\right)$ room $\left(\begin{array}{l}\text{perfect}\\\text{aspect marker}\end{array}\right)$

"He has put (it) in your room."   (3;6)

In the first two examples, *dʒɔ* is separated from the verbs *sɐi* "wash" and *dʒœk* "put on" by the object *sɐu* "hands" and *ŋɔ gɛ fu* "my pants" while in the last example, it is separated from the verb *dʒɐi* "put" by the adverbial *hai nei gɛ* room "in your room". It would appear that this idiosyncratic positioning of *dʒɔ* was a result of transfer which the child made from English to Cantonese resulting from the parallel Elvoo saw between the English "already" and the Cantonese *dʒɔ*.

An interesting corollary to this is that the position of "already" in Elvoo's English was affected too. The data from Elvoo shows that apart from using "already" in the sentence final position or in the position immediately before the verb (without an auxiliary) as in colloquial Singapore English, Elvoo also used it in an idiosyncratic position after the verb and before an object as though it were a verbal suffix like *dʒɔ* in adult Cantonese. Examples of this idiosyncratic use are:

The giant make *already* your house.   (4;0)
Now he kill *already* all the shark.   (4;0)

Such examples suggest that while the position of *dʒɔ* in Elvoo's Cantonese was affected by that of "already", the position of "already" was likewise affected by that of *dʒɔ*. It would seem therefore that in simultaneous language acquisition, the recognition of a semantic parallel between two items in the two languages would lead to a syntactic transfer, at least temporarily until the two systems are clearly sorted out.

Specification of Termination of Event

The way Elvoo expressed the concept of terminated event in the two languages he was learning also throws an interesting light on how transfer
operates in simultaneous language acquisition. In adult Cantonese, the
notion of terminated event is expressed by the verbal suffix *jyn*. At 3;6,
Elvoo was able to comprehend this grammatical marker, as reflected in the
following dialogue between him and his mother where he was able to
respond appropriately to his mother's question, thus showing his understanding of the aspectual meaning in his mother's utterance:

Mother: *dʒiŋ jyn*   *mei a?*
            (terminative   )   (interrogative)
         do (aspect marker) no (particle   )
         "Have (you) finished doing it?"

Elvoo: *dʒiŋ hou dʒɔ*   *la   ma*
                       (perfect   )
         do good (aspect marker) (modal particle)
         "(It) has been done, don't you know?"   (3;6)

At 3;7, he was able to use it in imitation, as demonstrated in the following
exchange where he appropriately incorporated in his response the verb *sik*
"eat" plus the terminative aspect marker *jyn* used in his father's utterance:

Father: *dɐŋ guŋ guŋ sik jyn*   *sin la*
                              (terminative   )
         wait Grand-dad eat (aspect marker) first (modal particle)
         "Wait till Grand-dad has finished eating."

Elvoo: *dim gai guŋ guŋ   m sik jyn*   *a?*
                              (terminative   ) (interrrogative)
         why   Grand-dad not eat (aspect marker) (particle   )
         "Why doesn't Grand-dad finish eating?"   (3;7)

However, while he was able to use this marker in imitation, he was not able
to use it productively on his own. Instead, to denote termination of event,
he would use the English lexical verb "finish" in the position occupied by
jyn in adult Cantonese, as in:

ŋɔ sik finish   la
I   eat finish   (sentence-final particle)
"I have finished eating."   (4;7)

when ŋɔ dei sik   finish   go   cake, ŋɔ dei hœy bin?
                   (terminative)(noun   )
when we   eat (aspect marker)(classifier) cake, we   go   where
"Where shall we go when we finish eating the cake?"   (4;7)

What must have happened in the above cases was that Elvoo had confused the Cantonese terminative aspect marker *jyn* with the lexical verb *jyn*, the latter translatable as "finish" in English. Since he was more proficient in his English and therefore found it easier to retrieve the English rather than the Cantonese form, he fell into the habit of using the English lexical verb for the Cantonese verbal suffix.

However, what is particularly interesting is that he transferred the idiosyncratic way he denoted the terminative concept in his Cantonese utterances into his English, to produce sentences such as:

I eat *finish* already.   (4;0)
When you eat *finish*, can you play with me?   (4;0)
When I drink *finish*, can I eat ice-cream?   (4;0)

Here it would appear that Elvoo had applied the Cantonese system of marking aspect with a verbal suffix to his English. It is possible that this transfer was facilitated by the fact that in English, aspect marking is in some cases done by using a verbal suffix, as in the case of the -ing form. In other words, the condition is favourable for such a transfer.

Positioning of the Interrogative Word

English and Cantonese show a marked difference in the position of the interrogative word. The way Elvoo handled this difference sheds an interesting light on the subject of transfer in simultaneous acquisition. In an English interrogative word question, the wh-word is preposed whereas in the Cantonese version, the corresponding word is not preposed. At 3;6, Elvoo was using a wide range of interrogative word questions in Cantonese with the interrogative words appropriately placed in different positions

according to their grammatical function in the sentence. When they substituted for the subject, they were placed before the verb and when they substituted for the object or the complement, they were placed after the verb,
as in the following examples:

> *bin gɔ mai gɔ di* cookies?
> who   buy those cookies
> "Who bought those cookies?"   (3;6)

> *ŋɔ jiu   wak   bin gɔ?*
> I   want draw who/what
> "Who/what do I want to draw?"   (3;6)

> *dʒɛ dʒɛ hɐi bin dou   a?*
> $\left(\begin{array}{l}\text{interrogative}\\\text{particle}\end{array}\right)$
> Je-Je   be where
> "Where's Je-Je?"   (3;6)

In other words, Elvoo had at 3;6 acquired the appropriate word order for
interrogative word questions in Cantonese and there was no evidence of
any interference from the different English word order. One probable
reason for Elvoo's early acquisition of the placement of the Cantonese
interrogative word is that the order is the same as that of the declarative
counterpart and no transposition is involved.

When attention is turned to how Elvoo at 3;6 asked interrogative word
questions in English, it is found that Elvoo had less success in getting the
appropriate word order here. Research on native English speaking children
as well as children speaking other languages as their first language shows
that they readily acquire the wh-word preposing rule and by 3;6 have no
difficulty in applying it (Brown 1968; Hatch 1974; Ravem 1975). This, however, was not the case with Elvoo, whose interrogative word questions from
3;6 to 3;9 fell into two groups: in one, the wh- word was apparently preposed and in the other, it was not. Examples of questions with the wh-word
placed initially are:

> *Who's* that?   (3;8)
> *What's* it?   (3;7)
> *Where's* the tree?   (3;6)
> *Where's* your mummy and daddy?   (3;8)

Examples of questions where the wh-word was not pre-posed are:

You are doing *what*?   (3;6)
This is for making *what*?   (3;9)
Your name is *what*?   (3;9)
Je-Je is *where*?   (3;9)
We're going to eat *where*?   (3;9)

The existence of a large number of questions where the wh- word was not preposed suggests that at this age, between 3;6 and 3;9, Elvoo had not acquired the preposing rule. What he seemed to have acquired were certain prefabricated questions in the form of "who's", "what's" and "where's" where the copula appeared invariably in the contracted *'s* form. It is suggested here that these prefabricated question forms with "who's", "what's" and "where's" were learned by imitation as a result of the high frequency of occurrence of such question forms. In other words, these early preposed forms were learned within the English language, through imitation, but did not represent the internalisation of the preposing rule as it was not generally applied to all wh- questions. Elvoo's relative difficulty in acquiring the preposing rule can be attributed to influence from colloquial Singapore English where the wh- word is not preposed and possibly influence from interrogative word questions in Cantonese. However, the cause of this difficulty is not a main concern in this paper. What is of interest here is what happened after Elvoo had acquired the preposing rule in English. Elvoo began to prepose the wh- word from 4;3 to 4;9, as he was also exposed to standard Singapore English where the preposing rule applies. The first wh- word to be preposed was "where", then followed by "what", as in:

Where I will hide?   (4;3)
What you want to do?   (4;6)

Even embedded clauses came to have the wh- words preposed, as in:

I don't know *where* he goes.   (4;8)
See *what* we'll make then.   (4;9)

What is particularly noteworthy is that with the internalization of the preposing rule in his spoken English, Elvoo transferred this rule to his Cantonese and came up with idiosyncratic forms such as:

<u>mɛ</u>   nei jiu   mai?
what you want buy?
"What do you want to buy?"   (4;9)

mɛ   hɐi li   gɔ?
what be   this (noun classifier)
"What is this?" (4;10)

bin   gɔ   nei dʒuŋ yi?
      (noun classifier)
which   you like
"Which one do you like?"   (4;10)

However, this preposing rule originating from English was not applied consistently to his Cantonese and preposed as well as unpreposed question forms appeared side by side, even within the same turn, as in:

ma ma, bin   gɔ   nei dʒuŋ yi? nei   dʒuŋ yi bin gɔ?
Mama, which(classi-)you like   you like   which(classi-)
            (noun)   (noun)
                fier   fier

bin   gɔ   nei dʒuŋ yi?
      (noun classifier)
which   you like

Here there is clear evidence of transfer from English to Cantonese. In this case, the transfer took place after the child had acquired the appropriate structures in the two languages. It would appear that the English preposed structure was so fully internalised that it was transferred to Cantonese temporarily, until the child learned to set up clearer boundaries between the two languages. (For a fuller treatment of this point, see Kwan-Terry 1986.)

Acquisition of the Relative Clause

Another area to look at is Elvoo's development in the use of the relative clause in English and in Cantonese, for relative clauses in these two languages display marked syntactic differences. In English, the relative clause is a right-branching clause linked to the preceding head noun with a relative pronoun. In Cantonese, on the other hand, the relative clause is a left-branching clause linked to the following head noun with either a determiner plus classifier or a linking particle. What form did Elvoo's first relative clause take? At 3;6, there first appeared what could be taken as a proto-relative clause in the English data. It took the form of

OK, go and tell the man *make the TV* come.   (3;6)

where the relative pronoun "who" is missing. It was only at 4;6 that the linking relative pronoun was added, in the form of the invariant "that", and this form continued to be used into the sixth year, after 5;0. The following are some examples:

I find a coconut *that* hanging in this tree.   (4;6)
I want nice bird *that's* a fire bird *that* is not angry.   (4;8)
I give you a medicine *that* can make it won't, won't dead.   (4;8)
I want the mouse *that* is circle, have or not?   (4;11)

In Elvoo's highly mixed Cantonese sentences, there was a similar pattern of development within the same period of time. What he had developed was not the left-branching Cantonese relative clause linked to the head noun with either a determiner + classifier or a linking particle, but the English proto-relative clause structure which he relexicalised in Cantonese. First he used the form without the linking "that", as in the following dialogue:

Annette: I say I don't want a dog that will bite the master. I want a dog that will not bite a master.
Elvoo: OK.

Mother: *nei jiu mε gɐu a*, Elvoo?
         (= "What dog do you want, Elvoo?")
Elvoo: *m   jiu   jɐt gɔ*   dog bite *gɔ*   master.
                            ⎛noun   ⎞   ⎛noun   ⎞
         not want a   ⎝classifier⎠ dog bite ⎝classifier⎠ master.
         "(I) don't want a dog (that) bites its master."   (4;6)

So here is a case of the transfer of an English proto-relative clause structure into Cantonese: although Annette included the linking pronoun in her utterance, Elvoo, not having developed the use of this linking pronoun, dropped it from his own utterance. Following the transfer of the English proto-relative clause into his Cantonese, Elvoo developed the use of the English linking relative pronoun in his Cantonese utterances, as in:

Tomorrow *ŋɔ hœy dʒou gɔ di* good dog that *m   hɐi* noisy *ha?*
tomorrow I   go   make those good dog that not be   noisy ⎛modal ⎞
                                                          ⎝particle⎠
"Tomorrow I will make a good dog that is not noisy, alright?"   (4;6)

nei   m   ŋɔi   li   gɔ   boat that *jɐu*   one chimney?

you   not   want   this ⎛noun   ⎞ boat that have one   chimney
                        ⎝classifier⎠
"Don't you want this boat that has a chimney?"   (4;9)

It can be seen from the above that as far as the relative clause is concerned, Elvoo developed first the English right-branching structure, which he relexicalised and borrowed into his Cantonese, and the pattern of development in his use of the structure in his Cantonese utterances followed the same pattern as in his English utterances.

The data shows that Elvoo did not develop the left-branching Cantonese relative clause until much later. At 4;9, he had no difficulty comprehending the Cantonese relative clause structure but the productive use of this structure developed only after 5;6. His first observed use was:

ŋɔ   jiu   tɐu   sin   nei   gɔŋ   *gɔ*   *gɔ*   king that *hɐi*

I   want just now you mention ⎛deter-⎞⎛noun ⎞ king that be
                                  ⎝miner ⎠⎜classi-⎟
                                          ⎝fier   ⎠

hou   strong.
very   strong.
"I want the king that you mentioned just now who was very strong."
(5;6)

Here the head noun "king" is modified by two clauses: "*tau sin nei gɔŋ gɔ gɔ*" (that you mentioned just now) and "that *hɐi hou* strong" (who was very strong). One is placed before the head noun in the fashion of the Cantonese left-branching clause linked to the head noun with the determiner plus classifier *gɔ gɔ* "that", and the other is placed after the head noun in the fashion of the English right-branching clause linked to the head with the relative pronoun "that". Here it would appear that the desire to modify the head noun in two clauses forced Elvoo to resort to the Cantonese relative clause structure in addition to the English structure, one branching to the left and the other to the right, thus avoiding the clumsiness of two right-branching relative clauses one after another.

Conclusion

The examples discussed in the above show that transfer plays an important role in bilingual language acquisition. This transfer may manifest itself in different ways and occur at different stages of acquisition. A learner may first acquire or internalise a particular linguistic structure found in one of the two languages he is exposed to (although he may not be aware of the source language from which the structure comes) and then apply the structure to both the languages he is learning. This is exemplified in Elvoo's use of the terminative aspect marking system in Cantonese which he borrowed into his English and in his use of the English relative clause which he relexicalised and adopted in his Cantonese. In the case of Elvoo's acquisition of the English relative clause, the process went through two stages: first the development of the proto-relative clause without the linking relative pronoun, then the development of the full clause with the linking pronoun; and these two stages were also reflected in Elvoo's adoption of the clause in his Cantonese. This suggests that a structure need not be fully developed before it is transferred or applied to the languages being learned. It might be argued here that the structure first learned for a particular function may not be a language specific structure (that is, taken from one of the languages being learned) but a language neutral structure, and that it is the first to be learned before any language specific structures are developed because it is closer to a language universal. The problem with this argument is that it is difficult to establish that the first structure that is learned is a language neutral structure, since it closely resembles the structure in one of the two languages being learned. The learner might not perceive the structure as specific to either of the two languages. However, the fact that it is a structure found in one of the two languages the learner is exposed to suggests that it is probably learned via exposure to this language and the structure is then transferred to the other language or applied to both languages. Alternatively, two different structures having the same function found respectively in two languages may be learned individually within each of the languages concerned, and with the acquisition of two parallel structures, the recognition of similar functions may lead the learner to transfer the syntactic property of one to the other. This is exemplified in Elvoo's use of the English and the Cantonese devices for the specification of the concept of event completed at a prior time and in the position he gave the interrogative word in speaking English and in speaking Cantonese. In both cases, the recognition of a parallel semantic function, between $d\textipa{Z}\textipa{O}$ and "already" and between the English wh- word and its Cantonese equivalent, led Elvoo to transfer the syntactic position characteristic of one to the other. The transfer may go in both directions, so that the parallel items in the two languages may each exhibit the syntactic property characteristic of the other. This transfer of syntactic property may occur from the beginning when a structure is being acquired, as in the case of Elvoo's use of *dʒɔ* and "already" (when the syntactic confusion was apparent from the start), or it may occur only after the structure in each of the two languages has already been established, as in the case of Elvoo's transfer of the English wh- word preposing rule to Cantonese after he had learned to use the interrogative words in Cantonese in appropriate positions.

References

Brown, Roger. 1968. "The Development of Wh- Questions in Child Speech". *Journal of Verbal Learning and Verbal Behaviour* 7(2). 279-290.

Hatch, Evelyn. 1974. "Are there Second Language Learning-Universals?" *Working Papers on Bilingualism* 3. 1-18.

Kwan-Terry, Anna. 1986. "The Acquisition of Word Order in English and Cantonese Interrogative Sentences: A Singapore case study". *RELC Journal* 17(1). 14-39.

Ravem, R. 1975. "The Development of Wh-questions in First and Second Language Learners". *New Frontiers in Second Language Learning* ed. by J. Schumann & N. Stenson, 153-175. Rowley, Mass.

A Sociolinguistic Interpretation of Everyday Talk between Mothers and Children[1]

Ruqaiya Hasan and Carmel Cloran

1. Introduction

Recent work in sociolinguistics has put to rest the fiction of language as a homogeneous system: the heterogeneity that Saussure tried to banish from the concerns of "linguistics proper" is now at the centre of the field. However, Saussure was a master of antinomies; and among these was one which is particularly relevant to this paper, his contrast between the social and the individual. Saussure gave substance to these terms, as he did to many of his key concepts, by relating them to language (*langue*) and speaking (*parole*):

> In separating language from speaking we are at the same time separating (1) what is social from what is individual, and (2) what is essential from what is accessory and more or less accidental.
>
> (Saussure 1966:14)

Speaking, for Saussure, was "an individual act", essentially "wilful and intellectual", where "the speaker uses the language code for expressing *his own thoughts*" (ibid; emphasis ours). What banished speaking from linguistics proper, according to Saussure, was its irregularity and unpredictability. Yet it is arguable that the idea of talk as irregular, accidental and unpredictable is actually an artefact of his own imagination. Despite his repeated claims about the social nature of language, Saussure continued to ignore the social nature of human talk, while highlighting individual volition, and individual ownership of thoughts, ideas and concepts, as perhaps the only important facts about speaking. But how true a model of human talk is this? Is speaking truly irregular, accidental and unpredictable?

In this paper, which reports on a small part of a wider programme of research,[2] we shall attempt to show that the nature of human talk is essentially social, and that it is this fact that explains its non-accidental and reasonably predictable character. The research project was called "The Role of Everyday Talk between Mothers and Children in Establishing Ways of Learning"; and one of our central concerns was to ask: Is there any evidence of systematic semantic variation in everyday dialogue? and if so, does it correlate with the social class position of the speakers? These research questions were embedded, in turn, in a more general concern with the effect of semantically different interactive practices on the formation of human consciousness, and their possible consequences for future interaction. In order to be able to examine this question, we needed to focus on dialogues where one member of the dyad would be already 'naturalized' into some socially recognized ways of saying and meaning, while the other would be at a formative stage, as yet uninfluenced by other significant modes of interaction.

It seemed clear that the most suitable subjects would be mother-child dyads with the children aged 3;6 to 4;2. Up to this age, at least in Australia, the mother is the most important 'other' in the child's interactive life, and peer group influence is not yet a significant factor. The average age of the children who participated as subjects in this research was in fact 3;8.

The question of social class is much more problematic. It could be argued that since children, and at least those mothers that are unemployed, do not form part of the labour force they should not be seen as belonging to any social class (see for example Horvath 1985). But in our view this is not a viable interpretation. Belonging to a social class is tantamount to gaining access to the possibility of active participation in a specific set of social processes (Connell 1983:148). Such access is not identical across the whole population; and it is not exclusive to the breadwinning member of the family — it encompasses the family as a whole. Thus, for example, infant mortality is much higher among working class than among middle class families in Sydney; and equally significant differences will be found in the incidence of unemployment, malnutrition, miscarriages and accidents. When the life chances of women and children are determined by the social status of the family to which they belong, it would seem extraordinary to deny them membership of a social class.

A more real problem is the definition of social class. Marx criticized "vulgar common sense" for turning "class differences into differences in the size of one's purse, and class conflict into a quarrel between handicrafts"

(Bottomore and Rubel 1976:208).

Criteria such as occupation, education and income are not only circular; they are also implicationally related. And while these criteria could be used heuristically, it seemed best to use more fundamental concepts in determining the social class of the subjects for this project. The questions that we took as criterial concerned the extent to which a person's position might permit him/her to take decisions in the day-to-day conduct of work-related practices, and to pass on these decisions to be executed by others. Thus it was the exercise of power, and access to control over others, of the main breadwinner that decided the class position of the family to which our research subjects belonged.

Clearly this has to do with autonomy at the place of work. This is not a simple question of having or not having autonomy; it is very much a matter of degree. Nevertheless we were able to identify two distinct groups, "LAP" (Lower Autonomy Profession) and "HAP" (Higher Autonomy Profession). Where the autonomy at work was none or very little, as with a council truck-driver or a contract bricklayer, the family was considered to belong to the LAP group; where it was considerable, as with a bank manager or a doctor, the family was considered to belong to the HAP. The population for this research consisted of 24 mother-child dyads equally distributed between the two groups.

Likewise, as the interaction of social class and sex has long been recognized in sociological studies, the children were equally distributed into female and male. Table 1 shows the distribution of the subjects by class and sex.

All mothers were born and brought up in Australia, and none had lived abroad for a length of time greater than six months. Their first language in all cases was English. (All were, in fact, white Australians.)

Table 1: Distribution of dyads by social group and sex of child

	LAP	HAP	Total
Girls	6	6	12
Boys	6	6	12
Total	12	12	24

2. Recording the Mother and Children

While it is generally accepted, following Labov's lead, that (except where the context is one that leads to self-monitoring) phonological patterns are beyond the speaker's conscious control, it might be thought that semantic patterns would be much more susceptible of conscious choice. But this would be true (if at all) only if 'semantic' is understood in the restricted sense of the choice of words and word meanings. In our research, however, where the concern is with language in the formation of social consciousness, semantics has to be understood as the deeper, cryptotypic grammatical meanings that Whorf (1956) showed to be much below the level of conscious awareness. It was, of course, important to avoid the kinds of situation that might lead to self-monitoring: for example if the speakers were being required to do something they would not normally have done in that particular time, place or company, or if some outsider was present in a context that was typically private and domestic.

What we did, therefore, was to seek the mothers' help in collecting the data. Each mother was given a small and powerful audio recorder, which once turned on did not need attending to. We asked the mothers to turn the recorder on whenever they felt they would like to, when they were talking to the child who was the subject. They did not have to worry about turning the machine off and on if the child disappeared briefly, but should turn it off only when they thought the child had now become engaged in something else and would not be talking to them again for some considerable time. They were specifically asked not to do, or make the child do, anything special since our purpose in collecting the data was to find out what the children say when left to themselves, not being prodded into talking. We did however ask them to do the recording at different times of the day so that the children's talk would be represented during the different kinds of activity they engage in as a matter of course, such as eating a snack, getting dressed, playing with the mother and so on.

Much to our surprise and delight, we found allies in the children in maintaining the naturalness of the data. Since the tape recorder was quite unobtrusive, and since there was no researcher/outsider present at the time of the recording, the children had no sense of being in a situation that was in any way other than normal. And whilst mothers did know that whatever was being said was for others' ears, they were unable to act in ways other than usual, because their children forced them to present that same maternal face with which they were already familiar. Further, the mothers were doing this recording at a time when they were engaged in their normal household chores. Anyone who has juggled the many balls that mothers juggle every day in coping with an immature human and the world of objects would realize how difficult it is to behave other than habitually under such circumstances.

3.   The Data

Each dyad was given six hours' worth of recording tape, but due to the recording instructions mentioned above, there was bound to be some wastage. The total amount of talk collected is approximately 100 real hours. As the resources of this project were limited, and the semantic analysis was labour intensive, all of this data could not be subjected to analysis. Criteria for deriving a viable smaller sample were based on a consideration of the nature of the 100 hours of talk. The systemic functional model provides a framework for describing the context of situation in which some historically located speaking has taken place. The three relevant parameters are (1) field of discourse; (2) tenor of discourse; and (3) mode of discourse (Halliday 1978:Ch.6,7). Could the 100 hours of talk be described in general terms, using the framework provided? To consider the nature of the dialogues, the more detailed account of the three parameters by Hasan (1985) is used here.

Beginning with the field of discourse, let us look at the *goal orientation of social activity*. Over the 100 hours, if we consider only the long term goal, the social activity would appear invariant: it could reasonably be maintained that the activity in which the dyads were engaged was one of socialization. As long term goals are seldom conscious ones, we suggest that, without necessarily realising the fact, the mothers were giving their children early lessons in ways of being, behaving and saying. However, in view of the recording instructions to mothers, not surprisingly the short term goals displayed a great deal of variation: they baked cakes, they cleaned rooms, they washed up, they "read" books, they played all sorts of games etc., etc. Each dyad did a myriad of things; and no two could be said to be exactly identical in the choice of such activities. However, informally speaking, all 24 dyads were found to interact in somewhat similar material situational settings (Hasan 1973), which can be globally characterised as (a) mother giving care to the child, e.g. providing food, giving a bath, dressing etc.; (b) mother and child engaged in some cooperative action, e.g. playing with building blocks, reading picture books, cooking, cleaning up some part of the house etc.; and (c) mother engaged in day-to-day household chores, while child is present in the same location doing something or just watching. It would be wrong to confuse these material situational settings with the notion of social activity relevant to the discourse; a situational setting such as telephoning may cover social activities as diverse as extending an invitation, making a medical appointment, or enquiring about the availability of some goods.

The second aspect of 'field', i.e. its *experiential domain*, is subservient to that social activity that is oriented to short term goal (Hasan in press). Thus if the short term activity is to invite someone to a dinner party, the experiential domain relevant to this would certainly be different from that where the short term goal of the activity is to find out the availability of some goods from a department store. This aspect of the field is ultimately expressed in the lexicogrammar of a discourse, via the experiential metafunction, as an organization of naming and specific states of affairs. We believe that Martin et al.'s *activity structures* (1988) capture this aspect of discourse organization. Hasan (1985, in press) has argued that the short term goal of an activity is typically conscious; by contrast, long term goals of activities often remain covert, below the surface of participants' consciousness. If the comments about the relationship of short term goal to domain of experience and of the latter to lexical selections are correct, then it would follow that the lexical aspects of a text are the least suitable materials for an examination of semantic variation. In this study, the selection of lexicon is completely ignored, except in as much as it might be implicated in the realization of some semantic configuration. By contrast, the long term activity of socialization is a better candidate for the study of semantic variation, because of the unconscious nature of its goal.

While the material situational settings (a)-(c) are not such as to indicate the experiential domain, they are not entirely irrelevant to the study. In fact these settings are like malleable frames which are shaped by the workings of the discourse into some specific fields. This possibility is relevant in the context of socialization. If over an equal amount of talk between the individual dyads, we find some that, for example, use these frames more often for issuing threats, while others use these same frames for providing reasons, then we would be justified in postulating the existence of semantic variation in the socializing activity of the two groups. This strategy has been followed in this study.

The description of the tenor of discourse appears much simpler. So far as the *social status* relation is concerned, we have a hierarchic dyad formed by (superordinate) mother and her (subordinate) child; and it is in the nature of this relationship that the *social distance* between the two would be near-minimal. As the long term goal is socialization, the *agentive roles* of socializer for mother and socialized for the child appear reasonable. Since in our study activities with a short term goal orientation were ignored, the action-based agentive roles are irrelevant. If, then, a pattern of semantic variation is found, such that it exists independently of the variations arising from differences in the experiential domain, it becomes reasonable to ask: what does this variation correlate with, particularly as it would seem that the relation between participants remains invariable?

Finally, the mode of discourse: here, the channel used is *phonic*; there was in the majority of cases also visual contact: the two speakers were where they could see and hear each other. The medium is *spoken* and *dialogic*; note that the linguistic patterns of the dialogue conform to those characteristic of speech (Halliday 1985), and there is the frequent turn-taking that is typical of dialogue. Since the role of language is sensitive, amongst other things, to the short term goal orientation, this too varied both within and across the many recorded dialogues. The description of the context of situation for the dialogues recorded is presented in summary form below:

Field of Discourse
> *Long term goal orientation*: socialization into ways of being, behaving and saying.
> *Short term goal orientation*: (varied across dialogues).
> *Experiential domain*: (varied across dialogues).

Tenor of Discourse
> *Agentive roles*: (varied across dialogues).
> *Social relation*: hierarchic; mother knowing, child novice.
> *Social distance*: near-minimal.

Mode of Discourse
> *Role of language*: (varied across dialogues).
> *Channel for access*: phonic with visual contact.
> *Medium of interaction*: spoken and dialogic.

In deriving the sample from the 100 hours of mother child talk, first those discourses were set aside which, for some reason such as household noise, were not intelligible. From the remainder, 46 minutes of talk per dyad was selected as the sample to be analysed. Each dyad was within reason equally represented for each setting (a)-(c), keeping in mind the malleability of the situational settings and the relevance of this to semantic variation. All results are based on this sample, which was transcribed as dialogue in ordinary orthography (for conventions see Hasan 1986; Butt 1989; Cloran 1989), and consisted of 20,544 messages. Message was defined as in Halliday (1984) and Hasan (forthcoming).

4.   Analytic Categories: An Example

Since the principle of paradigmatic organization applies at all levels of language, it is reasonable to suppose that the facts at the semantic level can also be represented as systems of interlocking choices (Halliday 1973). Our research design demanded a network that represented the semantic choices available to speakers of English regardless of the occasion of its use; i.e. what would be described as a *context-independent* system of semantic options. In fact, given the relationship between linguistic meanings and the context of situation, a particular set of semantic options chosen from such a network in the speech of some speaker could itself be used as a means for identifying the nature of the speech event. This must follow logically from, for example, Hymes' notion of language as constitutive of context (Hymes 1971), and from the postulated relationship between meaning and context in the systemic-functional model.

The construction of the semantic networks is one point in the model where Halliday's (1978:Ch.2,7) postulate of both multifunctionality and the equality of status between the functions can be further examined. It transpires that, if one is interested in the meanings of the messages, one cannot ignore any of these aspects, nor can one claim greater centrality for one kind of meaning in comparison with the others (Hasan Mss). The interpersonal and textual functions of the messages are just as important as the ideational function: it is equally important to know whether someone is making a statement; whether that statement is in response to something said by someone else or not; whether the message is logically related to another as, say, effect is to some cause; whether it describes a voluntary action or one

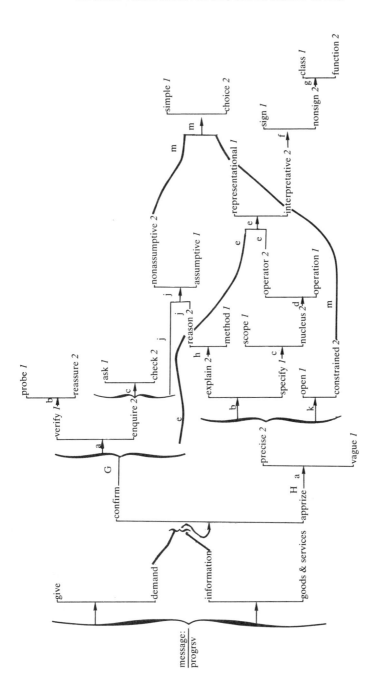

Figure 1: A simplified network of semantic choices for asking questions

Table 2: Demand information: realizations and examples

I: OPTIONS AND THEIR REALIZATIONS

ACCESS > H = [DEMAND; INFORMATION: APPRIZE]
(interrogative:non-polar; wh- conflated with Theme)

a1 [vague]	ellipsis of Finite and Predicator; AND Theme MUST BE initiated as *what/how about* with nominal group following
a2 [precise]	interrogative:non-polar
b1 [specify]	wh-element MUST NOT conflate with Circ:Reason OR Circ:Method:Principle
b2 [explain]	wh- is Adj *why/../how/..*
c1 [scope]	wh- is Adjunct; conflates with any Circ EXCEPT Reason or Principle
c2 [nucleus]	wh- is Subj or Comp *who/what../which..*
k1 [open]	interrogative:non-polar MUST NOT be followed IN SAME TURN by an elliptical clause whose single element matches wh-element in function
k2 [constrained]	non-polar interrogative, followed by elliptical clause with single element whose function is the same as that of wh- in the non-polar interrogative; turn change between the two NOT ALLOWED

ACCESS > H a2:k2 [apprize:precise:constrained]

m1 [simple]	elliptical clause MUST NOT enter into parataxis with another elliptical clause with identical structure
m2 [choice]	elliptical clauses MUST enter into parataxis with at least one more elliptical clause with identical structure

ACCESS > H a2:b1:c2 [apprize:precise:specify:nucleus]

d1 [operation]	wh- =*what* is Comp; Lex Vb in Pred MUST BE *do/happen/go on*
d2 [operator]	wh- is Subj or Comp *who/what../which..* AND *do* NOT ALLOWED as (non-substitutive) Lex Vb in Pred; *happen/go on* NOT ALLOWED as Lex Vb in Pred

Table 2 (cont.)

e1 [representational]	Pro [rel:intensv:attrbtv] NOT ALLOWED IF (1) Carr is sign and Att its meaning OR (2) Carr is non-sign and Att its class name
e2 [interpretative]	Pro MUST BE [rel:intensv:attrbtv] AND (1) IF Carr is sign Att MUST BE its meaning OR (2) IF Carr is non-sign Att MUST BE its class name
f1 [sign]	Carr MUST BE a sign e.g. *word/number*.. AND Att its meaning
f2 [non-sign]	Carr MUST BE *this/that...* (i.e. implicit reference device)
g1 [class]	Att MUST BE class name of Carr
g2 [function]	wh- =*what..-for* MUST conflate with Circ:Purp
	ACCESS > [apprize:precise:explain]
h1 [reason]	wh- =*why/for what reason/what for*
h2 [method]	wh- =*how/by what method/on what principle*
j1 [assumptive]	polarity negative
j2 [non-assumptive]	polarity positive

II. SELECTION EXPRESSIONS (=SE) AND EXAMPLES

SEs are grouped together on the basis of some feature(s) common to that group. These features are called assumed options. The assumed options for a group are listed at the head of the group; they are not displayed in each SE individually.

1. *Assumed Options H [apprize]*

SE1 *a1* [vague]
      (can't you remember anyone else's name?)
      how about the boys?

SE2 *a2:b1:c1:k1* [precise:specify:scope;open]
      where shall we put him?/who can I play with?...

SE3 *a2:b1:c1;k2:m1* [precise:specify:scope;constrnd:simple]
      where shall we put him? up here?

SE4 *a2:b1:c1;k2:m2* [precise:specify:scope;constrnd:choice]
      where shall we put him? up here, or in your room?

Table 2 (cont.)

---

2. *Assumed Options H a2:b1:c2 [apprize:precise:specify:nucleus]*

SE5   *d1;k1* [operation;open]
       what are you doing?/now, what's happening here?

SE6   *d1;k2:m1* [operation;constrnd:simple]
       what are you doing? colouring your pictures?

SE7   *d1;k2:m2* [operation;constrnd:choice]
       what are you doing? eating or playing with your food?

3. *Assumed Options H a2:b1:c2;d2 [apprize:precise:specify:nucleus;operator]*

S8   *e1;k1* [representational;open]
       who gave you those?/what are you eating?

S9   *e1;k2:m1* [reprsnt;constrnd:simple]
       who gave you those? Nanna?

S10   *e1;k2:m2* [reprsnt;constrnd:choice]
       who gave you those? Nanna, or daddy?

4. *Assumed Options H a2:b2:c2:d2:e2 [apprize:precise:specify:nucleus:operator:inter-pretative]*

SE11   *f1;k1* [sign;open]
       what's handsome boy? (= what does handsome boy mean?)

SE12   *f1;k2:m1* [sign;constrnd:simple]
       what does this say? David?

SE13   *f1;k2:m2* [sign;constrnd:choice]
       what's this sign? add, or take away?

SE14   *f2:g1;k1* [non-sign:class;open]
       what's that?

SE15   *f2:g1;k2:m1* [non-sign:class;constrnd:simple]
       what's that? a boat?

SE16   *f2:g1;k2:m2* [non-sign:class;constrnd:choice]
       what's that? a boat, or a catamaran?

SE17   *f2:g2;k1* [non-sign:function;open]
       what's that for?

SE18   *f2:g2;k2:m1* [non-sign:function;constrnd:simple]
       what's that for? for baking cookies?

Table 2 (cont.)

SE19   *f2:g2;k2:m2* [non-sign:function;constrnd:choice]
          what's that for? for baking cookies, or scones?

4. *Assumed Options H a2:b2 [apprize:precise:explain]*

SE20   *h1;k1* [method;open]
          how does this work?

SE210   *h1;k2:m1* [method;constrnd:simple]
          how does this work? by battery?

SE22   *h1;k2:m2* [method;constrnd:choice]
          how does this work? by battery or electricity?

SE23   *h2:j2;k1* [reason:assumptive;open]
          why don't you want to kiss me?

SE24   *he:j1;k2:m1* [reason:assumptive;constrained:simple]
          why don't you want to go there? because of the other kids?

SE25   *h2:j1;k2:m2* [reason:assumptive;constrained:choice]
          why don't you want to go there? because of the other kids, or something else?

SE26   *h2:j2;k1* [reason:nonassumptive;open]
          why can you light fires?

SE27   *h2:j2;k2:m1* [reason:nonassumptive;constrnd:simple]
          why did it die? because it was old?

SE28   *h2:j2;k2:m2* [reason:nonassumptive;constrnd;choice]
          why did it die? because it was sick, or because it was old?

---

that is imposed by some external agency. If all metafunctions are seen as equally important to the semantic potential of a language, then the system network must represent them all.

   Such a network was prepared by Hasan (1983). Obviously the network does not represent all or nearly all the semantic options available to speakers of English. To prepare such a network would be an enormous enterprise, quite beyond the resources of this investigation. A cut-off point in delicacy was chosen such that it would permit us to ask the kind of questions we are interested in exploring. Certainly this cut-off point in delicacy is quite gross when compared to what would be necessary if, for example, one were to use such a network for the machine generation of meaningful dialogues. But gross though the network is judged by that standard, it is still too vast to be presented within the scope of one article. Figure 1 is a simplified version of a fragment from Hasan (1983), displaying semantic options available to speakers of English if what they want to do is to find out some information from an addressee.

Since the systemic functional model conceives of meaning as constituted by lexicogrammar, it follows that nothing can be entered in the semantic network that cannot be expressed lexicogrammatically. To be valid, each semantic option in the network must be accompanied by some realization statement(s). Table 2 presents the realization statements for some of the options in the network, and provides examples of the relevant Selection Expressions (possible combinations of options from the system).

5.   Answer: The Point of a Question

Although for lack of space we have only presented that fragment of semantic choices which is concerned with the act of seeking information from an addressee, the results to be discussed below concern not simply these but also the semantic choices in giving information in response. Thus the focus of the results discussed below (Section 6) is on dyadic behaviour: how mothers answer children's questions, and how children answer their mother's questions. But before we turn to these results, it may be useful to examine a few extracts to see some of the ways in which questions and answers can be used. The most typical use of a question is to receive some information, this being the "preferred" or "expected" response (Levinson 1983:307). But while it may be true that most questions are paired with an answer, the term 'answer' itelf is not invariable; the kind and extent of information received can differ a good deal. Mothers — and even children as young as those ones used as subjects here — can treat a question as a point of departure for providing information that far exceeds what was strictly asked for, as the following example shows:

Ex: 1   (M = mother; K = Kristy)

    M: (1) can you try and remind me to ring Pam this afternoon?

    K: (2) mm (=yes) (3) why?

    M: (4) I'm going to ask her if she'll mind you one night next week

K: (5) mm

M: (6) 'cause I'm going out to dinner with some of the ladies from playgroup (7) because Sue is leaving

K: (8) pardon? (9) pardon?

M: (10) I'm going out with some of the playgroup ladies (11) because Sue is leaving

K: (12) mm

M: (13) did you know that they're going to leave?

K: (14) no

M: (15) they've been building a house

K: (16) mm

M: (17) oh they haven't been building it (18) someone else has been building it for them (19) and it's nearly finished (20) and they're going to move to their house in May

K: (21) why in May?

M: (22) they're going to wait until the end of the school term

K: (23) mm

M: (24) because Cathy goes to school now (25) and then she will change to her new school after the holidays

K: (26) mm

M: (27) if they'd moved earlier (28) she'd only go to the new school for a week or two (29) and then they'd have holidays you see (30) it would mess it up a bit for her

This extract provides a good illustration of the variability of answers. Note in passing that the very first message would not be treated as a demand for information, but rather as a particular kind of demand for service, i.e. a command. Kristy's message (2) is thus a case of *compliance*, since it is a positive response to a command. The mother interprets Kristy's message (3) as a search for explanation; and strictly speaking, her response (4) does provide this information. But the mother does not stop there; she goes on to give the reason for the reason. The demand for information here produces not simply the information sought, but also information that had not been explicitly sought. By contrast, the mother's own question (13) receives a minimal response in Kristy's (14): the child could not have said less than this without appearing to ignore her mother's question.

5.1 As answers, the mother's (4) and (6-7) on the one hand, and the child's (14), on the other, present two extremes: the mother elaborates upon what, without such elaboration, would still have been an appropriate *non-mini-mal* answer, by giving more information that is related to the matter in hand but has not been specifically sought, while the child provides the barest amount of information that is necessary and sufficient to be treated as a possible answer, and does not go on to add anything else. These two situations appear clearer by contrast with how Kristy's question in (21) is fielded by the mother. Here it is not so very easy to decide what constitutes sufficient information. Perhaps the mother's (22) is enough? But enough for what? The information that Kristy receives from her mother — and she tracks this information closely: note for example her *mm* (23, 26) — reveals to her the significance of May as a time for moving to the new house.

An elaborated answer is then not just "jargon and empty elaboration" (Labov 1972b:203), displaying the speaker's unfortunate tendency towards verbosity. If an answer is an attempt to provide a response that in the respondent's view meets the enquirer's specific need, then elaborated and unelaborated answers display two different estimates of the enquirer's needs. So far as speakers in a natural dialogue are concerned, if they provide elaborated answers, they are not providing information that is just an 'optional extra'. Equally, if they do not elaborate, they are not withholding information that they consider essential to the ongoing discourse. Rather, through the semantic features of their answers, they are indicating what they themselves understood to be the point of the question. Not surprisingly, elaborations typically provide some kind of condition, explanation, reservation, alternative etc. to what would have been just a necessary and sufficient answer, whether minimal or non-minimal.

5.2 Whether an answer would be considered adequate or inadequate is closely related to the concept of the "point" of a question. In the analysis of the data for this research we have attempted to keep the idea of adequacy separate from factuality. Consider the following example:

Ex: 2   (M = mother; K = Karen)

    K: (1) you read it mum
    M: (2) it says "this book belongs to Karen Megan"
    K: (3) (*repeating mother*) this book belongs to Karen Megan
    M: (4) that's right
    K: (5) and that says Karen Megan, doesn't it?
    M: (6) that's where you scribbled on it

K: (7) where? .. (8) where?

M: (9) mummy wrote that

Karen's question (5) seeks confirmation, simply needing reassurance that the state of affairs is as she sees it; and it may be that what the mother says in (6) is factually correct: at that particular place in the book Karen might have scribbled. But this statement of the mother's neither supports nor denies the thesis of the child's question, which is simply that at a specific spot in the book there is some mark/writing which stands for "Karen Megan". Had we not had (7)-(9), we might have been tempted to think that perhaps this is an indirect way of saying: yes this does say Karen Megan, because that's where you have scribbled (something by way of indicating your name). But obviously this interpretation is not possible, for the child does not recognize the spot that the mother is talking about as identical to the one she herself was talking about. The mother's answer is therefore inadequate; it fails to address the point of the question. And, so far as the response to the child's (7) and (8) is concerned, it would be difficult to assign it the status of an adequate answer. A very frequent variety of inadequate answer in our data is that attracted by the explanation-seeking question, e.g. in the following:

Ex: 3   (M = mother; K = Karen)

M: (1) put it (=torch) up on the stove (2) and leave it there

K: (3) why?

M: (4) 'cause

K: (5) that's where it goes?

M: (6) yeah

The mother's (4) *'cause* as an answer to the child's (3) *why* is inadequate, since all it manages to say is something like: the cause is. Note how in (5) the child provides what would be a possible adequate answer to her own question. Yet another variation on this type of question and answer is provided in the following exchange by the same dyad:

Ex: 4   (M = mother; K = Karen)

M: (1) but you'll be glad (2) when you go back to school, won't you?

K: (3) no

M: (4) why?

K: (5) 'cause

M: (6) 'cause why?
K: (7) 'cause Rebecca don't go to my school anymore

5.3 So while it is true that questions are normally used to elicit information that a speaker might need for some purpose or other, the success of this venture depends a great deal upon what the addressee does in response to the question. For example, there are various ways of *responding* but not *answering* (Halliday and Hasan 1976:206ff.). So, one may simply disclaim knowledge of the facts, and/or plead failure of memory, as in the following exchange between Karen and her mother. Again we are not concerned with the factuality of assertions of this kind; what matters is that for the questioner behaviour of this kind could very well be a closure, so far as that avenue of enquiry is concerned.

Ex: 5   (M = mother; K = Karen)
      K: (1) you — you — you try guess a name, alright?
      M: (2) um .. there's John ... isn't there?
      K: (3) who else?
      M: (4) I don't know (5) I can't remember

Here, the mother's last two messages disclaim knowledge of fact, and use failure of memory as the reason for not being able to provide the requisite information. There are also occasions in the data where what looks very much like a disclaimer is actually used as a kind of qualification, warning the questioner that the answer being provided is not necessarily the correct one. This is the case in this short exchange between Nathan and his mother:

Ex: 6   (M = mother; N = Nathan)
      N: (1) ah .. yes (2) where is it (= toy ladder) standing
      M: (3) I don't know darling (4) I'm just suggesting perhaps you
             look there (= downstairs) (5) it could be there .. (6) go and
             have a look.

Here although the mother begins by denying knowledge of the whereabouts of the toy ladder, she does so not, as it were, to evade answering; rather, her message (3) is more like an attempt to absolve herself from being held responsible for what is in her opinion just a guess. In the analysis of the data, such cases would not be treated as evasion.

5.4 It is not our intention to identify here all the ways in which an answer may be evaded; however, it is important to point out the logical end-point of evasion. This happens when the addressee simply ignores the question, failing to give any response whatever, as happens in another exchange between Nathan and his mother:

Ex: 7 (M = mother; N = Nathan)

N: (1) mummy, oh-oh, where does this go?** (2) I know where ..
(3) d'you know where this goes?

M: (4) no (5) do you?

N: (6) yes .. (7) look (*arranging a piece of the jigsaw*)

M: (7) oh yes

N: (8) that's where [?   ] (9) what does right in the corner mean? (10) what does right in the corner mean?

M: (11) what does right in the corner mean? (= is that your question?)

N: (12) yeah (13) where's the little bit?

M: (14) it means go as far as you can possibly go

N: (15) oh, here's the little bit (*begins to chant to self*) .. (16) mum see that's the bit up here, isn't it, mum? (17) mum, that's the little bit up here, isn't it mum? .. (18) mum, this is the little bit off there, isn't it mum? .. (19) there mummy lets —

The concept of ignoring is meaningful if the listener has been given a reasonable chance to reply; the absence of an answer has a different meaning if such an opportunity is not present. So for example, Nathan's message (1) is not answered by the mother, but the ** indicates that the child did not stop to let the mother answer; when in fact he does so in message (3), the mother does answer. By contrast, Nathan's questions (16)-(18) are ignored by the mother; there was enough opportunity for her to answer (as shown by the dots, indicating small pauses). Our data shows that in some families this is a typical mode of "fielding" questions. As can be seen from this very short extract, Nathan and his mother are often parties to such exchanges (cf. Nathan's message (9-10)). The effect of such ignoring is typically that the questioner is forced to repeat the question, as Nathan is in example 7, and Karen was in example 2 (messages 7-8)). When, in an exchange, the questions are not being repeated, this suggests that response is being provided.

6.   Asking and Telling: Some Results from an Empirical Investigation

With these brief comments, we turn to the statistical analysis of the semantic features pertaining to questions and responses to questions. The total
number of questions asked by mothers and children in the sample was
3,358, with children asking a little over one third of the questions (1,350)
and the mothers the remainder (2,008). This figure does not include those
interrogative clauses whose function was to realize some kind of command,
e.g. message (1) of example 1: *can you try and remind me to ring Pam this
afternoon?*, or offer as in *shall I do your laces up?*. Nor does the number
include formulaic questions asked by way of channel repair, e.g. *what?* or
what did you say? and its semantic variants.

    A principal components procedure was used for the statistical analysis
of the data. (For a more detailed discussion, see Horvath 1985; Cloran
1989; Hasan 1988.) The chief attraction of this method was its ability to iso-
late sub-classes in the research population. The use of this statistical procedure enabled us to answer the question: if the only criteria to be used were
the habitual selection of certain semantic features, how would the subjects
in this research compare with one another? Once a group of subjects having
a similar pattern of choice is identified, we can examine how it compares
with some extralinguistic grouping (LAP v. HAP, or male child v. female
child). From the total set of semantic features used as input, the analytic
procedure isolates specific bundles, with each such bundle accounting for
some degree of variance in the data. Each such bundle is known as a Principal Component (or just PC) and subjects are allocated scores on each PC.
It is thus the PCs as a whole that might be found to correlate with social factors; but since the highest degree of variance is accounted for by the first
PC (PC1), we shall limit ourselves to this. We shall consider here PC1 from
two analyses: (1) the semantic features of questions asked by children and
the answers to those questions provided by the mothers; (2) the semantic
features of questions asked by the mothers and of the answers provided by
the children. We are thus focussing on dyadic behaviour in both instances.

6.1 Table 3 shows details of PC1 from the first input. Note that the first letter of each semantic feature in the table is either Q or A: Q stands for *question attribute*, A for *answer attribute*. As analysis (1) is concerned with children's questions and mothers' answers, this implies that the question attributes are found in the speech of the child, and the answer attributes in the

Table 3: PC-A1: Children's questions and mothers' answers

	PC1	PC2	PC3	PC4
Q [REPEAT]	-0.85	0.01	-0.28	-0.06
A [PROVIDE]	0.81	-0.19	0.07	0.03
A [ELABORATED]	0.66	-0.33	-0.01	-0.24
Q [EXPLAIN]	0.65	-0.61	-0.19	0.06
Q [CONFIRM]	0.37	0.77	-0.04	0.05
Q [PREFACED]	0.38	0.58	0.32	0.04
Q [ASK]	-0.01	-0.18	0.75	-0.58
A [ADEQUATE]	0.47	0.10	-0.65	-0.34
Q [ASSUMPTIVE]	-0.08	-0.55	0.19	0.66
Q [RELATED]	0.44	0.40	0.13	0.46
Eigenvalues:	2.98	1.99	1.28	1.18
% Variance:	29.90	19.90	12.90	11.90

mothers' sayings. We shall refer to this PC as *PC1-A1*.

Two more points need to be made clear: first, if a semantic feature used as input is in systemic contrast with only one other feature (i.e. the system consists of a binary choice) then entering one such feature as input provides information regarding both. For example, in Table 3 Q[EXPLAIN] is one term from a binary system, the other term being Q[SPECIFY] (see Figure 1 Ha2b for the system and Table 2 for realization and examples of each term). We note that the loading for Q[EXPLAIN] is positive at .65; from this we can deduce that if the feature Q[SPECIFY] had been entered as input instead of Q[EXPLAIN], the loading for the former feature would have been negative at -.65, i.e the exact opposite of its contrasting term in the system. Thus the semantic features used as input not only state information; they may also imply information that is not explicitly asserted in a table such as Table 3. The second point to note is that not every semantic feature used as input bears relevance to a PC; only those features are considered relevant which reach a certain statistical criterion: thus for this research, only those features were considered relevant which load at or above .40. It is important to add that practice in this respect is varied (for example compare Horvath 1985).

6.2 The semantic features that load criterially on PC1-A1 are shown in Table 4.

Table 4: The structure of PC1-A1: Children's questions and mothers' answers

Q [REPEAT]	-.85
A [PROVIDE]	.81
A [ELABORATED]	.66
Q [EXPLAIN]	.65
A [ADEQUATE]	.47
Q [RELATED]	.44

Let us first present a brief description of each of the semantic features that enters into the structure of PC1-A1. Q[REPEAT], with its negative loading of -.85, implies that child-subjects scoring high on this PC do not repeat their questions. One important incentive for repeating questions is the absence of an answer (cf. 5.4). The absence of repeated questions raises the expectation that answers are provided without delay, and the positive loading of .81 for A[PROVIDE] indicates that indeed mothers in high scoring dyads do answer rather than ignore. A[ADEQUATE] with positive loading of .47 indicates that such answers are adequate. These loadings indicate quite clearly that dyads scoring high on this PC have mothers who answer without unreasonable delay and provide adequate answers. This is more remarkable in view of the fact that children in dyads scoring high on this factor are more likely to ask how/why questions — note the feature Q[EXPLAIN], which has a positive loading of .65 — than they are to ask questions with the features Q*[CONFIRM]* or Q[SPECIFY] (for these terms see Figure 5; for their realizations and examples see Table 2). That the mothers in high scoring dyads would be highly likely to elaborate is shown by the positive loading of .66 for the feature A[ELABORATED]. In keeping with this, children in the high scoring dyads would select the feature Q[RELATED] more often than not. This semantic feature is a more delicate sub-set of the feature [ELABORATED]. What it implies is that the question is logically related to some other message by an overt indication of hypotaxis or parataxis. An example of Q[RELATED] with hypotaxis is Kristy asking her mother *why <<if you're on a picnic>> you can light fires too?* (= why can you also light a fire if you're on a picnic?). An example of parataxis is provided again by Kristy when she says *I'm so quick, aren't I, with this cooking? and I also make scones.* When the features A[ELABORATED] and Q[RELATED] are interpreted together, the implication is that in dyads scoring high on PC1-A1 the speaker considers the addressee as more in need of verbally provided information than is the case in dyads who score low.

6.3 Since groups in the population are isolated by reference to the entire PC, it is the PC as a whole that should be treated as one socio-semantic variable, provided that it significantly correlates with some social factor. PC1-A1 accounts for 29.9% of variance in the data, and correlates significantly with social class, while it is barely short of significant correlation with the sex of the child. Informally the typical dyadic selection of meanings may be stated as follows:

Child:
– does not repeat his/her questions;
– is much more likely to ask *how/why* questions than *who/what/ where/when* .. questions or *is it/does it* kinds of question;
– is more likely to relate her/his question to some other message, thus elaborating on the question itself;

Mother
– is much more likely to answer than ignore question;
– is much more likely to answer adequately than inadequately;
– is very likely to elaborate upon the minimally sufficient answer.

The kind of dyadic behaviour specified above turns out to be much more typical of HAP dyads than of the LAP ones (HAP > LAP: p<.01). At the same time, there is a near-significant correlation between this behaviour and the sex of the child. These ways of asking questions and of being responded to are more typical of mother-daughter dyads (=F) than mother-son ones (=M) (F > M: p<.06). Figure 2 shows the location of LAP and HAP dyads by reference to their scores on PC1-A1 and PC2-A1, with the horizontal axis representing the former and the vertical the latter.[3] *L* stands for LAP dyad, *H* for HAP.

6.4 Let us turn now to the results of the analysis with the second input, where we look at the attributes of mothers' questions and children's answers. The implication is that any semantic feature tagged by Q represents maternal semantic choices in questioning, while those tagged by A represent children's semantic choices in answering. Again, we shall concern ourselves here only with the first PC, which will be referred to as PC1-A2. Like PC1-A1, this PC constitutes a socio-semantic variable, as it correlates

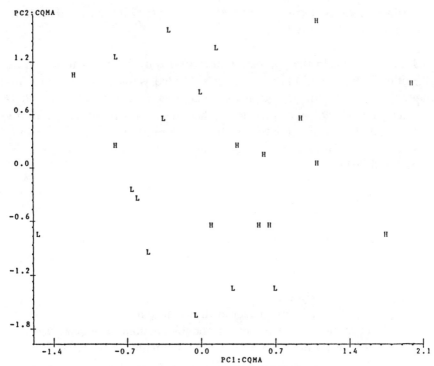

Figure 2: PC1-A1 and PC2-A1 scores and LAP and HAP dyads

significantly with both the social class of the dyad and the sex of the child, while accounting for 32.1% of variance in the data. The total input specification for the second analysis is shown in Table 5.

Three of the semantic features from the total input do not reach the criterial loading of .40 or above. The structure of PC1-A2 is as shown in Table 6. Most of the terms in Table 6 have already either been discussed in connection with Table 3, or explained in Figure 1 and Table 2. (For Q[AS-SUMPTIVE] see example 10 below.) The only exception is the term Q[PREFACED], which is an option in a system pertaining to the logical metafunction. A message is said to have the semantic feature [PRE-FACED], if it is introduced as some saying, thinking, preference etc. Thus in example 6 (see 5.3) Nathan's mother produced a message with the feature [PREFACED], when she said (4) *I'm suggesting perhaps you look there*. Here *perhaps you look there* is presented as a suggestion. Similarly in examples 8 and 9, we have answers that are [PREFACED], but this time both answers are presented as *thoughts*:

Table 5: PC-A2: Mothers' questions and children's answers

	PC1	PC2	PC3
Q [CONFIRM]	*0.73*	-0.09	-0.17
A [ADEQUATE]	*0.73*	-0.33	-0.25
A [ELABORATED]	*0.67*	0.11	-0.41
Q [ASSUMPTIVE]	*-0.67*	0.45	-0.25
Q [EXPLAIN]	*-0.62*	0.39	-0.07
Q [REPEATED]	*-0.59*	-0.36	0.00
Q [RELATED]	*0.47*	0.70	0.04
Q [PREFACED]	*0.45*	0.59	0.45
Q [ASK]	0.11	-0.41	0.71
A [PROVIDE]	0.11	0.16	0.55
Eigenvalues:	3.21	1.68	1.37
% Variance:	32.1	16.9	13.8

Table 6: The structure of PC1-A2: Mothers' questions and children's answers

Q [CONFIRM]	.73
A [ADEQUATE]	.73
A [ELABORATED]	.67
Q [ASSUMPTIVE]	-.67
Q [REPEAT]	-.59
Q [EXPLAIN]	-.62
Q [RELATED]	.47
Q [PREFACED]	.45

Ex: 8 (Mo = mother; Mk = Mike)

   Mk: (1) why are you putting the torecaider (=*taperecorder*) upstairs?

   Mo: (2) oh I just thought I'd bring it up

Ex: 9 (M = mother; K = Kristy)

   M: (1) that might be enough for two sandwiches there mightn't it?

   K: (2) mm .. I think a little bit more lettuce [?I might have] (3) 'cause I love the lettuce and blue vein mum.

The semantic features that make up PC1-A2 are in some respects like those found in PC1-A1. Thus just as in the high scoring dyads for PC1-A1, children are not likely to repeat their questions, so also in the high scoring dyads for PC1-A2, mothers are not likely to repeat their questions. Further, just like the children in the high scoring dyads for PC1-A1, mothers in the high scoring dyads for PC1-A2 are likely to relate their questions to some other message.

However, there are respects in which the semantic features of children's questions and those of the mother differ: as Tables 4 and 5 show, children in the high scoring dyads were more likely to ask why/how questions than either who/what/when/where or yes/no questions. This tendency is reversed for the mothers in the high scoring dyads for PC1-A2: here mothers are not very likely to ask how/why questions, which have a negative loading (-.58), thus implying that questions with the semantic feature Q[APPRIZE] (who/what/when/where) are more likely to be asked; further in the mother's sayings, questions with the feature Q[CONFIRM] (yes/no questions) are very much more likely to occur (positive loading .75). In our results we have noted a differential selection and patterning for the how/why questions: in mothers' talk such questions are more often than not associated with challenge, and so they tend to occur in a control situation with direct commands that do not allow discretion (Hasan 1988; Cloran 1989). An example is provided below:

Ex: 10 (M = mother; K = Karen)
   (*The mother has been trying to get Karen into bed, reasoning, scolding, threatening and slapping her to make her obey*)
   M: (1) Karen do as you — (*slaps child*) (2) put your legs down (3) or I'm going outside right this minute without a kiss (4) now put your legs down (*angry voice*)
   K: (5) mmhm (*refusing to comply*)
   M: (6) now give a kiss good night
   K: (7) I'm not (=I won't/I'm not going to)
   M: (8) you're not gonna kiss me?** (9) why?
   K: (10) 'cause
   M: (11) 'cause why?
   K: (12) 'cause I don't like you (*voice very loud*)

It is clear from the mother's threat in (3) and from the form of her question in (8) that she assumed the child would want to kiss her. The *why* in (9) is thus both a search for explanation for the child's refusal and a challenge against the child's position; the same is true of (11). In fact, the mother does finally force the child into giving her a goodnight kiss. Note in passing that (8) is a good example of a question with the feature [ASSUMPTIVE]; the hidden thesis of this question is *I assume you're gonna kiss me*. The selection of the feature [ASSUMPTIVE] typically implies a closeness of relationship by virtue of which another's beliefs, attitudes, motives and actions are treated as if they were already known and not subject to negotiation.

Two other semantic features which characterize the mothers' questions if they belong to the high scoring dyads for PC1-A2 are Q[ASSUMPTIVE] and Q[PREFACED]; of these, neither is criterial for high scoring children's questions for PC1-A1. Note that Q[ASSUMPTIVE] has a negative loading (-.63), so that high scorers would not be likely to choose this feature; however, the feature Q[PREFACED] has a positive loading (.46) and is thus likely to be present in the talk of the high scoring mothers. When we turn to the attributes of the answers given by children of high scoring dyads, it is notable that the answers are very likely to have the feature [ADEQUATE] and [ELABORATED]. It will be recalled that answers to children's questions too displayed these characteristics (see Table 5). Informally, the dyadic behaviour singled out by PC1-A2 as sociolinguistically significant can be summarized as follows:

Mother
- is highly likely to ask yes/no questions;
- is not likely to ask why/how questions, which implies that she is more likely to ask who/what/when/where questions;
- is not likely to make unspoken assumptions in asking;
- is not likely to repeat her questions;
- is likely to relate her questions to other messages, thus elaborating on its thesis;
- is likely to introduce the question together with someone's point of view, by presenting the question as a saying or an idea.

Child
- is highly likely to offer adequate answers;
- is likely to elaborate her/his answer, so that the sayings provide much more information than is necessary and sufficient in view of the question.

The kind of behaviour specified above is again more typical of the HAP dyads than it is of the LAP ones (HAP > LAP: $p < .002$); further, mother-

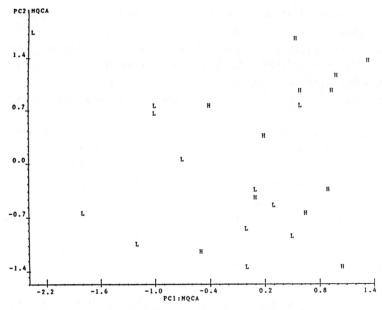

Figure 3: PC1-A2 and PC2-A2 scores of LAP and HAP dyads

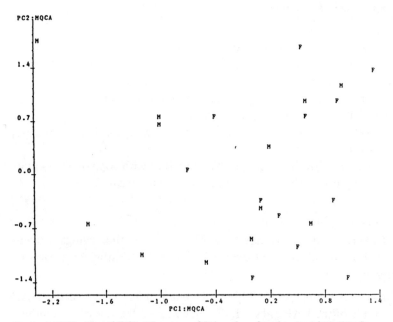

Figure 4: PC1-A2 and PC2-A2 scores of F (mother-daughter) and M (Mother-son) dyads

daughter dyads are more likely to behave this way than are the mother-son ones (F > M: p<.02). Figure 3 presents the plotting of the HAP and LAP dyads by reference to PC1-A2 and PC2-A2.

Figure 4 presents the location of the mother-daughter (=F) and mother-son (=M) dyads by reference to the same two PCs from analysis 2. The conventions for reading both Figures 3 and 4 are the same as for Figure 2.

6.5 If there is this degree of closeness between the two results, it would be reasonable to expect that a high positive correlation would obtain between them; and this is indeed the case (PC1-A1 v. PC1-A2: r = .59). The semantic coherence of the two factors discussed shows that a specific kind of orientation to meaning is to be found in the two groups, as shown by their semantic behaviour. Thus, for example, the kind of responsive behaviour that is displayed by high scoring HAP dyads would be inexplicable, if the mothers, in the act of making their children do what they want them to do, used threats rather than reasons, and did not elaborate their commands or the rationale for their commands. For this would indicate that there was a critical semantic dissonance between the mothers' responsive behaviour and their control behaviour. This is of course not the case. The control behaviour of the mothers is also a socio-semantic variable, with significant differences between the HAP group and the LAP group (Hasan Mss). So when the mothers' responsive behaviour is correlated with their control behaviour, a high correlation is obtained (r = .68); while children's responsive behaviour also correlates positively with their mothers' control behaviour (r = .69). It would be interesting to compare our results with those cited in Turner and Mohan (1970), Robinson and Rackstraw (1972), Wootton (1974), and others. The degree of semantic consistency found in the behaviour of the two social classes requires a higher order concept than semantic variation. Such a concept, we suggest, is *semantic orientation* which is directly deriveable from Bernstein's theory of *code orientation*.

7.   Conclusion

We would argue that the above results provide a convincing argument for the recognition of semantic variation as an important sociolinguistic phenomenon. Thinking of the semantic category QUESTION as a verbal

expression of the contextual act *find out some information* and ANSWER
as a verbal expression of the contextual act *provide information on demand*,
we can look at the various semantic features of questions and answers as
variant expressions of these higher level units. And when we do so, as in
this research, we find that speakers' semantic choices co-vary with some significant social factor. To us it appears that this is a classic case of sociolinguistic variation, in which the variation is not a matter of 'style' or 'expression' but a systematic selection of different ways of meaning in the service
of a definable long-term goal.

In view of our results, we reject Saussure's belief that in separating
speaking from the system of language, we are also separating what is individual from what is social: since our results show that belonging to a particular social class makes the selection of certain semantic features highly
probable, we must conclude that speaking is essentially social. Otherwise,
we cannot conceive of any means whereby the system of language itself
could come to be social. If we were to focus on the "essential", as opposed
to that which is "accessory and more or less accidental", we would certainly
not be able to write off the kind of regularities described above as anything
else but essential aspects of both speaking and language, since the meanings
people choose by virtue of who they are and what the system of their language is like cannot be seen as either accessory or accidental. Following the
drift of Saussure's thought, it would seem that he wished to point out the
accidental nature of phonation as a sign-manifesting modality. This may be
so; but speaking is not simply phonation. Its essential character resides in
its meaningfulness, and the meanings selected in speaking are not typically
describable as unpredictable, accidental, or wilful.

Nor do we feel convinced that Saussure's emphasis on the individual
ownership of thoughts, beliefs and attitudes is above question. This debate
is complex, but at least two remarks are necessary. First, we agree with
Vygotsky that in the life of an individual, all higher mental functions must
at first have been external (i.e. social) before they became internal, a part
of the individual's inner make-up (Vygotsky 1962, 1978; Wertsch 1985). It
is therefore facile to talk about the external and the internal as if they were
contraries. Second, as Bernstein (1987) has pointed out, we do need to
explain "how the outside becomes the inside and how the inside reveals
itself and shapes the outside". If the speaker's "own thoughts" are an
instance or a product of higher mental functions, it would seem to follow
that they are not as much his own possession, by an act of nature, as they

are a social gift. And if they are social gifts, then it is important to understand where such gifts come from, what is the means by which the social structure, the semantic orientation of communication and the inner consciousness of speakers are linked to each other. By closing with this issue, we wish to signal how central to this research are both the conceptual framework provided by Vygotsky and that provided by Bernstein's theory of code.

Notes

1. This paper is a revised and abridged version of a Special Interest Seminar presented at AILA87. Our thanks are due to Rhondda Fahey, who transcribed the proceedings. Hasan is responsible for the theoretical underpinnings of this paper; Cloran for the linguistic and statistical analysis; Hasan and Cloran for the interpretation of the statistical results.

2. The research project (1983-1986) was supported by the Australian Research Grant Scheme, and by a Macquarie University Research Grant. It was initiated and directed by Hasan, who was responsible for the overall research design and the preparation of the analytic framework. Cloran was responsible for the entire linguistic analysis of the data from Phase I of the project as well as the application of statistical procedures. The interpretation of the statistical results is the joint responsibility of Hasan and Cloran. We received help from too many colleagues to permit mention of each name; but our special thanks are due to Anne Eyeland and Allan Taylor for help with statistics, to David Butt, Michael Oerlemans, Rhondda Fahey and the staff of the Speech Hearing and Language Research Centre, in particular John Telec and Harry Purvis, all at Macquarie University; as well as to Barbara Horvath, Greg Guy and Chris Nesbitt at Sydney University.

3. PC2, or Principal Component Factor 2, is the one that accounts for the second highest degree of variance in the data; in this case, a bundle of semantic features having to do with the degree of imperative control. In the graphs (Figs. 2-4), the distribution of PC1 is plotted against that of PC2. Discussion of PC2, however, is beyond the scope of the present paper.

References

Bernstein, B. ed. 1973. *Class, Codes and Control*, Vol. 2: *Applied Studies Towards a Sociology of Language*. London: Routledge & Kegan Paul.

Bernstein, B. 1987. "Social Class, Codes and Communication". Chapter 68 in *Sociolinguistics: An international handbook of the science of language and society*, Vol. 1, ed. by U. Ammon, N. Dittmar & K.J. Mattheier. Berlin & New York: Walter de Gruyter.

Bottomore, T.B. & M. Rubel eds. 1963. *Karl Marx: Selected writings in sociology and social philosophy*. Harmondsworth: Penguin Books.

Butt, D.G. 1989. "The Object of Language". *Language Development: Learning language, learning culture* ed. by R. Hasan & J.R. Martin. Norwood, N.J.: Ablex.

Cloran, C. 1989. "Learning through Language: The social construction of gender". *Language Development: Learning language, learning culture* ed. by R. Hasan & J.R. Martin. Norwood, N.J.: Ablex.

Connell, R.W. 1983. *Which Way is Up? Essays on class, sex and culture*. Sydney, London & Boston: George Allen & Unwin.

Halliday, M.A.K. 1973. *Explorations in the Functions of Language*. London: Edward Arnold.

―――. 1984. "Language as Code and Language as Behaviour: A systemic-functional interpretation of the nature and ontogenesis of dialogue". *The Semiotics of Culture and Language*, Vol. 1, ed. by R.P. Fawcett et al. London & Dover, N.H.: Frances Pinter.

―――. 1978. *Language as Social Semiotic: The social interpretation of language and meaning*. London: Edward Arnold.

―――. 1985. *Spoken and Written Language*. Geelong, Vic.: Deakin University Press (Oxford: Oxford University Press, 1989).

Halliday, M.A.K. & R. Hasan. 1976. *Cohesion in English*. London: Longman.

Hasan, R. 1973. "Code, Register and Social Dialect". *Class, Codes and Control*, Vol. 2: *Applied Studies Towards a Sociology of Language* ed. by B. Bernstein. London: Routledge & Kegan Paul.

―――. 1983. *A Semantic Network for the Analysis of Messages in Everyday Talk between Mothers and their Children*. Mimeo.

―――. 1985. *Language, Context and Text: Aspects of language in a social-semiotic perspective, part B*. Geelong, Vic.: Deakin University Press (Oxford: Oxford University Press, 1989), with M.A.K. Halliday.

―――. 1986. "The Ontogenesis of Ideology". *Semiotics, Ideology, Language* ed. by Terry Threadgold et al. Sydney: Sydney Association for Studies in Society and Culture.

―――. 1988. "Language in the Processes of Socialization: Home and school". *Language and Socialization: Home and School* ed. by L. Gerot, J. Oldenburg & T. van Leeuwen (Proceedings from the Working Conference on Language in Education 17-21 November 1986). Macquarie University.

―――. in press. "Situation and the Definition of Genres". *What's Going on Here: Complementary studies of professional talk* ed. by A.D. Grimshaw. Norwood, N.J.: Ablex.

―――. mss. "Meaning in Sociolinguistic Theory". Plenary Paper presented at the First Hong Kong Conference on Language and Society, 25-28 April 1988. Hong Kong University.

―――. forthcoming. *Offers in the Making: A systemic-functional perspective*.

Hasan, R. & J.R. Martin (eds.). 1989. *Language Development: Learning language, learning culture*. Norwood, N.J.: Ablex.

Horvath, B.M. 1985. *Variation in Australian English: The sociolects of Sydney*. Cambridge: Cambridge University Press.

Hymes, D.H. 1971. "Competence and Performance in Linguistic Theory". *Language Acquisition: Models and methods* ed. by R. Huxley & E. Ingram. New York & London: Academic Press.

Labov, W. 1972. *Language in the Inner City: Studies in the Black English vernacular.* Philadelphia: University of Pennsylvania Press.

Levinson, S.C. 1983. *Pragmatics.* Cambridge: Cambridge University Press.

Lemke, J.L. 1985. *Using Language in the Classroom.* Geelong, Vic.: Deakin University Press (Oxford: Oxford University Press, 1989).

Martin, J.R. et al. 1988. "Secret English: Discourse technology in a junior secondary school". *Language and Socialization: Home and school* ed. by L. Gerot, J. Oldenburg & T. van Leeuwen (Proceedings from the Working Conference on Language in Education 17-21 November 1986). Macquarie University.

Robinson, W.P. & S.J. Rackstraw. 1972. *A Question of Answers.* London: Routledge & Kegan Paul.

Saussure, F. de. 1966. *Course in General Linguistics*, trans. W. Baskin. New York: McGraw Hill.

Turner, G.J. & B.A. Mohan. 1970. *A Linguistic Description and Computer Program for Children's Speech.* London: Routledge & Kegan Paul.

Turner, G.J. 1973. "Social Class and Children's Language of Control at Age Five and Age Seven". In Bernstein (ed.), 1973.

Vygotsky, L.S. 1962. *Thought and Language*, trans. E. Hanfmann & G. Vakar. Cambridge, Mass.: M.I.T. Press.

Vygotsky, L.S. 1978. *Mind in Society: The development of higher psychological processes* ed. by M. Cole et al. Cambridge, Mass. & London: Harvard University Press.

Wertsch, J.V. 1985. *Culture, Communication and Cognition: Vygotskyan perspectives.* Cambridge: Cambridge University Press.

Whorf, B.L. 1956. *Language, Thought and Reality: Selected writings* ed. by J.B. Carroll. Cambridge, Mass.: M.I.T. Press.

Wootton, A.J. 1974. "Talk in the Homes of Young Children". *Sociology* 8.

Are Mothers Really the Main Mediators of Language?

Susanne Döpke

Introduction

Mothers have traditionally been the main target of studies exploring adult influence on children's language development. Nash (1965) argued that the U.S.A. was a matrio-centric child-rearing society (cf. Rebelsky and Hanks 1971). Moerck (1972:230) stated quite explicitly that the fathers' influence on children's language development was not worth studying since mothers spent more time with young children, had more opportunities to model language for them, and therefore were more important for the children's language acquisition than fathers.

In this paper, I will report a number of studies challenging the overwhelming importance of mothers as well as studies comparing the verbal input provided by mothers and fathers. Following that, I will present some of my own results which suggest that fathers may have a greater impact on their children's language development than mothers.

Mother-Child and Father-Child Relationships

Research into the type and quality of interaction between mothers and their young children indicated that mothers at home spent surprisingly little time actively playing, cuddling, and exploring stimulating objects with their children (Clarke-Stewart 1972). Moreover, the emotional relationship between working mothers and their children could not be shown to be qualitatively different from that of mothers-at-home (Clarke-Stewart 1982:71ff.). Hoffman (1974) suggested that working mothers' deliberate efforts at spending time with their children in direct positive interaction might make the quality of interaction in the working mother-child dyad superior to the home mother-child dyad.

By the same token, it is unreasonable to expect that a father who spends the evenings (and weekends) interacting with his children would be unable to form a close relationship with them (Lamb 1975a). Lamb (1975a:249) suggested that "The opportunity for brief yet highly emotionally charged interaction with the father each evening may offset the longer hours spent with a harrassed and dissatisfied mother during the day."

Lamb further reported studies undertaken by others as well as himself which investigated the type and extent of father-child interactions. These studies indicated that fathers were indeed highly accessible to their children, but tended to avail themselves more to play than to caretaking activities. The children in Lamb's own study (1975b) responded more positively to play as well as physical contact with their fathers than with their mothers. He related that to the fact that the fathers' play was more physical and their physical contact more play-related than that of mothers, who spent a much higher proportion of the time they had with their children in caretaking activities.

Maternal Language versus Paternal Language

The discussion of maternal language features and their relation to child language acquisition eventually led to an examination of fathers' language behaviour and whether fathers speak like mothers. The implicit understanding was that only if fathers do speak like mothers (see Snow and Ferguson 1977; Newport, Gleitman and Gleitman 1977; Cross 1978; Furrow, Nelson and Benedict 1979, for features of "motherese") are children likely to learn language from fathers as well. The results obtained in these studies indicated that mothers' and fathers' speech was both similar and different. Fortunately, only a few results were mutually exclusive.

Similarities in Mothers' and Fathers' Speech

No differences were found in linguistic complexity, as measured in MLU (mean length of utterance) and in the complexity of preverbs, in the speech of mothers and fathers to their young children (Gleason 1975; Golinkoff and Ames 1979; Masur and Gleason 1980; Kavanaugh and Jen 1981). Discourse measures like repetitions and expansions (Gleason 1975; Kavanaugh and Jen 1981; Masur 1982) also proved to be similar. A number of studies looked at the types of sentences employed by mothers and fathers and found no differences in the usage of declaratives and interrogatives (Giattino and Hogan 1975; Golinkoff and Ames 1979; Kavanaugh and Jen 1981; for contradictory results see Rondal 1980).

In a study by Rondal (1980), both mothers and fathers displayed an increase in syntactic complexity and lexical diversity as well as a decrease in repetitions and expansions along with the developing linguistic abilities of the child. Masur (1982) found that mothers as well as fathers increased the frequency of symbolic play utterances, and of suggestions that the child should come up with problem-solving ideas, with increasing language development.

Studies by Golinkoff and Ames (1979) and Rondal (1980) showed that the situation had corresponding effects on mothers' and fathers' speech. Both parents talked more in a structured play situation, during which the parent was supposed to teach the child how to play with a complex toy, than in free play situations (Golinkoff and Ames 1979); similarly, story telling had the effect of increasing the amount of parental talk as compared with free play, whereas the meal situation motivated less talk than free play (Rondal 1980). Free play and story telling elicited more words, lower utterance complexity, fewer declaratives, more questions, fewer joint and indirect requests for action, more verbal approvals and more expansions of child utterances from both parents than did the meal situation. However, the lexical diversity was greatest in the story telling situation and decreased over meal situations to free play (Rondal 1980).

Differences in Mothers' and Fathers' Speech

The differences which were found in fathers' and mothers' speech to their young children can be related to talkativeness, degree of linguistic adjustment and general interactive style. Mothers took more turns (albeit shorter ones) than fathers in dyadic interaction (Friedlander, Davis and Wetstone 1972; Rebelsky and Hanks 1971; Gleason 1975; Rondal 1980). In triadic interaction, mothers talked more than fathers in general (Golinkoff and

Ames 1979; Rondal 1980). Golinkoff and Ames (1979) questioned mothers and fathers as to how often they thought children wanted to be talked to. Interestingly, mothers thought that children wanted to be talked to all the time, whereas fathers thought they wanted to be talked to sometimes.

The mothers in McLaughlin's study (McLaughlin, White, McDevitt and Raskin 1983) increased the structural complexity of their speech and decreased expansions with the children's growing linguistic development more than did fathers (yet fathers did adjust to some degree, as reported above). Mothers asked fewer questions of linguistically less able children, and formulated requests more directly with younger children but more implicitly with older children. Fathers did not exhibit these adjustments to the same degree mothers did. Kavanaugh and Jen (1981) found that mothers adjusted the semantic content of their utterances more than fathers in terms of extending the child's utterances through attribution, absent objects and temporal past. In summary, mothers appeared to put less demands on children than did fathers (Gleason 1975; Gleason and Weintraub 1978; Rondal 1980; Masur 1982; McLaughlin, White, McDevitt and Raskin 1983).

The mothers' focus of interaction tended to be more on their relationship to the child, whereas the fathers concentrated more on the activity *per se* and therefore involved the children less (Gleason 1975; Pieper 1984). While mothers were more indirectly guiding, fathers exerted more explicit control (Masur 1982); i.e. fathers used more imperatives (Giattino and Hogan 1975; Gleason 1975) and more attentional utterances (Rondal 1980), but fewer joint and indirect requests for action (Rondal 1980) than did mothers. Moreover, mothers encouraged children more to analyze the situation or to consider alternative solutions (Masur 1982).

Reasons for Differences Between Mothers' and Fathers' Speech

Pieper (1984) related these differences in interactive styles of mothers and fathers to their sex roles rather than their roles as fathers and mothers. In earlier studies by Gleason and Weintraub (1978) and Rondal (1980) the different roles which mothers and fathers occupied in the family were believed to be of crucial importance for the development of different interactive styles of men and women towards their children. The linguistic data indicated that mothers were in charge (Golinkoff and Ames 1979): they talked more than fathers when all three were together, but not necessarily so in dyadic interaction (Golinkoff and Ames 1979; Rondal 1980). Moreover, mothers uttered more implicit requests and more polar interrogatives than fathers during meal times, whereas fathers asked more yes/no questions than mothers during free play (Rondal 1980). Liddell, Henzi and Drew (1987) observed that mothers' dyadic behaviour differed considerably from mothers' triadic behaviour, yet fathers' behaviour was similar in these two interactional settings; they related that to the fathers' spending less time with their children in dyadic interaction than mothers. Gleason (1975), however, suspected that if fathers took on a nurturant role, their linguistic behaviour would become more like that of mothers.

Hypothesis

Up to now, the question as to which features of adult language promote language development in young children has not been answered conclusively. Some of the features which have been related to accelerated language development, or which have proven successful in the treatment of language-delayed children, have not yet been tested with regard to whether they are favoured by fathers or mothers or employed by both parents to the same extent. Among them are semantically related utterances (Cross 1978; Wells and Robinson 1982), conversation rather than control-oriented behaviour (Wells 1980; McDonald and Pien 1982) and general sensitivity to the child's focus of attention and lead in play (Hubbel 1977). These features are realisations of child-centred behaviour by the parent (Döpke 1986).

I would like to pose the hypothesis that the different roles occupied by mothers and fathers, i.e. that of homemaker versus that of breadwinner, and the related differences in contact time between mothers and children as compared with fathers and children, foster different activities to be undertaken by mother-child dyads than by father-child dyads. Mothers spend proportionally more time with their children in caretaking activities than fathers, whereas fathers engage in relatively more play and fewer caretaking activities during the few hours they see their children each day. Caretaking activities of child and home tend to elicit comparatively high proportions of control-oriented verbal behaviour and lack of response; they are not conducive to topic elaborations and therefore result in comparatively short exchanges and few exchanges per topic. Play activities, on the other hand, allow the parent to concentrate on topic elaborations, to be responsive to the child's verbalizations and to converse with the child rather than control him/her. Such verbal behaviour on the side of the parent results in relatively longer exchanges and more exchanges per topic. If the former is typical of mother-child interaction and the latter is typical of father-child interaction, then it is feasible that children find the interaction with their fathers more rewarding and enjoyable and choose to orient their own language behaviour on that of the father rather than the mother. In such a case the father is the more important language mediator in that family.

Method

Evidence for this hypothesis is derived from a study of six bilingual German-English families in Melbourne, who pursued the one person-one language principle with their children. All the children were first-born and aged either 2;4 or 2;8 at the time of the first audio-recording. Recordings were made twice over an interval of six months. They took place in the children's homes and covered a wide range of activities, all of which occurred unguided and spontaneously over roughly the last two hours before the children's bedtime. In all six families, the mothers carried the main responsibilities for home chores and the fathers worked the greater part of the day outside the home. In five of the six families it was the mother who spoke German to the child, but in one family the father transmitted the minority language.

The recordings were transcribed and each interactional move which was made by a parent to the child, or by the child to a parent, was assigned to a theoretical discourse category. The discourse categories reflected the function of the particular move in the ongoing interaction: they indicated whether a move was initiative or reactive, whether it referred to a new or an already introduced topic, whether it was accepting or rejecting, whether it was meant to elicit a verbal or a non-verbal response, or whether it was not directly geared towards eliciting a response at all; they also showed how difficult it was for one of the interacting partners to get through to the other. Stubbs' (1983) and Keenan and Schieffelin's (1976) discourse models served as the frame into which the categories derived from parent-child verbal interaction were integrated through sub-classifications. The resulting large number of functionally different moves were combined into seven interactionally relevant groups (see Döpke 1986 for a more detailed discussion):

Conversational drive: This group comprised all of a parent's moves to his/her child which drove the ongoing conversation further on by re-introducing the existing topic with new initiative moves or semi-initiative moves, such as feedback questions, which passed the turn to the original speaker.

Responsivity: This group reflected the extent of a parent's interactional effort regarding direct reactions towards the child's contributions to the conversation. It included measures like expansions, repetitions, positive reinforcements and verbal reflectives.

No-response: The degree to which a parent interrupted a child and failed to respond to sequential initiations of the child was represented by the group "no-response".

Communication problems: Summonses, attentionals, queries, behaviour-modelling openings and re-initiations are all devices to make a speaker's conversational move more likely to succeed. An accumulation of them indicated communication problems between the interactants. Inappropriate reactions were also counted in this group.

Conversation-oriented initiations: The parents' intention to elicit continuing verbal participation from their children was accounted for in the group "conversation-oriented initiations". In contrast to the group "conversational drive", this group included all questions and tag-questions in addition to the topic-incorporating moves which constituted the first group.

Control-oriented initiations: The parents' orientation towards controlling the children rather than conversing with them was reflected in the group "control-oriented initiations". This group comprised all types of directive and attentional moves as well as non-sequential moves which initiated new topics. The latter were attributed to a parental orientation towards controlling the child because of their adult-centred rather than child-centred nature.

Control orientation plus no-response: Since to interrupt or not to respond to a conversational partner is a form of exerting control as well, a group "control orientation plus no-response" needed to be established. Negative reactions were incorporated into this group, too, because of their controlling functions. In contrast to the group "control-oriented initiations", this group comprised initiative and reactive measures which constituted parental control.

The seven interactionally relevant groups, thus formed, were concerned with the ways in which parents sustained conversations with their young children, as well as with the parents' needs and methods for exerting verbal control over their children. Four additional measures gave an indication of how much parent-child dyads pursued topics, how intensive the verbal exchange was and how strongly the parent participated in the conversations. These measures were "exchanges per topic", "moves per topic", "moves per exchange" and "moves per topic: parent to child".

The frequency with which the parents made use of strategies in each of the seven interactionally relevant groups as well as the dyads' rates of topic maintenance were calculated. Subsequently, each child's mother and father were compared in order to determine whether mother or father interacted in a more child-centred way.

I understand a child-centred mode of interaction as one which is responsive to the child's contributions to the conversations, which works on maintaining a once introduced topic, and which is more oriented towards conversing with the child than controlling the child. The frequency of communication problems was taken as an indication of how approachable the child was for the parent. In the second column of Tables 1 and 2, the direction of the hypothesis is marked for each group. The father could be considered as behaving in a more child-centred way than the mother when he scored higher than the mother in the groups "conversational drive", "responsivity", "conversation-oriented initiations" and the four measures of topic length, and lower than the mother in the groups "no-response", "communication problems", "control-oriented initiations" and "control orientation plus no-response".

The effect of the parents' interactive styles on the children's language acquisition was related to the children's willingness and ability to speak German originally and intentionally. In other words, it was believed that the child would orient his/her language acquisition on the English-speaking parent rather than the German-speaking parent if he/she did not speak German actively.

Results

Traditionally, one would immediately suspect that the children would be learning German from their mothers as a matter of course, but that it should be difficult for the father to accomplish the same. This, however, was not the case. Kenneth, who was spoken to in German by his father, used German originally and intentionally, but four of the five children whose mothers were the transmitters of the minority language did not.

Table 1 shows that Kenneth's German-speaking father behaved in a

Table 1: *Comparison of fathers and mothers with regard to their discourse behaviour — first recording*

Groups	Hypo-theses	Alanna	Kenneth	Jonas	Anna	Felicity	Tanja
Conversational drive	+	+16.2%*	−0.4%	+6.4%*	+9.2%*	− 6.5%	+8.9%*
Responsivity	+	+17.0%*	+10.1%*	+3.1%*	+13.2%*	+13.6%*	−4.0%
No-response	−	−0.6%*	−17.7%*	+0.1%	−1.2%*	−12.6%*	+5.8%
Communication problems	−	−6.1%*	−0.9%*	−1.6%*	−10.9%*	−0.4%*	+1.1%
Conversation ori-ented initiations	+	+9.5%*	+14.2%*	+13.8%*	+26.7%*	+1.2%*	+5.8%*
Control oriented initiations	−	−5.3%*	−5.3%*	−13.8%*	−27.4%*	−3.3%*	−3.7%*
Control orientation plus no-response	−	−3.4%*	−4.9%*	−6.5%*	−12.0%*	−8.0%*	− 3.7%*
Exchanges per topic	+	+1.13*	+0.57*	+0.28*	+0.34*	−0.03	+0.39*
Moves per topic	+	+3.19*	+2.44*	+1.47*	+0.98*	+0.52*	+0.53*
Moves per exchange	+	+0.25*	+0.6*	+0.32*	+0.18*	+0.33*	−0.23
Moves per topic: parent to child	+	+1.27*	+1.77*	+0.92*	+0.31*	+0.41*	−0.24
Number of items scored by father		11	10	10	11	9	6

Notes to Tables:
1. The sign indicates the direction of the relationship between the fathers' and the mothers' scores required to confirm the hypothesis. A "+" sign indicates that the feature is present more frequently in the father's discourse. A "−" indicates that the feature is present more frequently in the mother's discourse.

2. * indicates that the comparison of features in the father's discourse and features in the mother's discourse supports the hypothesis, i.e. that the father behaves in a more child-centred way than the mother.

Table 2:　Comparison of fathers and mothers with regard to their discourse behaviour — second recording

Groups	Hypo-theses	Alanna	Kenneth	Jonas	Anna	Felicity	Tanja
Conversational drive	+	+7.7%*	+1.1%*	+12.4%*	+13.4%*	+1.0%*	+5.6%*
Responsitivity	+	+3.1%*	+10.6%*	−0.9%	+21.1%*	+2.5%*	+7.0%*
No-response	−	−3.6%*	−10.5%*	+3.2%	−20.8%*	−7.2%*	+9.9%
Communication problems	−	−14.7%*	+4.0%	−0.4%*	+5.7%	+0.1%	−5.1%*
Conversation oriented initiations	+	+16.8%*	+17.9%*	+15.3%*	+4.1%*	+0.7%*	+8.7%*
Control oriented initiations	−	−20.9%*	−24.2%*	−19.2%*	−17.6%*	+3.6%	−9.6%*
Control orientation plus no-response	−	−10.6%*	−10.7%*	−8.5%*	−12.3%*	−1.3%*	− 8.4%*
Exchanges per topic	+	+0.65*	+0.21*	+0.42*	+0.07*	+0.09*	−0.01
Moves per topic	+	+1.43*	+1.2*	+1.44*	+0.79*	+0.25*	−0.52
Moves per exchange	+	+0.04*	+0.48*	+0.28*	+0.1*	+0.01*	−0.33
Moves per topic: parent to child	+	+1.13*	+0.9*	+0.71*	+0.12*	+0.05*	−0.88
Number of items scored by father		11	10	9	10	9	6

more child-centred way than his English-speaking mother in 10 out of 11 measures. Most of the differences exceeded 3% for the interactionally relevant groups and 0.6% moves for the measures of topic maintenance. With respect to the eleventh group, namely conversational drive, the parents behaved practically the same. The same was true for Alanna's, Jonas' and Anna's English-speaking fathers. All three behaved in an overwhelmingly more child-centred way than the children's German-speaking mothers. The second recording six months later (Table 2) confirmed the relative stability of the parents' verbal behaviour.

The results obtained from Felicity's and Tanja's families are not as clear. Felicity was the only child, apart from Kenneth, who used German originally and intentionally. However, her English-speaking father seemed to engage in more child-centred verbal behaviour than did the German-speaking mother. A closer look at the parents' differences in each group reveals that the differences in four of the nine groups in favour of the father, during the first recording, are so small that in these the parents' verbal behaviour can be considered the same. During the second recording (Table 2), the similarities between the parents were even stronger. In 8 out of 9 groups Felicity's father's score must be considered equal to that of her mother.

Tanja spoke a considerable amount of German during the first recording, but hardly any during the second recording. In only a small majority of groups did Tanja's English-speaking father appear more child-centred than her German-speaking mother. However, nearly all of his scores were in the interactionally relevant groups and displayed a clear difference between his and the mother's verbal behaviour.

All fathers, except for Felicity's, were clearly more oriented towards conversing with the children, and less towards controlling them, than the mothers were.

Discussion

The advantages of the present data were three-fold. Firstly, since the type of speech generated in parent-child interaction is closely related to the activities performed by the participants, observations in the families' normal environment and lack of intervention as to what activities have to take place provide the researcher with more representative speech samples for each particular parent-child dyad. Secondly, due to the one parent-one language principle exercised in the families, it was possible to view the effects which mothers' and fathers' verbal behaviours had on the children's language development separately. Thirdly, since we are comparing parent-child dyads which involve the same child, the argument as to whether it is the parent who influences the child's language development or the child who determines the parent's verbal behaviour can be put to rest for the moment.

The children in the present sample failed to acquire the minority language German parallel to the major language in the community, English, unless the German-speaking parent displayed a verbal behaviour which was at least as child-centred as that of the English-speaking parent. Interestingly, in five out of the six families it was the father who engaged in more child-centred verbal interaction than the mother. Consequently, only the child who was spoken to in German by his father acquired an active command of German, whereas the four other children whose mothers spoke German with them did not. The only child who learned German from her mother was the one who was involved in similar types of verbal interaction by both her parents.

In conclusion, even if mothers can be shown to be more child-centred than fathers in play activities, the overall quality of interaction may well be higher in father-child dyads than in mother-child dyads, if mothers play relatively less with their children. As a result of my studies on bilingual children who are raised by the one person-one language principle, I have reason to suspect that children learn more from father-child interaction that is less in quantity but qualitatively better than they do from greater quantities of "business oriented" mother-child interaction.

References

Clarke-Stewart, K.A. 1972. *Interactions between Mothers and their Young Children: Characteristics and consequences.* Unpubl. Doctoral Thesis, Yale University.

————. 1982. *Day Care.* Glasgow: Fontana Paperbacks.

Cross, T.G. 1978. "Mothers' Speech and its Association with Rate of Linguistic Development in Young Children". *The Development of Communication* ed. by N. Waterson & C. Snow, XXV. Chichester: Wiley.

Döpke, S. 1986. "Discourse Structures in Bilingual Families". *Journal of Multilingual and Multicultural Development* 7. 493-507.

Friedlander, B., B. Davis & H. Wetstone. 1972. "Time-sampling Analysis of Infants' Natural Language Environments in the Home". *Child Development* 43. 730-740.

Furrow, D., K. Nelson & H. Benedict. 1979. "Mothers' Speech to Children and Syntactic Development: Some simple relationships". *Journal of Child Language* 6. 423-442.

Giattino, J. & J.G. Hogan. 1975. "Analysis of a Father's Speech to His Language-Learning Child". *Journal of Speech and Hearing Disorders* 40. 524-537.

Gleason, J.B. 1975. "Fathers and Other Strangers: Men's speech to young children". *Developmental Psycholinguistics: Theory and application* ed. by D. Dato, 289-297. Washington, D.C.: Georgetown University Press.

Gleason, J.B. & S. Weintraub. 1978. "Input Language and the Acquisition of Communicative Competence". *Children's Language* vol. I, ed. by K.E. Nelson, XVI. New York: Gardner.

Golinkoff, R.M. & G.J. Ames. 1979. "A Comparison of Fathers' and Mothers' Speech with their Young Children". *Child Development* 50. 28-32.

Hoffman, L.W. 1974. "Effects of Maternal Employment on the Child: A review of the research". *Developmental Psychology* 10. 204-228.

Hubbel, R.D. 1977. "On Facilitating Spontaneous Talking in Young Children". *Journal of Speech and Hearing Disorders* 42. 216-231.

Kavanaugh, R.D. & M. Jen. 1981. "Some Relationships between Parental Speech and Children's Object Development". *First Language* 5. 103-115.

Keenan, E.O. & B.B. Schieffelin. 1976. "Topic as a Discourse Notion: A study in the conversations of children and adults". *Subject and Topic* ed. by C.N. Li, 335-385. New York: Academic Press.

Lamb, M.E. 1975a. "Fathers: Forgotten contributors to child development. *Human Development* 18. 245-266.

————. 1975b. "Infants, Fathers and Mothers: Interaction at eight-months-of-age in the home and in the laboratory". *Proc. Meet. Eastern Psychology Association.*

Liddell, C., S.P. Henzi & M. Drew. 1987. "Mothers, Fathers and Children in an Urban Park Playground: A comparison of dyads and triads". *Developmental Psychology* 23. 262-266.

Masur, E.F. 1982. "Cognitive Content of Parents' Speech to Pre-schoolers". *Merrill-Palmer Quarterly* 28. 471-484.

Masur, E.F. & J.B. Gleason. 1980. "Parent-Child Interaction and the Acquisition of Lexical Information During Play". *Developmental Psychology* 16. 404-409.

McDonald, L. & D. Pien. 1982. "Mother Conversational Behaviour as a Function of Interactional Intent". *Journal of Child Language* 9. 337-358.

McLaughlin, B., D. White, T. McDevitt & R. Raskin. 1983. "Mothers' and Fathers' Speech to their Young Children: Similar or different?" *Journal of Child Language* 10. 245-252.

Moerk, E. 1972. "Principles of Interaction in Language Learning". *Merrill-Palmer Quarterly* 18. 229-257.

Nash, J. 1965. "The Father in Contemporary Culture and Current Psychological Literature". *Child Development* 36. 261-297.

Newport, E., L. Gleitman & H. Gleitman. 1977. "Mother, I'd Rather do it Myself: Some effects and non-effects of maternal speech styles". *Talking to Children* ed. by C.E. Snow and C.A. Ferguson, 109-149. Cambridge: Cambridge University Press.

Pieper, U. 1984. "Is Parental Language Sexually Differentiated". *Studia Anglica Posnaniensia* 17. 71-80.

Rebelsky, F. & C. Hanks. 1971. "Fathers' Verbal Interaction with Infants in the First Three Months of Life". *Child Development* 42. 63-68.

Rondal, J.A. 1980. "Fathers' and Mothers' Speech in Early Language Development". *Journal of Child Language* 7. 353-369.

Snow, C.E. & C.A. Ferguson. eds. 1977. *Talking to Children: Language input and acquisition.* Cambridge: Cambridge University Press.

Stubbs, D.M. 1983. *Discourse Analysis.* Oxford: Basil Blackwell.

Wells, C.G. 1980. "Apprenticeship in Meaning". *Children's Language* ed. by K.E. Nelson, vol. 2, 45-126. New York: Gardener Press.

Wells, C.G. & W.P. Robinson. 1982. "The Role of Adult Speech in Language Development". *Advances in the Social Psychology of Language* ed. by C. Fraser & C.R. Scherer, 11-76. Cambridge: Cambridge University Press.

"Artificial" Bilingualism: Must it Fail?

George Saunders

Introduction

The title of this paper was inspired by comments made by Kielhöfer and Jonekeit (1983:15, 95) in their book *Zweisprachige Kindererziehung* (Raising children bilingually), in which they specifically warn parents to avoid what they call "artificial" bilingualism, saying rather ominously that all such attempts by families to establish this type of bilingualism which they know of have failed ("Uns sind nur Mißerfolge dieser Art von künstlicher Zweisprachigkeit bekannt"). I will be examining what is meant by "artificial bilingualism" and looking at, and evaluating, the possible reasons for the warning given by Kielhöfer and Jonekeit. In doing so, I will make particular reference to an actual case of artificial bilingualism.

"Artificial" Bilingualism

Kielhöfer and Jonekeit (1983:15) distinguish between what they call "natural bilingualism" and "artificial bilingualism". In *natural bilingualism* children acquire two languages naturally, i.e. without any special tuition, from *native speakers* of the two languages, either one language from their mother and the other from their father, or one language from their parents and the other from the environment. *Artificial bilingualism*, or at least the type they specifically mention, occurs when such a situation is imitated by parents and one (or both) of the parents speaks to the children in a *non-native* language.

There are, of course, many parents in the world who, for a variety of reasons, speak to their children in a language which is not their native language, but usually this occurs when immigrants use the language of their new country to their children rather than their own native language. In Australia, for instance, the 1976 Census showed (see Clyne 1982) that 28% of first generation German immigrants had shifted to using English only, which means that *at least* that many German-speakers in Australia speak English to their children. This is borne out if we look at how many Australian children with German parents actually speak German. Only 38% of children who have two German parents speak German. The figure is even lower in families with one German-speaking parent and one English-speaking parent: only 4% of the children speak German. However, this kind of use of a *non-native* language by parents would seem to fall outside Kielhöfer's and Jonekeit's concept of artificial bilingualism, since in such cases the children obviously do not become bilingual; moreover, their monolingualism is acquired not only from the non-native speaking parent(s), but also from the native speaking community.

There are also parents whose native language is the language of the community but who have learnt their spouse's native language and have chosen to speak to their children in that language. A typical example is described by Fantini (1985, 1986). Fantini, the son of Italian immigrants in the USA, speaks Spanish, his wife's native language, with her and with his two children. Such a family situation would probably also fall outside Kielhöfer's and Jonekeit's concept of artificial bilingualism, since although one parent is a non-native speaker, the other parent *is* a native speaker of the home language, and in addition the children are acquiring the other language also from native speakers in the community outside the home.

There are also quite a few examples of bilingualism which would fit Kielhöfer's and Jonekeit's definition of "artificial" bilingualism, and which have by no means all ended in failure. Indeed, some countries have relied on large numbers of their citizens speaking a non-native language to their children to enable the creation of a national language. A good example of this is the revival of Hebrew as a spoken language with native speakers using it in all aspects of life. For many centuries it had not been spoken as a native language, its use having been reduced to a language used by Jews for public and private readings of religious writings and for prayers. Its revival as a native language meant that many parents spoke to their children not in their own native languages but in Hebrew, a language they knew only from books and religious activities. And it worked. Their children grew up speaking Hebrew as their native language, and now there are several million native speakers of the language. Some other languages which are at present in danger of dying out (e.g. Scottish Gaelic, Irish) will also probably have to rely to some extent on the assistance of non-native speakers who have, or acquire, a good command of the languages and then consciously pass them on to their children, if the languages are to be conserved or revived. I have met, for example, in Ireland a number of parents who, although themselves from English speaking homes, speak only Irish to their own children.

Case studies of this type of bilingualism are not plentiful in the literature. Apart from my own detailed longitudinal study (Saunders, 1980a, b, 1982a, b, c, 1984, 1986, 1988), which I will be referring to soon, there are only a few other reports. Past (1976) reports on how he and his wife, both native speakers of English and living in the USA, speak Spanish to their daughter for a specified part of each day. Dimitrijevic (1965), a native speaker of Serbian living in Yugoslavia, speaks English to his son, whilst his wife speaks Serbian with him. Facey (1986) and her husband, both native speakers of English living in Australia, speak German to their two children. Corsetti and Taeschner (1986) and Brennan (1987) report on an interesting case involving Esperanto as one of three languages being acquired by two children in Italy; the children's Italian father speaks to them and his wife in Esperanto, their native English speaking mother speaks to them in English, and they acquire Italian from the environment.

Objections to Artificial Bilingualism

Kielhöfer and Jonekeit (1983:95) do not explain the rationale behind their warning "Vermeiden Sie künstliche Zweisprachigkeit" (*Avoid artificial bilingualism*), beyond saying that they know of no cases where it has been successful. However, since their book is a guide explaining how "natural" bilingualism can succeed, the implication is strong that there must be significant differences between the two types of bilingualism. The obvious major difference is that in "artificial" bilingualism, one of the languages involved is being passed on to the children by a parent who is not a native speaker of that language. This is something which seems to disturb not only Kielhöfer and Jonekeit, but also, as my own research has revealed, troubles some native speakers of both that particular language and of the other language. In the literature on bilingualism there are many recommendations that parents should speak to their children in their own native language, because this is the language which is closest to one, the language in which one can express oneself most automatically, the language which is warmer, more familiar, richer in words, the language which awakens the deep layers of one's personality, the language in which one is more oneself (see Skutnabb-Kangas 1984:49). Moreover, this language is linked with a particular culture. Can all this be duplicated in a second language learned later, and is such duplication necessary for the successful passing on of this second language as a family language? These questions will now be considered in the light of my own study of three children growing up in Australia.

A Case of "Artificial" Bilingualism

For the past 12 years I have been engaged in a longitudinal study of my three children, Thomas (now 13), Frank (11) and Katrina (6) who were all born in Australia. (This study is documented in some detail in Saunders (1982c, 1988).) My wife, Wendy, and I are both native speakers of Australian English, but the children and I have always communicated with each other in German. Otherwise family communication (husband-wife, children-mother, children-children) normally occurs in English. The procedure followed is very similar to the now well-known one-person-one-language method used by Ronjat (1913) and Leopold (1939-49). None of the children has been outside Australia except in 1984, when the family spent six months in Hamburg. Their mother has a good knowledge of German and also speaks it fluently, although she rarely does so within the family itself. Each family member, therefore, understands both English and German, which means that there is no danger of friction or resentment arising because someone feels left out of a conversation. My proficiency in German is high. I began learning it at school at age 14 and have been learning it ever since. It is also my profession, since I teach the language at tertiary level. Although my proficiency in my native English is superior, I have very few problems communicating in German and speak it with a near-native accent.

Whilst the term "artificial" bilingualism is probably useful in that it distinguishes this particular kind of bilingualism, it is also somewhat unfortunate, since "artificial" often has negative connotations, implying unnaturalness, lack of genuinenes, or affectation. However, we need to consider the situation from three points of view: (a) from the point of view of the non-native speaking parent; (b) from the children's point of view; and (c) from the point of view of outsiders.

a. From my point of view, as a parent involved, the family's linguistic situation has long ceased to feel artificial or unnatural in any way. Only in the beginning, with the first child, before he could speak, did it seem more of a game to address him in German (which was done for a number of reasons, among them out of a sense of fun and an interest in what would happen). However, virtually from the moment he began to respond to my German and then uttered his first German word to me, my use of German to him suddenly felt quite natural, at least in the privacy of the home, and then rapidly also outside the home. German quickly became "our" language. Some people who are sceptical about what I am doing have said that I, as a non-native speaker of German, would not know how to speak to my children in German, that I would not be able to express a full range of emotions, etc., in the language, since my own childhood was completely in English. It may well be true that I do not speak to my children in exactly the same way as a native speaker of German, but from my observations there is considerable variety in the way German parents speak to their children, anyway. But I have always spoken German with them, my own variety of German, and for us it has become a family language, a natural means of communication.

My not being a native speaker of German has rarely proved to be a disadvantage. It is true that particularly as the children have grown older, there have been some gaps in my German vocabulary revealed when I have had to discuss things, or assist my children to discuss things, which I normally do not read or talk about, e.g. physics. However, this has been only a comparatively minor problem, and the children accept that at times dictionaries etc. may have to be consulted to locate the German terminology needed. Nevertheless, it would seem desirable that non-native speakers wishing to pass on a language to their children have a fairly good command of the language so that they can communicate reasonably easily, confidently, and naturally with their children in a wide range of situations and on a wide range of topics. This would mean minimal frustration for the parents and ensure that the children are exposed to a reasonably developed variety of the language.

b. The children do not regard it as artificial or unnatural that their father speaks German with them, since this is the way things have been for as long as they can remember. Their realization, after beginning school, that their father is not a native speaker of German had done nothing to alter their view of their linguistic situation; they can see that it is an unusual situation, but that does not make it unnatural. Even in cases where a parent speaks with a non-native accent or intonation, initially children would not be aware of this or, if they were, it would not necessarily concern them unduly. The important thing is that the parent speaks to them in this language, it is the language of intimacy between them and the parent — it is *their* language.

c. To some outsiders this type of bilingualism does indeed seem artificial. There exists, for example, among native speakers what Christopherson (1973) calls a widespread "proprietary feeling" towards their language, i.e. a native speaker is allowed to take liberties with the language which are not conceded to the non-native speaker, no matter how well he or she has mastered the language. Among these "liberties" would seem to be the right to pass the language on to one's children, especially when one represents the only or major input the children receive in the language.

Artificial and Natural Bilingualism — Similarities and Differences

Both kinds of bilingualism have much in common. One of the concerns of the non-native speaker without perfect mastery of the language is that he or she is passing on to the children a non-genuine version of the language (see Facey 1986). However, if one looks at the linguistic behaviour of immigrants who speak their native language to their children in a foreign environment (see, for example, Haugen 1953; Clyne 1967), it is clear that the language of such immigrants is quickly influenced by the language of the new country so that it begins to diverge from the variety spoken in the linguistic homeland: words may be adopted from the language of the new country to refer to new concepts, when a word in the home language is momentarily forgotten, for expressiveness, etc. Thus the language which the children of immigrants acquire from their parents is somewhat different from the same language spoken by their peers in their parents' country of origin. If these children in turn pass the language on to *their* children, the differences will be even more noticeable. Linguistically, at least, the non-native speaker speaking the language to his or her children has much in common with the immigrant and the immigrant's offspring.

In some ways the non-native speaker parent may have certain advantages over the immigrant parent. In an "artificial" bilingualism situation the children are adding a second language and the risks associated with failure are minimal. If the attempt at bilingualism should fail, although sad for the participants, little has been lost, since the children will still speak their parents' own language as a native language. (Because of this, Skutnabb-Kangas (1984:148) refers to my own case as an example of élite bilingualism.) For this reason, I prefer to refer to "artificial" bilingualism as "home immersion", since there are many similarities between it and the early immersion programs in Canada and elsewhere, where majority language children are immersed in a minority language at school. For immigrant children, however, the consequences of not acquiring their parents' language can be more serious: they can become excluded from effective communication with their parents, from their origin and culture, perhaps being linguistically cut off from the family's relatives and homeland.

In my own case, not being a native speaker of German does also have a certain psychological advantage, in that I do not have the same emotional attachment to the language as do many native speakers and can perhaps be more tolerant of the way my children are acquiring German, more accepting of aberrations in their German and of the fact that their German may lag behind the German of children in a German speaking country. After all, I can see that they do have a native speaker's mastery of my own native language, English — their ability to communicate in German is a pleasing bonus. It would also seem to be an advantage that the children know that their father is indistinguishable from a native speaker of Australian English. In families with immigrant parents the children often reject the home language and try to assimilate as much as possible, because "the parents, with their fixed values and speech habits, will always remain 'different' from the community" (Clyne 1967:101).

Skutnabb-Kangas (1984:78) mentions as one of the consequences of a child not successfully acquiring a parent's language that "the child may have a less satisfactory relationship with one or both of the parents if s/he does not share a mother tongue with them." In my case, this does not apply, since I do share a mother tongue with my children, although we do not speak it to each other. Nor does the relationship we have established with each other through German seem any less satisfactory than it would have been if we had spoken English to each other. In a way it may even be more satisfactory, since, being conscious of the responsibility of being the children's principal source of German, I have perhaps spent more time with them than if I had spoken English with them. The children are aware that communication with their father might be a little easier in English, but obviously regard German as an integral part of their relationship with him and have expressed the view that a shift to English would not only be psychologically very difficult for them but would also mean the loss of an important part of their life. As Dorian (1981:107) has shown in her study of semi-speakers of East Sutherland Gaelic, there are factors other than just linguistic proficiency which can influence language choice. The factor most influencing her semi-speakers' conscious choice to use their imperfect Gaelic in certain communication situations, although they and their inter-locutors are fully proficient speakers of English, is "a strong attachment to some kinsperson".

How Effective is "Artificial" Bilingualism?

I would now like to look at the linguistic results of my own "home immersion program" and consider its degree of success. A number of tests have been carried out over the years to monitor the children's progress:

Receptive Vocabulary

The children's receptive vocabulary in English has been measured at approximately two-year intervals using the Peabody Picture Vocabulary Test (PPVT). This test is not ideal for testing speakers of Australian English (see Saunders (1982:159-161) for discussion), since it was standardized in the USA and the difficulty ranking for some items does not coincide with Australian usage; but it does provide a good comparison with monolingual speakers of English and makes it possible to monitor the children's progress in extending the range and complexity of their English vocabulary.

As can be seen in Table 1, the results obtained are fairly consistent. They indicate that the children have an above average receptive vocabulary in English. The lowest percentile recorded for Thomas is a high 93 (indicating even here that his receptive vocabulary was superior to 93% of his monolingual peers). Even the lowest percentile in the whole table, 71 scored by Frank at age 9;7, is above average. The children's performance at school confirms these findings: English expression is the subject in which

Table 1 PPVT — Standardized English-language version

Child and age		Form A		Form B	
		Raw Score	Percentile	Raw Score	Percentile
Katrina	2;4	36	93	32	89
Katrina	4;3	52	80	55	91
Katrina	5;3	62	95	55	76
Frank	3;7	50	94	–	–
Frank	5;5	56	75	60	91
Frank	7;9	78	94	73	78
Frank	9;7	84	82	81	71
Frank	11;7	103	95	96	81
Thomas	5;5	60	93	63	95
Thomas	7;3	78	98	76	97
Thomas	9;7	95	97	99	97
Thomas	11;7	117	99+	100	98

Table 2: First 100 items of PPVT — English vs German

Child and age		No. of items correct			
		English		German	
		Form A	Form B	Form A	Form B
Katrina	5;3	66	66	61	65
Frank	5;5	66	70	70	74
Thomas	5;5	76	69	75	80
Frank	7;9	78	81	75	83
Thomas	7;3	80	79	82	92
Frank	9;7	86	86	85	87
Thomas	9;7	92	97	90	99
Frank	11;7	90	93	85	92
Thomas	11;7	94	97	96	97

they all do best and are ranked at or near the top in their classes.

To compare the children's receptive vocabulary in their two languages, a German version of the first 100 items of forms A and B of the PPVT (see Saunders 1982:159ff.) has also been administered at regular intervals. As can be seen in Table 2, the children performed approximately equivalently

Table 3: Forms A (100) + N (100) = 200 vocabulary items in each language

Child and age		Items known in English	Items known in German	Items known in either English or German
Katrina	5;3	132	126	152
Frank	5;5	136	144	163
Thomas	5;5	145	155	169
Frank	7;9	161	158	173
Thomas	7;3	159	174	182
Frank	9;7	172	172	191
Thomas	9;7	189	189	196
Frank	11;7	183	177	190
Thomas	11;7	191	193	198

in their two languages. This is interesting and encouraging, because it suggests that the considerable imbalance in favour of English in the children's linguistic input (at present probably as high as 6:1) is not as significant a factor in the acquisition of receptive vocabulary as in the acquisition of oral fluency and grammatical accuracy (see below).

Merrill Swain (1972) suggests that when both a bilingual's languages are examined, his or her total conceptual vocabulary may exceed that of a monolingual child. This would seem to be so in this case, for, as can be seen in Table 3, the vocabulary items not known by each child were not exactly the same ones in each language. As can be seen, in every case the total number of concepts known by the children *in at least one* of their languages exceeds the number known in each language individually by quite a significant margin. A look at one example will make this clear. At age 9;7 Frank scored 172/200 for both English and German. However, out of the 28 concepts which he did not know in each language, only 9 were the same in *both* languages, e.g. he missed both *coil* and its German equivalent *Spirale*. This means that there were also 19 concepts which he missed in English but knew in German (e.g. he knew *Kelch* but not its English equivalent *goblet*), and another 19 *different* concepts which he missed in German but knew in English (e.g. he knew *beam*, but not its German equivalent *Balken*). This means that if *all* Frank's correct answers were counted, irrespective of language, the total number of concepts known would rise quite dramatically to 191/200. Similar comments could be made about both the other tests done by Frank and also about the tests done by Katrina and Thomas. Such results show the unfairness of assessing bilinguals for verbal intelligence as if they were simply two monolinguals. They also give rise to the question whether in this case the children's bilingualism has not, as found by researchers such as Doyle *et al.* (1978), caused a vocabulary lag in each of their languages. This is difficult to prove one way or the other, but it is possible that in some cases they would have acquired the English word from their father if they had not spoken German to him. However, even if there is some vocabulary lag, it would appear to be small, since, as already seen, the children compare very well with monolingual English speakers of the same age. Moreover, they have the added bonus of having a German receptive vocabulary of similar standard to their English.

Degree of Bilingualism

The language dominance of the children has been tested using Edelman's (1969:175) contextualised measure of degree of bilingualism. Children are asked to name in 45 seconds, first in one language, then in the other, as many things as possible that can be found in various domains, the assumption being that they will produce more words in the language in which they are dominant for a particular domain. Results are given on a scale from 0.00 to 1.00, where 0.00 would indicate *no* responses at all in *English*, 1.00 would indicate *no* responses at all in *German*, and 0.50 would indicate balance, i.e. an equal number of responses in English and German. How Thomas, Frank and Katrina performed in this test at various ages can be seen in Table 4. The results indicate that overall the children are slightly more dominant in English: of the 20 scores in the table, 11 indicate dominance in English, 6 (asterisked) indicate balance between the two languages, and 3 (italicised) indicate dominance in German. Some of the results are a little surprising, e.g. Katrina's score of 0.45 for the school

Table 4: Degree of bilingualism

Domain	Score						
	Thomas 5;6	Thomas 7;6	Thomas 12;6	Frank 4;0	Frank 5;7	Frank 10;7	Katrina 5;3
Home	0.58	0.58	0.56	*0.44*	0.55	0.67	0.73
School	0.50*	0.67	0.50*	0.50*	0.55	0.55	*0.45*
Neighbourhood	0.56	0.56	0.50*	–	*0.47*	0.58	0.50*

domain; she was able to name 11 words in German and 10 in English, despite the fact that at that age she could talk more fluently about school in English. Again, given the far greater amount of exposure the children have to English, it is encouraging that German fares so well in comparison.

Accuracy

The children's grammatical accuracy (as measured against the adult standard) has been monitored diachronically. At present the three children make almost no errors in their English. In German the picture is somewhat different. In the years before they spent six months in Hamburg in 1984, Thomas averaged about 4.9 errors per 100 words in German, Frank averaged about 8.3 errors per 100 words, and Katrina 7.3 errors per 100 words. Since returning from Hamburg, the figures are approximately (up till the end of 1986) 3.5 (Thomas), 5.2 (Frank) and 7.6 (Katrina). (The effects of their stay in Hamburg are discussed below.) At least half of the errors in any taped sample of the children's German are due to the language's quite complex gender and case system. To put the children's frequency of errors into perspective, it is interesting to make a comparison with Reitmajer's (1975) study of 30 grade 4 children who spoke predominantly Bavarian dialect at home: when speaking Standard German they made 11.8 errors per 100 words.

A Family Language Meets a National Language

In Australia the children's German is basically a family language used predominantly with their father, and it is adequate for this purpose. But how well would it serve the children in an all-German-speaking environment where they would need to use it in all spheres of life? The chance to find out came in July 1984 when the three children, then aged 10;7 (Thomas), 8;8 (Frank) and 3;4 (Katrina) left Australia for the first time to spend nearly 6 months in Hamburg. This would be their very first contact with people who spoke only German, so that recourse to an English word or expression in moments of linguistic difficulty would not be possible as it was in Australia.

A few precautions were taken before the family's departure from Australia to minimize any culture or linguistic shock for the children; e.g. I used role play to give the two boys practice in using formal forms of address (*Sie*), something they had not needed in Australia, since (a) they spoke

German mainly with me, and (b) there is a much wider use of the informal form of address (*du*) among immigrants in Australia than in German speaking countries, so that no adults had ever required them to address them with *Sie*. This raises the question of whether it is necessary for someone passing on a non-native language to his or her children to also pass on in its entirety the culture of native speakers of the language. Personally, I have not felt it necessary to try to become a carbon copy of a German father culturally as well as linguistically, although I have by no means divorced German language from German culture. There is also not such a sharp division between the culture of German speakers, particularly those in North Germany, and the culture of Anglo-Australians, as there is, for example, between Japanese and Anglo-Australian culture. Through using German with their father and a few other German speakers in Australia, through hearing German stories, watching German films, etc., the children had, while still in Australia, gained an awareness of the main differences between Anglo-Australian culture and that of the German speaking world. This awareness simply needed to be heightened a little. before arrival in Germany in order to avoid potential *faux pas* in an all-German environment. The same sort of thing would apply to English speaking Australian (and even adults) setting out to spend six months in England or the USA — even though they would share the same language .(more or less!), there would be a certain number of cultural surprises in store for them. Thomas, Frank and Katrina see themselves not as English and/or German, but as *Australians* who speak English and German. In much the same way, Malaysian friends' children who speak English as their main home language, go to Malay-medium schools, and as ethnic Chinese also have some knowledge of Hokkien, do not see themselves as English, but as Malaysians.

On arrival in Hamburg, the children's wonder and excitement that *everyone* spoke German was evident, and the two boys revelled in being able to use their "father tongue" in so many novel situations, e.g. buying ice-creams. Even in those first days there was over 95% mutual intelligibility between Hamburg German and the children's German. Most people were surprised to meet Australian children who could speak German so fluently and they received many compliments. The children understood most of what they heard, but, being used to their father's not very rapid speech, they initially had difficulty if someone spoke fast — as most children their age seemed to do!

One month after arriving in Hamburg, Thomas (10;8) began grade 5 in a *Gesamtschule* (comprehensive high school), and Frank (8;10) started grade 3 at a *Grundschule* (primary school). They had few difficulties communicating with their fellow pupils, and this introduced them to children's German, something which previously they had known virtually only from dialogues in books, films and recordings. However, communicating in German in an informal way with one's peers is not the same as being taught formally through the language and having to come to grips with all school subjects in German. (They were already reasonably competent in reading and writing in German, since they had been doing reading and writing exercises for me from the time they began school in Australia.) Some problems were solved relatively easily, as they were simply a matter of acquiring the necessary terminology, e.g. in mathematics. Others were more difficult to solve. Thomas, for example, had in Australia been among the top 5% in his grade (100 pupils) in English expression and composition writing; writing stories was one of his favourite school activities. Now he had to do this in German, and he became acutely aware that he did not have the same stylistic control of German as he did of English; his essays in German, he felt, lacked the richness and breadth of vocabulary he was able to display in English, and he also lost marks for grammatical and spelling mistakes which would not have been present in an equivalent piece of work in English. He found this rather demoralising. I tried to console him by:

  a. pointing out that to get a 3 (an average mark) for an essay in a German school in his weaker language was a considerable achievement;
  b. pointing out that it is not unusual for bilinguals to be more competent in the language they use more and have more exposure to, and that the father himself could also write complex English more easily and with greater stylistic flexibility than German;
  c. offering Thomas linguistic assistance when he was searching for the most apt way to put his thoughts into words, searching for appropriate adjectives, verbs etc.;
  d. reminding him that he would still be among the top in English when he returned to Australia.

These measures were effective to a certain extent, although the time was too short for him to become as competent in written German as in English; it is estimated that probably about two years in a German school would be required for this to come about.

But apart from the actual subject German, in which, as mentioned above, Thomas understandably performed less well than in the subject English in Australia, he did not feel that his German disadvantaged him in other subjects, and this seemed to be the case; e.g. in the report he received from the school when he left in December 1984 he received a 2 (the second best mark) not only in mathematics, music and art, subjects where performance is probably less dependent on language, but also in politics, where ability to express ideas in German is important. His German improved in grammatical accuracy, fluency, breadth of active vocabulary and in comprehension of fast, complex German. In a speech sample taken just before leaving for Germany, Thomas made 6.0 errors per 100 words; speech samples taken in Hamburg showed an average of 3.1 errors per 100 words. In the comments included in his report, the following reference was made to his German:

> In allen Fächern hat er sich sprachlich erstaunlich gut zurechtgefunden.
> (Linguistically, Thomas has coped amazingly well in all subjects.)

Frank's German, which deviated grammatically more than Thomas's from Standard German on arrival in Hamburg, also made similar improvements. In a recording made shortly before he left Australia he made a high 9.5 errors per 100 words; after 3 months in Hamburg this had dropped to 6.5 errors per 100 words. Certain grammatical features were even added to this German, e.g. the subjunctive. His linguistic achievements at school in Hamburg are perhaps best summed up by quoting some relevant parts of the school report he received when he left in December 1984:

> Frank kam mit guten deutschen Sprachkenntnissen in die Klasse und überwand so die Anfangsschwierigkeiten rasch. ... Im Rechtschreiben unterliefen ihm nur noch bei schwierigen Wörtern Fehler. Frank liest auch ungeübte Texte fließend und deutlich ... Seine Aufsätze schreibt er sprachgewandt und bereichert sie mit netten Ideen. ...
> (Frank joined the class with a good command of German and thus quickly overcame any initial difficulties. ... In spelling, he made errors only with difficult words. Frank reads even previously unseen texts fluently and clearly. ... He writes his compositions articulately and enriches them with good ideas. ...)

Since the children's return to Australia, their German has not stood still, although their fluency and speed of delivery have decreased a little. The following are examples of Frank's speech in both languages at age 11;11,8. This is 23 months after returning from Germany. He is the most fluent speaker of the children, although not the most grammatically accurate. The

German sample was recorded shortly after Frank had taken part in a 12
kilometre fun run and he was telling his father how he had performed. The
English sample was taped later the same day as he was making a cassette
for his grandparents to tell them about the same event.

German	*English*
… und man muß zwölf Kilometer laufen.	… and it's twelve kilometres. And
Und, ah, am Anfang war es sehr e-, eng,	when we got there we lined up and the
weil es gab sehr viele Leute, und ich	bloke, um, and the bloke sounded the
bin beinahe ins Bach gefallen, aber dann	gun and we were off. And I — I nearly
mußte ich ziemlich — sehr schnell laufen,	ran into the creek because you get
um all — , durch all die Leute zu kommen,	almost crushed, 'cause there's a — over
und, ah, dann war es leicht. Und ah,	two thousand people running in it. And
man mußte ein' sehr steilen Hügel	then gradually you make your way
hinauflaufen, aber dann gab es	through the people and they get
Getränke und so weiter. Ich habe	dropped back. And, um, and I
viele Männer und Frauen, ah, überholt.	overtook um, all these men and that.
Und, ah, dann war der Hälfte des	And I was aiming to overtake this
Wettbewerbs, ah- hat der Mann ge-,	bloke in this red, um, shirt and all the
mir mein-, meine, ah, Zeit gesagt,	way I was behind him — most of the
und er hat gesagt: "Neunundzwanzig	I was behind him — and then he ran up
Minuten und fünfzig Sekunden." Und	the hill, and you could get drinks, and
ich hab gedacht: "Sehr gut. Jetzt	I washed myself down with a sponge …
muß ich, ahm, schnell auf den	And when I got to the half-way point
Heimweg laufen." Und, ahm, ich bin	I, um, I started — the bloke there said
den Hügel ziemlich schnell hinauf-	that I did the six kilometres in twenty-
gelaufen, und dann noch ein Getränk	nine minutes and fifty seconds, and I
geholt. Und es gab ein Mann in	thought, "Oh, that's pretty good." And
einem roten, ah, Hemd vor mir, Bert,	then on the way back I overtook that
und ich wollte ihn besiegen, und, ah,	bloke in the red shirt, and I overtook
ungefähr die letzten zwei Kilometer	all these people. And then on the
hab ich ihn überholt. Und dann bin	last bit where I could see the bridge
ich sehr schnell gegangen, und ich	near the end — and then, um, I ran
konnte die Brücke sehen — weißt du	real fast, and I was feeling sick in the
diese Brücke? — Ja, und ich fühlte	head, but I kept on going. And then
mich krank in den Kopf, aber ich	when I got to the finish my time was
wollte immer noch — ich mußte immer	sixty minu-, my time for twelve
noch laufen. Und dann, ein paar	kilometres was sixty minutes and
Minuten später bin ich angekommen.	eighteen seconds, and I was real
Und ich wollte meine Zeit kriegen,	pleased. And after — ah, when I went
und, ah, ich bin zur Frau gegangen,	to get my time I was sick, because I
und dann hab ich mich erbrochen.	felt sick in the head, and I vomited
Und die Frau hat mich gesagt, was	up. Yeah, yeah, it was a real good
meine Zeit war: es war sechzig	run….
Minuten und achtzehn Sekunden.	

Translation of the German version:
... and you have to run twelve kilometres. And, um, at the start it was very cr-, cramped, because there were lots of people, and I nearly fell into the creek, but then I had to run fairly — very fast to get through all the people, and then it was easy. And, ah, you had to run up a very steep hill, but then there were drinks etc. I, ah, overtook lots of men and women. And, ah, then half of the competition was, ah — the man to — , ah, told me my — my time, and he said: "Twenty-nine minutes and fifty seconds." And I thought: "Very good. Now I'll have to, ah, run fast on the way home." And, um, I ran up the hill fairly quickly and then got another drink. And there was a man in a red, ah, shirt in front of me, Dad, and I wanted to beat him, and, ah, about the last two kilometres I overtook him. And then I went very fast, and I could see the bridge — you know that bridge? — yes, and I felt sick in the head, but I still wanted to — I had to keep on running. And then, a few minutes later I arrived. And I wanted to get my time, and, ah, I went to the lady, and then I vomited. And the lady told me what my time was: it was sixty minutes and eighteen seconds.)

The results of comparing the German and English versions are summarized in Table 5. The two versions are remarkably similar both in content and the fluency with which they are told. The similarity in rate of delivery is even more striking if, instead of counting words (on average English words are shorter than German words), we count *syllables*: in the German version Frank speaks at a rate of 179.4 syllables per minute, and in the English version at a rate of 182.9 syllables per minute. The speech samples are reasonably typical of the way he speaks both his languages, although on some topics he may sometimes strike a few vocabulary problems in German which slow down his rate of delivery. The number of errors is higher in German, but none of them hinders understanding. (*Real* used as an adverb instead of *really* e.g. "I was *real* pleased" has been counted as an error here in the English version, although it is acceptable in colloquial English, since in the German version the *weil* sentence without the verb at the end of the clause has also been counted as an error, although nowadays it is probably acceptable colloquial German — see Perrin (1982).)

When Thomas was aged 13;5,7 and Frank 11;6,11, they were asked to

Table 5: Comparison of English and German versions of sample text

	Errors per 100 words	Words per minute	Filled pauses with 100 words	Repeats per 100 words	Length in words	Time (min:sec)
English	0.4	151.2	2.3	1.9	258	1:42
German	4.7	129.4	3.8	1.7	235	1:49

Table 6: Self-assessment

	Frank		Thomas	
	English	German	English	German
Listening comprehension	100	95	96	89
Speaking	100	95	92	78
Reading	100	100	95	82
Writing	100	90	89	76

assess their own proficiency in their two languages in the four skills of listening comprehension, speaking, reading and writing. They were asked to give themselves a mark out of 100, with 100 representing perfect mastery, and 0 indicating zero proficiency. They considered the matter very carefully and then awarded themselves the marks summarized in Table 6. The results reflect in part the different attitudes of the two boys. Frank, more confident and less self-conscious about making mistakes, has taken his ability in English to be perfect (even though he does admit that there are English words which he does not understand and English words which he cannot spell correctly, etc.). Thomas, however, is more cautious, more self-critical, and perhaps more realistic, in judging his linguistic ability; he, for example, revealed that he compared his own English with that of adults when making his assessment, whereas Frank compared his English with that of his peers.

Conclusions

The three children have acquired a good level of proficiency in German at no expense to their English. Their English is not only indistinguishable from that of their monolingual peers, but is well above average with regard to receptive and active vocabulary.

So, is this case of "artificial bilingualism" successful? I would say so (although I may be a little biased!). To the perfectionist, the children's German is perhaps inadequate, because it does not match monolingual German children's proficiency. But, as we have just seen, it is a German which is serviceable and which has enabled them to function well in an all-German-speaking environment.

Provided a parent has a good and confident command of the non-native language and speaks it consistently and with commitment with his or her children, the chances of success would seem similar to those in cases of "natural bilingualism".

References

Brennan, Anne. 1987. "Teaching a Trilingual Child to Read". *Bilingual Family Newsletter* 4(3).

Christopherson, Paul. 1973. *Second-Language Learning. Myth and reality*. Harmondsworth: Penguin.

Clyne, Michael. 1967. *Transference and Triggering: Observations on the language assimilation of postwar German-speaking migrants in Australia*. The Hague: Nijhoff.

———. 1982. *Multilingual Australia: Resources, needs, policies*. Melbourne: River Seine Publications.

Corsetti, Renato & Traute Taeschner. 1986. "Early Language Differentiation in a Trilingual Child". Ms.

Dimitrijevic, N. 1965. "A Bilingual Child". *English Language Teaching* 20. 23-28.

Dorian, Nancy. 1981. *Language Death. The life cycle of a Scottish Gaelic dialect*. Philadelphia: University of Pennsylvania Press.

Doyle, A., M. Champagne & N. Segalowitz. 1978. "Some Issues on the Assessment of Linguistic Consequences of Early Bilingualism". *Aspects of Bilingualism* ed. by M. Paradis, 13-20. Columbia: Hornbeam Press.

Facey, Andrea. 1986. "Bilingualism with a Difference". *Bilingual Family Newsletter* 3(3). 5-6.

Fantini, Alvino. 1985. *Language Acquisition of a Bilingual Child: A socio-linguistic perspective to age 10*. Clevedon: Multilingual Matters Ltd.

Fantini, Alvino. 1986. "Developing Bilingualism: Two world views?" *Bilingual Family Newsletter* 3(3). 1-3.

Kielhöfer, Bernd & Sylvie Jonekeit. 1983. *Zweisprachige Kindererziehung*. Tübingen: Stauffenberg Verlag.

Leopold, Werner. 1939-49. *Speech Development of a Bilingual Child: A linguist's record*, Vols. 1-4. Evanston: Northwestern University Press.

Past, Al. 1976. *Preschool Reading in Two Languages as a Factor in Bilingualism*. Ph.D. thesis, University of Texas at Austin.

Peña, A. & E. Bernal. 1978. "Malpractices in Language Assessment for Hispanic Children". *Occasional Papers on Linguistics*, No.3. 102-116. Southern Illinois University at Carbondale.

Penfield, W. & L. Roberts. 1959. *Speech and Brain Mechanisms*. Princeton: Princeton University Press.

Perrin, Geoffrey. 1982. "Divergences between Spoken and Written Language — Their implications for the classroom". *The British Journal of Language Teaching* 20(1). 55-57.

Reitmajer, V. 1975. "Schlechte Chancen ohne Hochdeutsch". *Muttersprache*. 310-324.

Richards, Jack & Mary Tay. 1981. "Norm and Variability in Language Use and Language Learning". *English for Cross-Cultural Communication* ed. by L. Smith. New York: St. Martin's.

Ronjat, Jules. 1913. *Le développement du langage observé chez un enfant bilingue*. Paris: Librairie Ancienne H. Champion.

Saunders, George. 1980a. "Adding a Second Native Language in the Home". *Journal of Multilingual and Multicultural Development* 1(2). 113-144.

————. 1980b. "Creating Bilingualism". *Australian Review of Applied Linguistics* 3(2). 122-130.

————. 1982a. "Infant Bilingualism: A look at some doubts and objections". *Journal of Multilingual and Multicultural Development* 3(4). 277-292.

————. 1982b. "Der Erwerb einer zweiten ,Muttersprache' in der Familie". *Bilinguale und multikulturelle Erziehung* ed. by James Swift. Würzburg: Verlag Königshausen & Neumann.

————. 1982c. *Bilingual Children: Guidance for the family*. Clevedon: Multilingual Matters Ltd.

————. 1984. "Creating Bilingualism Revisited". *Australian Review of Applied Linguistics* Series S, No.1. 24-35.

————. 1986. "'Artificial' Bilingualism". *Bilingual Family Newsletter* 3(3). 3-4.

————. 1988. *Bilingual Children: From birth to teens*. Clevedon: Multilingual Matters Ltd.

Skutnabb-Kangas, Tove. 1984. *Bilingualism or Not. The education of minorities*. Clevedon: Multilingual Matters Ltd.

Swain, Merrill. 1972. *Bilingualism as a First Language*. Ph.D. thesis, University of California at Irvine.

The "Bilingual" Child as Interlanguage Hearer: Implications for Migrant Education

Marta Rado and Lois Foster

0. Introduction

Undoubtedly, language is regarded as a key issue in the education of children generally, but perhaps its significance is nowhere more evident than in the education of children whose home language differs from the school language. The purpose of this paper is to provide information which should prove useful in fashioning language programs in terms of curriculum planning and classroom teaching methodology and in formulating policies regarding ethnic language maintenance in the domains of home and school.

The empirical data on which the discussion is based have been collected by the authors in the course of the last decade in Australia where the official school language is English. Per force it is the characteristics of the English language use of the children and that of the significant adults in their lives which inform this discussion. Findings are explained and illustrated in terms of the English language and recommendations concern mainly, but not exclusively, English language education across the curriculum in Australia. However, as the emphasis is on the underlying universal meanings, findings should be of interest to others concerned with the language education of children in comparable bilingual situations. The language data consist of interview protocols of primary age students with a non-English speaking (NES) and an English-speaking (ES) background and their parents. In the case of children, there are additional data in the form of narrative discourse and the results of a language awareness test.

Of particular interest are two aspects of the NES parents' speech. Firstly, in what way it differs from the language of comparable ES parents. This serves the double purpose of highlighting the difference in the language environment of NES and ES background children respectively. At the same time, it documents the type of interlanguage immigrant parents are likely to use in Australia. Secondly, the NES parents' interlanguage is discussed from the point of view of the hearer's decoding task. With respect to the NES background children, it is not hypothesised that the same interlanguage features will be found in their language as in that of their parents. The contention is that the NES background may have a subtle general influence affecting their decoding and encoding strategies in a more global way. With respect to the parents, it is hypothesised that they are mature speakers of their mother tongue.

In conclusion, we argue firstly, that our findings point to bilingual language development as a good solution for children exposed to interlanguage in the home; secondly, that we have some evidence for believing that the language development of bilingual children growing up in an interlanguage home environment is not necessarily affected in an adverse way in all its aspects; thirdly, that a comparative analysis of the language of bilingual and monolingual children provides useful information for designing the language component of school curricula.

0.1 *Data*

The data for this paper are drawn from taped interviews with year 5 and 6 primary-age children with an NESB and an ESB, and their parents. The children were attending both government and Catholic schools in the northern suburbs of Melbourne. They were matched for sex, age and school achievement. The NESB children came from family backgrounds in which Italian, Greek, Macedonian, Spanish, Turkish and Vietnamese were spoken. Because priority was placed on detailed analysis of individual language use, the number of participants is relatively small — eight in each group.

The majority of parents had primary schooling only and had a lower socio-economic background. All the NESB parents used some English with their children in the home despite the fact that they were all *interlanguage* speakers of English in that they used non-standard, idiosyncratic forms in English, albeit with varying density. Indeed one question this paper addresses is what significance this has for their children as *hearers*.

The parents interviews covered ten topic areas; some of these were included in the child interviews. The topics shared across the four groups were: (1) personal data (e.g. schooling); (2) attitude to language maintenance/ bilingualism; (3) importance of education; (4) appraisal of the contribution of immigrants to Australia; (5) child's leisure activities; (6) identification with own group and stereotyping. The additional topics included in the parent interviews were suggestions for improving the quality of life in Australia and questions relevant to one of the groups only (e.g. early experiences in Australia; helping with English expression).

1.   The Role of Shared Knowledge in Conversation: Parents and Children

1.1 *Knowledge of the Topic*

Language is an interactive process. Effective communication is the result of a cooperative act between speaker and hearer (Grice 1975). The more skilled the speaker, the easier the hearer's task will be. A skilled speaker knows how to signal the conceptual, formal and pragmatic aspects of the message effectively by making good use of the shared pre-knowledge between the conversational partners. It can be assumed that parents talking with their children in their mother tongue know how to tune their speech to the conceptual level of their children. As mature speakers, they share the rule system with other speakers of their dialect and exploit the resources of their language. If parents use an interlanguage, the situation is different. This is discussed in detail below.

1.2 *Shared Linguistic Knowledge*

Language simultaneously expresses factual, social and affective information. This is economical but adds to the complexity of language. Speakers and hearers cope with the complexity and hence with the richness of verbal messages on the basis of a shared rule system, which is a prerequisite for successful communication. One characteristic of the rule system is that some of it is obligatory and some optional, or perhaps more precisely, avoidable. For example, speakers of English must always mark tense in a finite verb phrase or number in a noun phrase. Obligatory marking has advantages because by predetermining that certain notions are to be marked, language becomes more predictable for the hearer who as an active participant appears to shadow the speaker in some way. Obligatory marking also benefits the speaker who, relieved of the need to choose, can concentrate on other aspects of the message. In Brown's words

> I speculate that it is necessary for any language to make obligatory and
> automatic certain meanings in order to leave central channeling capacity
> free to cope with the exigencies of each particular communicative prob-
> lem. (1983:65)

1.3 *Obligatory Marking*

The term obligatory marking refers to all the semantico-grammatical signals
that must be present in a well-formed string of words whether they be complete or ellipted clauses; that is, grammatically well-formed clauses despite
the absence of a finite verb. If the message is to be understood despite the
absence of obligatory marking (e.g. grammatically ill-formed, wrong choice
of words), the missing element must be restored by the hearer. What the
nature of the repair work is does not concern us here. What is of import is
the fact that the hearer has to supply some of the information that according to Grice's (1975) Co-operative Principle should have been given by the
speaker. If this is the case then interlanguage speakers increase the processing load for their hearers (e.g. NES parent: "No much people make too
many job").

Of course, mother tongue speakers also make errors requiring repair,
due to some temporary difficulty such as inattention or fatigue. As a rule,
however, there is a marked difference between native speakers and interlanguage speaker error rates. The language data drawn from the parent
interviews support this claim (e.g. ES parent: "but I don't think it should
ever been a subject").

The language material judged for acceptability on the basis of grammatical, semantic and pragmatic appropriateness was selected by first
establishing a sampling fraction for clauses and then systematically sampling 50 complete or ellipted finite clauses uniformly across the sample in the
case of parents and 25 such clauses in the case of children. The lower error
rate of ESB children compared with their parents (as shown in Table 1) is
due to their relatively frequent bare yes/no responses. Both groups of children were at times content not to elaborate their yes/no answers.

It can be argued that despite errors, many messages can be understood
because of their context. Taking this into account, clauses were rated as
containing single errors, multiple errors, or impossible to repair. Significantly there were only two ESB parent clauses where the manner of repair

Table 1: Faulty clauses

	Parents' clauses (n = 400)	Children's clauses (n = 200)
NESB	66%	37%
ESB	11%	7%

Table 2: NES parent message restoration

	Restoration	
	Clauses (n = 400)	Faulty clauses (n = 264)
Single	46%	70%
Multiple	8% ⎫	12% ⎫
	⎬ 20%	⎬ 30%
Impossible	12% ⎭	18% ⎭

was in doubt. In contrast, one fifth of the NESB parent clauses could have been repaired in various ways or were impossible to repair, in other words incomprehensible (see Table 2). Clearly much of the NESB parent speech is difficult to interpret accurately. It can be hypothesised that exposure to interlanguage puts NESB children in a position conducive to accepting inordinate vagueness in messages as a matter of course. This could be a disadvantage when faced with learning tasks where accuracy of interpretation is at a premium.

Consider the following NESB parent responses from the point of view of repair.

Single error
NES Parent: "She working a lot".

Multiple errors
NES Parent: "Because maybe after she go somewhere".

Impossible to repair
NES Parent: "I think the Australian government matter matter to think everything".

Alternative repair possible
NES Parent: "The way we like to grow up the children".
Repair A: "The way we like the children to grow up".
Repair B: "The way we like to bring up the children".

It can be assumed that impairment in obligatory marking increases the processing load for the hearer; perhaps it can be also assumed that choice and uncertainty in repair will further increase this load. Moreover, it is often impossible to interpret such clauses accurately.

1.4 *Optional Marking*

Failure to carry out obligatory marking can be considered as impeding communication, whereas optional marking can be seen as enriching it. The elements selected for observation should illustrate this. The data base in this instance are the full answers given to 17 questions by the parents and 10 questions by the children. Again the unit chosen for analysis was the clause as this can be regarded as the primary perception unit in speech processing (see Bever 1972:104).

1.5 *Verbal Output*

The volume of responses (as can be seen in Table 3) varies considerably across the four groups. One can speculate that this is due to language competence rather than attributing greater talkativeness to native speakers of English. It may be worth noting that whereas ESB parents say three times as much as NESB parents, the number of clauses uttered by ESB children was greater by only one seventh.

1.6 *Connectives*

Connectives can serve as a good example for optional language elements because their absence does not necessarily constitute a mistake. Connectives help the listener to *track relations between events* while providing *extra*

Table 3: Number of clauses

	Total no. of clauses	Average per person
NESB parent	1098	137
ESB parent	3150	394
NESB child	362	45
ESB Child	417	52

planning time for the speaker. Gap fillers and *boundary markers* also *lighten the planning/processing task* by diluting information density. At the same time, they help *to maintain* the impression of *fluency.* Although they are not essential for the intelligibility of a text, their very existence and variety is significant.

There are two overlapping systems expressing relations between clauses. One is the *grammatical* system of *subordination* and *coordination.* The other is the *semantic* system of *connecting clauses "logically" to their context* (see Halliday and Hasan 1976:226-273). The *"logical" conjunctions* identified in the parent protocols were categorised according to Martin (1983:21) illustrated here with examples from the protocols. The list of examples is not complete.

> Additive: and, or;
> Temporal: when, before;
> Consequential: but, because;
> Comparative: whereas.

In addition, Halliday and Hasan's *"continuative"* category was also used (Halliday and Hasan 1976:267-271). Parents used connectives from all five categories, but ESB parents made greater use of them than NESB parents.

Table 4 is remarkable in that it shows great similarity between parent and child use of single connectives. If one considers connectives in speech as place holders indicating to the children that a connection should be made between clauses, they may well direct non-conscious attention to these signals. This could be useful given the importance logical conjunctions play in expository prose, a discourse genre many NESB children find difficult to handle.

1.7 *Examples of Connectives*

Conjunction
ES Parent: "I might be wrong but I used to think".

Table 4: Connectives

	NESB Parent	ESB Parent	NESB Child	ESB Child
No. of clauses	1098	3150	362	417
Connectives	31%	41%	29%	41%

Continuative
ES Parent: "Well I think the freedom side of it".

Connective cluster
ES Parent: "He was behind a bit and then I taught him to read".

Scarcity of connectives
NES Parent: "If you start today job tomorrow may be give you sack. No guarantee you know. This not fair. Maybe I buy one house 100,000 dollars. I start job my wife together. One week after factory say sorry, no have job, you finish."

1.8 *Unpredictable Elements*

The use of "fillers" and "routines" is not obligatory and is totally unpredictable. The label *routine* refers to all types of stereotyped words or phrases totally or practically predetermined "covering the full range of utterances which acquire conventional significance, for an individual, group or whole culture" (Hymes cited in Coulmas 1981:4). For the purposes of this discussion, *fillers* were considered separately from other types of routines. Words or expressions were classified as fillers if their sole function was to fill a gap giving the speaker time to plan the next verbal sequence and giving the hearer extra processing time. Where an expression also had a communicative function (e.g. when "I think" is used to emphasise the speaker's personal opinion), the expression was not classified as a filler. Typical fillers were "I think" and "you know". ESB parents used a greater variety of fillers than NESB parents.

Coulmas explains the widespread use of routines as follows:

> ... man says the same thing a number of times not because he is a tedious bore. It happens because man has socially shared intentions stimulated to a great extent by contexts of situation which recur and so does linguistic expression because it is economical, functionally required and satisfactory. (1981:67)

Generally it can be said that *gambits*, a sub-category of routines, provide a semantic frame but do not convey a specific meaning (Keller 1981:107). They can function as *semantic introducers* (e.g. a topic can be framed in terms of personal opinion "My personal opinion is", "I honestly believe" or "I would imagine"). They can *signal the special context* in terms of *turn-taking signals* or as indications of the *speaker's social role*. Typical of the

Table 5: Unpredictable elements

	NESB parent	ESB parent	NESB child	ESB child
No. of clauses	1098	3150	362	417
Fillers	7%	12%	0%	2%
Routines: gambits	11%	18%	9%	13%

former are expressions of wanting to abandon a turn, e.g. "That's all". Further, they can indicate a person's *state of consciousness*, that is readiness to receive or provide new information, opinions or emotions, suggesting that some knowledge or concern is being shared, "I didn't think that"; "That's a different question".

The above can serve as an illustration of some of the variety of functions wholly or partially *prefabricated chunks* can fulfil. In fact there is now growing evidence that in order to achieve native-like fluency, speakers must make extensive use of such sequences. Peters (1983:3) maintains that it is a shortcutting device: "It saves processing time and effort, allowing the speaker to focus attention elsewhere, for instance, on the social (as opposed to the linguistic) aspects of interaction". In view of the usefulness of routines and the important role they play in first language acquisition according to Peters, it is interesting to note that eighteen percent of the total verbal output of the ESB parents was classified as belonging to gambits whereas that of NESB parents was eleven percent. Moreover, every ESB parent used several gambits. In the case of NESB parents, four gambits were recorded in all (see Table 5).

If NESB parents do not avail themselves of routines, they increase the processing load of their children, because the verbal material to be analysed is denser. Further, the children miss an opportunity in experiencing the way *social relations* and *discourse features* can be indicated. In other words, they miss out on witnessing how language can be enriched.

1.9 *Examples of Fillers and Gambits*

> *Fillers*
> ES Parent: "I sort of find that they spend sort of more time with their families".

Gambits
– To introduce
ES Parent: "I don't think I ever caught an exam after that".

– To mark off
ES Parent: "I couldn't read the newspaper and things like that".
NES child: "Because you don't pass your test or something".

– To indicate personal opinion
NES Parent: "After will be very easy to understand, I reckon".

Up to this point, the language data were viewed from the point of view of the *hearer*. What emerged was that the NESB child has a more difficult task in interacting with parents in English than the ESB child. This is the case because of the additional processing load interlanguage imposes on the hearer and because the parents' interlanguage is denser.

It appeared that NESB children uttered relatively more faulty clauses than ESB children. In the use of optional elements, the former were closer to their parents than to their peers. Nevertheless, the NESB children's English, according to the measures we have applied, seemed much easier to process than that of their parents.

That the difference between the two groups of children is not greater is astounding given the NESB children's situation. In the home these children are constantly exposed to linguistic data they must disregard as a source of valid information about the lexicogrammatical rules of English. They must do this during an important period of language development when they are probably more sensitive to input data than they would be later as mature speakers of English.

Besides analysing the language data from a *hearer perspective* we also studied some of the data from a *pedagogical* point of view, in other words, what practical conclusions teachers could draw from the findings. With this objective in mind, the children's oral and written stories were analysed in various ways.

2.   Communication Through Narrative: Children and Their Stories

2.1 *Methodology*

This section is based on the completion of stories by the two groups of children. They were given a printed text in big characters and well set out so that they were eminently legible. Two texts were used of approximately the same length (35-40 words). Their subject matter was similar in that they introduced a stranger who assumed a threatening role. The story broke off at the crisis point leaving it to the narrator to provide the subsequent events and resolution. The setting was a familiar one experientially and linguistically, namely the home and milk bar. The former was entitled *Balcony*, the latter *Milk Bar*. The protagonists were the narrator in the first person and a strange man. Other probable participants who could subsequently be easily introduced by a narrator completing the story were members of the family, police, the shopkeeper and customers. In this way, it was ensured that the completion of the story was cognitively and linguistically well within the reach of the children so that they could pay full attention to the needs of the hearer. They were made aware of hearer needs by being told in advance that they and their partner would be asked to reproduce both completed versions in writing.

The children were asked to read the beginning of the story out aloud and then to invent the rest. Once read out, the printed material was withdrawn.

The two stories were evenly distributed between the two groups so that four children in each group completed the *Balcony* story and the other four the *Milk Bar* story. Each child besides completing a story wrote down his/her story and that of the partner. The oral story was taped and transcribed. In sum, the data base consists of three stories per child, in other words, a total of 48 stories.

2.2 *Discussion*

The analysis reported here is based on the story completion of the 1985 respondents. It is strictly exploratory, the intention being to discover trends to be studied further.

Comparisons are made within the two groups, across the two groups and in some instances between boys and girls. The latter grouping did not take ethnicity into account.

Table 6 indicates that the total number of clauses across the three versions produced by the ESB children was greater than that of the NESB children (NESB children 241 vs ESB children 279). The range of clauses for the NESB children was 18-47 and that of the ESB children 21-35. So the range of the latter group was narrower.

Table 6: Comparison of total narrative clauses

Children	Sex	No. of clauses			
		Oral story	Written: own story	Written: partner's story	Total
NESB	G	5	6	6	17
	G	16	10	7	33
	G	6	6	6	18
	G	25	12	21	58
	B	16	11	11	38
	B	6	5	4	15
	B	6	13	11	30
	B	6	5	8	19
ESB	G	15	11	9	35
	G	23	13	14	50
	G	9	6	8	23
	G	14	10	10	34
	B	29	15	16	60
	B	10	9	9	28
	B	15	10	14	39
	B	9	7	7	23
Totals:		210	149	161	520
NESB totals:		86	68	74	228
ESB totals:		124	81	87	292
NESB average:		10.7	8.5	9.25	28.5
ESB average:		15.5	10.1	10.8	36.5
Boys' totals:		97	75	80	252
Girls' totals:		113	74	81	268

Comparing the output of girls and boys, it is the girls who produced more clauses (girls 268 vs boys 252).

Treating the three versions as one text might appear strange to those who strongly hold the view that the written mode is radically different from the oral mode. Farr sums up this position neatly:

> ... for written language, meaning primarily resides in the text itself, whereas for oral language, much meaning is communicated in the context in which the language is used. In this sense, written language is more autonomous, or decontextualized, than spoken language. (1986:197)

But as Farr points out, recently researchers have tended to highlight the connection rather than the difference between the two modes. They stress that "all language use, whether oral or written, is embedded in a social context that affects both its form and its function (1986:197)".

Since the various text versions were produced in the same social context, the assumption was that some of their characteristics would not vary significantly across the oral and written modes. Consequently, it would be reasonable to compare the overall results for each group as well as the characteristics of the three stories composed by the same individual.

When the three versions were compared individually it appeared that the NESB children's oral version was significantly shorter ($\chi = 6.88$, p< .001) and the boys as a group said less than the girls. Comparisons of the two written versions within and across ethnic and sex groups yielded no remarkable differences in number of clauses. In other words the children sustained their writing at similar length.

The analysis of the three story versions focussed on some selected discourse features such as the structural patterns of the oral versions, types of clauses and accuracy of reproduction.

2.3 *Structural Patterns*

The classification scheme adopted for the structural patterns of the stories was based on that used by Peterson and McCabe (1983:37). This approach, inspired by Labov's work, considers the high or crisis point as the main organiser of a personal narrative. Our classification system had to suit stories that started at the crisis point, hence the difference.

The ranking order of the oral stories was established from best to worst narrative pattern according to the following criteria:

> *Evaluative*: the narrative comments on the crisis point(s), and then resolves it/them;
>
> *Disjointed*: the narrative leaves out major events that must be inferred by the hearer, but the crisis is resolved;
>
> *Chronological*: the narrative uses a simple description of successive events, then stops, and the crisis is not resolved;
>
> *Impoverished*: the narrative presents or reiterates only two events;
>
> *Disoriented*: the narrative is too confused for the hearer to understand.

Table 7: Story distribution according to structural patterns

	NESB	ESB
Evaluative	2	5
Disjointed	1	2
Chronological	3	0
Impoverished	1	0
Disoriented	1	1

Table 7 shows that the majority of the ESB children's stories belong to the two highest ranking categories. Compared with the NESB children's stories the former were more sophisticated on this measure.

2.4 *Narrative Clauses*

Besides such a global evaluation, the narratives were also studied at the clausal level to document the hearer-oriented informative aspects of the different story versions. The classification scheme used for this analysis was also influenced by the Labovian-based Peterson and McCabe method of analysis but differs from it in some essential ways because the stories are not complete personal narratives as the narrator was given the beginning of the story.

Definition of narrative clauses used in the analysis:

> *Action*: refer to the chronologically ordered events. This is the information component of narratives, and is the only essential type. Action clauses can also serve to resolve the crisis or cap off the experience (e.g. ES girl and boy "The police came").

> *Orientation*: statements that provide the setting or context of a narrative, including participants, time, location, general conditions, imminent events, objects or features of the environment (e.g. NES boy "Then got the money from the counter", ES boy "He had tools").

> *Evaluation*: statements that tell the hearer/reader what to think about a person, place, thing, event, or the entire experience, for example, guesses, causal explanations, subjective judgments and internal emotional states (e.g. NES girl "She got really mad", ES girl "He never came back again"). (Based on Peterson and McCabe 1983:31-34)

Table 8: Overlapping clause types

	Oral:own story			Written:own story			Written:partner's			All versions		
	Total no. of clauses	Overlapping clauses		Total no. of clauses	Overlapping clauses		Total no. of clauses	Overlapping clauses		Total no. of clauses	Overlapping clauses	
		No.	%		No.	%		No.	%		No.	%
NESB	86	25	29	68	24	35	74	22	30	228	71	31
ESB	124	44	35	81	29	36	87	29	33	292	102	35
Boys	97	41	42	75	30	40	80	27	34	252	98	39
Girls	113	28	25	74	23	31	81	24	30	268	75	28

A similar categorisation scheme is probably used by most teachers teaching narrative composition and in assessing such compositions. According to Peterson and McCabe, even very young, primary school-age children use these three types of clauses in their narratives.

Not surprisingly there was some overlap of clause types in that a single clause contained a combination of action, orientation or evaluation elements. In such instances, the same clause was counted twice; in other words, it was included in more than one category. Table 8 shows that when the three versions were considered as a group the proportion of clauses with overlapping elements was about one third. But when the versions were considered individually about half to one third of the clauses belonged to more than one type. Clauses containing more than one element have greater information value and so it can be said that they are richer. There was almost no difference between the two ethnic groups in the use of such enriched clauses. But there was a difference between the boys and girls in that the girls consistently used fewer of these. In the oral versions and the partner's written version the difference is significant ($z = 2.69$, $p<.01$ and $z = 2.64$, $p<.01$). Apparently the girls spread the orientation elements across clauses rather than presenting them in the same clause.

A detailed analysis of the different types of clauses yields the following information. In the case of both the NESB and ESB children somewhat over half of the clauses contain an action and an orientation element and 16 percent or somewhat fewer an evaluation element. This differs from the Peterson and McCabe observations in that the orientation element more closely approximates the action element than in their estimation. They state that action clauses are the most frequent, being the backbone of a narrative, whereas orientation clauses can be expected to occur less frequently (about one third of the narrative clauses). They estimate that about 15 percent would be purely evaluative but that almost half of narrative comments express some evaluation (1983:48-61).

What is of interest to us here is the fact that there is hardly any difference between the two groups except for the proportion of action clauses in the oral versions. The ESB children's stories were not only longer, they also used a significantly greater proportion of action clauses ($z = 2.09$, $p<.05$) so that relatively more happened in their oral stories. Curiously in the written version of their own story the NESB children increased the proportion

Table 9: Comparison of Action, Orientation and Evaluation clauses in oral version: own

Children	Sex	No. of clauses	Act		Orn		Evn	
			No. of clauses	%	No. of clauses	%	No. of clauses	%
NESB	G	5	4	80	1	20	1	20
	G	16	6	38	6	38	6	38
	B	16	14	88	11	69	0	0
	B	6	4	67	3	50	0	0
	B	6	4	67	3	50	1	17
	G	6	6	100	6	100	0	0
	G	25	5	20	13	52	6	24
	B	6	3	50	5	83	4	67
ESB	G	15	7	47	7	47	6	40
	G	23	15	65	12	52	0	0
	B	29	25	86	20	69	1	3
	B	10	7	70	5	50	2	20
	B	15	9	60	9	60	2	13
	G	9	7	78	6	67	1	11
	G	14	10	71	10	71	0	0
	B	9	4	44	7	78	1	11
Totals:		210	130	62	124	59	31	15
NESB totals:		86	46	53	48	56	18	21
ESB totals:		124	84	68	76	61	13	10
Boys' totals:		97	70	72	63	65	11	11
Girls' totals:		113	60	53	61	54	20	18

Act = Action; Orn = Orientation; Evn = Evaluation.

Table 10: Comparison of Action, Orientation and Evaluation clauses in written version:
own

Children	Sex	No. of clauses	Act		Orn		Evn	
			No. of clauses	%	No. of clauses	%	No. of clauses	%
NESB	G	6	5	83	1	17	1	17
	G	10	4	40	4	40	3	30
	B	11	8	73	6	55	0	0
	B	5	4	80	4	80	0	0
	B	13	11	85	9	69	1	8
	G	6	5	83	5	83	0	0
	G	12	8	67	6	50	4	33
	B	5	4	80	3	60	1	20
ESB	G	11	6	55	6	55	2	18
	G	13	8	62	9	69	0	0
	B	15	13	87	8	53	1	7
	B	9	5	56	3	33	2	22
	B	10	5	50	5	50	1	10
	G	6	6	100	4	67	0	0
	G	10	6	60	6	60	1	10
	B	7	3	43	5	71	1	14
Totals:		149	101	68	84	56	18	12
NESB totals:		68	49	72	38	56	10	15
ESB totals:		81	52	64	46	57	8	10
Boys' totals:		75	53	71	43	57	7	9
Girls' totals:		74	48	65	41	55	11	15

Act = Action; Orn = Orientation; Evn = Evaluation.

of event clauses, approximating that of the ESB children.

As Tables 9, 10 and 11 indicate, there are significantly ($p<.05$) fewer evaluation clauses compared with the other two. As evaluation clauses draw the attention of the listener/reader to the meaning of the experiences narrated, they make an important contribution to the quality of the narrative. If Peterson and McCabe are correct that about half of the clauses in children's narratives are wholly or partially evaluative, then the children in our sample are not doing as well as they should. In other words this analysis tells us that we should pay special attention to the development of this element in the compositions of children of similar age, ability and background.

Table 11: Comparison of Action, Orientation and Evaluation clauses in written version: partner's

Children	Sex	No. of clauses	Act		Orn		Evn	
			No. of clauses	%	No. of clauses	%	No. of clauses	%
NESB	G	6	5	83	5	83	1	17
	G	7	6	86	9	129	0	0
	B	11	13	118	10	91	1	9
	B	4	5	125	5	125	2	50
	B	11	6	55	6	55	2	18
	G	6	6	100	6	100	0	0
	G	21	7	33	6	29	0	0
	B	8	3	38	6	75	1	13
ESB	G	9	4	44	1	11	1	11
	G	14	3	21	4	29	2	14
	B	16	8	50	7	44	1	6
	B	9	4	44	3	33	0	0
	B	14	6	43	8	57	2	14
	G	8	5	63	5	63	0	0
	G	10	9	90	8	80	5	50
	B	7	5	71	8	114	0	0
Totals:		161	95	59	97	60	18	11
NESB totals:		74	51	69	53	72	7	9
ESB totals:		87	44	51	44	51	11	13
Boys' totals:		80	50	63	53	66	9	11
Girls' totals:		81	45	56	44	54	9	11

Act = Action; Orn = Orientation; Evn = Evaluation.

In order to do this, further details on the informativeness of the stories might be useful. An analysis of the orientation clause sub-categories could serve as one source of pertinent information.

2.5 *Orientation Clauses*

Orientation clauses provide contextual information which the story teller must share with the listener in order to make the narrative comprehensible.

Orientation clauses were subdivided into nine categories: participants, time, location, general conditions, ongoing events, tangential information, general cases, imminent events, objects or features of the environment (adopted from Peterson and McCabe 1983:32).

1. *Participants*: The most important element. It tells the listener who was involved including animals and animated objects. (NES girl: "It was the painter outside.")

2. *Time*: This type can refer to specific time or time in relation to other events.
    (NES girl: "This time he just made sure.")

3. *Location*: This type locates events, people and objects.
    (ES boy: "I hid behind the door.")

4. *General conditions*: These refer to environmental conditions such as weather, noise, etc.
    (ES boy: "I left the door open.")

5. *Ongoing events*: These tell the listener/reader what is happening at the same time.
    (ES girl: "A man that was standing there.")

6. *Tangential information*: This provides relevant but not necessary information.
    (ES girl: "The house was just across the road.")

7. *General cases*: These refer to habitual actions and general attributes relevant to the story.
    (NES girl: "She sulks for everything.")

8. *Imminent events*: These inform the listener/reader of what may happen next.
    (ES girl: "He was just about to get away.")

9. *Objects or features of the environment*: This type of clause mentions and describes objects and other details of the environment.
    (ES boy: "He had a thing on like Ned Kelly.")

(Based on Peterson and McCabe 1983:221-222)

An analysis of the children's orientation clauses yielded the following results.

1. *Participants*: Treating the three versions as one text one finds that both the NESB and the ESB children mentioned participants in about one-fifth of their clauses. If one compares the stories individually, it appears that the NESB children referred to participants proportionally more often in the oral and written versions of their own story but not in recording the partner's story. In the latter instance, the ESB children mentioned participants

Table 12: Orientation clauses referring to participants, location and objects

	Oral version			Written version of own story			Written version of Partner's story		
	Total no. of clauses	Orientation clauses		Total no. of clauses	Orientation clauses		Total no. of clauses	Orientation clauses	
		No.	%		No.	%		No.	%
NESB	57	44	82	48	41	85	58	46	79
ESB	84	48	57	54	25	46	44	34	77

proportionally more often.

2.   *Time*: The proportion of mentions is small and similar across the two groups of children.

3.   *Location*: Location is mentioned in about one-third of the orientation clauses in the texts of both groups. It drops back to one-fifth in the written version of the NESB children's own story and in the written version of the ESB children's partner story.

4.   *General conditions*, 5.   *Ongoing events*, 6.   *Tangential information*, 7.   *General cases*, and 8.   *Imminent events*: appeared sporadically in all versions or were non-existent.

9.   *Objects or features of the environment* outnumbered participant mention in practically every case. This reflects the fact that once the identity of participants is established pronouns and ellipsis can be used in referring to them (see Rado and Foster 1986a, 1986b).

The elements of contextual information can be ranked according to the more or less essential role they play in story comprehension. If one looks at the proportion of orientation clauses (see Table 12) referring to participants, location and objects, one can see that a substantial majority of clauses overall belong to this group. However, these indispensible elements do differentiate between the NESB and ESB spoken and written versions of the children's own stories. (These differences are statistically significant: $z = 3.15$, $p<.05$ in the case of the oral versions and $z = 4.75$, $p<.01$ in the case of the written versions.) Whereas the NESB children concentrated more on these essential elements to the exclusion of others in their narratives, the ESB children behaved in the opposite manner.

To sum up, the analysis of types of clauses and their sub-categories shows that in the use of these, the two groups of children are remarkably similar. They satisfy the minimum requirements for comprehension in giv-

ing the essential factual information. However, the stories are rather bare
in several respects. They don't enrich the context by giving environmental
details and other relevant information so that a great deal is left to audience
imagination. Further there is little attempt to help the listener/reader in
interpreting the narrative by drawing attention to certain features by means
of similes, for example, by giving explanations, expressing feelings, passing
judgments and so forth. Clearly there is room for developing these children's narrative skills.

2.6 Accuracy of Story Reproduction

One type of comparison of the written with the oral version was that of
accuracy of reproduction. The questions posed were whether one of the
groups followed the story line of the oral versions more closely than the
other; and whether there was any difference in the amount of material they
introduced which did not occur in the original version but was invented in
the process of writing.

The comparison was made by matching the written and oral clauses of
the same story on the basis of their propositional content. Clauses were
categorised according to the degree of similarity and dissimilarity. The
clause categories used were grouped as:

Close   *identical*: exactly the same wording is used

paraphrased: the clause is reworded but the propositional content is not altered significantly

extended: some additions are made to the original wording but
with little change in meaning

reduced: some of the original wording is omitted but with little
change in meaning.

Distant   *different*: participants and/or events are transformed

original: the clause is part of the stimulus material but not part of
the oral version

new: entirely novel participants and/or events are introduced

unused: these oral clauses have no counterparts in the written
version.

The two ethnic groups and the boys and girls reproduced each other's
stories and their own story in a similar way. About half the clauses in the
original oral versions were reflected in some way in the written versions,

whereas the other half were radically altered or ignored. On the similarity or closeness scale (see Tables 13 and 14), approximately ten to fifteen percent of the clauses were repeated word by word and about one-fifth to one-third were reworded by both groups. On the dissimilarity or distance scale (see Tables 15 and 16), just over 40 percent were ignored, to be partly replaced by extraneous material which was totally new or had appeared in the original text used as stimulus material. The NESB children introduced more of such elements into the written version of their own story. In contrast, the ESB children recorded more novel material when writing down the partner's story compared with writing their own. It is interesting to note that the NESB children elaborated their partner's story more in writing. One might hazard the guess that the act of speaking might divert their attention more from what they want to say compared with their ESB peers.

Table 13: Close measures for own written version

		Id		Para		Ext		Red		Clt
		f	%	f	%	f	%	f	%	f
NESB	G	1	20	1	20	0	0	1	20	3
	G	0	0	1	6	1	6	5	31	7
	B	2	13	5	31	0	0	1	6	8
	B	1	17	3	50	0	0	0	0	4
	B	1	17	2	33	0	0	0	0	3
	G	5	83	1	17	0	0	0	0	6
	G	0	0	7	28	0	0	1	4	8
	B	3	50	0	0	1	17	0	0	4
ESB	G	2	13	4	27	0	0	3	20	9
	G	2	9	4	17	1	4	4	17	11
	B	4	14	9	31	1	3	1	3	15
	B	4	40	3	30	0	0	1	10	8
	B	1	7	1	7	1	7	3	20	6
	G	1	11	0	0	0	0	5	56	6
	G	3	21	3	21	1	7	2	14	9
	B	1	11	4	44	0	0	0	0	5
Totals:		31	15	48	23	6	3	27	13	112
NESB totals:		13	15	20	23	2	2	8	9	43
ESB totals:		18	15	28	23	4	3	19	15	69
Boys' totals:		17	18	27	28	3	3	6	6	53
Girls' totals:		14	12	21	19	3	3	21	19	59

Id = identical; Para = paraphrased; Ext = extended;
Red = reduced; Clt = clause totals; f = frequency.

Table 14: Close measures for partners' written version

		No. of clauses	Id f	Id %	Para f	Para %	Ext f	Ext %	Red f	Red %	Clt f	Clt %
ESB	G	15	0	0	2	13	1	7	0	0	3	20
	G	23	0	0	5	22	0	0	2	9	7	30
	B	29	6	21	9	31	0	0	0	0	15	52
	B	10	1	10	1	10	1	10	3	30	6	60
	B	15	1	7	3	20	0	0	1	7	5	33
	G	9	1	11	5	56	0	0	1	11	7	78
	G	14	0	0	3	21	0	0	1	7	4	29
	B	9	1	11	5	56	0	0	0	0	6	67
NESB	G	5	1	20	2	40	1	20	0	0	4	80
	G	16	1	6	3	19	0	0	0	0	4	25
	B	16	3	19	3	19	0	0	0	0	6	38
	B	6	0	0	3	50	0	0	0	0	3	50
	B	6	1	17	2	33	0	0	0	0	3	50
	G	6	2	33	4	67	0	0	0	0	6	100
	G	25	3	12	5	20	0	0	1	4	9	36
	B	6	0	0	1	17	0	0	0	0	1	17
Totals:		210	21	10	56	27	3	1	9	4	89	42
ESB totals:		124	10	8	33	27	2	2	8	6	53	43
NESB totals:		86	11	13	23	27	1	1	1	1	36	42
Boys' totals:		97	13	13	27	28	1	1	4	4	45	46
Girls' totals:		113	8	7	29	26	2	2	5	4	44	39

Id = identical; Para = paraphrased; Ext = extended;
Red = reduced; Clt = clause totals; f = frequency.

Table 15: Comparison of oral with own written version: distance measure

	Own written version					Own oral version				
	Total no. of clauses	New f	New %	Original text f	Original text %	Total no. of clauses	Different f	Different %	Unused f	Unused %
Total	149	11	7	13	8	210	11	5	89	42
NESB	68	10	15	9	13	86	6	7	35	41
ESB	81	1	1	4	5	124	5	4	54	44
Boys	75	4	5	12	16	97	4	4	41	42
Girls	74	7	9	1	1	113	7	6	48	42

Table 16: Comparison of oral with partner's written version: distance measure

	Partner's written version					Own oral version				
	Total no. of clauses	New		Original text		Total no. of clauses	Different		Unused	
		f	%	f	%		f	%	f	%
Total	161	25	16	16	10	210	26	12	93	44
NESB	74	13	18	12	16	86	13	15	40	47
ESB	87	12	14	4	5	124	13	10	53	43
Boys	80	5	6	16	20	97	12	12	39	40
Girls	81	20	25	0	0	113	14	12	54	48

A comparison of the distance measures within the two written versions shows that the difference between these and the oral versions is mainly due to the fact that a significant proportion, close to half the clauses of the oral versions, were ignored. This was the case not only when the children wrote down their partner's story but also when they recorded their own. Both ethnic groups and the boys and girls as a group behaved in a similar way (see Tables 17 and 18).

Table 17: Comparison of different distance measures within same group: oral/own written version

	NESB			ESB			Boys			Girls		
	Total no. of clauses	f	%	Total no. of clauses	f	%	Total no. of clauses	f	%	Total no. of clauses	f	%
New	68	10	15	81	1	1	75	4	5	74	7	9
Original	68	9	13	81	4	5	75	12	16	74	1	1
New	68	10	15	81	1	1	75	4	5	74	7	9
Different	86	6	7	124	5	4	97	4	4	113	7	6
New	68	10	15	81	1	1	75	4	5	74	7	9
Unused	86	35	41	124	54	44	97	41	42	113	48	42
Original	68	9	13	81	4	5	75	12	16	74	1	1
Different	86	6	7	124	5	4	97	4	4	113	7	6
Original	68	9	13	81	4	5	75	12	16	74	1	1
Unused	86	35	41	124	54	44	97	41	42	113	48	42
Different	86	6	7	124	5	4	97	4	4	113	7	6
Unused	86	35	41	124	54	44	97	41	42	113	48	42

Table 18: Comparison of different distance measures within same group: oral/partner's written version

	ESB			NESB			Boys			Girls		
	Total no. of clauses	f	%	Total no. of clauses	f	%	Total no. of clauses	f	%	Total no. of clauses	f	%
New	87	12	14	74	13	18	80	5	6	81	20	25
Original	87	4	5	74	12	16	80	16	20	81	0	0
New	87	12	14	74	13	18	80	5	6	81	20	25
Different	124	13	10	86	13	15	97	12	12	113	14	17
New	87	12	14	74	13	18	80	5	6	81	20	25
Unused	124	53	43	86	40	46	97	39	40	113	54	48
Original	87	4	5	74	12	16	80	16	20	81	0	0
Different	124	13	10	86	13	15	97	12	12	113	14	17
Original	87	4	5	74	12	16	80	16	20	81	0	0
Unused	124	53	43	86	40	46	97	39	40	113	54	48
Different	124	13	10	86	13	15	97	12	12	113	14	17
Unused	124	53	43	86	40	46	97	39	40	113	54	48

To sum up, there is no clearly demonstrable difference between the two groups in the way they reproduce in writing a short oral narrative. Approximately half the clauses are directly connected with the original text and half are entirely new or strikingly different. The question is whether these children treat expository prose the same way, that is omit or change the propositional content of about half the clauses in a text they encounter. What is of import here is the fact that the propositional content of the clause was fully understood by the children and yet they reproduced the stories inaccurately, including their own. So this was not a matter of language comprehension but rather the task of recording a familiar text. If such material is reproduced inaccurately, one wonders how conceptually new material would be treated by these children. The question that needs to be pursued is whether the children don't consider accuracy important or whether they find it difficult to record what they know.

3.   Conclusion

In general, the lack of significant difference (when the length of the narratives is controlled by comparing proportions of clauses) between the narratives of NESB and ESB children is a startling finding. It indicates that both groups of children approach the construction of a narrative text in similar ways. In other words, they share the same strengths and weaknesses. They have some appreciation of how clauses should be sequenced and linked and what essential information the listener needs. But their narratives lack quality. In concentrating on the most essential details, they make their stories intelligible on the literal level but fail to invest them with a particular meaning. In other words the stories tend to be colourless and pointless.

The fact that the results are not very different is reassuring in that it is one indication that the NESB and ESB children are similar in the ability of handling discourse. If this is the case, the same language teaching program should suit both groups. At this point it might be wise to pause and reflect that on the whole, in absolute frequency, the ESB children outperformed the NESB. On a given task with no time limit imposed, the output of the NESB children was smaller. This has a certain significance since shorter texts tend to contain fewer enriching details. The NESB children by providing shorter texts get less practice in elaborating their stories in the direction of more mature narratives. This should be kept in mind when planning programs so that they can be fine-tuned to cater for individual needs. In order to do this, one can analyse the quality of the students' narrative prose in ways we have discussed. Categorisation schemes such as ours are within the reach of teachers.

To sum up, the *discourse characteristics* we have selected and the *evaluation tool* we have adopted can serve teachers, whether mother tongue or foreign/community language teachers, well. They can use them to identify student needs in some detail and to assess the quality of compositions from the discourse point of view in a systematic way. The method would enable them to compare student compositions of varying length. At a time when teachers are given increasing assessment responsibilities coupled with demands of accountability, the method presented here should be of interest.

References

Bever, T.G. 1972. "Perceptions, Thought and Language". *Language Comprehension and the Acquisition of Knowledge* ed. by J.B. Carroll & R.O. Freedle, 99-112. Washington, D.C.: V.H. Winston & Sons.

Brown, R. 1973. *A First Language*. Cambridge, Mass.: Harvard University Press.

Coulmas, F. (ed.). 1981. *Conversational Routine*. The Hague: Mouton.

Farr, M. 1986. "Language, Culture and Writing: Sociolinguistic foundations of research on writing". *Review of Research in Education* 13, ed. by E.Z. Rothkopf. Washington, D.C.: American Educational Research Association.

Grice, H.P. 1975. "Logic and Conversation". *Syntax and Semantics* Vol.3 ed. by P. Cole & J. Morgan, 41-58. New York: Academic Press.

Halliday, M.A.K. & R. Hasan. 1976. *Cohesion in English*. London: Longman.

Keller, E. 1981. "Gambits! Conversational strategy signals". *Conversational Routine* ed by F. Coulmas, 93-113. The Hague: Mouton.

Martin, J.R. 1983. "The Development of Register". *Developmental Issues in Discourse* ed. by J. Fine & R.O. Freedle, 1-40. Norwood, N.J.: Ablex.

Peters, A.M. 1983. *The Units of Language Acquisition*. Cambridge: Cambridge University Press.

Peterson, C. & A. McCabe. 1983. *Developmental Psycholinguistics. Three ways of looking at a child's narrative*. New York: Plenum Press.

Rado, M. & L. Foster. 1986a. "Migrant Children's Language, Parental and Peer Language Environments and their Implications in the Australian Intercultural Context". *ARAL* 9(1). 62-91.

Rado, M. & L. Foster. 1986b. "The Language of Migrant Parents, their Children and Anglo-Celtic Peers: An interlanguage perspective". *Working Papers on Migrant and Intercultural Studies* No.4. Monash University.

Acquiring a Sense of the Story Genre:
An Examination of Semantic Properties

Christine C. Pappas

Acquiring a sense of story (Applebee 1978) is learning story discourse — it involves acquiring many interrelated aspects of the written story genre. During the past decade or so, research (two excellent reviews are Sulzby 1985, and Teale 1986) has indicated that a major way by which young children learn about the written story genre "naturally" is by being read to, by hearing written story language read aloud (Cambourne 1981; Doake 1984; Holdaway 1979, 1986; Smith 1982; Teale 1984; Wells 1981, 1986). This emergent literacy research has also noted that when young "prereading" children are read storybooks, they frequently and independently "re-enact" or "pretend to read" their favorite books (Butler 1980; Crago and Crago 1983; Holdaway 1979, 1986; Schickedanz and Sullivan 1984; Sulzby 1985; Taylor 1984). Young children's successive "pretend readings" (elsewhere termed 'protoreading' by Pappas 1987) approximate more closely the text of the book read to them (McKenzie 1977) so that by the end of the process they can even recite almost verbatim their favorite book. What is the nature of this approximation process? What does it tell us about how children acquire a sense of the written story genre? This paper reports on a quasi-experimental investigation of certain aspects of this reading-like behavior at the beginning of this approximation process to gain insights into early literacy.

During the preschool years young children learn a lot about the lexicogrammatical realizations of the language system. This linguistic knowledge has been acquired in rich contexts of interpersonal interaction where language accompanies action (Bruner 1983; Donaldson 1978; Wells 1981). Here, attention is focused only partially on what is said; other nonverbal, paralinguistic cues or parameters in the material situational setting contribute to and support the meaning constructed (Halliday 1977; Hasan 1984b; Wells 1986) — that is, in typical everyday conversations, "words fit the world" (Wells 1986). It is through such experiences that children acquire not only considerable event knowledge or "scripts" (Nelson 1986) about a variety of familiar experiences (for example, getting dressed scripts, birthday party scripts, restaurant scripts, and so forth), but they also learn a range of oral language registers to express meanings in these contexts. In other words, children learn to adjust their linguistic choices to meet the features of particular social contexts in their culture — the setting, the participants, and the specific task at hand.

In contrast to this "ancillary" role of oral language, the role of typical written language is "constitutive" (Halliday 1977; Hasan 1984b). As Halliday (1977) has characterized it, a written text "creates its own immediate context of situation, and the relating of it to its environment in the social system is a complex and technical operation" (1977:198). In other words, written discourse relies less on immediate context factors or interpersonal contributions, but instead is more *message-focused* (Tannen 1985). Thus, the registers (Halliday 1985; Halliday and Hasan 1976) of written language are different from those of speech; the written text itself is a greater carrier of meaning — as Wells (1986) has argued, in typical written language "words create a world of meaning." To become literate, then, the young child must come to terms with certain characteristics of written communication — its sustained organization, its characteristic rhythms and structures, and the disembedded quality of written language (Wells 1985, 1986).

A picture storybook — the type of nursery tale or storybook read to young children — is defined as a book which has pictures, but the illustrations are only extensions of the text or linguistic message (Huck 1976). That is, the pictures may enrich the interpretation of the story, but they are not necessary for its understanding. The text of the book "stands on its own," the role of language is constitutive. In other words, because the *pragmatic environment* for verbal art like picture storybooks is different from that of typical face-to-face conversational encounters, the characteristic structure of the storybook text itself has a major role in providing the clues to access meanings (Hasan 1984b).

A major aspect of learning about the written story genre is learning what researchers call macro-structures, the big "chunks" or global elements which serve as an outline of story discourse (e.g., Hasan 1984a, b; Pappas

1985; Pappas and Brown 1987; Stein and Glenn 1979). This paper uses Hasan's (1984a, b) scheme and terminology to describe the elements of this structure. Twenty kindergarten children (who were not reading in the traditional sense) were read a picture storybook — *The Owl and the Woodpecker* (Wildsmith 1971) — on three occasions, and then, after the book was read to them each time, were invited to take their turns to "read" (or "pretend read") the book. The focus in this paper will be on the children's developing an understanding of the nature of the first two global elements realized in *The Owl and the Woodpecker*, what Hasan (1984a, b) calls the Placement and the Initiating Event. Using Hasan's work as a guide, twelve semantic properties expressed in the Placement and the Initiating Event of the book have been identified. The major purpose of the present paper is to show how the absence/presence of these properties in the kindergarteners' three readings of the first part of the book provides important information about the process by which young children might learn about the written story genre. Later in this paper, I will propose that a particular written genre, like the story genre, represents a complex, abstract structure — it is a type of macro-category or -concept. Thus, another objective of this paper is to relate the process of learning about the written story genre to concept development in general.

Method

Subjects

The data to be reported about semantic properties have been extracted from a larger study which examined the ontogenesis of the registers of written story language by kindergarten children (see Pappas 1986, and Pappas and Brown 1988, for details of the larger study). These children were middle-class children who attended either morning or afternoon kindergarten sessions at a public school in a small university city in the northwestern United States. They were taught by the same teacher (my co-principal investigator in the project), who used children's literature as the basis for her reading program. In this larger study, which occurred during the spring of their kindergarten year, children read two picture storybooks written by Brian Wildsmith — they read *The Lazy Bear* (1973) first and then read *The Owl and the Woodpecker* (1971) approximately three weeks later. Twenty children (10 girls and 10 boys) who read *The Owl and the Woodpecker* are the subjects of the present paper.

Procedure

The picture storybook was read to the children three times, usually on consecutive days. They were taken out of their classroom for these reading sessions. Each time the book was read to a child, the child was then invited to take a turn to "read" it. We merely told the children, who did not as yet read in the traditional sense, that we were interested in their good ideas about reading books. We acknowledged that they might not be able to read the book "for real," but suggested that they could read it "their own way" — they could "pretend read" it if they wanted. Nothing specific about the book (initially unfamiliar to them) was pointed out to the children before reading to them, but the adult reader did respond to any questions or comments they had about the book. When the children took their turns to "read," they were in charge of the book; they held the book, turned the pages, and so forth. All of the children in the study used a "reading" voice, not a "telling about the pictures" voice — that is, they did indeed pretend to *read*. The three child "readings" of the book were audio-taped.

Global elements of story discourse

The global text structure scheme developed by Hasan (1984a, b) was used in this study. In this scheme there are obligatory or necessary elements which any story has to include, and optional elements which may or may not be realized in a particular story. The Initiating Event, Sequent Event, and Final Event of the global text structure are considered to be obligatory global elements; the Placement, Finale, and Moral are optional ones. A Placement is an element where characters are introduced and where information about what these characters habitually do or what attributes they may have is provided. The Initiating Event is the global element in which the conflict or problem emerges. This conflict or problem causes the characters to attempt to resolve it, and the description of these attempts constitutes the Sequent Event element. The Final Event is the global element where resolution of the problem/conflict gets settled. The Finale element is like a restoration or reestablishment of equilibrium (Todorov 1971).

It goes beyond the resolution in the Final Event element by adding conventionalized statements about the main protagonists — e.g., "they lived happily ever after" or "they were friends for the rest of their lives." Since the Finale hints at a habitual or normal state of affairs, it could logically function as the Placement for another tale (Hasan 1984a). Finally, the Moral global element is where a moral claim is made relative to the message of the story.

Elements of *The Owl and the Woodpecker*

The Owl and the Woodpecker possesses the three necessary global elements — an Initiating Event (IE), a Sequent Event (SE), and a Final Event (FE) — as well as two optional elements — an explicit "discrete" Placement (P), one which precedes the Initiating Event element, and a Finale (F), which follows the Final Event. (See the appendix for a copy of the text of *The Owl and the Woodpecker* marked with these global elements.)

As already indicated, this paper focuses on the first two global elements, the Placement and Initiating Event, with special attention to the Placement. Figure 1 shows part of the text of *The Owl and the Woodpecker*: the first two units[1] constitute the Placement; units 3 and 4 are the beginning of the Initiating Event and unit 30 is the last unit of that global element. Hasan's (1984b) recent work was used to identify and describe the impor-

Figure 1: The placement and part of the initiating event of "The Owl and the Woodpecker"

Global Structure Element	Unit	Text of *The Owl and the Woodpecker* (Wildsmith 1971)
Placement	1	Once upon a time, in a forest, far away, there lived a Woodpecker.
	2	The Woodpecker lived in a tree in which he slept all night and worked all day.
Initiating Event	3	In the tree next door, there came to live an Owl, who liked to work all night and sleep all day.
	4	The Woodpecker worked so hard and made so much noise that his tapping woke the Owl.
	30	He began to be so crotchety and rude that all the other animals decided that something must be done.

tant features — which Hasan terms semantic properties — of the explicit discrete Placement and Initiating Event realized in the story.

The Placement Element

The explicit discrete Placement of the story has certain semantic properties and lexicogrammatical realizations that distinguish it from different types of Placements in other stories. The most crucial semantic property in this type of Placement is a type of 'character particularization.' Here, it is achieved by the indefinite modification of the animate noun — *a woodpecker* — which serves as a participant in the process found in the first unit. Such an indefinite modification implies that there are other entities of the class named by the noun that has been used. Two other associated semantic properties are also realized in this unit — what Hasan calls 'temporal distance' (the formulaic *once upon a time* and *a forest far away*), and 'impersonalization' (the third-person noun *woodpecker*). These two additional features remove the events and the character of the tale "from the axis of the biographical to that of the general and hypothetical" (Hasan 1984b:86). Thus, these are the properties that distinguish the story from narratives of personal experience discussed by Labov and Waletzky (1967).

Hasan (1984b) has also identified two kinds of elaborative semantic properties that are possible in this type of Placement. The first is 'habitude' and it is expressed in *The Owl and the Woodpecker* by the habitual acts or states of the particularized woodpecker. One realization is found in the first unit through *lived*, which asserts the woodpecker's existence. Other habitude realizations are in unit 2 — they consist of the woodpecker's living in a tree and those acts which involve sleeping all night and working all day.

The second possible elaborative semantic property is termed 'attribution.' Potentially, it could have been realized in the type of Placement found here in *The Owl and the Woodpecker*, but was not. For example, certain characteristics could have been assigned to the particularized character woodpecker — like the color of his feathers, etc. — by the author. More will be said about this semantic property when excerpts from the children's three reading texts are reviewed.

The Initiating Event Element

As indicated in Figure 1, the third unit of *The Owl and the Woodpecker* is the beginning of the Initiating Event element. The Initiating Event element of the book is too long to discuss in the same detail as has been done for the Placement. It is important, however, to review the essential characteristics of the Initiating Event to understand how these features are related to the explicit discrete Placement in the book.

According to Hasan (1984b), the Initiating Event can be potentially conceived of as three parts — a 'frame,' a 'main act' and a 'sequel.' The frame, the first ·of these semantic properties, is an optional feature in Hasan's scheme, but is realized in *The Owl and the Woodpecker* book. The frame is defined as the state of affairs which serves as the background for the main act. In this book, it is expressed by the moving-in of the owl — who happens to have the opposite sleeping/working habits of the wood-pecker. The frame has to occur either anterior to (which is the case here), or at the same time as, the main act.

The main act and the sequel are essential parts of the Initiating Event. The main act is a one-time happening event that sort of breaks the cycle of the habitual state of affairs; it gets the whole story going. That is, semanti-cally speaking, the main act is characterized as a punctiliar, non-relational process where the tense of the verbal group is non-progressive. In *The Owl and the Woodpecker*, the main act can be found in unit 4 when the wood-pecker's tapping woke the owl. It is that act that gets expanded into the problem/conflict in the story. The sequel follows this main act and is related to it in three different ways — as a temporal sequence, as a tangential rela-tion, and (the most frequent type) as a causal dependence. Not every rela-tion realized in the book has been considered in the present analysis. Instead only the most significant causal relation of the owl's being awakened by the woodpecker's tapping — namely, the owl's being crotchety and rude (as realized in unit 30 in Figure 1) — has been examined. The Initiating Event in a story closes when the main act of expectancy becomes frustrated. In the case of *The Owl and the Wood-pecker*, the animals of the forest cannot endure the owl's poor disposition any longer and decide to act, which triggers the onset of the Sequent Event (see unit 31 in the Appendix).

Only five units of the book have been discussed, but it is clear that these units represent much learning about story discourse. There is ample evidence, for example, from the work of Nelson and her colleagues (1986), that young children bring to bear considerable knowledge of their world — its spatial-temporal structure, the people and objects that occupy it, and their activities — to the task of understanding the story genre. However, what will be argued in this paper is that even more is involved in this

Table 1: Points identified for the semantic properties and lexicogrammatical realizations found in the placement and initiating event of "The Owl and the Woodpecker"

Global Structure Element	Realization	Semantic Property	Point
PLACEMENT:	*once upon a time*	temporal distance	1
	a forest, far away	temporal distance	1
	a woodpecker	character particularization impersonalization	1
	lived	habitude (assertion of existence)	1
	he lived in a tree	habitude	1
	he slept all night	habitude	1
	(he) worked all day	habitude	1
INITIATING EVENT:	*in the tree next door there came to live an owl*	frame	1
	who liked to work all night	frame	1
	(who liked to) sleep all day	frame	1
	his tapping woke the owl	main act	1
	he began to be so crotchety and rude	sequel	1
		Total	12

development. Learning about the written story genre, as a type of verbal art, represents — to use a term from Karmiloff-Smith (1979) — a certain kind of *linguistic* problem-space, too.

Table 1 summarizes the semantic properties and lexicogrammatical realizations of these semantic properties found in the Placement and Initiating Event of *The Owl and the Woodpecker*. Table 1 also shows the points that were identified to document children's acquisition of these semantic properties.

In the Placement element, two different points were possible regarding temporal distance, and four points were possible relative to habitude. The realization, *a woodpecker*, which represents two semantic properties — character particularization and impersonalization — was given only one point to avoid overestimating children's acquisition of these properties. In the Initiating Event element, there were three possible frame points, one point for the main act, and (as already noted above) only one point was possible for the sequel.

If listening to stories read aloud fosters the acquisition of a sense of the written story genre, some indication of this learning in terms of these semantic properties should be found in the children's subsequent (second and third) pretend readings. The general aim of the study, therefore, was to see whether these semantic properties of the book (a possible twelve points) appeared in their texts. A more important and specific objective was to ascertain *how* the absence/presence of these properties were expressed by the children in their readings. That is, if the written story genre can also be conceived of as a linguistic problem-space, it was crucial to discover (and illustrate) the *process* by which young children accomplish this endeavor.

Results

General Pattern of the Acquisition Process

The results indicated a gradual increase of the semantic properties across the three readings — the mean use was 6.35 in Reading 1, 7.10 in Reading 2, and 8.15 in Reading 3. The scores (1-12 semantic properties) constituted the dependent variable in a one-factor repeated ANOVA (using the Geisser-Greenhouse conservative F test) with Reading (One, Two, Three) serving as the within-subjects treatment comparison. A significant effect for Reading resulted: $F(1,19) = 6.30$, p < .05. Tukey follow-up tests indicated that there was a significant increase in the use of the semantic properties between the first and third readings (the increase observed between the first and second readings and between the second and third readings was not significant).

Many might argue, however, that the absence/presence of these twelve semantic properties could be explained merely in terms of the simple recall (or lack of recall) of specific details of the book. In other words, the increased use of the properties may reflect little about the children's acquisition of a *sense* of the story genre. It is only through a more detailed examination of some of the children's three reading texts that it can be demonstrated that more than rote memory is involved. The rest of this paper, therefore, will discuss some excerpts from the children's readings to better clarify the process of learning the written story genre.

Examples of the Process of Learning the Story Genre

The first example to be examined is Robert's three "readings" of the first three pages of the book.

Example 1: Robert
Page Unit

Reading #1
Placement
1   1   once upon a time there was a owl and a woodpecker [*who* who
            lived at] who lived right next to each other
2   2   every day the woodpecker would keep on pecking and pecking
            [*ah* every day]
      3   and sometimes in the night he would go to sleep

Initiating Event
3   4   and [*acro*] across from that tree there was a rusty old owl
      5   [*he was*] he was so grumpy and so rude that he could not stand
            the noise from the woodpecker pecking along on his tree

Reading #2
Placement
1   1   once upon a time [*there*] there was a owl and a woodpecker
      2   they did not live very far from each other
      3   [so they] [and they had] and they needed that home to be happy
2   4   [but all] [but some] [but all the night] but [*the woodpec*] the
            woodpecker would peck on his tree [all *ah*]
      5   he would work all day and sleep all night until the next day

Initiating Event
3   6   and across from the woodpecker's tree not very far [was a *cr*]
            lived a crusty old owl [*in a*] in a hollow tree
      7   [*he he*] he was so patient sometimes and [so] sometimes so rude
            that he could not stand the noise

Reading #3
Placement
1   1   once upon a time [*in*] in a forest not far from here lived a owl
            and a woodpecker
2   2   every day the woodpecker would tap away
      3   and every night he would sleep

Initiating Event
3   4   and not far from that tree lived a crotchety and rude owl
      5   and every day he could not stand the noise
      6   and he always had to stay awake and try to make the
            woodpecker stop

The most striking feature of Robert's pretend readings is that he places or introduces *both* the woodpecker and the owl in the first unit of the Placement and then later on in the Initiating Event "reintroduces" the owl. Although Robert's Placement includes *a owl* (in unit 1), he does *not* use the definite form of the modifier (*the ... owl*) later on in his texts. Instead, in all of the three readings, Robert also uses the indefinite modification (*a rusty old owl* in Reading 1, *a crusty old owl* in Reading 2, and *a crotchety and rude owl* in Reading 3) in his second introduction in each of his Initiating Events. Presenting the owl with the woodpecker in the Placement is not consistent with the book, but it does reflect an understanding on Robert's part that in many stories all of the major characters are presented at the beginning. And, the repeated use of the indefinite modification of the owl character in both the Placement and Initiating Event can be seen as an overextension of the semantic properties of character particularization and impersonalization. The "extra" habitual information and the inclusion of attribution — *they needed that home to be happy* — in Robert's Placement of the second reading could also be seen in this way. In other words, that unit indicates that he understands that the 'habitude' semantic property could have been realized several ways in this type of Placement and that, although it was not included in the book, the semantic property of attribution could also have been expressed there.

Another interesting feature of Robert's readings is how he deals with the semantic properties in the Initiating Event. Robert does not include important frame information regarding the owl's working/sleeping habits, which are opposite to those of the woodpecker's expressed in the Placement, in any of his three reading texts. Moreover, he does not include the main act information — that the woodpecker's tapping woke the owl — in most of his readings either. Instead, Robert's texts jump ahead in the story to include more sequel information — that the owl was grumpy or crotchety and rude and could not stand the woodpecker's noise — see the very first units of his Initiating Event in each reading. In fact, in his readings, he states this sequel information over and over again throughout his three Initiating Events (not included in the excerpt above). In other words, it is as if he is trying to overcompensate for his omission of the frame and main act information through redundancy of the sequel information. Even Robert's "creative constructions" (Lindfors 1986) — *a rusty old owl* (Reading 1), *a crusty old owl* (in Reading 2), and finally *a crotchety and rude owl* in Reading 3 — reflect his attempts to express this sequel information early on in his readings.

Although it is a risky business to infer understanding or competence from what children say or do not say in story reproductions (that is why much of the story grammar research includes a probe technique following story retelling), the ways in which Robert expresses certain semantic properties of *The Owl and the Woodpecker* and includes and then drops certain features not found in the book suggest that the task for the children measured more than just their memory of particular facts in the book. Children's realizations of the semantic properties were considered to reflect how they might learn about the written story genre in general. Consequently, when a child included a particular property in one of his or her readings of the book, that inclusion was considered to be convincing (albeit not necessary or conclusive) evidence of that child's tacit story genre understanding. Conversely, when a particular property was not included, it suggested that the child might lack such understanding.

Several features found in Robert's readings were also observed in other children's texts. Several children, for example, introduced the owl with the woodpecker in the Placement. Most, though, used the definite article in subsequent references to it (*the* owl). A couple did what Robert did, however — namely, they reintroduced the owl using the indefinite article again. Tessie provided only a general "animals" introduction in her Placement in her first two readings (*once there was some animals*), and then employed such a strategy in her third reading (Example 2).

Example 2: Tessie
Reading #3
2   and there was a woodpecker and a owl
.
.
.
4   and a new neighbor [*um*] moved in
(Note: Tessie specifies this new neighbor as that of the owl in subsequent units in her
        text.)

The inclusion of extra habitude information and of attribution also were observed in other children's texts. An example of the addition of habitude can be found in Annie's third reading — see Example 3.

She introduced both the owl and woodpecker in a "bare-bone" Placement in her first two readings — she stated something like *there was an owl and a woodpecker* — and then provided this Placement in her third reading.

And, an interesting example of attribution elaboration can be seen in

Example 3: Annie
Reading #3
1.   there was once a woodpecker who loved the animals and tapped all day
                in his tree.

Example 4: Nancy
Reading #1
3   and once a time there was a little woodpecker who was black
4   [and she *ha*] and he had [white] black polka dots on the white

Nancy's first reading (Example 4). Presumably relying on picture details, she provides a description of the physical attributes of the woodpecker.

Although the 'frame' semantic property of the Initiating Event element is an optional feature in Hasan's scheme, in *The Owl and the Woodpecker* the relationship of the frame information regarding the owl's working/ sleeping habits to the habitude information concerning the woodpecker's working/sleeping activities in the Placement was important in that it provided tension in the story. Some children indicated their understanding of this relationship of tension by their comments to the adult reader during the first reading of the book. A few actually explicitly stated something like "there is going to be a problem" after page 3 of the book had been read (after unit 3 of the book in Figure 1), and then added, "I told you" when the main-act information — that the woodpecker's tapping woke the owl — had been read to them on page 4 (after unit 4 of the book). Half of the children included the Placement information regarding the woodpecker's working/sleeping habits in their first reading — and that information gradually increased in the second and third reading. A much fewer number of children included the frame information concerning the owl's habitual activities in their Initiating Events, although an increase of that information was also observed across the three readings. A number of children did attempt to include this frame information, but did it incorrectly by stating that the owl worked all day and slept all night. Since some children commented that it was "funny" that the owl slept during the day and worked at night, it could be that some children may not have known about nocturnal animals and consequently did not appreciate the significance of the opposite sleeping/working habits of these two major characters.

Although many children (like Robert in Example 1) did not include the frame information about the owl's activities in their texts, almost all of the children consistently expressed the main act relative to the woodpecker's tapping waking the owl in the three readings. In contrast, the

sequel information — that the owl became crotchety/rude — was included
by fewer children, although the number of children who included this information almost doubled in the second and third reading (6 in Reading 1 and
11 in Readings 2 and 3).

The next example indicates that different children seemed to focus on
different semantic properties in their readings. Note that the frame information about the owl's working/sleeping activities omitted in Robert's texts
(Example 1) is included here (Example 5), and that Brad appears to be
addressing the problem of how to realize another part of the frame in the
Initiating Event element, the owl's moving into the tree next door. He also
attempts to deal with aspects of temporal distance. Example 5 shows the
first units of Brad's three readings.

Example 5: Brad
Reading #1
Placement
1   [there] once upon a time there was a woodpecker that was very kind
            and loving
2   [he pecked all] he slept all night and [pecked] worked all day
Initiating Event
3   there was an owl that slept all day [work] and worked all night
4   [*he* he was] the woodpecker was pecking one day
5   [he] and the owl woke up and said "stop pecking you nerd"

Reading #2
Placement
1   [*there once was*] there once was a woodpecker that [*umm*] lived in a
            forest far far away in a hollow tree [*he* he] which he worked all day
            and slept all night
Initiating Event
2   once [live] came to live an owl [he like] which he slept all day and
            worked all night
3   he said "screech"
4   [*um* he screeched *um* "that pecking makes me"] [the pecking would] [*the
            ta*] the tapping was so loud [*that it*] that it woke the owl up
Reading #3
Placement
1   once upon a time far far away in the forest there lived a woodpecker
            which he worked all day and slept all night
Initiating Event
2   there came to live an owl which he worked all night and slept all day

As already noted, Brad's texts illustrate how he dealt with temporal
distance in the book. In Reading 1 only the *once upon a time* marker is pro-

vided; in Readings 2 and 3 some version of the second realization of the temporal distance property in the book (viz., *a forest far away*) can also be seen. By the third reading all of the children included the first realization of temporal distance. In contrast, Brad was among the few who expressed this second expression of it (e.g., only six children expressed it by their third reading). Examples 6 and 7 show two other children's efforts regarding this second semantic property of temporal distance.

Example 6: Helen
Reading #1
1   once upon a time there was a woodpecker deep down in a forest
Reading #2
1   [once *de*] once there was a woodpecker *makes buzzing sound* that
             lived deep down in the forest
Reading #3
1   [*once up*] once upon a time there lived a woodpecker deep down in a
             forest

Example 7: Jeanne
Reading #1
1   once upon a time in a dark forest there lived a woodpecker
Reading #2
1   once upon a time in a dark forest there lived a woodpecker
Reading #3
1   once upon a time in a far far forest lived a woodpecker

Helen includes it in all three of her readings through her use of an approximation ("deep down") for "far away"; whereas Jeanne accomplishes it in her third reading, only after employing "dark forest" in her first two readings.

To return to Example 5, once again, an instance of the semantic property of attribution (*woodpecker ... was very kind and loving*) can be observed in one of Brad's texts (in his first reading), but note that it is different from those used by children in earlier examples. Brad's inclusion of this attribution was probably motivated by the fact that the woodpecker character "saves the day" in the story (see the Final Event in the Appendix). Note that Brad did not include this elaboration in his subsequent readings.

Unlike Robert's three texts (Example 1), the beginnings of Brad's Initiating Event include the frame information regarding the owl's working/ sleeping habits. Extra units in the first two readings have been provided to show the unique ways Brad expressed the main act information — the owl waking up and saying "stop pecking you nerd" in Reading 1 and all of his false starts and repairs in Reading 2.

Brad's texts also show his attempts to include the owl's coming-to-live part of the frame. This feature of the frame is nonexistent in his first reading, but limited versions can be found in the second and third readings — the *coming to live* is there but no mention of living next door to the woodpecker exists. Only six children included this aspect of the semantic property in their first reading, but twice that many expressed it in their subsequent readings (11 in Reading 2 and 13 in Reading 3). Repairs were frequent in children's attempts to tackle this part of the frame, indicating that this feature of the book appeared to pose a special challenge for the children. An excerpt from Mark's second reading is an example of these repairs — see Example 8.

Example 8: Mark
Reading #2
3   [*um* the next door neighbor] it was [*the owl um*] the owl lived into [the next door] the [tree] next door neighbor's tree

Discussion

Not all of the twelve semantic properties have been covered in the eight examples in the previous section, but these examples do represent the typical responses of the children's three pretend readings. For a couple of the semantic properties (one aspect of the frame and the sequel, as were noted above), a sharp increase across the readings existed; but, in general, children's increased use of the semantic properties was a gradual one.

It is important to note that this study involves only twenty children reading one book, so conclusions based on these data must be made with caution. Nevertheless, I believe that the children's three readings of a book unfamiliar to them do provide a means for shedding light into how children might learn story understandings.

To summarize and conclude, three interrelated points about the study of children's use of the semantic properties will be discussed. None of these points results directly from the examples of children's three readings of *The Owl and the Woodpecker*. Instead, the points serve as a framework to examine what the findings of the study imply regarding how children might learn about written story discourse.

First, the examples show the constructive ways by which children employed the semantic properties in their readings. Their approximations, overextensions, elaborations, repairs, and so forth, clearly indicate that children did not acquire a sense of written story discourse in any rote fashion. With repeated exposures to the story, the children attempted to construct — using what they know about the world, language, and books — the message of the author. In other words, the children were developing a concept of written story by trying to understand how the semantic features were realized in the book that was shared with them.

This characterization of this developmental process of acquiring a sense of story underscores the second and third points to be made here — namely, the written story genre appears to represent a kind of linguistic problem-space or macro-concept so that the acquisition of the sense of story is analogous to concept development in general. To understand stories children clearly draw on what they know about both the 'people world' and the 'object world,' to apply the terminology and the distinctions made by Karmiloff-Smith (1979). For example, an understanding of conflict in a particular story "implies understanding characters'˙ goals, how their goals interrelate, and how plans to achieve goals mesh or clash" (Bruce 1984:157). These understandings represent knowledge of the human world, of the social and interpersonal aspects of a character's actions — what can be inferred about someone's beliefs, purposes or motives. Knowledge of the object world also contributes to understanding a particular story when the words describe the *physical* aspects of characters' actions on, or movements towards, objects, for example. What is suggested here is that the acquisition of the sense of the written story genre also includes children's constructive interaction with their 'language world,' or, more specifically in our case, the 'language world of the written story genre.' Karmiloff-Smith (1979) has argued,

> Whilst very general, common cognitive mechanisms may underlie the children's interaction with all three 'worlds,' linguistic developments are not simply the outcome of non-linguistic cognition. Emphasis must also be placed on language-specific developments. (1979:19)

This is an important point, for while current theories of reading comprehension characterize the process as being interactive, one involving a reader's schemata and a text, these theories depict the reader's knowledge usually only in terms of what the reader knows or needs to know about a topic the text is about (e.g., Anderson and Pearson 1984). Very little is said in these models about how the reader's *linguistic* knowledge of the structure of a particular written genre (that is, the way information on a topic is expressed by certain lexicogrammatical patterns in the text) also contributes to understanding that text.

However, it is not being suggested here that these language-specific understandings about the written story genre are developed by children separate from their knowledge of the other two worlds. Instead, children's three worlds — the object world, people world, and language world — all interact and influence each other in complex, synergistic ways (Bloom 1976; Pappas 1983). Such interactions between knowledge of the three worlds, indeed, seemed to be reflected in the examples included in this paper. For example, perhaps Brad (Example 5) could tackle the coming-to-live part of the frame in the Initiating Event because he already knew about the nature of nocturnal animals. Or, other children (like Mark in Example 8) might have actually learned something about nocturnal animals from the text itself — a case of learning about the world *through language* (Halliday 1982) — so that not until the later readings could these children realize the significance of the owl's moving in, and note how that information was expressed linguistically. That these interrelations (among the worlds) exist in development does not alter the importance of the language-specific contributions in children's acquisition of the sense of the written story genre.

If, then, we accept the notion that the written story genre can be conceived of as a linguistic problem-space for children, then it might be useful to consider that specific problem-space as a macro-concept. In this view, then, children learn story discourse by reading[2] (or having read to them) more variations of the genre — stories having a similar type of Placement, a different type of Placement, or no Placement at all, for example, as well as examples of nonstory genres (like information books). In such a framework, learning the story genre is therefore analogous to concept development in general. That is, recalling (or not recalling) particular facts from a particular book, as exemplified in the language samples provided in this paper, is similar to noting (or not noting) certain attributes or features of a particular dog, and it is these kinds of individual instances of the various versions of the story genre/dog — or of the information-book genre or cat, for example — that contribute to children's concept of the story genre/dog in general.[3]

To sum up, children's acquisition of the sense of the written story genre can be described as follows: (1) It is a very constructive cognitive/linguistic process characterized by overextensions, approximations, elaborations, and so forth. (2) While children's knowledge of their human and object world influence this process, learning a sense of story also involves children's interaction with a particular linguistic problem-space, a specific type of language world. (3) The process by which children develop their understanding of the written story genre is consistent with, and analogous to, concept development in general.

Notes

1.   The text of the book, as well as the children's reading texts, was parsed into complex clause units called T-units (Hunt 1965; O'Donnell 1967). A T-unit is defined as a single independent clause together with any subordinate clauses grammatically related to it. Sometimes a parsed clause unit coincided with the sentence used by the author; sometimes two clause units were made out of a particular sentence. *The Owl and the Woodpecker* consisted of 62 clause units.

2.   Although the focus in this paper is on reading, it is not being implied that the acquisition of the sense of the written story genre is accomplished only through reading (or being read to). Instead, being read to (or reading) is considered to be a necessary condition that must be complemented and extended by other language experiences, such as children's retelling stories and creating and writing their own stories, thereby providing the sufficient conditions for fostering children's sense of the written story genre.

3.   Viewing a written genre as a macro-concept has also been examined in Pappas (1987b). Here, a typicality approach or model of concept formation has been used to describe the "information book" genre specifically and to account for the probabilistic nature of genres in general.

Appendix

The Owl and the Woodpecker (Wildsmith, B., 1971)

GSE Unit
P   1   Once upon a time in a forest, far away, there lived a Woodpecker.
     2   The Woodpecker lived in a tree in which he slept all night and worked all day.

IE   3   In the tree next door, there came to live an Owl who liked to work all night and sleep all day.
     4   The Woodpecker worked so hard and made so much noise that his tapping woke the Owl.
     5   "I say, you, there!" screeched the Owl.
     6   "How can I possibly sleep with all that noise going on?"

7   "This is my tree," the Woodpecker said,

8   "and I shall tap it as I please."

9   The Owl lost his temper.

10   His screeches and hoots echoed through the forest,

11   and animals for miles around came running to see what was the matter.

12   "You carry on tapping, Master Woodpecker," squeaked the mouse.

13   "Owl is always bossing and chasing us about."

14   "Oh, do be quiet," growled the Bear.

15   "Woodpecker, stop tapping, and let Owl sleep.

16   We like a peaceful life around here."

17   Angrily, the Owl swooped down on the small animals, who ran for their lives and hid in all kinds of curious places.

18   "Bully," they shouted, when they were sure they were safe.

19   Then the Owl asked the bigger animals what he could do to stop the noise,

20   but they all shook their heads.

21   "How should we know?" they said.

22   "You are the wise and clever one.

23   Perhaps you could move to another tree."

24   "Why should I?" snapped the Owl.

25   "I like living in this tree.

26   That noisy Woodpecker must move."

27   But the Woodpecker would not move.

28   Day after day his noisy tapping kept the Owl awake.

29   And day after day the Owl became more tired and more and more bad-tempered.

30   He began to be so crotchety and rude that all the animals decided that something must be done.

SE   31   So they held a meeting.

32   "Something must be done," said the Badger.

33   "Woodpecker was here first,

34   so Owl must leave."

35   "But he says he will not leave his tree," replied the Deer.

36   "In that case we shall have to push down the tree,

37   and then he will have to leave," said the crafty Fox.

38   That night while the Owl was out hunting they all tried to push down his tree.

39   But no matter how hard they pushed and puffed and panted they could not move the tree the smallest bit.

40   So they gave up, and went back home.

41   Some time later two strangers came to the forest.

42   They were a pair of beavers,

43   and they took a fancy to the Owl's tree, and started to gnaw at the trunk.

44   Every day they gnawed a little more, until it seemed as if they would gnaw the trunk right through.

FE 45   Then one day a great storm shook the forest.
    46   The wind roared through the trees.
    47   It was so strong the Woodpecker gave up tapping,
    48   and so for once the Owl slept in peace.
    49   The Owl's tree began to creak and crack and groan as the wind grew more and more fierce,
    50   but the tired Owl slept soundly on.
    51   Suddenly the Woodpecker saw the Owl's tree begin to sway and fall.
    52   At once he struggled bravely through the storm and tapped loudly close to the Owl's ear to wake him.
    53   The Owl woke up in a fury, hearing the Woodpecker tapping on his tree,
    54   but when he realized his tree was being blown down his anger quickly disappeared.
    55   Together the Woodpecker and the Owl struggled to safety just as the tree crashed to the ground.
    56   Then the storm died away,
    57   and the Owl thanked the Woodpecker for saving his life.
    58   Now he was glad that the Woodpecker had been his neighbour.

F   59   So the Owl and Woodpecker became good friends,
    60   and the Woodpecker helped the Owl to find another tree in a quiet part of the forest, where he could sleep all day without being disturbed.
    61   Peace and quiet returned to the forest
    62   and the Owl and the Woodpecker remained good friends all the rest of their lives.

References

Anderson, R.C. & P.D. Pearson. 1984. "A Schematic-Theoretic View of Basic Process in Reading Comprehension". *Handbook of Reading Research* ed. by P.D. Pearson, 255-291. New York: Longman.

Applebee, A.N. 1978. *The Child's Concept of Story*. Chicago: University of Chicago Press.

Bloom, L. 1976. "An Integrated Perspective on Language Development". *Papers and Reports on Child Language Development* 12. 1-22. Department of Linguistics, Stanford University.

Bruce, B.C. 1984. "A New Point of View on Children's Stories". *Learning to Read in American Schools: Basal readers and content texts* ed. by R.C. Anderson, J. Osborn & R.J. Tierney, 153-174. Hillsdale, N.J.: Erlbaum.

Bruner, J. 1983. *Child's Talk: Learning to use language*. New York: W.W. Norton.

Butler, D. 1980. *Cushla and her Books*. Boston: The Horn Book.

Cambourne, B. 1981. "Oral and Written Relationships: A reading perspective". *Exploring Speaking-Writing Relationships: Connections and contrasts* ed. by B.M. Kroll & R.J. Vann, 82-98. Urbana, IL: National Council of Teachers of English.

Crago, M. & H. Crago. 1983. *Prelude to Literacy: A preschool child's encounter with picture and story*. Carbondale: Southern Illinois University Press.

Doake, D.B. 1985. "Reading-like Behavior: Its role in learning to read". *Observing the Language Learner* ed. by A. Jaggar & M.T. Smith-Burke, 82-98. Newark, DE: International Reading Association.

Donaldson, M. 1978. *Children's Minds*. Glasgow: William Collins Sons.

Halliday, M.A.K. 1977. "Text as Semantic Choice in Social Contexts". *Grammar and Descriptions* ed. by T. van Dijk & J.S. Petöfi, 176-225. Berlin: de Gruyter.

————. 1982. "Three Aspects of Children's Language Development: Learning language, learning through language, and learning about language". *Oral and Written Language Development Research: Impact on the schools* ed. by Y. Goodman, M. Haussler & D. Strickland, 7-19. Urbana, IL: National Council of Teachers of English.

————. 1985. *Spoken and Written Language*. Victoria: Deakin University Press.

Halliday, M.A.K. & R. Hasan. 1976. *Cohesion in English*. London: Longman.

Hasan, R. 1984a. "The Structure of the Nursery Tale: An essay in text typology". *Linguistica Testuale* ed. by L. Coveri, 95-114. Bulzoni: Roma.

————. 1984b. "The Nursery Tale as a Genre". *Nottingham Linguistic Circular* 13. 71-102.

Holdaway, D. 1979. *The Foundations of Literacy*. Sydney: Ashton Scholastic.

————. 1986. "The Structure of Natural Learning as the Basis of Literacy Instruction". *The Pursuit of Literacy: Early reading and writing* ed. by M. Sampson, 56-72. Dubuque, IA: Kendall/Hunt.

Huck, C.H. 1976. *Children's Literature in the Elementary School*. New York: Holt, Rinehart & Winston.

Hunt, K.W. 1965. *Grammatical Structures Written at Three Grade Levels* (Research Rep. No. 3). Champaign, IL: National Council of Teachers of English, Detroit, MI.

Karmiloff-Smith, A. 1979. *A Functional Approach to Child Language: A study of determiners and reference*. Cambridge: Cambridge University Press.

Labov, W. & J. Waletzky. 1967. "Narrative Analysis: Oral versions of personal experience". *Essays on the Verbal and Visual Arts* ed. by J. Helm, 12-44. Georgetown: University of Washington Press.

Lindfors, J.W. 1987. *Children's Language and Learning*, second edition. Englewood Cliffs, N.J.: Prentice-Hall.

Nelson, K. 1986. *Event Knowledge: Structure and function in development*. Hillsdale, N.J.: Erlbaum.

O'Donnell, R.C. 1967. *Syntax of Kindergarten and Elementary School Children: A transformational analysis* (Research Rep. No. 8). Champaign, IL: National Council of Teachers of English.

Pappas, C.C. 1983. "The Relationship between Language Development and Brain Development". *Journal of Children in Contemporary Society* 16. 133-169.

————. 1985. "The Cohesive Harmony and Cohesive Density of Children's Oral and Written Stories". *Systemic Perspectives on Discourse: Selected applied papers from the 9th International Systemic Workshop* ed. by J. Benson & W.S. Greaves, 169-186. Norwood, N.J.: Ablex.

————. 1986. *Learning to Read by Reading: Exploring text indices for understanding the process*. Final Report to Research Foundation of National Council of the Teachers of English. ERIC Document No. ED 277 971.

————. 1987a. "Exploring the Textual Properties of 'protoreading'". *Language Topics: Essays in honour of Michael Halliday*, Vol. 1 ed. by R. Steele & T. Threadgold, 137-162. Amsterdam: John Benjamins.

————. 1987b. *Exploring the Generic Shape of "Information Books": Applying 'typicality' notions to the process*. Paper presented at the 14th International Systemic Workshop, Sydney, Australia.

Pappas, C.C. & E. Brown. 1987. "Young Children Learning Story Discourse: Three case studies". *Elementary School Journal* 87. 455-466.

————. 1988. "The Development of Children's Sense of the Written Story Language Register: An analysis of the texture of 'pretend reading' texts". *Linguistics and Education: An international research journal*.

Schickedanz, J.A. & M. Sullivan. 1984. "Mom, What Does U-F-F Spell?" *Language Arts* 61. 7-17.

Smith, F. 1982. *Understanding Reading*. New York: Holt, Rinehart & Winston.

Stein, N.L. & C.G. Glenn. 1979. "An Analysis of Story Comprehension in Elementary School Children". *New Directions in Discourse Processing* ed. by R.O. Freedle, 53-120. Norwood, N.J.: Ablex.

Sulzby, E. 1985. "Children's Emergent Reading of Favorite Storybooks: A developmental study". *Reading Research Quarterly* 20. 458-481.

Tannen, D. 1985. "Relative Focus on Involvement in Oral and Written Discourse". *Literacy, Language and Learning: The nature and consequences of reading and writing* ed. by D.R. Olson, N. Torrence & A. Hildyard, 124-147. Cambridge: Cambridge University Press.

Taylor, D. 1983. *Family Literacy*. Exeter, N.H.: Heinemann.

Teale, W.H. 1984. "Reading to Young Children: Its significance for literacy development". *Awakening to Literacy* ed. by H. Goelman, A.A. Oberg & F. Smith, 110-121. Exeter, N.H.: Heinemann.

————. 1986. "The Beginnings of Reading and Writing: Written language development during the preschool and kindergarten years". *The Pursuit of Literacy: Early reading and writing* ed. by M.R. Sampson, 1-29. Dubuque, IA: Kendall/Hunt.

Todorov, T. 1971. "The Two Principles of Narrative". *Diacritics* 1. 37-44.

Wells, G. 1981. *Learning Through Interaction: The study of language development*. Cambridge: Cambridge University Press.

————. 1985. "Preschool Literacy-Related Activities and Success in School". *Literacy, Language and Learning: The nature and consequences of reading and writing* ed. by D.R. Olson, N. Torrence & A. Hildyard, 229-255. Cambridge: Cambridge University Press.

————. 1986. *The Meaning Makers: Children learning language and using language to learn*. Portsmouth, N.H.: Heinemann.

Wildsmith, B. 1971. *The Owl and the Woodpecker*. Oxford: Oxford University Press.

————. 1973. *The Lazy Bear*. Oxford: Oxford University Press.

Cohesive Ties in Written Narratives:
A Developmental Study with Beginning Writers

Philip Yde and Marc Spoelders

In written communication, writers construct a cognitive representation of meaning and produce texts to express that meaning for their readers. As Nystrand (1986:13) states: "Both readers and writers make sense — the one of print, the other in print." Written texts can therefore be considered as traces constructed by writers for their readers. To ensure that the meaning the reader constructs is what the writer originally intended, some specific text-forming strategies must be applied. The writer's mastery of these strategies will finally be revealed in the text itself. In this respect comparative text studies contribute to a better understanding of written language acquisition.

Meaning is seldom resolved in a single word or phrase, but mostly through longer structures that cross or intertwine the written text. These structures can only be understood when their elements are connected to one another. Connectedness is at the core of meaning. Consequently writers should have at their disposal a repertoire of linguistic clues to signal to their readers this connectedness. In general, the linguistic elements making explicit the semantic links between one sentence and another are called cohesive devices. In this paper we focus on cohesion, an important aspect of textual interrelatedness. Psycholinguistic models of text comprehension view cohesive devices as a set of text-level linguistic clues which writers provide for readers to guide or control their construction of the intended meaning of the text (di Sibio 1982).

Learning to write effectively implies learning to order a series of sentences, linked by common properties to form an integrated whole. Consequently, learning to write implies learning to handle cohesive devices appropriately. A cohesive tie is a semantic relation between an element in a text and some antecedent that is crucial to its interpretation. There is indeed a set of expectations between reader and writer so that in processing information of an utterance in context, the reader can discover the intended antecedent in that context. A kind of contract between both requires the writer to use language structures appropriate to effective written communication. Therefore research on textual cohesion provides some insight into the extent to which writers exploit writing as a communicative process. It points to the writer's assumption of the reader as a co-creator of text.

If effective communication depends on the clarity of the text and if appropriate cohesive ties provide clarity, then using cohesive devices appropriately is a critical skill in creating effective texts. In this respect, the type and distribution of the cohesive devices in a text are important. But the distance between the cohesive devices and their antecedents is also essential. According to Chafe (1974, 1976) this distance must be limited, since writers can only refer to the entities present in the consciousness of their readers. To account for difficulties in finding antecedents, Chafe attributes a limited capacity to consciousness. During the reading of a text, old items are being pushed out of consciousness as new ones come in. The factors influencing an item's stay include the number of intervening sentences in which it was not mentioned. Effective writers must observe these limits on future readers' capacities in using cohesive devices.

How do children cope with these fundamental requirements in producing written texts? It seems plausible that they encounter many difficulties in this respect. In the initial stages of learning to write they draw upon linguistic resources gathered principally through oral speech (cf. Britton 1983). They imitate in writing the oral telling of a story, where their audience is immediate and where, if the audience does not comprehend a given point it can say so, thus allowing the teller to insert information on demand. Young children have difficulty sustaining an endophoric text for a nonpresent audience. They also have difficulty conceptualizing what information is and is not available to a reader who does not share the immediate context (cf. Kress 1982). Beginning writers may also find it difficult to recall information they provided previously in their texts (cf. Freedle and Fine 1983). In these cases cohesive problems are attributed to limitations in children's cognitive capacities. But linguistic factors may also be at work: a child may realize that a cohesive device has to be used but fail to select the correct linguistic item.

In order to provide a basic description of beginning writers' control of cohesive devices we conducted a text analysis to survey the type and distribution of cohesive devices used by beginning and somewhat more advanced writers. We also assessed textual compactness. This concept refers to the distance between a cohesive element and its antecedent as this is an important variable in the acceptability of a cohesive tie.

Before focussing on children's ability to handle cohesive devices, we want to stress that cohesion is only one aspect of good writing. It is quite possible for a piece of writing to contain cohesive devices in explicit detail and still be unsatisfactory because the writer does not develop a theme which provides a purpose to the text. Cohesion and coherence are related, but cohesive texts are not necessarily coherent or vice versa (cf. Hasan 1979; Scardamalia, Bereiter and Goelman 1982). Cohesion is a surface level feature of the text, whose main function is to signal some aspects of coherence, which in its part is more in the minds of writers and readers than in the text itself. Coherence refers to the conceptual connectedness of a text and its fitness for the extra-textual or rhetorical situation. Since it is a relation between the text-world and the world outside the text, it is impossible to discover and quantify precisely what in a text alone creates coherence. Readers and writers bring to their work a lot of world-knowledge that is not actually marked in the text itself.

Purpose

Although the purpose of our research is much more ambitious, in this report we highlight just three questions: 1. What is the degree of cohesiveness demonstrated in the texts from beginning and advanced writers? Is there a significant difference? 2. What kind of cohesive devices do beginning and advanced writers select to guide the reader in relating new information to old? Are there significant differences? 3. What is the degree of compactness demonstrated in the texts from beginning and advanced writers? Is there a significant difference?

Method

Subjects

Our subjects were 161 Dutch-speaking pupils, who attended elementary schools in the area of Ghent, Belgium. The first sample consisted of 76 children aged 8-9 years (mean age: 8;7), 34 boys and 42 girls. These subjects had mastered the basic mechanical and transcriptional aspects of writing and had started to produce the kinds of narrative valued in our culture. We compared the texts from these subjects with those produced by somewhat older children who had already received more writing instruction. The second sample consisted of 85 children aged 10-11 years (mean age: 11;8), 31 boys and 54 girls. According to Perera (1984:213), children in this age category are becoming increasingly aware of the differences between speech and writing.

Stimulus Materials

In order to control the texts for discourse type and topic, we provided a stimulus for the writing task: children in both groups were asked to write a story based on a series of 8 pictures.

We controlled for discourse type because the mode and the field of a text determine the kind of cohesive relations which dominate (Eiler 1983). We focussed on narrative text production, which is emphasized in the early school curriculum. Bereiter (1980) reports that narrative writing is established by the age of eight or nine, but that expository writing develops "much later". This may be explained by the fact that narrative text production exhibits greater affinities to oral story telling than does expository text production, which is first presented to children in the later primary school years. Narratives are an important part of everyday life and a critical source of information about language and the world. We also provided a stimulus in order to reduce variation in the actual content of text produced.

The picture prompts feature a group of boys and girls returning from school. On their way home they ring the doorbell of a house and run for it. The inmate is furious. The next time they pass by, one of the boys decides to tease the man again. But he has taken his precautions and stands on the first floor with a bucket full of water. The moment the teaser rings, the inmate pours the water on the boy's head. The boy looks crushed, while the other children have the laugh on him.

Procedures for Data Collection

The children were tested as a group in their own proctored classrooms. The researcher told them that they would be given a cartoon to look at and that they would be asked to write down the story after returning the cartoon. The children were assured that their stories would not be graded, but were to be shared with peers from another school who did not share the sequence of pictures. It was emphasized that the pictures were only a kind of springboard. Pupils were free to write about things that might have happened. There were no constraints as to length of text, nor was there a time limit. After the subjects had finished their writing, they were given the opportunity to proofread their texts.

The younger children took on average 25 minutes to write their texts, whereas the mean writing time for older children was 32 minutes.

Instruments

The screening and coding of the cohesive relations in the text followed the classification suggested by Halliday and Hasan (1976), who introduced one of the most exacting and complex of all text analysis systems. Dutch has almost the same cohesive devices as English. Kittredge (1978) points out that parallel sub-languages, such as narratives, are much more similar structurally than are different sub-languages of the same language. Our data did not warrant substantial additional distinctions regarding cohesive relations beyond those suggested in the nearly exhaustive classification system developed by Halliday and Hasan. They discuss the different kinds of cohesion under the five headings: reference, substitution, ellipsis, conjunction and lexical cohesion.

Reference includes pronominals (hij = he, hem = him, ze = she, haar = her, etc.), demonstratives and definite articles (dit = this, dat = that, de = the, etc.) and comparatives (meer = more, ander = other, etc.).

Substitution replaces one item (noun phrase, verb phrase or clause) with another to avoid repetition.

Ellipsis omits an item (noun phrase, verb phrase or clause) which is assumed and can be supplied by the reader using information from the linguistic context.

Conjunction is a semantic connection. It can be additive (en = and, verder = furthermore, etc.), adversative (maar = but, toch = yet, etc.), causal (omdat = because, dus = so, etc.) or temporal (dan = then, onder-tussen = meanwhile, etc.).

Lexical cohesion includes reiteration and collocation. An item is reiterative when it is repeated or a synonym is used (e.g. kat-poes = cat-kitty). Collocation refers to the fact that lexical items are linked in terms of association (e.g. water-nat = water-wet).

Cohesiveness is not a matter of all or nothing, but of more or less. As a means for assessing the degree of cohesiveness of each text, an index was computed using a formula adapted from Scinto (1983):

$\lambda = (\Sigma W(A)) / V$, in which
λ = degree of cohesiveness,
$\Sigma W(A)$ = the number of cohesive ties,
V = the number of sentences.

Compactness is given by another formula adapted from Scinto (1983):

$C = (\Sigma W(adj)) / V$, in which
C = degree of compactness,
$\Sigma \quad W(adj)$ = the sum of the weighted values of the cohesive ties between the sentences for adjacency. When there are no intervening sentences between the cohesive elements and their antecedents, the value 3 is assigned. When there is one intervening sentence the value 2 is assigned. When there are two or more intervening sentences, the value 1 is assigned,
V = the number of sentences.

In most cases the segmentation of text into sentences was established by the pupils themselves, using conventional markers: initial capitals and periods. Some of the texts, especially from younger children, were not consistently segmented into sentences. In these cases we divided the texts into segments consisting of a main clause with a finite verb and any minor clauses attached to it (cf. Dillinger 1985). In difficult cases we followed the segmenting and coding procedures suggested by Scinto (1983):
- a single theme-rheme nexus consistent with a grammatical pattern of noun phrase-verb phrase constitutes a single sentence;
- a theme-rheme nexus with subordinate clause constitutes a single sentence;
- where 'and' conjoins two theme-rheme nexuses that can be shown to be otherwise syntactically and semantically independent (i.e. each con-

stituting an independent theme-rheme pattern) each is counted as a single sentence.

Since our data-base was to be used only for studies of cohesiveness and compactness, we omitted any attention to spelling, punctuation or capitalization.

Results and discussion

Cohesiveness and Compactness

As Table 1 indicates, the total of the cohesive ties in our corpus numbers 7,672. Older children use on average almost twice as many cohesive ties, primarily because they write longer narratives. We notice a very strong positive correlation between text length, as measured by the number of

Table 1: *Number of cohesive ties for the two age groups and for the whole sample. Percentage of intrasentential ties for the two age groups and for the whole sample.*

Group	N	Ties	Ties per text			Intrasentential ties per text		
			Mean %	SD	t	Mean %	SD	t
Younger	76	2554	33.60	14.82		12.79	6.93	
Older	85	5118	60.21	18.73	**	17.55	7.35	**
Total	161	7672	47.65	21.55		15.30	7.52	

* p < .05 ** p < .01

Table 2: *Mean text length, measured by number of words (W) and number of sentences (S) for the two age groups and for the whole sample. Mean sentence length, measured by the number of words for the two age groups and for the whole sample.*

Group	Text length (W)			Text length (S)			Sentence length		
	Mean	SD	t	Mean	SD	t	Mean	SD	t
Younger	88.15	30.21		14.14	5.10		6.19	1.15	
Older	152.17	45.42	**	19.92	6.56	**	7.77	1.35	**
Total	121.95	50.38		17.19	6.57		7.02	1.48	

* p < .05; ** p < .01

*Table 3: Mean scores for cohesiveness and compactness for the two age groups and for
the whole sample*

Group	Degree of cohesiveness			Degree of compactness		
	Mean	SD	t	Mean	SD	t
Younger	2.0724	0.5152		2.8557	0.6100	
Older	2.4826	0.4355	**	3.1266	0.4733	**
Total	2.2889	0.5160		2.9987	0.5571	

* p < .05; ** p < .01

words, and the number of cohesive ties (Pearson, r = .89). The difference between the two means for number of words is significant (t = 10.63, p < .01).

Our results in Table 2 indicate however that the older children write sentences that are only slightly longer than those from their younger counterparts. So their longer texts result primarily from an increase in number of sentences, rather than from an increase in number of words per sentence.

One of our main concerns is to determine if there is a significant difference in the degree of cohesiveness demonstrated in the narratives from beginning and somewhat more advanced writers. Our findings indeed indicate that older children's texts show a significantly higher degree of cohesiveness (t= 5.47, p < .01). The same applies to the compactness scores, which indicate the degree to which each successive sentence feeds off an immediately preceding sentence in text building. These scores were significantly higher for the older children (t = 3.17, p < .01). In their narratives, the mean distance between a cohesive element and its antecedent is significantly smaller than in the narratives of the younger children. We also noticed a strong positive correlation between the degree of cohesiveness and compactness (Pearson, r = .77). These results suggest that children get better with age and instruction in the construction of tightly woven, compact narrative texts. As can be noticed in Table 3 there is a rather strong decrease in the standard deviations associated with the grade means for cohesiveness and compactness. The older the children, the more their scores cluster together around the mean. This indicates that as a group children handle textual interrelatedness more consistently as they get older.

We also want to survey the kind of cohesive devices beginning and somewhat more advanced writers select to guide their readers in relating new information to old. Because texts varied rather dramatically in length, simple counting of cohesive devices would not be a valid technique for comparisons. Data transformations were necessary to prevent spurious findings. Our analysis and discussion of the different cohesive devices are therefore based on percentages. Table 4 gives summary distributions of each type of cohesion (reference, substitution, ellipsis, conjunction, lexical cohesion) as percentages of the total ties for the whole sample and for each group separately.

Halliday and Hasan (1976) stress that cohesion is a general text-forming relation and that cohesive relations have in principle nothing to do with sentence boundaries. The same cohesive devices may be found just as well within a sentence as between sentences. Halliday and Hasan state, however, that cohesive relations attract less notice within a sentence, because of the cohesive strength of grammatical structure. So they accept that in a sense the sentence is a significant unit for cohesion. It is the highest unit of grammatical structure that tends to determine the way in which cohesion is expressed. Cohesive ties between sentences stand out more clearly because they are the only source of texture; whereas within sentences there are the structural relations as well. We therefore distinguish intrasentential and intersentential cohesive ties.

Total Cohesion

First we examine the distribution of the different cohesive devices, without distinguishing intra- and intersentential cohesion.

As can be noticed in Table 4, every cohesive device appears at least minimally in each age group.

Table 4: *Percentage of each type of cohesion for the whole sample and for the two age groups*

	Total group	Younger	Older	t
Ref	35.58	33.36	37.58	**
Sub	1.31	1.74	0.93	*
Ell	4.55	3.96	5.07	--
Con	22.24	24.66	20.08	**
Lex	36.32	36.16	36.46	--

* p < .05; ** p < .01

Lexical cohesion is the children's preferred strategy for making cohesive links in their texts. The predominant subtype of lexical cohesion is word repetition. To a lesser degree do our subjects replace lexical items by semantically related words. Texts by beginning and somewhat more advanced writers do not differ significantly in terms of total lexical cohesion.

The second most frequently used cohesive device is reference, achieved predominantly through the use of pronominals and demonstratives. Although the age groups do not differ extremely in their distribution, reference cohesion is somewhat more frequent in the older group. We notice that younger writers often use nominal repetition where older writers would prefer a referential device. Young children often write repetitive texts, comparable to the kind of writing found in early reading books. Children may unconsciously model their writing style to this type of text. An adequate use of reference presents major hurdles for the younger children. We often notice pronominal confusion. A typical example is where the writer switches from describing a set of events as an outsider to playing a major part in it. Young children confuse the discrete roles of narrator and protagonist. They suddenly resort to familiar speech roles. Young children not only experience difficulties with a consistent use of pronouns; their readers are often confronted with referential ambiguity, causing serious comprehension problems.

In comparison to lexical and referential cohesion, we notice less conjunctive devices in the texts, although the percentage is still substantial. Since we asked our subjects to write narratives, temporal connectives are used most often. Conjunctive cohesion declines sharply and significantly in the older group. These children demonstrate much less linguistic explicitness in this respect. An explanation may be that older children possess better assumptions about the reader as a collaborator in the process of communication and as a sharer of knowledge. They are much more aware that a discourse with a chronological pattern of organization does not strictly require temporal connectives, since the reader simply assumes that the order of the sentences reflects the order of events. In general, older children strike a more careful balance between what needs to be said and what may be assumed. Another explanation may be that they write more complex sentences, treating intrasententially information that younger subjects treat intersententially.

Ellipsis is very rare and substitution is almost nonexistent. Substitutes are rather typical of spoken language and this may explain the decline in percentages we notice in texts written by the older children. In writing they draw to a lesser extent upon linguistic resources gathered through oral speech. Older children have more reading experience, which may provide them with the linguistic resources of written language. Younger subjects show some instances of nominal substitution, almost none of verbal or clausal substitution. Ellipsis occurs occasionally at both verbal and clausal level.

Intrasentential Cohesion

Halliday and Hasan (1976) notice that, although the cohesive devices used within a sentence or between sentences are the same, intrasentential cohesion needs to be regarded as a distinct phenomenon. Intrasentential devices are subject to certain restrictions, because the grammatical condition of being a sentence already ensures that the parts are related to one another.

Young elementary school children often write their narratives in discrete event units: each sentence is perceived as an autonomous whole, containing a complete action. In the definition of sentence topical connectedness is the primary motivating factor. The sentence often has a similar function to that of the paragraph in adult writing, with cohesion handled largely within it.

Halliday and Hasan (1976) stress that a sentence gets cohesive strength through its grammatical structure. We therefore expect that in our relative distributions the percentages of grammatical cohesive devices (reference, ellipsis and substitution) will be much higher with intrasentential cohesion. The same may apply to conjunction, which is on the borderline between grammatical and lexical cohesion.

Our findings strongly confirm our expectations. Intrasentential reference, a grammatical relationship, far outnumbers any other intrasentential cohesive device (see Table 5). As can be noticed in Table 6 the relative proportion of intrasentential reference for the whole group is significantly higher than that of intersentential reference ($t = 2.70$, $p < .01$).

Conjunction is the second most preferred strategy for creating intrasentential cohesiveness (see Table 5). In the older age group the relative proportion of intrasentential conjunction is more than twice that of intersentential conjunction (see Table 6). The difference between the means is statistically significant ($t = 10.31$, $p < .01$). The same applies for

Table 5: Percentage of each type of intrasentential cohesion for the whole sample and for the two age groups

	Total group	Younger	Older	t
Ref	41.06	41.16	40.96	--
Sub	0.43	0.91	0.00	--
Ell	14.29	13.83	14.71	--
Con	33.61	32.14	34.92	--
Lex	8.74	8.00	9.40	--

* p < .05; ** p < .01

Table 6: Percentage of each type of intra- versus inter-sentential cohesion for the whole sample and for the two age groups

	Intra	Inter	t
Total sample			
Ref	41.06	34.72	**
Sub	0.43	1.48	**
Ell	14.29	2.37	**
Con	33.61	19.52	**
Lex	8.74	41.31	**
Younger			
Ref	41.16	32.49	*
Sub	0.91	1.86	*
Ell	13.83	1.99	**
Con	32.14	22.61	**
Lex	8.00	40.20	**
Older			
Ref	40.96	36.71	*
Sub	0.00	1.15	**
Ell	14.71	2.71	**
Con	34.92	16.76	**
Lex	9.40	42.30	**

* p < .05; ** p < .01

the younger children, although the difference is less substantial (t = 3.13, p < .01). An explanation may be that since older children write more complex sentences, they rely to a higher degree on intrasentential conjunction.

In the relative proportions of intra- versus intersentential ellipsis, younger children use on average almost seven times as many intrasentential devices; older children more than five times as many (see Table 6). The differences between the means are statistically significant for both age groups (younger: t = 6.08, p < .01; older: t = 8.24, p < .01). These results are not surprising since ellipsis works within event units rather than between them.

Intrasentential substitution is negligible and even disappears completely in the older group (see Table 5).

We notice an extremely high difference between the relative proportions of intra- versus intersentential lexical cohesion (see Table 6). The relative proportion of intersentential lexical cohesion is more than five times as high as that for intrasentential lexical cohesion. The difference between the means is statistically significant for both age groups (younger: t = 16.1, p < .01; older: t = 23.2, p < .01).

We conclude that intrasentential cohesiveness is signalled by grammatical cohesive devices rather than by lexical ones; with intersentential cohesiveness we notice the reverse.

Texts by younger and older children do not differ significantly in terms of the relative proportions of each intrasentential device. So quantitatively speaking, younger and older children parallel one another in their intrasentential cohesive patterning.

Intersentential Cohesion

Writers must break their texts into manageable information units and carefully mark relevant text boundaries. Cohesive ties do occur within sentences, but it is those across sentence boundaries that really allow sequences of sentences to be understood as a text. As a consequence intersentential cohesive devices attract more attention and are of particular

Table 7: *Percentage of each type of intersentential cohesion for the whole sample and for the two age groups*

	Total group	Younger	Older	t
Ref	34.72	32.49	36.71	**
Sub	1.48	1.86	1.15	*
Ell	2.37	1.99	2.71	--
Con	19.52	22.61	16.76	**
Lex	41.31	40.20	42.30	--

* p < .05; ** p < .01

interest in our study. We are interested in a summary distribution of each type of intersentential device as a percentage of the total ties for the whole sample and for each age group separately.

As can be noticed lexical cohesion is by far the most popular strategy for creating intersentential cohesive links in narratives. The predominant types of lexical cohesion are repetition and collocation. Younger children use to a lesser degree synonyms, superordinates or general items. Intersentential lexical cohesion tends to increase slightly over time.

The second most popular intersentential cohesive device is reference, achieved predominantly through the use of pronominals, demonstratives and definite articles. A particular problem young children experience with intersentential reference is the alternation of the subject of several consecutive sentences. Young children very often repeat the same pronoun, a phenomenon that characterizes immature narratives.

Conjunction comes in third place as intersentential cohesive device. Crystal (1979) reports that teachers of primary school children are particularly concerned about their pupils' inability to handle connectives skilfully. Some are overused, others underused. Since narratives are organized chronologically, we are not surprised to find the highest incidence of temporal connectives.

As Table 7 indicates, intersentential substitution and ellipsis are marginal. The predominant type of intersentential ellipsis used is propositional ellipsis: the omission of a propositional element in answer to a Wh- or a Yes/No question.

Comparisons between the age groups indicate both similarities and differences. Although the age groups do not differ extremely in the relative proportion of any cohesive device, intersentential reference is statistically more frequent in the older group ($t = 2.75$, $p < .01$).

We further notice a sizeable and significant drop in intersentential conjunction as the pupils grow older ($t = 4.71$, $p < .01$). Young children are fascinated with conjunctions. Most frequently used is *and* (Dutch *en*). In some narratives by younger children this device accounts for more than 50% of all conjoining. This finding is not surprising in view of the fact that *and* is very frequently used when children are telling a narrative orally.

The serious decrease of intersentential conjunction in the older group may be explained by the fact that older children write more complex sentences. It may signal a rise in structural versus non-structural ordering of information in a text. Older children have acquired a more elaborated style and demonstrate a more parsimonious use of intersentential conjunctive devices. They realise to a higher extent that a structurally harmonious discourse cannot be achieved by a purely additive type of composing where each sentence grows out of its predecessor. This may be due to writing instruction since run-on sentences are one of the teachers' pet peeves.

Though the incidence of intersentential ellipsis is low, the older group uses this device to a somewhat higher degree. This increase can be explained by the fact that with age children become more aware of the inferential processes involved in understanding and the role of ellipsis in regulating them.

Intersentential substitution appears even more rarely and tends to decline as the children grow older.

We conclude that quantitatively speaking the older writers deploy intersentential cohesive resources in their narratives in a different way from their younger counterparts.

Conclusion

Written literacy implies knowing how to write a particular text for specific purposes in specific contexts of use. The effectiveness of written communication depends on the successful interaction between writer and reader by way of the text. Although a text can only be evaluated appropriately in its context, some key variables of good writing depend on specific text features.

We focussed on the narrative writing skills of elementary school children. They are in the process of learning how to translate a complex network of ideational relationships into a series of sentences, linked by common properties to form an integrated whole. We therefore studied some aspects of cohesion, an important text feature that facilitates the sense-making capacity of a text by signalling the interrelatedness of its elements.

Our comparison of the cohesive patterning by third and sixth grade children indicates some developmental trends:
1. The older the children, the higher the degree of cohesiveness and compactness.
2. Narratives by beginning and somewhat more advanced writers do not differ significantly in their distribution of intrasentential cohesive devices.

3. However, they show significant differences in their intersentential patterning.
4. There are significant differences between the relative distribution of intrasentential versus intersentential cohesive devices for both age groups.
5. The decline of the standard deviations for most variables in the older age group indicates that their cohesive patterning becomes more consistent.

We want to warn against generalizing about written language acquisition in a very global way since so many factors contribute to how children pattern their written texts. There are many gaps in our knowledge, so many questions still need to be studied in the years ahead.

It would be interesting to determine if children vary their cohesive patterning according to varied writing situations. Different type, purpose or audience may require other thinking and planning strategies, with the consequence that the cohesive patterning of their texts will differ significantly.

We also found strong indications that certain kinds of errors accompany certain stages in learning to write. However the sources of error in written discourse are often complex and difficult to trace. Many of these problems have not been studied yet, because it is hard to find an appropriate methodology.

Some think that pupils will absorb the appropriate cohesive patterning just by reading and writing. We believe that teachers should take deliberate steps in this respect. To do so, they require knowledge of both what the pupils cannot yet do and what they are already capable of doing. Teachers should have a framework of knowledge to assess their pupils' cohesive abilities. It is only with an explicit, systematic knowledge that they can be aware of what is beneath the surface of a text and identify its strengths and weaknesses.

We therefore believe that text studies do have something in them for teachers. They can suggest new ways and appropriate terms for directing the pupils' attention to some aspects of their writing. Text studies can lead to new ways for teachers to respond and provide cues for pupils' text revisions. Of course we do not suggest at all that such a framework should be formally taught.

The ability to identify key trouble sources and to intervene appropriately implies familiarity with the cohesive patterning typical for a certain age group. In their feedback teachers often refer to some kind of ideal text.

As a consequence pupils get constantly corrected, and often the teacher's advice and comments are restricted to some vague generalities. These do not contribute to the acquisition of a relevant and flexible range of cohesive devices from which the writer can select the appropriate ones as the occasion demands. We believe that the best use of cohesion terminology is in the teacher's responding to student writing after a tentative version of a text has been written. From the foregoing arguments and our findings so far there is good reason to pursue the study of cohesive patterning. Our intention is to provide much more refined profiles of children's cohesive skills for narratives at different ages.

We finally want to stress that there is no virtue in appropriate cohesiveness for its own sake. Ability to handle textual interrelatedness is worth emphasizing, but it is only one aspect of written language acquisition. Cohesive skills are a means, not an end in themselves. Cohesiveness is a necessary though not a sufficient condition for the creation of effective text. Good writing depends first and foremost on having something to write about.

Text studies cannot provide a complete pedagogy for writing, but they certainly contribute to a better understanding of written language acquisition. We believe that cohesive skills are major text-creation skills; that they are susceptible to educational influence, and therefore ought to have an important place in the writing curriculum.

References

Bereiter, C. 1980. "Development in Writing". *Cognitive Processes in Writing* ed. by L.W. Gregg & E.R. Steinberg, 73-93. Hillsdale, N.J.: Laurence Erlbaum Associates.

Britton, J. 1983. "Shaping at the Point of Utterance". *Learning to Write: First language, second language* ed. by A. Freedman, I. Pringle & J. Yalden, 13-19. London: Longman.

Chafe, W. 1974. "Language and Consciousness". *Language* 50. 111-113.

———. 1976. "Giveness, Contrastiveness, Definiteness, Subjects, Topics and Point of View". *Subject and Topic* ed. by C. Li, 27-55. New York: Academic Press.

Crystal, D. 1979. "Language in Education — A linguistic perspective". *Language, Reading and Learning* ed. by A. Cashdan, 13-28. Oxford: Basil Blackwell.

Dillinger, M. 1985. *Segmentation and Clause Analysis*. Montreal, McGill Discourse Processing Laboratory Report 3.

di Sibio, M. 1982. "Memory for Connected Discourse: A constructivist view. *Review of*

Educational Psychology 52. 149-174.

Eiler, M.A. 1983. "Meaning and Choice in Writing about Literature". *Developmental Issues in Discourse* ed. by J. Fine & R.O. Freedle, 169-223. Norwood, N.J.: Ablex.

Freedle, R.O. & J. Fine. 1983. "An Interactional Approach to the Development of Discourse". *Developmental Issues in Discourse* ed. by J. Fine & R.O. Freedle, 143-168. Norwood, N.J.: Ablex.

Halliday, M.A.K. & R. Hasan. 1976. *Cohesion in English*. London: Longman.

Hasan, R. 1979. "On the Notion of Text". *Text vs. Sentence* ed. by J.S. Petöfi, 369-390. Hamburg: Helmut Buske.

Kittredge, R. 1978. *Textual Cohesion within Sublanguages: Implications for automatic analysis and synthesis*. Bergen: Coling.

Kress, G. 1982. *Learning to Write*. London: Routledge & Kegan Paul.

Nystrand, M. 1986. *The Structure of Written Communication. Studies in reciprocity between writers and readers*. Orlando, Florida: Academic Press.

Perera, K. 1984. *Children's Writing and Reading*. Oxford: Blackwell.

Scardamalia, M., C. Bereiter & H. Goelman. 1982. "The Role of Production Factors in Writing Ability". *What Writers Know* ed. by M. Nystrand, 173-210. New York: Academic Press.

Scinto, L.F.M. 1983. "The Development of Text Production". *Developmental Issues in Discourse* ed. by J. Fine & R.O. Freedle, 225-268. Norwood, N.J.: Ablex.

Spoelders, M. & Ph. Yde. 1981. "Van stellen naar schrijfvaardigheidsonderwijs: een opstel over het opstel". *Persoon en Gemeenschap* 34(3). 139-149.

Yde, Ph. 1982. "Beschouwingen bij het onderwijs in de schriftelijke formuleervaardigheid". *Scientia Paedagogica Experimentalis* 19(1). 159-174.

―――. 1986. "Steldidactiek en schrijfonderzoek: een overzicht". *Interface. Journal of Applied Linguistics* 1(1). 43-60.

Yde, Ph. & M. Spoelders. 1985a. "Some Pragmatic Aspects of Teaching and Learning to Write". *Language Acquisition and Learning. Essays in educational pragmatics 2* ed. by M. Spoelders *et al.*, 79-90. Leuven/Amersfoort: Acco & Gent: C&C.

―――. 1985b. "Teaching Writing: A brief discussion of some approaches". *Proficiency Training in Language Education* ed. by W. Decoo, 213-226. Antwerpen: ABLA.

―――. 1985c. "Text Cohesion: An exploratory study with beginning writers". *Applied Psycholinguistics* 6. 4-7-415.

Metalinguistic Activities and the Development of the Use of Formal Register Among Elementary School Children

Luc Ostiguy, Gilles Gagné and Jean-Guy Blais

1. Problem

The work we report on is pedagogical research focussing on linguistic variation in oral discourse; that is, the same meaning being conveyed by different linguistic forms. The use of one form instead of another depends on different well-known factors: geographical, social (age, sex and socioeconomic status of the subjects) and situational factors. This research deals with situational factors. It is recognized that a speaker has a tendency to use different variants depending on the characteristics of the speech event (Hymes 1972; Gumperz 1971; Halliday *et al.* 1972; Labov 1972). Furthermore, speakers show a general tendency to use formal variants in formal situations and informal or casual variants in casual speech situations.

Elementary school children seem to be able to understand formal variants when used in sentences or discourse at their level. Research by Gleason (1973) and Andersen (1978) indicates that even preschoolers make use of situational variation. The use of such stylistic variation by elementary school children has also been reported by Houston (1970), Jensen (1973), Reid (1978), Gambell (1981) and Lucas and Borders (1987). No such research has been carried out on French-speaking children in Québec. But what emerges from descriptive research and general impressions is that children do not use formal variants fluently in formal speech events.

One of the aims of mother tongue education in school should be to develop among the children the ability to use formal variants in formal speech situations. Obviously, this can be done and has to be done without any rejection or condemnation of the colloquial register of the Québec way of speaking. Thus, the pedagogical problem is to develop among elementary school children the use of formal variants when the situation requires them to do so.

In order to collect some data related to the problem, preliminary research was conducted with 9- and 10-year-old French-speaking children. The results presented at the 1985 UNESCO meeting in Venice (Gagné and Ostiguy 1989) showed that these children (1) vary their language spontaneously according to the formality of the situation, (2) are aware of situational factors which make speakers vary their language, (3) are not aware, however, of precise variants, (4) may become aware of many variants following specific activities.

2.   Aims

These preliminary findings enabled us to formulate more relevant aims for the present research: (1) proposing and testing a linguistic content, the use of which could be developed; (2) elaborating and experimenting with two ways of developing the use of formal variants; (3) providing data on the question of the relationship between metalinguistic knowledge and linguistic use.

2.1 *Elaboration of Linguistic Content*

At the moment, there is no precise oral linguistic content in the Québec curriculum. Therefore we propose a linguistic content and try to evaluate its relevance as a matter of learning. Gagné (1983) has suggested three sociolinguistic criteria for learning relevance. Those criteria have guided the elaboration of this content: (a) formal variants corresponding to sociolinguistic markers instead of indicators, first, because the use of the former is conditioned by situations as well as social factors whereas the use of the latter is only conditioned by social factors, second, because speakers are more aware of the former than the latter (Labov 1972); (b) formal variants whose use is frequent in the formal speech of the community; (c) formal variants perceived positively by the speakers of the community.

The variants were chosen on the basis of results of sociolinguistic and descriptive research on French spoken in Québec. The linguistic content (see below, Section 4.1) is limited to phonemic, morphemic and syntactic variants. Lexemes were not included because the probability of their occurrence in the discourse is too small.

2.2 Elaboration of Two Ways of Developing the Use of Formal Variants

The second aim of the research concerns the development of the use of formal variants. Broadly speaking, mother tongue curricula in francophone countries use three ways to develop the use of formal variants: pattern drills, contact with texts and formal oral speech and metalinguistic activities.

The two approaches we experimented with in class are based on the production of speech preceded and followed by metalinguistic activities. Metalinguistic activity can be defined as a cognitive activity on language, the conditions of its use, its meaning or its form (Boutet *et al.* 1983).

Authors who have worked on metalinguistic activity among children do not share the same conception with regard to its nature. For example, in her taxonomy of the types of metalinguistic awareness, Clark (1978) considers speech self-monitoring as a metalinguistic activity. On the other hand, others like Hakes (1980) and Tunmer and Herriman (1984) state that metalinguistic activity is a conscious, voluntary action. According to Bredart and Rondal (1982) and Boutet *et al.* (1983), to be labelled metalinguistic, an activity should imply an explicitation of knowledge. We have adopted the latter conception. It seems more appropriate to label the implicit knowledge inherent in self-monitoring as linguistic knowledge rather than metalinguistic knowledge.

The development of metalinguistic consciousness and activities seems to begin at the age of five (Hakes 1980; Tunmer and Herriman 1984), middle childhood being the period during which the child develops metalinguistic behaviour as Cazden (1975) observed. More specifically Barbarie (1981) and Van de Craen (1981) have shown that 9- and 10-year-old children can be aware of stylistic variations.

We have elaborated two ways of making children aware of formal variants and able to use them in formal situations. Both ways consist of asking children to present individually five oral communications in a formal situation in front of the whole class. The speeches are video-taped. The five speech events with interlocutors, physical settings, and function remaining the same, are the following: report on documentary research, news bulletin, report on an event, description of a peculiar or rare object, report on a second documentary research.

Each speech event is embedded in this pedagogical sequence: (1) collective preparation of general content and form of the speech to be produced, that is, activities intended to help the children discover what might be the appropriate information to be presented in the speech as well as what might be the appropriate language to use; (2) individual preparation; (3) the children's oral presentation; (4) after each child's speech, collective "feedback" about the content and the language used, by using the following questions: Did our friend give relevant information in order to be clearly understood? With a view to improving understanding, are there any relevant pieces of information missing in his speech? Which ones? Did he use the language ordinarily used in this kind of speech event? Tell us which pronunciations, words or expressions make you think that he used or did not use careful speech?

The second approach (*B*) is identical to the first one, except that it includes more specific metalinguistic activities following the collective "feedback". These activities aim to develop more precise knowledge in a more systematic way. They do not focus on the speech event, but they are related to it in a certain way. They consist in viewing video-taped puppets which are first shown preparing their speech in casual style and then, presenting it in front of the class in formal style. The speech topics of the puppets are always similar to the ones the children produced, that is, documentary research, a news bulletin and so on. Metalinguistic tasks to be performed by the students are the identification of casual and formal variants in the puppets' speeches, and the production of formal variants corresponding to the puppets' casual variants.

We wanted to see if the children, after the completion of each of these two experiments (approach *A* implying an analysis of the language used by the children themselves, and approach *B* implying in addition a systematic analysis of the language used by the puppets) would have increased their use of formal variants, and also to see which one of these two approaches was more efficient.

2.3 *Role of the Development of the Explicit Knowledge of Formal Variants in the Development of their Use*

The third aim of this research is related to the second. There is agreement as to the role of metalinguistic knowledge in the development of language performance. It seems that this role is recognized in reading acquisition (Tunmer and Bowey 1984; Bowey 1986). However, it is not clear if linguistic awareness is a prerequisite to learning or a consequence of it (Ehri 1979). On the other hand, teaching grammar as a means for developing language abilities has been condemned by many authors (Moffet 1968; Wesdorp 1983). Nevertheless, some authors believe that it might depend on the type and object of the meta-knowledge. In this respect, Odlin (1986) reports that metalanguage observed in research on first language and in anthropological linguistics tends to describe more accurately the linguistic functions of forms than the forms themselves. She concludes that formal linguistic knowledge is often less accessible and less useful than functional metalinguistic awareness. For Odlin, metalinguistic knowledge regarding facts of language which play a more important function in communication is useful when it comes to monitoring and planning speech. One may think that linguistic variants functioning as markers are more accessible to the speaker's consciousness because of their significant function in communication, since they are related to careful or casual speech, that is, to stylistic variation.

In the absence of an agreement on the relationship between explicit knowledge and language use, we postulate that explicit knowledge plays a role in the development of the use. Since approaches A and B aim at developing explicit knowledge of the variants, a comparison of the results obtained by each approach as to the use and the knowledge can bring some empirical information about the issue we are interested in: does explicit knowledge of the formal variants increase the use of these variants in appropriate speech events? If knowledge has an influence on utilisation, could it be that the more the approach develops explicit knowledge of the formal variants, the more it develops their use?

3. Methodological Scheme

The experiment was conducted with middle-class students living in a small industrial town in Québec during a period of three months in the winter of 1986. It was conducted in two regular classes of 9- and 10-year-old children and involved their regular teachers. Both teachers were participating in a training program. Both groups were comparable as far as socioeconomic aspects were concerned.

As we want to verify the effect of the pedagogical approaches on the development of the use of formal variants and to study the relationship between explicit knowledge of the formal variants and their use, the evaluative scheme consists of a pre-test and a post-test measuring use as well as knowledge. The utilisation test consisted of the performance of the children in the first and last speech events (reports on documentary research), both sharing the same communicative function. Each child is marked according to the frequency of use of formal variants in relation to his overall use of the linguistic variables involved. The knowledge pre-test covers 18 linguistic variables, each of their casual variants occurring three times in 20 utterances. For the post-test, the casual variants are the same but the utterances are different. The score for each child is based on the frequency of production of formal variants, the child being asked to say each utterance in a more formal style.

4. Results

4.1 *Content*

To evaluate the linguistic content, we used two pedagogical criteria regarding learning relevance, which were suggested by Gagné (1974): (a) formal variants are not fluently used by children of a certain age; (b) the use of these formal variants can be increased after specific activities.

First of all, five formal variants were fluently used by all the children in the pre-test; and, thus, have to be considered as irrelevant (see Table 1).

Second, 20 variants were used more frequently in the post-test (see Table 2).

Table 1: Formal variants consistently used by all subjects

Levels	Formal variants	Casual variants	Examples
Phonemic	(oi) [wa]	[we]	*moi, il voit*
	(ɛ #) [ɛ]	[æ]	*jamais, il avait*
Morphemic	(leur, Pro) [lœR]	[lø(z)]	*j'leur ai donné ...*
	(leur(s), Det.) [lœR]	[lø[z]]	*leurs enfants, leur maman*
	(la, les, Det.) [le(z)]	[a], [e(s)]	*on voit la/les maison(s)*

Table 2: Formal variants used more frequently in the post-test than in the pre-test

Levels	Formal variants	Casual variants	Examples
Phonemic	(ɑ#)[ɑ]	[ɔ]	*chat, repas*
	(ɛ:)[aᵉ]	[aⁱ]	*fête, mère, neige*
	(ɑ:)[ɑ:]	[aᵘ]	*canard, tâche, sable*
	(oi C)[wɑ]	[waᵉ]	*poèle, framboise, croire*
	(final consonant clusters)		
	autre chose, autre enfant	aut'chose, aut'enfant,	
	triste, table	*tris', tab'*	
Morphemic	(prep+article)		
	[syRla], [suRle]	[sa:], [se:]	*sur la table, sur les tables*
	[ala]	[a:]	*à la*
	[dãla], [dãle]	[dã:], [dẽ:]	*dans la/dans les maison(s)*
	(il) *il*	[i]	*il avait;*
	(ils‿C) (ils‿V) *ils*	[i]	*ils prenaient, ils avaient*
	(elle) [ɛl]	[a]	*elle prend*
	(il y a) *il y a*	[jɔ];	*il y a des enfants...*
	(il y en) *il y en...*	[lnn..]/[jãn...]	il y en avait, aurait...
	(ce sont) *ce sont les...*	*c'est les...*	*ce sont les chiens*
	(j'vais) *j'vais*	*j'vas / ma*	*j'vais faire ça*
	la, les (pronoun)	[a], [e(z)]	*il va la/les prendre;*
	(quand‿V) [kã] [kã(t)]	[kãk]	*quand il y avait..;*
	(Wh)	[kOmãsk] / [usk]	*j'sais comment//ou vous êtes*
Syntactic	(noun+verb)		
	le chat boit du lait	*le chat, i' boit du lait*	

Only one formal variant (*elles*) showed no increase. The children still used the casual variant [i] as in the following utterance *on dit qu' i' sont grandes et belles*.

Third, eight variants did not show enough occurrences in the corpus; yet an analysis of the data concerning the increase in knowledge shows that knowledge of six of them has increased (for example: (œ:)[œ:]~[aʸ] *sœur, peur*, (tout,s) [tu]~[tUt] *tous les hommes*; (verbs: oi) [ãvwa], [swa]~[ãvwɛj], [swɛj] *ils envoient, il faut qu'il soit*). On the other hand, knowledge of two did not increase, that is the formal variants (ce Wh) *c'que* (instead of *qu'est-c'que: j'sais c'que tu veux*) and the auxiliary *être* (instead of *avoir* when used with a few verbs such as *partir, sortir: j'suis parti ce matin, il est sorti à 4h*). One may think that the use of the former eight variants would have increased had these variables been used. However, we have to verify first if there is a relationship between explicit knowledge and use. If such a hypothesis is true, we could propose a new criterion for pedagogical relevance: (3) for lack of figures regarding use, variants about which explicit knowledge could be increased should be taught. Since the data regarding use cannot be obtained easily from oral performances, this new criterion would be useful.

Therefore, many of the proposed variants were relevant. At first their use was not very frequent but it was more developed at the time of the post-test. On the basis of this research, these variants can be considered as suitable content for 4th grade students. On the other hand, the increase of knowledge about some of the variants not found in the performance data suggest that their use could be developed; therefore they could also be proposed as relevant content.

4.2 *Pedagogical Approaches and Development of the Use*

In order to know if there was an increase in the use of formal variants at the end of the sets of classroom activities, an analysis of gain variations has been done.

According to the results obtained after approach *A*, it seems that communication in formal situations and collective questioning on the language to be used and the language actually used produced an increase in the use of formal variants. The increase in the use in group *A* could be explained by suggesting that the children might have implicit and passive knowledge of the implied formal variants (Barbarie 1981) which could have been stimulated under the influence of formal speech events and collective questioning.

In group *B*, there was also an increase in the use. A covariance analysis of the results of both groups has been performed to verify if there is a significant difference between increases.

Table 3: *Use and increase in the use of the formal variants by students from two groups in the pre-test and the post-test*

Test	Group	Mean	Standard deviation	N	Group	Mean	Standard deviation	N
Pre	*A*	.24	.09	20	*B*	.30	.13	22
Post		.58	.23			.61	.24	
+		*.34*	.22			*.31*	.20	

Table 4: Explicit knowledge of formal variants in pre-test and post-test and increase in the knowledge

Test	Group	Mean	Standard deviation	N	Group	Mean	Standard deviation	N
Pre	A	.46	.19	20	B	.45	.20	22
Post		.54	.20			.63	.18	
+		*.08*	*.09*			*.19*	.12	

Results show that the increase in the use obtained with approach *B* is not significantly different (F = .042, p = .839) than the one obtained with approach *A*. Thus is seems that both approaches are equally efficient with regard to the development of the use of formal variants.

4.3 *Effect of the Increase in Explicit Knowledge on the Use of Formal Variants*

According to the postulated relationship between explicit knowledge and use of formal variants, an increase in the knowledge should be accompanied by an increase in the use. In order to know if there was an increase in the knowledge of formal variants at the end of the sets of classroom activities, an analysis of gain variations has been performed.

According to the results in Table 4, both approaches contribute to increased explicit knowledge. Nevertheless, approach *B* seems to be more efficient than approach *A* with regard to the development of knowledge. A covariance analysis performed on the results of both groups shows that the increase of knowledge obtained with approach *B* is significantly larger (F = 11,505, p = .002) than the one obtained with approach *A*. It shows that the metalinguistic activities of approach *B* have had a greater impact on the development of knowledge. But such an increase was not accompanied by a statistically more significant increase in the use. Does this mean that there is no relationship between knowledge and use?

To study the relationship between knowledge and use, a more refined analysis is necessary. Some variables appearing in the utilisation test were not included in the knowledge test. Conversely, other variables, of which the knowledge had been tested, were not found in the children's speech. Therefore, we have kept for analysis only the linguistic variables which showed scores for both use and knowledge and among these scores, only

Table 5: Analysis of correlations between knowledge and use of formal linguistic variants

Group	Test	Mean	Standard deviation	r	Significance of r	N
A	Pre use	.20	.14			
	Pre know	.49	.24	.46	.02	20
	Post use	.53	.24			
	Post know	.60	.21	.54	.007	
B	Pre use	.28	.17			
	Pre know	.44	.20	.48	.013	22
	Post use	.57	.27			
	Post know	.69	.22	.60	.002	

the ones produced by the same children. A Pearson's correlation test was applied to the data obtained.

Results show that there is a significant positive relationship between knowledge and use four times out of four. In other words, when the knowledge increases, the use tends to increase also, at least for the variables under study and the children concerned. This relation is in accordance with the fact that in group *B*, the increase in knowledge was actually accompanied by an increase in use. Why was the increase in the use in group *B* not greater than the increase in group *A*, which showed no significant development of the knowledge?

One may observe in Table 5 that for the same variables, children from group *A* have used in the pre-test many fewer formal variants than children from group *B* (0.20 vs 0.28), even though, surprisingly, the knowledge is higher in group *A*. (0.49 vs 0.44). So, did children from group *A* underperform in the utilisation pre-test? This seems to be confirmed by an analysis of the gain variations (Table 6) made on the oral performances of all the children in mid-experiment speech event 3 (events report).

The gain for group *A* is 0.36 compared to 0.24 for group *B*. Compared to this performance, results of group *A* in the post-test show a decrease of 0.02, whereas results of group *B* show an increase of 0.07. So the gains in use for group *A* were all made after two speech situations. This could be explained more by a below-standard performance in the pre-test than by the activities themselves, or by a combination of both factors. Such an explanation is also supported by the fact that the following activities did not increase the students' utilisation of formal variants. Children of group *B*, by

Table 6: Use of formal variants in pre-test, third speech event and post-test, and increase in the use

Group	Test	Mean	Standard deviation	Increase	N
A	Pre use	.24	.09		20
	3rd speech	.60	.26	+.36	
	Post use	.58	.23	−.02	
B	Pre use	.30	.13		22
	3rd speech	.54	.25	+.24	
	Post use	.61	.24	+.07	

contrast, went on increasing their use of formal variants after the third speech event.

If the children from group *A* underperformed in the utilisation pre-test, then it is also possible that the children in group *B* performed better in the pre-test than they would normally have. Such was probably the case since the conditions in which the children performed their first oral presentation were slightly different from one group to another. One week before the first speech (utilisation pre-test) we asked the children from both groups to present to us, privately, part of their reports in order to verify how they were doing. In fact, the speeches made by the children from group *B* did not contain enough information to include a sufficient amount of linguistic variables. We then had a meeting with the teacher to find an appropriate way to make the children work more on their topic. The children were then over-encouraged by their teacher, which might have had an effect on their performances. In contrast, speeches by the children from group *A* already included enough information, so we did not need to do anything for this group except the regular preparation before the pre-test.

Therefore, it seems that the children from group *A* underperformed in the utilisation pre-test while children from group *B* might have overperformed in the same test. This combination of factors offers a very plausible explanation for the absence of significant differences in the results with regard to the increase in the rate of utilisation within the two groups. So, at this point of our analysis, no valid conclusion can be put forward as to the effect of the development of metalinguistic knowledge on increase in the use of formal variants.

Conclusion

As a general conclusion of the research we might say that, first, the two pedagogical approaches that we elaborated and experimented with did contribute to the increased use of formal variants by the 9- and 10-year-old children involved in the research. Second, the approach which includes specific metalinguistic activities seems to be more efficient for the development of explicit knowledge. Third, there seems to be a positive relationship between use and knowledge among these children, but because of experimental shortcomings, it was not possible to be affirmative in our conclusions about the effect of the specific metalinguistic activities of approach *B* on the increase in the use of formal variants in appropriate situations.

Fourth, the criteria used for the choice of the variants to be taught seemed to be operational and pedagogically relevant. The use of many of the proposed variants was not very developed in the beginning but it was more developed at the time of the post-test. As there seems to be a relationship between explicit knowledge of formal variants and their use in formal speech events, we may suggest a third criterion for pedagogical relevance: variants of which the children can develop explicit knowledge.

It would be interesting to undertake further research in order to investigate the relationship between factors such as socioeconomic origin, intelligence quotient and sex of the children and the development of the use of formal variants. In other respects, the results of this research seem to show that communication in formal speech events followed by metalinguistic activities of two types does have an impact on the development of use. However, it would be interesting to gather empirical information on the impact of simply communicating. In other words, would the children develop the use of formal variants as much merely by communicating in formal situations?

References

Andersen, E. 1978. *Learning to Speak with Style: A study of the sociolinguistic skills of children*. Doctoral thesis, Stanford University.
Barbarie, Y. 1981. "Destination: la norme — attention: détour". *Liaisons* 5(5). 27-28.
Berko-Gleason, J. 1973. "Code Switching in Children's Language". *Cognitive Development and the Acquisition of Language* ed. by T.E. Moore, 159-167. New York: Academic Press.

Boutet, J., F. Gauthier & M. St-Pierre. 1983. "Savoir dire sur la phrase". *Archives de Psychologie* 51. 205-228.

Bowey, J.A. 1986. "Syntactic Awareness and Verbal Performances from Pre-school to Fifth Grade". *Journal of Psycholinguistic Research* 15(4). 285-308.

Bredard, S. & J.-A. Rondal. 1981. *L'analyse du langage chez l'enfant.* Bruxelles: Pierre Mardaga.

Cazden, C.B. 1975. "Play with Language and Metalinguistic Awareness: One dimension of language experience". *Dimensions of Language Experience* ed. by C.B. Windsor. New York: Agathon Press.

Clark, E.V. 1978. "Awareness of Language: Some evidence from what children say and do". *The Child's Conception of Language* ed. by A. Sinclair, R.J. Jarvella & W.J.M. Levelt, 17-43. Berlin: Springer-Verlag.

Ehri, L.C. 1979. "Insight: Threshold of reading acquisition". *Reading Research: Advances in theory and practice* ed. by T.G. Waller & G.E. Mackinnon. New York: Harcourt Brace Jovanovich.

Gagné, G. 1974. "L'enseignement télévisé du français langue maternelle à l'élémentaire: présentation, critique, évaluation". *Vingt-cinq ans de linguistique au Canada: Hommage à Jean-Paul Vinay* ed. by G. Rondeau, G. Bibeau, G. Gagné & G. Taggart, 493-517. Montréal, C.E.C.

————. 1983. "Norme et enseignement de la langue maternelle". *La norme linguistique*, 463-509. Paris: Le Robert; Québec: Gouvernement du Québec.

Gagné, G. & L. Ostiguy. 1989. "The Development of Metalinguistic Awareness and the Acquisition of Formal Speech in Mother-Tongue Education". *Literacy in School and Society* ed. by E. Zuanelli Sonino, 147-157. New York: Plenum Press.

Gambell, T.J. 1981. "Sociolinguistic Research on Children's Language: The culture of the classroom". Conference presented at the annual congress of the Canadian Society for the Study of Education, Halifax.

Gumperz, J.J. 1971. "Social Meaning in Linguistic Structures: Code switching in Norway". *Language in Social Groups: Essays by John J. Gumperz* ed. by A.S. Dil, 274-310. Stanford, California: Stanford University Press.

Hakes, D.T. 1980. *The Development of Metalinguistic Abilities in Children.* Berlin: Springer-Verlag.

Halliday, M.A.K., A. McIntosh & P. Strevens. 1972. "The Users and Uses of Language". *Readings in the Sociology of Language* ed. by J. Fishman, 139-170. La Haye: Mouton.

Houston, S.H. 1970. "A Reexamination of Some Assumptions about the Language of the Disadvantaged Child". *Child Development* 41. 947-963.

Hymes, D. 1972. "Models of the Interaction of Language and Social Life". *Directions in Sociolinguistics* ed. by J.J. Gumperz & D. Hymes, 35-71. New York: Holt, Rinehart & Winston.

Jensen, J.M. 1973. "A Comparative Investigation of the Casual and Careful Oral Language Styles of Average and Superior Eighth Grade Boys and Girls". *Research in the Teaching of English* 7. 339-350.

Labov, W. 1972. *Sociolinguistic Patterns.* University of Pennsylvania Press.

Lucas, C. & D. Borders. 1987. "Language Diversity and Classroom Discourse". *American Educational Research Journal* 24(1). 119-141.

Moffet, J. 1968. *Teaching the Universe of Discourse*. Boston: Houghton Mifflin Company.

Odlin, T. 1986. "On the Nature and Use of Explicit Knowledge". *International Review of Applied Linguistics in Language Teaching* 24 (2). 123-144.

Reid, E. 1978. "Social and Stylistic Variation in the Speech of Children: Some evidence from Edinburgh". *Sociolinguistic Patterns in British English* ed. by P. Trudgill, 158-171. London: Edward Arnold.

Tunmer, W.E. & J.A. Bowey. 1984. "Metalinguistic Awareness and Reading Acquisition". *Metalinguistic Awareness in Children* ed. by W.E. Tunmer, C. Pratt & M.L. Herriman, 144-168. Berlin: Springer Verlag.

Tunmer, W.E. & M.L. Herriman. 1984. "The Development of Metalinguistic Awareness: A conceptual overview". *Metalinguistic Awareness in Children* ed. by W.E. Tunmer, C. Pratt & M.L. Herriman, 12-35. Berlin: Springer Verlag.

Van de Craen, P. 1981. "Social and Situational Constraints on Communicative Performance". *Revue de phonétique appliquée* 57. 51-55.

Wesdorp, H. 1983. *Research vs Tradition: The unequal fight: The evaluation of the traditional grammar curriculum*. SCO-cahier No. 20. Amsterdam, The Netherlands.

Learning to Read in a Second Language: A Window on the Language Acquisition Process*

Catherine Wallace

In this paper I should like to discuss the influence of the stage of L2 language development on the learning to read process. My interest, as a teacher as much as a researcher, is in the kinds of resources drawn on by L2 learners in learning to read in English; also in trying to account for some of the difficulties which apparently simple reading texts may provoke for such learners. My aim is to show that difficulties encountered by L2 learners in reading should not be perceived as deficiencies in the learner; rather they can be exploited as an opportunity for both learner and teacher to react to and reflect on some of the features of written English texts, in particular the relationship between written and spoken language modes.

One way in which difficulties are made apparent is through the occurrence of learner miscues. A miscue is defined by Goodman (1973) as "an actual observed response in oral reading which does not match the expected response", the expected response being the print on the page. Goodman (1969) proposed that readers make use of three cuing systems simultaneously, namely graphophonic, syntactic and semantic. These cuing systems reflect three levels of language inherent in all texts. That is, all texts consist of actual physical marks on the page, structure or grammar carried by morphemes, function words and word order, and meaning carried by both content items and grammatical items. More recently interest has centred on a fourth level of language and a fourth cuing system, namely pragmatic (cf. Rigg 1986), which involves our drawing on certain kinds of knowledge of the world, often culture-specific, and which for an experienced reader would also include knowledge of the world of texts, for instance a knowledge of the typical structure and content of certain genres.

An extended version of this paper has appeared in *Reading in a Foreign Language* (5(2), Spring 1989.

Second language learners may have difficulty with all these levels, because of a mismatch between the text's language and assumed knowledge of the world and the learner's own language and knowledge systems.

Inherent in the concept of textual cues and learner miscues are two major principles. Firstly, miscues should not be regarded negatively. All learner readers and all experienced readers miscue. Secondly, learner reading behaviour is not random. Just as we can uncover patterning to L2 learners' oral language development, through error analysis for example, so miscue analysis can reveal a patterning in L2 reading behaviour.

In this paper I shall use as illustrative data, samples of the language and reading behaviour of one young adult learner, new to both English and to literacy at the start of her instruction. The teaching situation described was one to one with a teacher, i.e. myself. What the one-to-one reading aloud situation offers, as well as a chance for teacher and learner to read together and talk about stories in an interaction focussed around a particular text, is also an opportunity to observe and record how the learner tackles particular features of written English texts. The reading aloud activity is thus potentially a window not only on the learning to read process (as Goodman 1973 describes it) but also on the language acquisition process.

A dilemma for ESL teachers in considering the source of unexpected difficulty with apparently simple items of language is whether one is talking of a reading problem or a language problem. In fact, the two are necessarily interlinked if one has a view of reading as a process which essentially involves using one's language competence to predict structural, semantic and pragmatic features of texts. If the learner is unable to predict even basic structures in the second language because control of the English language system is still weak, reading, that is reading for sense, will not take place. What may occur is mechanical decoding, especially with L2 learners who are literate in their L1 and have therefore learnt or acquired decoding skills which may equip them to decode English, without, however, necessarily understanding what they read. It is frequently observed that ESL learners often have highly developed graphophonic skills (cf. Rigg 1986). For this reason learners new to literacy as well as to English and not taught through decoding methods of reading instruction, are interesting to observe. Points of special interest are not only the nature of miscues but comments made by the learner herself. In the shared reading situation a learner's thinking aloud through a text can shed light on both her expectations of texts and key features of the texts themselves, which may be "taken for granted" by more experienced readers.

One should add, moreover, that the oral reading event not only offers insights into the learner's existing language and reading competence but is potentially a language learning activity, in the sense that an opportunity is offered the learner to discover more about English because certain linguistic features are more salient and therefore observable in written than in typical oral forms of the language. As Holdaway (1986) observes, "spoken words cannot be held in front of attention, cannot be studied, cannot be pointed to in any direct way".

One way, then, in which metalinguistic awareness can be developed is through access to written texts which allows learners to focus attention on (Simons and Murphy 1986:193) "the phonological, lexical, syntactic, semantic and pragmatic levels of language, to notice anomalies at these different linguistic levels and to comment on them". Simons and Murphy are particularly interested in phonological awareness. My interest in this paper is in ways in which learners' awareness of syntactic, semantic and pragmatic features may be enhanced through interacting with written language, with the teacher on hand to confirm or disconfirm learners' hypotheses.

Subject and Data Collection

Amna was a nineteen year old Pakistani woman who had been in England for about one year at the start of instruction. She had not in that time, however, had much contact with English speaking people and was a near beginner to English in September 1985. She could not read in her mother tongue, Urdu, and had no experience of school in Pakistan before arriving at the local college of further education where I taught her. She was also a total beginner to reading in English at the start of our lessons.

At our college, the Havelock Centre in Southall, West London, Amna was a full time student acquiring English in both classroom and naturalistic contexts, as English tended to be the peer group language, along with Punjabi, the main community language. Nearly all the students were bilingual, many multilingual, and most of the classroom contact was of the English immersion type (as described by Ellis 1985) where focus is on meaning in L2 medium subject lessons, such as Maths or Science, with few interactions focussed on form.

Amna was a particularly interesting learner in that she was ready to take the initiative in learning situations. She was a learner who, as Rivers (this volume) describes it, "seeks opportunities to communicate". Our sharing of texts offered an opportunity for one to one interaction which Amna was eager to take advantage of. While much of our talk related the experiences described in the story to our own, Amna continually commented on the structure as well as the content of the texts we read together. Moreover, these comments were largely unsolicited by me. It is important that the conversation around texts allows the learner an "initiating role" as Dombey (1983), talking of child/adult interaction around a text, describes it. I should add that Amna herself asked for extra lessons in reading, which provided the opportunity for this study.

I recorded nearly all the reading and conversation sessions between myself and Amna over a period of 17 months in all. I also kept notes. However, most of the recordings took place within an eight month period of more regular weekly one-to-one reading sessions. I have selected for analysis eleven of these hour-long sessions recorded at monthly intervals over a period of one year from February 17, 1986 to February 18, 1987. It includes both reading aloud data, a small amount of elicited classroom language data and also informal spontaneous conversation between teacher and learner which occasionally also included contributions from other learners in a small group situation.

The Texts

Amna and the other students in the group usually selected texts themselves from a number of books made available to them. There was also some language experience work where texts were composed jointly by the group and then read back. While language experience approaches are likely to play a major role in the literacy classroom, the experience of print in commercially produced books and the achievement of completing even a simple book, with however much support, is also important. There then arises the question of which books. It is difficult to find books which are both predictably structured and culturally accessible and appropriate for adult L2 learners. In our case, teacher/learner consultation would result in a range of text types or genres being selected and the four samples given here in the appendix are representative of these.

1. *The Empty House* is part of a reading scheme, *One, Two, Three*

and Away.

2. *The Sly Fox and Little Red Hen* is a simplified folk tale and forms part of the supplementary books in the *Ladybird* reading scheme.

3. *A Woman on her Own* and 4. *Doing up my Flat* are books produced by adult learners for other adult learners in an adult literacy scheme.

It will be noted that these texts were produced with different kinds of readers in mind, though none of them can be said to be "natural" texts if by "natural" one means written by authors to entertain, inform or persuade, rather than for broadly educational purposes. The first is part of a widely used reading scheme in Britain and has a controlled vocabulary; *The Sly Fox and the Little Red Hen*, though recognisably part of the *Look and Say Ladybird* books, is designed to be read by adults to small children. *A Woman on her Own* and *Doing up my Flat* have been produced by adult learners for other adult readers on a "language experience" model. This means students have told their personal stories to a literacy tutor who acted as scribe. These stories have subsequently been produced in book form.

Though no explicit rationale is given for the selection and grading of language items, the texts suggest the operation of certain principles. The reading scheme book has a controlled vocabulary, with a calculated repetition of items; the folk tale accommodates a richer vocabulary base than the actual reading scheme books, though it is still structurally and rhetorically simpler than most authentic childrens' stories. In the last two "adult" books there is a shift of genre to autobiography so that the writer is the protagonist. The vocabulary is not controlled, on the language experience principle of keeping as close to the narrator's original spoken version as possible. Content words such as "depressed" and "frightened" are anyway both predictable in the context and readily explained by a literacy tutor if necessary. What possibly is not considered is that the selection of this particular genre may involve stylistic choices which initially create difficulty for early readers.

The Study

From the selected books, I took three examples of textual features which in Amna's oral rendering provoked:

> non-attempt or hesitation;

a miscue or miscues;
comment about the particular textual feature.

All these responses are potentially significant in that they can offer useful insights into, firstly the stage of second language development, secondly, developing reading strategies, thirdly developing metalinguistic awareness and finally areas of textual difficulty for L2 learners in particular but, arguably, for all learner readers.

I selected for focus two classes of grammatical items, morpheme and pronoun, and from these groups, the *-ed* morpheme and the personal pronouns *they* and *you*. As soon as learner readers begin encountering simple continuous narrative texts they will need to recognise the function of the *-ed* morpheme in marking past tense; pronouns are another of the most frequent items in any spoken or written text and an understanding of the way they give text cohesion is crucial to the comprehension of even the simplest of written texts. As Goodman (1984) points out, "the language requires the use of pronouns where the referents for noun phrases are established in the text or situational context". Although pronouns perform grammatical functions and are therefore part of syntax they are also part of the semantic system. Goodman (1983) notes: "The specific reference of a particular pronoun can only be determined from the total semantic and pragmatic context". It will be seen that in responding to pronouns in context Amna needs to bring both semantic and pragmatic judgements into play.

It is important to stress that what is at issue is not the manner in which words may be understood out of context (though many teaching approaches and materials continue to assume that difficulty lies at the word level); rather it is the learner's response to the items in context and the fact that in Amna's case this is typically variable. In the first case, that of the response to the *-ed* morpheme, this is because of a developing language competence and language awareness in the learner; in the second case, that of the response to *they* and *you* in particular contexts, this is because of the variable meaning, both propositional and pragmatic, which the items take on in the context of the texts. The "problems" then reside neither in the text nor in the learner, but in the interaction between text and learner.

1. *Past Tense -ed Morpheme*

The transcripts of Amna's spoken language show a development from the base form of the verb for simple past meaning, e.g. *he go road* "he went down the road" and *I finish this page* "I finished this page" with an increasing number of irregular past tense forms gradually being added (the progression being: *saw — went — lost — took — came — read*). As might be expected, the irregular past tense forms met in texts created little or no difficulty and were not miscued. The regular *-ed* forms were very slow to emerge in Amna's spontaneous oral production (partly because, as Ellis 1985 notes, past time reference is not required very much in communicative classroom speech). Only after seven months of fulltime classes at Havelock, which included our weekly one-to-one hour of reading, did I notice a clear use of past tense *-ed* in *College man maybe he locked all* "Maybe the college man, i.e. the caretaker, locked everything". And in all the data transcribed, I found only one other instance, namely on the last occasion when we had an extended conversation together — *I stayed to my sister house* "I stayed at my sister's house".

During the first recording of a reading lesson transcribed in detail on February 17, 1986 and indeed the first time a full narrative in past tense was attempted, Amna read "looked" as "look — it", isolating the *-ed* morpheme and then querying with "Miss?" (cf. Appendix 1, line 7). On the same occasion she totally failed to read other *-ed* forms, such as "lived" and "stopped". There appeared, that is, to be no understanding initially of the grammatical function of the *-ed* morpheme. However, after another similar rendering of the item in the same text as "look — it" (Appendix 1, line 13) on the next occurrence of the word "looked", Amna rendered the text as follows: *Ramu look up it the top window* "Ramu looked up at the top window" (Appendix 1, line 17). Moreover, she continued thus: *Something white fly across the window* "Something white flew across the window" (Appendix 1, line 19). This rendering clearly reflected Amna's current interlanguage. And the shift into interlanguage away from attempts at decoding marks on the page — or attempting to — was an encouraging sign that Amna was reading for meaning. For, as observed in Wallace (1988), it tends to be at times of greater fluency and confidence that L2 learners render texts directly in their interlanguage, much as native speaking non-standard readers do in the case of non-standard dialects.

However, it must of course be emphasised that learners' ability to read and make sense of structures is in advance of their own productive use of them in spontaneous face-to-face situations. And the next past tense narrative text we read nearly two months later seemed to indicate that Amna was now competent to understand the function of the past tense *-ed* morpheme though this was still absent from her own spoken English production. On this occasion Amna read the regular past tense forms of the text with no hesitation, so "walked", "jumped", "slipped" and "picked" were read with little or no difficulty as "wokt", "jumpt", "slipt" and "pikt" and there was no attempt to mark off the -ed morpheme.

Two weeks later, there seemed to be a further development in the process of conceptualising about the -ed feature. Again this was indicated by departures from the text. While most of the -ed forms in the text were again read with no difficulty (e.g. "lived", "worked", "picked" and "looked", with the -ed morpheme in "lived" being differentiated from that in the other three words to give the response "livd") there were two other kinds of responses: firstly, interlanguage forms were occasionally used along with the standard forms, the interlanguage form acting as a gloss, e.g., *None of the sly young fox's plans worked — work*. Also of interest was a new phenomenon, namely overgeneralisation (cf. Appendix 2). Amna began to read *He picked up a bag* ... at which point I provided the missing and almost certainly unknown word *slung*. Amna repeated it and then chose to retrace the text to read: *He picked up a bag and slunged it* ... (Appendix 2, line 4). A little earlier in the same text she read *he didn't live* as *he did -ent — didn't lived*. Her reading behaviour here thus appeared to mirror a stage observable in more advanced L2 learners' oral language development, but not so far with Amna.

In short, one notes, in Amna's case, varying kinds of responses to -ed marking for past time in texts i.e.

1. non-recognition of the grammatical form;
2. direct rendering in the text version;
3. overgeneralising the -ed marker;
4. rendering in text version with a gloss in interlanguage
5. direct rendering in interlanguage.

5, as already suggested, tends to characterise growing confidence and fluency in early L2 learner readers. 2 and 3 together suggest a developing understanding of how past is marked in written texts. And 4, most interestingly perhaps, is indicative of an awareness of alternates, of an equivalence of meaning between the learner's typical interlanguage version and the standard form of the text. For finally what is of interest is not recognition of form as such but a growing awareness of how form relates to meaning. This is even more apparent in the second example of a textual feature which I shall consider next.

2.   *The Pronoun "They"*

One of the items which created difficulty for Amna was the pronoun *they* in the text extracted in Appendix 3. Amna generally had some difficulty with this particular pronoun, either not attempting it at all or, occasionally, rendering it as *they're* (possibly having understood this as a chunk from the frequent occurrence in oral language of the contracted form, e.g. *they're outside*). The problem may be attributable to any one or all of several factors. Firstly, I nowhere noted in my data any use of *they* in either Amna's spontaneous speech or elicited classroom language. Where Amna used third person plural anaphoric reference (noted only six times in the data) she used *he*, e.g. *You know my nephew and niece. He told me you going Pakistan* "You know my nephew and niece. They told me that I (i.e. Amna) was going to Pakistan". Moreover, for the impersonal meaning of *they* Amna used *somebody*, e.g. *Somebody no give her time* "They don't give her time".

A second factor is that she was more familiar with *they* in situational uses than in referring uses (cf. Appendix 3, lines 38-40). That is, in the kind of spoken face-to-face interaction with which Amna was familiar, there is more use of exophoric reference than of endophoric reference, exophoric reference being reference which is outside the confines of the text but present in the situation (Halliday and Hasan 1976). Simons and Murphy (1986:190) suggest that intratextual or endophoric reference may create difficulty for early readers. They put it thus:

> The use of deictic items in written text [among which they include referring pronouns] requires different processing strategies of children whose language experiences are mainly oral and who are accustomed to using the physical and temporal situations to anchor deictic items.

I would argue that illiterate adults such as Amna may initially have similar difficulties with endophoric reference, especially where it is remote in the text.

However, the particular difficulty with this text is that *they* neither refers back in the text to specific characters in the story nor to accompanying pictures. Nor indeed is *they* an impersonal use as in *they say he beats his wife*. Here *they* refers to a class, i.e. "all women on their own", an abstract concept not representable through illustration. And Amna, like all early readers, was still heavily dependent on pictures to anchor reference items which occur in the text. Dombey (1983) notes how "the pictures provide continued deictic support for the child". And the same is likely to be true for the adult learner new to literacy.

The difficulty, in short, was a conceptual one, due to Amna's as yet limited awareness of how items refer in English, which in turn was partly due to her limited access to written texts where such uses of reference are highlighted. Certainly Amna expected texts to have cohesion and her comments (cf. Appendix 3, lines 19, 21 and 26) show her searching the text for referents for *they*. However, she expected reference to be tied closely to the pictures or immediate text, and it is likely that, initially at least, she understood "women on their own" as "a woman on her own", that is the individual woman shown in the pictures who is also the story teller in this first person narrative. The case of *they* suggests that it is not so much linguistic forms which create difficulty for Amna, but the way in which form relates to meaning, and the fact that this relationship is not one to one.

3. *The Pronoun "You"*

My third example of text-related difficulty is illustrated by the pronoun *you* in the text given in Appendix 4. Here the difficulty seems to be not so much a syntactic/semantic one as a pragmatic one. It was not the propositional meaning but the function of *you* which perplexed Amna. She had never before encountered this exophoric use of *you* in a written text and as a learner who looked to make sense of texts she sought clarification. Paradoxically, this interpersonal use where the addressee (here, the reader) is directly addressed is like speaking, where, of course, the interpersonal use of the second person pronoun would be very familiar to Amna. However, in most written genres the writer does not directly address the reader. For instance, in folk or fairy tales we typically get this kind of exchange:

> What big eyes you have Grandma!
> All the better to see you with.

The reference is endophoric and it was this use of second person reference in written texts, usually supported by an illustration of two characters, which Amna had become familiar with. She had no difficulty with the pronoun in: *"Did you see that", cried Peter* (cf. Appendix 1, line 11). However, the direct address from the writer, who is also the narrator in this first person autobiography, to the reader confused Amna, not yet familiar with the genre of first person true-life narratives which in mode may be close to "speaking written down". In other words, as an inexperienced reader, she was as yet unfamiliar with the different ways language may function in pragmatically different types of texts.

Amna's Comments on Texts

Amna's comments suggest that it is not only what learners do in response to texts, as evidenced by miscues for instance, which is of interest but what they say; the language they themselves use to talk about the language of the text. Firstly, such comments may show the second language learner verbally checking out differences between her own current interlanguage and the language of the text. So, for example, Amna who had never herself previously used the *do* auxiliary to form past tense interrogatives, on meeting this feature in written texts, commented thus:

> "Did you" mean past?
> "Did you sleep" means you sleep or no?

Secondly, the comments may throw light on the actual process of developing a greater understanding of written language. For instance, shortly after our conversation centering on the pronoun *they* Amna commented, sotto voce and more to herself than to me, as follows on this text extract later on in the same story:

> I go home and get a cup of tea.
> I sit down and drink it.
> Why not write here "tea"? Why write "it"? Short way. "It" means "tea".

In short, the kinds of comments and queries made by Amna on the forms and related meanings of written English reveal her checking out her hypotheses about the nature of English, using the written data as evidence and the teacher as a resource to confirm or disconfirm. They also reveal her interacting with the text, drawing on her as yet limited experience of other written texts, as well as her greater experience of spoken forms of English.

Conclusion

In conclusion, the one-to-one reading event offers the opportunity not merely to help develop the learner's reading strategies but to gain insights, through the way print is tackled, into the learner's current interlanguage development (not always accessible to teacher observation from informal or even more formal classroom contact). More importantly, the learner herself, if encouraged to explore and comment on textual, as well as topic, features, is advantaged in several ways. Firstly, access to written language, more stable, consistent and fully structured than typical day-to-day spoken language, visible as marks on the page and therefore more readily talked about, allows the learner the opportunity to develop an awareness of syntactic, semantic and pragmatic features of texts. Secondly, she is offered access to her own second language development through the opportunity to "stand back" and reflect on areas of difference between her own typical English usage and the way meaning is conveyed in written English. Arguably both learner language and language awareness is extended through the process, however halting and teacher supported, by which L2 learners render aloud simple texts in the second language.

Appendices

Texts referred to in the Appendices:
1. *One Two Three and Away: The Empty House* by Sheila McCullagh.
2. *Ladybird: The Sly Fox* and *The Little Red Hen* by Vera Southgate.
3. *Gatehouse: A Woman on her Own* by Margaret Fulcher.
4. *Centerprise: Doing my Flat Up* by Dalcy Edwards.

Notes on the transcription

∧	indicates an intervention from the teacher at this point
...	indicates a hesitation
-	indicates a immediate self-correction or repetition
capitals	indicates that a word or phrase is provided by the teacher
word italicised	indicates a student's response or comment
---	indicates that a word is omitted
•••••	indicates that a portion of transcription is left out

They came to the empty house.

"Look!" cried Peter. "Look up there!

Look at the top window!"

Ramu looked up.

Something white went by the window,

inside the room.

"Did you see that?" cried Peter.

"It's a ghost!"

3

Ramu looked up at the window.

There was something white inside.

He could see it flying

across the window.

"It can't be a ghost," he said.

"You go inside, then,

and see what it is," said Peter.

"One of the windows at the back

of the house is open.

You can get in there."

4

Appendix 1: Transcript

AMNA	*CW*
	… anyway so lets see if theres a ghost here. So THEY
1. They ∧ came to the empty house	CAME
2. Look ∧ cried Peter. Look up	CRIED - LOOK UP THERE
3. Look it - at the top wen …	AT Look at the picture whats this
4. Look at the top window	
5. *Miss Rhoda's father — Rhoda father*	
6. Look at the top window	
7. Ramu look - it - it Miss?	LOOKED
8. Looked up. Some … wen …	SOMETHING. Its a colour …..
9. something white went by the window,	INSIDE — Inside the r… ROOM
10. - inside room. ∧	DID
11. Did you see that ∧ cried Peter	CRIED
12. Its a ghost	Lets see if it really is a ghost
13. Ramu look - it ∧ looked up ∧ at	LOOKED AT
14. the window. There was some	THERE WAS SOME ….
	read the next word?
15. some --- white - something white	WHITE
16. in an …	There was something white in
	… - INSIDE
• • • • •	
17. Ramu look up it the top window	
18. *miss window*?	AGAIN
	SOME-
19. Something white fly - fly across the	ACR…
20. window. *Miss across this one*?	Well "across" means it flew that. I could say "I ran across the …?"
21. *Ah. Across the road*	So something white flew across the window

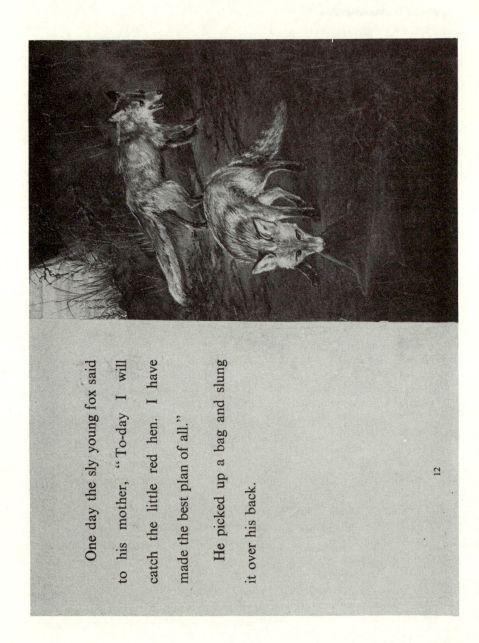

One day the sly young fox said

to his mother, "To-day I will

catch the little red hen. I have

made the best plan of all."

He picked up a bag and slung

it over his back.

12

Appendix 2: Transcript

AMNA	CW
1. He picked - he picked up a	
2. big — big ∧ bag	he picked up a ... ?
3. and ∧ slung it	SLUNG
	he picked up a bag
	and slung it ...
4. slunged ... Miss?	it - slung it means
	"threw it" over ...
5. Over her - no ∧ his black	HIS ... his?
6. - back	

3

When they do get a chance

to go out,

people think they are going out

just for men.

But they are not really

going out for men.

They get tired of sitting

in the house.

They get very depressed

and frightened.

They want to go out for company.

2

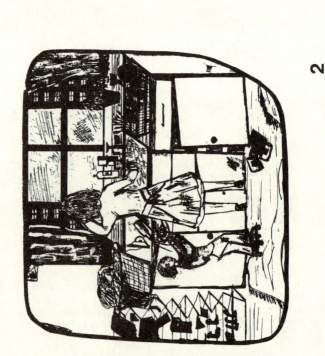

Women on their own
cannot really have a life
because of the world.

Appendix 3: Transcript

	AMNA	*CW*
1.	Women on their own ca.... ∧ cannot ∧	CANNOT REALLY
2.	really have a life because of the	
3.	wild ∧ world. When their - them ...	
4.		- Lets go back a bit. It
5.		says here: women can't have a
6.		good life because of the way
7.		the world is. When -
8.	them?	carry on: when ---
9.		do ...
10.	When --- do get a ∧ chance	CHANCE
11.	*I don't know this one*	Its THEY
12.	they	you know what "they" means
13.		don't you? When they do get
14.		a chance ....
15.	*they means?*	
16.		You don't know what "they"
17.		means? Who are they? Who
18.		are we talking about?
19.	*child - life*	It says "women on their own
20.		have a hard life" ...
21.	*her husband?*	
22.		... "when they do get a chance
23.		to go out people think they
24.		are going out just for men"
25.		they ...
26.	*they means "people"?*	
27.		Not just people in general.
28.		Women, it means women. Women
29.		- Women on their own with
30.		children. ..... So who are
31.		we talking about?
32.	*She?*	
33.		*They* not *she*. It's *they*. It
34.		means *all* women.
35.	*She telling all women?*	She's talking about all
36.		women, <u>all</u> women who live on
37.		their own.
38.	*Yeh "they" means 'nother woman*	
39.	*"they" means this one* (she points	Yes we can say they are
40.	outside to children in playground)	playing
41.	*the children*	Yes the children or women or
42.		other people together. So
43.		she's talking about women
44.		on their own.

I paint the ceiling.
You should see me.

8

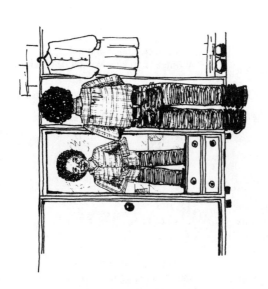

You should see me
when I put my jeans on
and my boy shirt.

7

Appendix 4: Transcript

AMNA	CW
1. I paint - I paint the	What's she painting? Look at
2.	the picture. What's this?
3.	CEILING
4. I paint the ceiling	
5. you ... said ... ∧	SHOULD
6.	you should
7. you should see me	
(repeats "you should see me")	
8. *Who telling?*	Who's ? ... ?
9. *Who's she - no who's she telling*	
10. "Your should" - *this is "your"?*	You
11. "You should see me"	
12. *Then who see her*	Yes. Who's she talking to?
13. *Yeh ...*	Well, she's talking to *you*
14.	the reader - I think. Do you
15.	think that's strange?
16. *Yeh, nobody here then who*	
17. *talk to her?*	That's right. Who's talking
18.	to her? She's the writer.
19.	She's writing the story for
20.	*you*. She's talking to *you*.

240 CATHERINE WALLACE

References

Dombey, H. 1983. "Learning the Language of Books". *Opening Moves: Work in progress in the study of children's language development. Bedford Way Papers*. University of London Institute of Education.

Ellis, R. 1985. *Understanding Second Language Acquisition*. Oxford: Oxford University Press.

Goodman, K.S. 1969. "Analysis of Oral Reading Miscues: Applied psycholinguistics". *Language and Literacy: Selected writings of Kenneth S. Goodman*, Volume One, *Process, Theory and Research* ed. by F.V. Gollasch, 1982, 123-132. London: Routledge.

————. 1973. "Miscues: Windows on the reading process". *Language and Literacy: Selected writings of Kenneth S. Goodman*, Volume One, *Process, Theory and Research* ed. by F.V. Gollasch, 1982. 93-101. London: Routledge.

Goodman, K.S. & L. Bridges Bird. 1984. "On the Wording of Texts: A study of intratext frequency". *Research in the Teaching of English* 18(2). 119-145.

Goodman, K.S. & S. Gespass. 1983. *Text Features as they Relate to Miscues: Pronouns*. Research report: program in Language and Literacy, College of Education, University of Arizona.

Halliday, M.A.K. & R. Hasan. 1976. *Cohesion in English*. London: Longman.

Holdaway, D. 1986. "The Visual Face of Experience and Language: A metalinguistic excursion". *Metalinguistic Awareness and Beginning Literacy: Conceptualizing what it means to read and write* ed. by D. Yaden & S. Templeton, 79-97. Portsmouth, N.H.: Heinemann.

Rigg, P. 1986. "Reading in ESL: Learning from kids". *Children and ESL: Integrating perspectives* ed. by P. Rigg & D.S. Enright. Washington, D.C.: TESOL.

Rivers, W. This volume. "Interaction: The key to communication".

Simons, A. & S. Murphy. 1986. "Spoken Language Strategies and Reading Acquisition". *The Social Construction of Literacy* ed. by Jenny Cook-Gumperz, 185-206. Cambridge: Cambridge University Press.

Wallace, C. 1988. *Learning to Read in a Multicultural Society: The social context of second language literacy*. New York: Prentice Hall.

The Development of Genre in the Writing
of Two Adolescent Lebanese Students of English
as a Second Language

Marietta Elliott

1. Description of the Study

Since the beginning of 1985, I have been conducting case studies of students learning to write in their second language at "Brewster" Language Centre.[1] Students were observed at least weekly for the whole of their stay at the Language Centre; usually about 6 months.

I have used the following data collection methods:
- weekly videotaping;
- observational diary;
- interviews with students, teachers and parents;
- analysis of all texts written during writing classes.

The teachers were attempting to follow a "process writing" approach, so that the students had considerable choice of topic and language, though topics were occasionally initiated by teachers.

2. The Two Students: Similarities and differences

The two students, Nasr and Rouba, are both Lebanese, so that Arabic is their L1. They had both had some exposure to French, so that they were familiar with Roman script. Whereas both students did write in their L1, much more of Rouba's writing in Arabic exists than of Nasr's. From the evidence it would seem that Rouba was the more competent L1 writer, even though she had had less time in school due to the war in Lebanon.

Whilst there were no great socio-economic differences in their situation, there were differences in *personality* which seem to have affected the way they approached the task. Rouba is the eldest of 5, and though she was the same age as Nasr (14), she seemed more mature and serious, and concerned with getting things right. Nasr had a playful attitude to learning, and was much less concerned with correctness, especially in the early stages.

The role of *input* for the two learners was also very different, and seems to be related to personality. Nasr was left free to adopt his particular learning style, and was not corrected unless he asked. Rouba, however, was always looking for confirmation and insisted on being corrected. After a conference with the teacher, who made major structural alterations to a self-translated text. Rouba decided to abandon translation and to "begin again", using only English. This decision had a profound effect on the type of discourse she produced in L2.

3.   The Nature of the Evidence

Studying ESL learners' written interlanguage involves attempting to combine research done in two different areas: writing development in English as an L1 and Second Language Acquisition (SLA), which has dealt predominantly with the phenomenon of spoken rather than written language. However, when applying SLA concepts to written interlanguage, several important differences must be taken into account.

Firstly, writing is never "natural" or "untutored".

Secondly, the learner's output over a comparable period of time is bound to be much smaller, so that it may be problematic to talk about "development" on the basis of only a few pieces.

However, as students had considerable choice as to what topic and genre they wrote, the sequence in which they attempted different genres is considered to be significant. Moreover, the data was gathered over a considerable period of time: six months. Over this period of time, the students' writing shows major changes which are analyzed below.

4. Terminology

4.1 *Genre*

Space does not permit a detailed discussion of the concept of "genre". My use of the term in the present context is to signify "discourse type", though I am well aware that the term as it is now used has a much broader meaning (cf. Christie 1984; Kress 1985; Martin 1986).

Martin and Rothery, in their (1981) description of the written genres acquired by English native speakers in the course of their primary and secondary education, posit a sequence which begins with an undifferentiated "observation/ comment" genre. This then splits into two strands: a "narrative" strand, which begins with "recount" and progresses to "narrative" and "thematic narrative", and an "expository" strand, which begins with "report" and progresses to "exposition" and "literary criticism".

I was interested in investigating whether the ESL writers would follow a similar sequence, and whether this sequence could be considered developmental, even though there seems to be some disagreement amongst those writing about genre on this point (cf. Martin and Rothery 1986; Martin 1985; Rothery 1984). Though the evidence is slim as yet, it seems that Nasr followed the sequence part of the way, but Rouba, because she used translation, had a different sequence.

In the course of their acquisition of English written genres, the ESL students produced non-target structures which can be regarded in the same way as spoken forms of interlanguage (Selinker 1972) with their own logic and systematicity.

4.2 *Transfer and Translation*

In general, the notion of a "transfer strategy" (Meisel 1983) seems plausible, but the question of what is evidence of such a strategy has not yet been conclusively determined. It seems likely, in any case, that there is not one "transfer strategy", but that some distinctions will have to be drawn between different strategies. One strategy used by the learners whose writing development is discussed here is *translation*. This discussion, therefore, is not concerned with a "transfer strategy" in general, but will restrict itself to translation, precisely because of the nature of the evidence at hand, although data from other learners may reveal evidence of different "transfer strategies" used when learning to write. Data from the present study suggest a causal link between the manner in which the text was generated, namely, if translation was used, and the presence of non-target L1-like features in the interlanguage. The term *translation* is used for the process of generating L2 text from an L1 model, and the noun *transfer* is used to indicate the presence of non-target L1-like features in the L2.

Several distinct *translation strategies* can be distinguished. The following have been found in the data:

a. The whole text first written in L1;
b. Oral L1 text written down in the L2 by the aide or an Arabic-speaking classmate;
c. L1 phrase spoken aloud and then translated with the help of a dictionary or classmate;
d. Single items translated alone with the help of a dictionary during the composition of a text in L2.

Whilst it is argued here that the number of non-target, L1-like features in the writing of the two students described here is closely related to their use of translation, the connection is not inevitable. Instances exist in the data where the student has actually achieved the target form of the desired item through translation, even though, as the data clearly shows, a more extensive use of translation will inevitably lead to more non-target, L1-like features. Conversely, non-target features bearing a resemblance to L1 forms have not always been arrived at through translation.

Nevertheless, the relationship between transfer and translation is clearly a close one, and one worthy of investigation. As the processes of written text generation are more deliberate and slower than those of spoken text generation, observation of ESL students' composing behaviour affords us a unique opportunity to further our understanding of the processes involved in second language use. Thus, rather than merely inferring a process from the appearance of a feature in the text, this discussion focuses on the strategy of translation and the resultant L1-like features in the students' written interlanguage.

Evidence from the present study suggests that the decision to use translation is made consciously by the learner. The learner has several possible ways of using translation, and the choice made affects the number of L1-like features present. Such a feature will be most frequently present if the first draft is written in L1 and the student has a very literal attitude to translation. There were fewer such features present when Rouba was translating mentally without having an L1 text on paper. Thus one factor creating variation in written interlanguage development is whether or not translation is used, and if so, what kind.

5. Nasr and Rouba

I shall now discuss the progress of each of the two learners, Nasr and Rouba, in some detail, focusing on the following questions:
1. What was the generic type and structure of the pieces they produced, both in L2 and in L1?
2. Can a developmental sequence be hypothesized, and is this similar to that suggested for L1?
3. What was the influence of L1 on the discourse structure?
4. What was the effect of input, particularly of teacher input?

5.1 *Nasr*

5.1.1 *Genre of Nasr's Pieces*
L1 writing: Nasr wrote the following pieces in his L1:
  (i) An autobiographical piece which bears some resemblance to the first L2 piece (*observation/comment*);
 (ii) Several *poems* — little verses he knew by heart;
(iii) A *report* of an Easter Church Service from which he adapted some material for *My Contry*;

Genre of L2 pieces (these represent his entire output in 6 months):
Term I:
(1) 21/2/85 *I like Australia* observation/comment
(2) 22/2/85 *I like T.V.* observation/comment
(3) 22/2/85 and 25/2/85 *I like boats* observation/comment
(4) 4/3/85 *My School B.L.C. is on the Moon* (*a Lie*) report
(5) 22/3/85 *I like ... I don't like* observation/comment
(6) 15/4/85 *My Contry* report-observation/comment
(7) 20/4/85 *My Teachers* observation/comment
(8) 22/4/85 *The first day I came to School* recount/narrative
Term II:
(9) 11/6/85 *The yellow and the red* observation/comment

(10) 11/6/85 *My house* observation/comment
(11) 2/7/85 *New Name for teachers* observation/comment
(12) 2/7/85 *My Memories* observation/comment
(13) 9/7/85 *I like dogs* poem
(14) 9/7/85 *I like stars* poem
(15) 14/7/85 *My Country* (draft 3 of *My Contry*: see (6))
(16) 18/7/85 *Boy in the Sea* narrative-observation/comment
(17) 23/7/85 *The names* observation/comment
(18) 6/8/85 *War in my Village* narrative

5.1.2 Developmental Sequence

Nasr can be seen as having progressed from observation/comment and recount to narrative. We can also see elements of report in one of the observation/comments. Pieces which are of mixed genre are considered as indicative of his stage of development at the discourse level. He is able to experiment with forms which he is as yet unable to sustain for sufficient length to create an independent text.

A factor which differentiates ESL writers from L1 writers is that they are learning spoken and written language simultaneously. Narratives and recounts, for example, require the past tense. The forms of the past tense are acquired over a long period, even in the spoken language (see Elliott 1986). While it is possible to write a recount in the present tense, and many students in fact do so, it is likely that Nasr, at least, did not follow this option, but delayed attempting a recount or a narrative until some of the more common forms of the past tense had become part of his interlanguage.

Nasr's writing development does not merely take place from one genre to another. Within the genre of observation/comment there is a world of difference between the first text in existence, which is close to labelling (see Martin and Rothery 1986) and where the predominant referent is Nasr himself:

> l'ime Nasr Nabbout l'me gaw scoule chis name Bronsvik languiche cintre
> ...

and

> My contry was lovely contry before 100 years ago it was the good contry of all contries.

In the later piece the observations and comments concern the situation in Lebanon, and there is also an attempt to back up the comments with reason.

Similarly, there is development from the first narrative to the final narrative (see Appendix) which is not merely one of genre but involves the seriousness of the subject, the way the orientation and the resolution are handled, and the consistency with which the point of view is maintained.

5.1.3 *Influence of L1 in Nasr's writing*

Whilst, as has already been stated, Nasr's basic strategy was "begin again", *My Contry* (see Appendix) is the one piece where non-target, L1-like features are evident, and where videodata show that he is using translation: namely, he had previously translated a part of his own L1 report of an Easter Church service into English, and he incorporated some of this material into the text of *My Contry* (see Elliott 1986).

This piece illustrates the difficulty inherent in applying notions of discourse structure developed for English writing to a piece which, while it is actually written in English, is written by someone who has internalized genres belonging to another culture.

The schematic structure of the piece is realized by different beginning/middle/end elements, and there is circularity in its thematic progression. Field, tenor and mode (see Halliday and Hasan 1985:30-34) are realized differently from the way they might be in English, especially in school-based writing. The mode could be called "oratorical". Although the language is written down, it sounds a little like a sermon. The field is not restricted to personal experience, rather it deals with group experience: "My Contry" includes the self. However, the self radiates out to include the family and the whole country, because Nasr does not set the individual apart from these groups, but identifies most strongly with them. The tenor is more formal than we might call solidary, but formality does not necessarily signify a great distance. The coda contains a prayer. Most of the above characteristics can also be found in Rouba's writing both in L2 and in L1. This is why they are considered evidence of L1 influence. Nasr ended several more pieces with a prayer before he caught on, without being told, that this was not a feature of English writing.

5.1.4 *Input*

Almost all the classroom input on record was initiated by Nasr, and he requested quite specific information from the teacher. For example, instead of asking the teacher to point out his errors, as Rouba used to do, he would ask if a particular word was correct or not. No particular topic or genre was imposed on him, and he was not corrected unless he asked. Whilst there were no models for Nasr's pieces about Lebanon, which were generated from his experience, he followed predominantly student models, from collections of other students' writing, or took ideas for topics from simple books.

Though it was important for models to be available, it seemed to benefit Nasr, at least, that he was able to choose those models which suited his particular stage of development and purpose.

5.2 Rouba

Rouba used three different methods of text generation:
  – L1 only;
  – Translation from L1 to L2;
  – L2 only.

5.2.1 Genre of Rouba's pieces

L1 Writing
  The following pieces were composed in L1:
    1 narrative
    3 recounts
    2 literary criticism
    2 recount/exposition
    1 narrative/recount
  Rouba is able to use a variety of genres, even literary criticism, though, in several cases, she has not been entirely consistent in maintaining one genre throughout, lapsing into recount at times. This may have been due to the fact that she was simultaneously attempting to satisfy two criteria: those inherent in the Lebanese and those belonging to the Australian classroom situation. For example, she prefaced many of her texts (whether in Arabic or in English) with "This is the story of ...". The teacher's instructions or comments commonly included the word "story".

  As in one of Nasr's pieces which shows L1 influence, there are no clear divisions between "personal/impersonal" in respect of field, and "formal/

informal" in respect of tenor in Rouba's Arabic writing. The field is predominantly personal experience, but the interpretation of "personal" seems to be less individualistic. The person seems very intimately connected with the family, and the country; so that "we" rather than "I" tends to be the protagonist. Particularly in the first piece, Rouba describes how she is lying in hospital, but she is aware that outside the shooting is still continuing:

> While this was happening outside the shelling and bombardment still continued ... Everyone went home they were frightened and scared for their children ... I was crying because of Lebanon. What was going to happen to Lebanon after I left? (6/6/86)
> (Translated by Mohammad Alman)

Similarly, while the tenor is predominantly solidary, the reader is addressed with politeness, even with oratorical tone:

> I like to remember Lebanon. Whenever I remember the tears come to my eyes ... In the summer we have school holidays for three months, and these three months pass with much suffering. (6/6/86)
> (Translated by Mohammad Alman)

It is precisely these qualities of her work, which also featured in Nasr's *My Contry*, and which are highly valued in the writing of her own country (Peter Tilley, pers. comm.), which cause her difficulty when she attempts to translate them into English.

5.2.2 *Generation and genre of the translated texts*

(1) "About my country" (16/9/86 and 23/9/86) (observation/comment)
    (a) Section 1 written in English.
    (b) Whole piece recomposed in Arabic (including the English section).
    (c) Section 2 self translated.

(2) "Today I'm writing sea sons Spring" (30/9/86, 7/10/86, 14/10/86, and 21/10/88) (observation/comment)
    (a) Draft 1 written in Arabic (30/9/86 and 21/10/86)
    (b) Draft 2 written in English (7/10/86, 14/10/86 and 21/10/86) with assistance from teacher, aide, peers and the dictionary.
    (c) Draft 3 composed by the teacher (21/10/86).

(3) "Today this story whit are I doing in Sea" (6/11/86, 11/11/86 and 18/11/86) (recount)

(a)   One draft only written in English (with assistance from teacher, peers and the dictionary).
(b)   Last section written by aide in consultation with Rouba (she dictated the Arabic).

5.2.3 *Discussion of a "translated" text: "... Sea sons Spring"* (see Appendix)

As translated by Rouba, the text reads as an observation/comment, but in the original it was more like a poem.

Compare (a), which was translated from the original by Peter Tilley, with (b), Rouba's own translation:

(a)   Indeed I love the season of spring, because it is beautiful the season of leisure and the beautiful season. Indeed I love it because it is enjoyable in its beauty and its flowers and its trees. Indeed in the season of spring the people, "all of her" (everyone) verily sees in it beauty and loveliness.
(b)   I love season spring. Beautiful seasons west (rest) seasons beautiful. I love very much. Because very beautiful in seasons spring flowers and trees in seasons spring the people everyone is welcame (welcomes) seasons spring. ("welcome" is not in the original)

This piece is an ode to spring, with three elements interwoven, rather than being presented in a strict beginning/middle/end sequence:
– observations about spring;
– comments about people's activities during this season; and
– expressions of emotion, both Rouba's own and those of the community, "everyone".

We can see that this piece caused Rouba difficulty in translation, not only at the lexical level, but in respect of generic structure and register features.

5.2.4 *Piece written in L2 only*

The last piece (see Appendix: "... Picnic ..." 25/11/86) was written entirely in English. Rouba did not use any translation strategies at all in composing this text. She did not look at the dictionary, nor ask any questions of the aide or peers in Arabic. This piece is a straightforward account of a school excursion. It does not show any of the non-target, L1-like discourse features found in the translated pieces.

5.2.5 *Developmental sequence?*
Rouba's development proceeded in three phases: an L1 only phase, a translation phase and an L2 only phase. Whether, with better backup facilities, she could have continued generating L2 text through translation, rather than being forced to "begin again", using only L2 and being much less ambitious in terms of content, must remain an open question for the moment.

The actual sequence in which Rouba wrote her L2 pieces is not considered developmental because the observation/comments have the same consistent, L1-influenced, generic structure and field/tenor/mode characteristics previously described for Nasr's writing. The developmental aspect is considered to be her manner of text generation, the gradual elimination of a translation strategy.

In the end, *how* Rouba wrote became more important to her than *what* she wrote, and the decision to concentrate on the process rather than the product had a profound effect on the discourse features of the pieces she chose to write. Thus her development consisted in using fewer L1-based strategies in her writing.

As a result of Rouba's decision to be less ambitious, her development in respect of field and tenor proceeded in the opposite direction to that posited by Rothery (1984:84) for English mother-tongue writers. Whereas the translated pieces deal with group experience, the focus of the L2 only piece is more on individual experience, and the tenor is solidary rather than formal. Rouba had abandoned the register she had learned from her L1.

5.2.6 *Input*
The teacher virtually rewrote Rouba's text about spring, giving it a report structure, adding facts and cutting out some of the oratory. He also cut out the more formal tenor. As a result of this feedback, Rouba abandoned any translation strategies altogether. In an interview early in 1987, she said the reason was that English and Arabic were "too different". Whilst it is not possible to *prove* a cause/effect relationship between the teacher's reaction to Rouba's translated text and Rouba's subsequent decision not to use translation, the evidence that such a link exists seems strong.

5.2.7 *Postscript*
Rouba is a confident writer in her first language. There is some evidence in her writing from her current school that she is progressing. Particularly a

personal narrative seems ot provide evidence that L1 literacy training has
finally transferred to L2, and that she has also learnt to adjust the tenor so
that it is more in line with the writing of her English speaking peers. The
following text is very similar to Nasr's final text:

> In lebanon there are many things that scare me at night. I'm scared
> of earthquakes one day an earthquake hit lebanon some people are
> sleeping, some people are watching T.V. ... while I was sleeping
> the bed moved from left to right but I thought I was dreaming.
> After that I heard something like a scream. I was very scared. I
> screamed "Oh my Got, what will I do ..."

Like Nasr's narrative, this piece has an orientation, complication, resolution and coda (see Martin and Rothery 1981:12). Like Nasr's, it is a narrative based wholly on personal experience, rather than partly, as Martin
and Rothery consider typical (1981:17). Though some non-target items are
still in evidence, such as inconsistencies in the use of the past tense, other
aspects have been controlled well, as for example the precise detail in her
description of the actual events.

Thus Rouba started by using a "translation" strategy, but she abandoned it and eventually followed the same path Nasr had taken: "begin
again". Though it took her somewhat longer, her writing eventually became
very similar to Nasr's.

6.   Conclusion

The writers whose progress is described above are considered to be representative of a broad selection of ESL students. They are reasonably competent in their L1 and have no special personal or literacy problems.

The above analysis has shown that it is possible to speak of written
interlanguage at the discourse level, and that there may be specific developmental sequences in which second language learners acquire written English genres. In the course of this development, learners produce non-target
generic structures which should be regarded as evidence of the particular
stage they have reached, and not as random deviations. The sequence could
depend on the kind of strategy being followed: whether "translation", or
"begin again". Of course the evidence of two learners is insufficient, and
more work is presently being done to see if similar patterns emerge.

Non-target, L1-like features are shown to have occurred at the discourse level, but their predominance seems to depend on the strategy adopted by the learner. A "transfer strategy" has been commonly inferred from the presence of L1-like features in the interlanguage. In the written interlanguage of the two learners presented here, L1 influence has occurred as a consequence of a conscious decision of the learner to use translation, even of the particular translation strategy being used. Though translation is used more predominantly by Rouba, Nasr did have recourse to it on occasion. Thus the decisions made by these two learners determined the genres they produced, and the way in which these were realised linguistically.

It is possible that learning to write and learning to speak are unalike and thus translation is a strategy available to the writer and not to the speaker, because of the opportunity to plan and revise. However, the question of whether translation is a possibility for the speaker is worthy of investigation. As a result, we may gain more insight into the actual processes through which L1 influences L2 use.

Note

1.   "Brewster" is an inner suburb of Melbourne. Newly arrived immigrant secondary students are offered an intensive ESL course there lasting 6 months, after which the students are placed in secondary schools.

Appendix

Two of Nasr's Texts:

1. *My Contry* (15/4/85)
       My contry was lovely contry before 100 years ago it was the good contry of all ,
   contries. but now
       My contry is Not good because lebenon I means My contry the israil soldier shooting the libanes. soldier and the people in My contry No just israil and palistin and syria evryone shoot My contry.
       and Now Lebenon crucified on the cross. Why? because My contry is the smaller of all the contries but His is the good and is the lovely of all the contries. an the end I pray to Jesus to protect My contry.

2. *War in My Village* (6/8/85)
       It was a good Morning when I waked up but it was Raining and very cold
       suddnely when we siting near the Fire somthing is (crossed out, "was" written)

happend one (crossed out, "one" written again) of My Village dead My uncle talled
us

My village yong they got the shooting gun and they went to protect the village.
and we went to My grand Father's house to stay their

after they (crossed out) because My Father was Not home

after My cosins talled us that someone killed that Mam

suddnely we hear someone is shooting so that was the yongs how had the shooting gun they found the Killer

and that's all My story and it's true

Two of Rouba's Texts:

1. *Today I'm writing sea sons Spring* (7/10/86 and 14/10/86)

I love sea sons spring ("in lebanon" added later). Beautiful sea sons west sea
sons Beautiful. I love very much. Because very beautiful in sea sons spring flowers
and trees in sea sons spring. the people. Every one is welcome sea sons spring it
Every one people. love spring and Every one people welcome spring. and Every one
peaple happy Because is camme sea sons spring. But after comme sea sons spring
Every (crossed out) oll people are (added later) going to park and my family are
going to the park in the mountains. and oll people go very happy. my family very
happy in sea sons spring Beautiful. and sea sonse spring in lebanon. flowers All of
the flowers open and the trees open the flowers in sea sons beautiful we my family
go in sea sons spring very happy. we A going to sea beautiful flowers and oll spring
we very happy very much in sea sone spring Beautiful oll people love sea sons flowers and trees in spring Beautiful all ("the things" added later) love spring. to beautiful. I love sea sone spring very much and I love, to sea sone spring. Trees and flowers and butterfly beautiful and Birds in moning Every day I woke up I listen Birds
(Arabic word inserted). I love season("s" then "e" overlaid) spring Because oll the
things beautiful. (Arabic word)

2. *The story for picnic langues centers* (25/11/86 and 2/12/86)

Brunswick langues centers went to a pickining. (revision: "picnic") and all
teacher went with studentr (sic) and all people very happy. When we arrived at yarra
river park the teacher very happy going (revision: "very happy" crossed out, "went"
to replace "going") to couck to it and the student going (revision: ªwent") take by
(revision: "bicycle") and I go (revision "went") take by I am very happy When we
finished went to it (revision: "eat"). I am very happy. The teacher said all students
came here and we go to the teacher. oll one student take meat and go (revision:
"went") sat on the floor and all student very happy (revision: "were" inserted) I love
pickining (revision: "picnic") very much. Because all people relax in the pickining
(revision: "picnic").

This story for picnic.

References

Christie, F. 1984. "Varieties of Written Discourse". *Language Studies: Children writing: Study Guide*, 11-51. Geelong: Deakin University Press.

Connor, U. & R.B. Kaplan. 1987. *Writing Across Languages: Analysis of L2 text*. Reading, Mass.: Addison-Wesley.

Elliott, M. 1986. "Nasr's Development as a Writer in his Second Language: The first six months". *Australian Review of Applied Linguistics* 9(2). 120-153.

Halliday, M.A.K. & R. Hasan. 1985. *Language, Context and Text: Aspects of language in a social-semiotic perspective*. Geelong: Deakin University Press.

Kress, G. 1985. *Linguistic Processes in Sociocultural Practice*. Geelong: Deakin University Press.

McLean, R. 1984. "Expository Writing". *Language Studies: Children writing: Study Guide*, 159-180. Geelong: Deakin University Press.

Martin, J.R. 1984. "Language, Register and Genre". *Language Studies: Children writing: Reader*, 21-30. Geelong: Deakin University Press.

————. 1985. "On the Analysis of Exposition". *Discourse on Discourse. ALAA Occasional Paper No. 7* ed. by R. Hasan, 61-91.

————. 1986. "Intervening in the Process of Writing Development". *Writing to Mean: Teaching genres across the curriculum. ALAA Occasional Paper No. 9* ed. by C. Painter & J.R. Martin, 11-43. Papers and workshop reports from the Writing to Mean Conference.

Martin, J.R. & J. Rothery. 1981. *Writing Project Report No.2*. Linguistics Department, University of Sydney. (Working Papers in Linguistics).

————. 1986. *Writing Project Report No.4*. Linguistics Department, University of Sydney. (Working Papers in Linguistics).

Meisel, J.M. 1983. "Transfer as a Second-Language Strategy". *Language and Communication* 3(1). 11-46.

Mohan, B.A. & W.A.-Y. Lo. 1985. "Academic Writing and Chinese Students: Transfer and developmental factors". *TESOL Quarterly* 19. 515-534.

Parbs, R.L. 1986. *Written Discourse Genres in Interlanguage Texts: An initial exploration*. Unpublished M.Ed. Thesis, La Trobe University, Melbourne.

Rothery, J. 1984. "The Development of Genres — Primary to junior secondary school". *Language Studies: Children writing. Study Guide*, 67-114. Geelong: Deakin University Press.

Scardamalia, M. 1984. "How Children Cope with the Cognitive Demands of Writing". *Language Studies: Children Writing: Reader*, 100-105. Geelong: Deakin University Press.

Selinker, L. 1972. "Interlanguage". *IRAL* 10(3). 209-231.

Oral and Written Language in the Educational Context

Jennifer Hammond

The original focus of my recent work was on children's literacy development. However it has become increasingly clear to me that in order to understand literacy development it is necessary to take account of the context in which written texts are produced. This realization has led me to focus on the oral as well as the written language that occurs within the educational context.

Recently I have spent much time recording the oral language interaction that occurs within the classroom, observing the class and collecting the written texts produced by children in that classroom context. This activity has convinced me of the importance of understanding the relationship between oral and written language. It has also convinced me of the importance of teachers' perceptions and assumptions about this relationship and of the fact that there are important educational implications that result from teachers' perceptions and assumptions.

I will begin this paper by referring to one of the lessons that I have recorded. The class in which this lesson was recorded consisted of 23 7-8 year old children in year 3 at school. They were grouped according to ability levels for Maths and Language, and then returned to their home class for "Process Writing". This writing session occurred between the mid morning recess and the lunch break. At the time this particular lesson was recorded, the children had just returned to school after a two week holiday. They were gathered together at the beginning of the writing session for a brief discussion. This lesson was typical of many other lessons in this class which began either with the teacher reading to the children, followed by a brief discussion of what had been read, or with a discussion between teacher and student about something that was happening at school or an event of local interest.

The lesson began once the children were comfortably sitting on the floor with the teacher saying:

T: Has anybody anything they would like to say about the holidays they've just had? Something that happened to them or they did, anything at all? Just some talking time about the holidays.

The teacher then nominated children to take turns in speaking about their holidays. One of the children was Vangeli. His contribution was as follows:

T: What did you do in the holidays Vangeli? I can see you are dying to tell us ..

V: I'm not dying ...

T: Well you're interested to tell us then, maybe not dying.

V: On Friday, I went, I caught, me and my mother and my friend caught the train four times to get to Circular Quay. From there we took the ferry twice to get to Taronga Zoo. We went past the Opera House and the Harbour Bridge and when we got there, I couldn't see no animals or nothing in all the trees that were grown. I said Mum, this isn't going to be a very good day. And when we got there we saw all these animals. We saw one hippopotamus open his wide mouth and we took a picture of it, and my mother took a picture of me feeding these birds with a yellow beak ...

Children: (discussion of what type of bird it was. Toucan ... no not toucan ... yellow beak ...)

V: Yeah, one of those.
      (more discussion about type of bird)

V: And then we went to see some reptiles, and then after that we went to see the chimpanzees, and they were so funny. One chimpanzee, a baby one, was running. He picked his nose, like he picked it and he put it in his mouth and he ate it.

Children: (Comments and giggles)

V: Then we went to feed the elephants and we took a picture of the elephants then we went to see the seals. And we saw lots of good things.

T: Have you been to the zoo before?

V: Yes.

T: Well you've been with the school haven't you?

V: No.

T: Oh didn't you go with the school? I thought most of you had been in the zoo.

Children: (various comments)

T: Well that was a very interesting day for Vangeli. What about you Vasco ...

Later during the same writing session, Vangeli wrote the following text:

Vangeli Taronga Zoo
on friday we went to
taronga Zoo. It was fun, we
saw some reptils, fish and
lots more. We came back with
the ferry. we went past the
opra houes and the houber bridge.

We saw kwales, gerafts,

The last sentence "We saw kwales, gerafts" was added after a conference with the teacher who suggested that more information could be included in the text.

Even a very brief comparison reveals significant differences between Vangeli's oral and written texts. The oral text has a structure of orientation (getting to the zoo), a brief complication and resolution (not being able to see the animals through the trees and then seeing them after all). The majority of the text, however, is a recount of what the participants did and saw on their trip to the zoo. Despite a rather abrupt ending, it is a well structured and clear oral recount of Vangeli's trip to the zoo.

The oral text is quite long (twenty seven clauses) and grammatically quite intricate. All but two of these clauses form part of larger clause complexes. For example:

i.   We went past the Opera House and the Harbour Bridge
     and when we got there
     I couldn't see no animals or nothing
     in all the trees that were grown.

ii. And then we went to see some reptiles
     and then after that we went to see some chimpanzees
     and they were so funny.

Cohesion within the spoken text is reflected through use of a variety of conjunctions such as "from there", "and when", "then when", "and then". Reference is used appropriately. The participants in the trip to the zoo are explicitly introduced "me my mother and my friend" and referred to thereafter as "we". Textual development is reflected in a variety of related themes such as:

On Friday me my mother and my friend
From there we
I
one chimpanzee
We   etc.

Overall the spoken text is a well developed, cohesive and interesting recount.

The written text is much less successful. Its structure is reasonably clear in that it contains a brief orientation (On Friday we went to Taronga Zoo), then a few details of what happened and what was seen. However it is very short (six clauses). It contains no clause complexes and hence no conjunctions. Each sentence consists of one clause: e.g.

On Friday we went to Taronga Zoo
We saw reptiles fish and lots more

Development of the text, such that there is, occurs largely through repetition of theme. "We" is theme in four of the six clauses. Participants in the trip to the zoo are not explicitly introduced but are simply referred to as "we".

The picture that emerges from this brief comparison is that the spoken text is well developed, rich in detail and comment and interesting to listen to, while the written text is underdeveloped, provides little information about what happened on the trip to the zoo and is not particularly interesting to read.

Why is this so? Why was Vangeli able (or why did he choose) to give a rich oral recount, but only a very brief and basic written recount of the same event? There are a number of possible answers to this question. One answer is that young children (year 3) have a greater command of oral than written language. They have, after all, been learning oral language for a longer period of time. Even though Vangeli is from a non English speaking background, his oral English has developed to a considerable level of fluency. He is an articulate and confident speaker. While he is also one of the more competent writers in his class, his control of oral language is clearly ahead of his control of written language. This situation is typical of the language development of other children in the class.

Another factor which contributes to differences between young children's oral and written texts is the physical effort involved in writing. It would have taken Vangeli a long time to write a text of the same length as his oral text. However, earlier in the year after a trip to Greece and Italy, Vangeli wrote a recount which extended over some seventeen pages, and which was divided into several chapters. Clearly when he perceived an appropriate purpose for writing, Vangeli was not deterred by the physical effort of writing long texts.

While much of the development of this long text occurred through repetition of "and then we did x", it was considerably better developed and more interesting than the one about his visit to Taronga Zoo. Thus while differences in command of oral and written language, and the physical effort involved in writing, probably contributed, it appears there must be a further explanation for the differences in quality between Vangeli's oral and written texts, and in particular for the rather poor quality of his written text.

I believe that at least part of the explanation for these differences lies in what happened in this particular lesson. The child's perceptions and the teacher's perceptions of the purpose of the lesson as a whole, and the purpose of writing within the context of this lesson, appear to be quite different. As I have suggested before, this lesson is typical of many that occurred in this classroom. It is also typical of many that occur in other classrooms and other schools, and hence an understanding of what was going on here has implications beyond this single lesson.

The child appears to regard the oral recount as the most important part of this lesson. He participates enthusiastically and very effectively in the oral recount, but then having done so, appears to find little purpose in writing about the same event. Some of the features of his written text support this hypothesis. For example in his spoken text he explicitly introduces the participants in the recount (me, my mother and my friend), whereas throughout the written text, he simply uses "we" to refer to the participants. He appears to assume that having already made explicit who "we" refers to in his oral recount, the reader of his text will already have that information, and it does not need to be repeated. He includes few details of the trip to the zoo, and apart from "It was fun", he includes no comment on the events. This is in contrast to his oral text, which is rich in details of the trip to the zoo, and the animals he saw there. The oral text also includes a number of comments on the events, for example:

> I said Mum this isn't going to be a very good day
> ... and they were so friendly
> We saw lots of good things

Overall the impression that Vangeli gives in his written text is that producing a written recount of an event immediately following an oral recount is not an adequate purpose for writing, except perhaps to satisfy the demands of the teacher.

On the other hand, the teacher clearly perceived that this was a writing lesson and that the class discussion of the children's holidays was a suitable and useful way of motivating the children to write. After each child had a turn of recounting his or her holiday experiences, the teacher encouraged the children to write about their holiday experiences by saying:

> T: Now it's time to do some writing ... I thought some of you might
>   do some writing about the holidays, whatever you did. It's just
>   an idea. You don't have to, you know that. You can write about
>   anything you like. Remember though, some of you still have not
>   reached the right number of published stories, so I think you'd
>   better start working and writing solidly. That means heads down
>   and working. Try and make yourselves work.

Of the twenty three children in the class, eight wrote about their holidays. Except for two other children who worked on texts already in progress, these eight were the most competent writers in the class. That is, it appeared that the most capable children had responded to the teacher's implicit directive, and had written about their holidays. Vangeli was one of these children.

The point is that the lesson was deliberately planned and organized. It had the clear purpose of using oral discussions as a means of motivating the children to write. Further, the lesson was based on beliefs and assumptions about language which I believe are held by many teachers and teacher educators. These are:

i.   that the teacher should use what the child knows in order to develop effective teaching programs. This includes the "language experience" notion of using the child's own experience and oral language as a starting point in teaching writing;

ii.   that writing is essentially speech written down. This assumes that discussion of personal experiences is a necessary and sufficient preparation for writing. It also assumes that there are no significant differences in purpose or linguistic realization between an oral text and a written text, except for the phonology/graphology distinction.

I believe the first assumption is an explicit one. If questioned about the purpose of the lesson, the teacher would respond that the lesson was deliberately planned with the purpose of using the children's personal experiences and oral language as a basis for writing. However, I believe that the second assumption is largely implicit. If questioned about this assumption many teachers would concede that there may be differences of purpose and linguistic realization between oral and written texts; yet clearly the message that children receive from lessons such as the one I have described in this paper is that written language is speech written down.

Before discussing these assumptions in more detail, I will digress to discuss the relationship between oral and written language, and in particular some of the differences between oral and written modes that have implications for the educational context.

The Relationship Between Oral and Written Language

In any literate society oral and written language modes have evolved to fulfil different purposes and functions. Because of this, generally they are used in different contexts. The oral mode is typically used in situations where participants are face to face, as in conversations, service encounters, recounts of personal experiences or, importantly for the educational context, in formal and informal learning situations. In such contexts there is a joint negotiation of meaning as the various participants offer input, give feedback, request clarification and so on. Because participants in such language interaction are physically in the same environment and are often known to each other, they can assume shared knowledge, either on the basis of previous experiences or from the shared context in which the language interaction occurs.

Written language however is used in situations where some kind of permanent record of facts, information or ideas is required. A written text enables readers to reflect on and refer back to the same text as frequently as they require. There is a temporal and geographical distance between writer and reader, as the reader is not present in a shared context with the writer. Because of this physical distance writing is essentially a monologue. The writer cannot assume shared knowledge with a reader, except perhaps when writing to a close friend — and even here the writer must make explicit who or what is being referred to, the sequences of events etc., as the reader is not present to request clarification should any confusion arise. More frequently writer and reader are unknown to each other. All written texts must contain details of setting, participants, sequence of events, thesis and line of argument in order to be comprehensible to the reader. A written text must create its own context for meaning. It must be independent of any context outside itself. In this sense it must be decontextualized. An oral text, on the other hand, can depend on the context of the language interaction for at least part of its meaning.

Because oral and written language are generally used for different purposes and in different contexts it is not surprising that they differ in their linguistic realizations. To demonstrate this point I will refer to three short texts that appear in M.A.K. Halliday's book *Spoken and Written Language* (Halliday 1985:79).

    i.   /// The <u>use</u> of this <u>method</u> of <u>control</u> <u>unquestionably</u> <u>leads</u> to <u>safer</u> and <u>faster</u> <u>train</u> <u>running</u> in the most <u>adverse</u> <u>weather</u> <u>conditions</u> ///

    ii.   /// If this <u>method</u> of <u>control</u> is <u>used</u>// <u>trains</u> will <u>unquestionably</u> (be <u>able</u> to) <u>run</u> more <u>safely</u> and <u>faster</u>// (even) when the <u>weather</u> <u>conditions</u> are most <u>adverse</u>///

    iii. /// You can <u>control</u> the <u>trains</u> this <u>way</u>// and if you do that// you can be quite <u>sure</u>// that they'll be able to <u>run</u> more <u>safely</u> and more quickly// no matter how bad the weather gets.///

The following symbols have been used on the above texts:

   /// : to indicate clause complex boundaries
   // : to indicate clause boundaries
   _____ : to indicate lexical items

While the information conveyed in the above three texts remains similar, there are significant differences between them. English speakers would have little hesitation in agreeing that text i is typical of a written text, while text iii is typical of a spoken text. They would also agree that text ii lies between the other two in terms of its "written" and "spoken" features. What are the linguistic features that distinguish oral and written texts?

Grammatical intricacy is one of the distinguishing features. Each of the above texts consists of a single clause complex, but whereas in text i this clause complex contains one clause, text ii contains three clauses and text iii contains five clauses. As the texts become more "spoken", the number of clauses increases and the relationship between these clauses becomes more intricate. This feature is typical of other spoken and written texts. That is, spoken texts generally are more grammatically intricate than written ones.

On the other hand lexical density decreases as a text becomes more "spoken". Halliday (1985:64) calculates lexical density by dividing the number of lexical items by the number of clauses in a text. If we follow this formula, then we see that text i, which has twelve lexical items distributed across one clause, has a lexical density of twelve. Text ii also has twelve lexical items, but these are distributed across three clauses, and hence the lexical density of text ii is four. Text iii has ten lexical items distributed across five clauses, and hence has a lexical density of only two. Again this is typical of other spoken and written texts. As grammatical intricacy in spoken texts increases, lexical density decreases.

It is interesting to note what happens to the lexical items that occur in text i as the texts become more "spoken". Many of the lexical items in text i occur as nouns. Examples of these include *use, method of control, train running* and *adverse weather conditions. Use* in text ii has become the verb *is used* and in text iii it becomes *if you do that* (i.e. use this method of control). *Method of control* remains a noun in text ii, but in text iii it has changed into a verb *control the trains this way. Train running* in text ii has become a verb *trains will ... run* and in text iii it appears as *they'll* (i.e. the trains) *be able to run. Adverse weather conditions* in text ii has become *weather conditions are most adverse* and in text iii it is *no matter how bad the weather gets.*

In each example, what appears in text i as a noun or a "thing" becomes transferred into a verb or a "happening", as the text becomes more "spoken". The nominalization that occurs in text i contributes to its lexical density and is typical of other written texts.

It should be pointed out that differences in grammatical intricacy, lexical density and nominalization that occur between oral and written texts are not absolute differences. In some contexts the distinctions become rather blurred. This is likely to occur for example in texts which are written to be spoken, as for radio, television, public lectures etc. Such texts will have features of both oral and written language. The differences referred to above represent clusters of tendencies along a continuum. However, generally the functions and contexts in which oral and written language are used are separate, and their linguistic realizations reflect this separation.

The situation is somewhat analogous to a bilingual society where different languages are used in different contexts. If separate contexts and separate purposes for the use of the two languages disappear, then the society may well become monolingual. There is no need to have two languages that fulfil the same functions. In literate societies the written mode exists because it fulfils functions and purposes that the oral mode cannot. Oral and written modes are used for different purposes and occur in different contexts.

How does this discussion of oral and written language relate to Vangeli? It seems to me that the point Vangeli was making in his oral and written texts was a directly related one. That is, writing a recount, immediately following an oral recount of the same event, is not an adequate purpose for writing, as the two texts are doing the same job. They are fulfilling precisely the same purpose, and hence the effort required to produce an effective written text is simply not worth while.

Teachers' Assumptions about Language

The discussion of oral and written language I believe is also relevant to the lesson as a whole in which Vangeli produced his texts, and to the assumptions upon which the teacher appeared to base this lesson. I argued earlier in this paper that these assumptions are ones that are commonly held by teachers and teacher educators, and therefore I believe an understanding of how they arose and of their educational implications is important.

The first assumption on which the lesson was based was that the teacher should use the child's own experiences and knowledge of oral language as a basis for teaching writing. In this lesson as in many others, the child's "own experiences" are interpreted as being personal experiences which occur outside the formal classroom setting. Inevitably writing about personal experiences means writing recounts of the kind Vangeli wrote in his "Taronga Zoo" text.

In the early stages of literacy development there appears to be considerable merit in this assumption. At this time the oral language used by young children, and what they are attempting to write, are in fact very similar. An emphasis on "writing down what you say" is useful in teaching young children that writing is a meaningful activity, and that language can be expressed through writing, as well as through speaking. It is also useful in teaching some of the conventions of writing, such as left to right progression, word spaces and spelling, within the context of meaningful written texts.

However, as children move beyond the early stages of literacy development, their spoken and written language becomes less similar. Mode differences become more important. A continued emphasis on writing based on personal experiences does not provide an adequate basis for teaching about the different purposes for which we use writing in a literate society, either at school or in the broader community. This is not to suggest that children should never write recounts based on personal experiences, but rather that problems exist if these recounts are the only genres that children write.

There are further implications that arise from this assumption. If the approach being used to teach children to write does not explicitly take account of purpose and mode differences between oral and written language, then children are not likely to be given any explicit assistance in moving beyond writing personal experience texts, and in fact this is what happened in Vangeli's class. The class writing program was based on "Process Writing", an approach which emphasizes personal responses and personal experiences as a basis for writing and for discussing written texts. During the year, the children wrote virtually only personal experience genres. While it may be argued that such young children have plenty of time to learn to write a range of other genres as they get older, the interesting thing is that the previous year these same children had been writing a greater range of genres, and doing so quite effectively. The difference was that during the previous year the children received explicit guidance and support in writing narratives and factual reports through oral discussions of particular topics, and then class-negotiated texts, which provided models on which the children could base their own writing. Without the continued explicit guidance and support which was provided in that previous year, the children reverted to writing easier genres which more closely resembled their familiar oral language.

The second assumption on which the lesson was based is that writing is essentially speech written down. As I suggested before, this assumption is probably implicit but nevertheless it is the message that children receive from lessons such as this one. It is also the message that is implicitly supported by much of the current literature on literacy development, specifically that which refers to Process Writing and "whole-language" teaching (e.g. Cambourne 1984, 1985; Harste *et al.* 1984; Goodman 1986). Very briefly, the argument relating to mode that runs through this literature is that listening, speaking, reading and writing are all part of the same thing — that is, they are all part of the "whole" that is language. Implications for the teaching of literacy are drawn from this argument. These implications stress the similarity of how oral and written language modes are learned, and suggest that classroom literacy-learning environments ought to be based as far as possible on the "natural" learning environment in which children learn their oral language.

It is undoubtedly true that listening, speaking, reading and writing are all part of language. It is also useful to stress the similarity of the linguistic system that underlies oral and written language, especially as a contrast to the fragmented behaviourist approach to language teaching which dominated for many years. However I believe this argument oversimplifies the matter. It fails to take account of the real and significant mode differences that exist between oral and written language, and it fails to take account of the different purposes for which we use oral and written language in society. The implications of this argument are that children are given little explicit guidance or support in making the mode shift from oral to written language. Children need to be able to make this shift in order to cope with the literacy demands placed on them in high school and in later life. That is, the implications of failing to recognize mode differences are that children are given little assistance in learning how to write effectively for the variety of purposes for which we use writing in a literate society.

I will attempt to draw together the various points I have been making in this paper. The main point is this: there are problems in lessons such as the one I have presented, which move directly from a discussion of personal experiences to writing about those personal experiences. There are two reasons for these problems.

i.   The types of personal experiences on which the lesson was based do not provide an adequate basis for extending the child's knowledge of the world, nor for exploring the different purposes for which we use writing in our society. I would suggest that in developing literacy programs we need to consider the kinds of experiences and oral discussions that are appropriate to use as a basis for writing. Such considerations will incorporate a language across the curriculum perspective, so that experiences and discussions in subject areas such as science and social studies form the basis for learning to write for different purposes. This is not to suggest that children should never write about their personal experiences and personal responses, but to suggest that teachers need to ensure their students are not restricted to this kind of writing.

ii.   Oral discussion is a necessary but not sufficient preparation for writing. In developing effective literacy programs it is necessary to take account of mode differences. This entails providing an extra step when teaching children to write. Thus a lesson may begin with an oral discussion of a particular topic, but instead of moving directly from this discussion to the children writing on that topic, an extra step needs to be inserted that will provide an opportunity for the children to obtain information about what a successful text, written for a particular purpose, actually looks like. Only after such information has been made available do the children attempt to write texts themselves.

The extra step in the process of teaching children to write may take a range of different forms. It may be that the children get this information through their own reading; i.e. the expressive and factual literature that the children are reading may provide them with models upon which their own writing can be based. If the teacher also discusses, reflects on and analyses such literature, the children will undoubtedly learn much from such models. As well, this extra step may entail teacher and class working together to jointly negotiate a model text which the teacher writes on the board. Such an activity has the advantage of not only providing a model, but providing a model that the children themselves have actively engaged in constructing. The extra step may occur as the teacher conferences with individual children about particular texts that they are working on. Such conferences enable teacher and pupil to clarify the purpose for writing the text, and the overall structure, development and linguistic features of individual texts. Effective conferences however are dependent on there being an on-going developing awareness of language and how language works. That is, they are dependent on the development of a shared class language for talking about language which will enable children to reflect on and discuss the texts that they are writing.

The extra step may include any or all of the activities referred to above. These activities need not occur every day in every lesson, but they do need to be a regular part of any literacy program. The important point is that there should be provision in literacy programs for the teaching of what successful written texts look like. Such programs need to take into account the different purposes and contexts in which we use oral and written language in our society. They also need to take account of the consequent linguistic differences between oral and written genres. If children are to successfully make the transition from their familiar oral language into the written mode then they need explicit guidance and support from a teacher who has an understanding of mode differences and of how purpose shapes both oral and written genres.

References

Cambourne, B.C. 1984. "The Origins of Teachers' Doubts about Naturalizing Literacy Education". *Selected Key Papers of 10th ARA Conference*, Vol. 2.

Cambourne, B.C. 1985. "Change and Conflict in Literacy Education. What's it all about?" *Australian Journal of Reading* 8(2).

Goodman, K. 1986. *What's Whole in Whole Language?* Portsmouth, N.H.: Heinemann Educational.

Halliday, M.A.K. 1985. *Spoken and Written Language*. Geelong, Vic.: Deakin University Press.

——. 1985. *An Introduction to Functional Grammar*. London: Edward Arnold.

Hammond, J. 1986. "The Effect of Modelling Narratives and Reports on the Writing of Year 2 Children from a non-English Speaking Background". *Australian Review of Applied Linguistics* 9(2).

——. 1987. "Process or Genre in Teaching ESL Students to Write". Paper presented at the 5th ATESOL Summer School, Sydney, January.

——. 1987. "An Overview of the Genre-Based Approach to the Teaching of Writing in Australia". *Australian Review of Applied Linguistics* 10(2).

Harste, J.C., V.A. Woodward & C.L. Burke. 1984. *Language Stories and Literacy Lessons*. Portsmouth, N.H.: Heinemann Educational.

Implications of Learnability Theories for Second Language Learning and Teaching[1]

Lydia White

1. Grammar Change and Positive and Negative Evidence

In this paper, I shall consider the relationship between different stages of second language (L2) development, and the kinds of data that are necessary to promote changes between stages. I assume that a task of any language learner is to make sense of input data and that this is done by internalizing a mental grammar, which, in effect, constitutes the learner's theory of the language being learned. This grammar must change over the course of time, since learners do not instantaneously achieve a grammar sufficient to handle all of the target language, and learners can be thought of as going through a series of grammars, or interlanguages (ILs), in the course of acquisition. If we consider the kind of grammar a learner has internalized at some stage X, and how this relates to a subsequent stage Y, we can look at the types of evidence necessary to bring about change from the grammar of stage X to the grammar of stage Y. I shall focus on the question of whether L2 acquisition can proceed solely on the basis of positive evidence, and I shall suggest that it cannot, that there will be cases where change from X to Y will require negative evidence.

In principle, there are two main kinds of evidence that can serve as input to a grammar: positive evidence which indicates that something is possible in the target language, or negative evidence which indicates that something is not possible. Positive evidence can serve to motivate new analyses, and, in certain circumstances, it can serve as disconfirming evidence for analyses that are in fact incorrect. Negative evidence can serve only the latter function.

There are three potential relationships between grammars X and Y to be considered here. The first is when X has simply failed to take into account some aspect of the input which is subsequently accommodated in Y. In other words, something is added to grammar X. In these circumstances, positive evidence can bring about change from X to Y. This circumstance is diagrammed in (1).

(1)

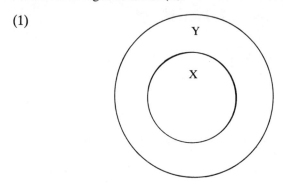

As an example, consider the acquisition of the complements of verbs. A verb like *see* can take a direct object noun phrase or a sentential complement, as in (2a) and (2b):

(2)   a.   Mary saw John
       b.   Mary saw that John was tired

Learners do not necessarily acquire all the complements of a particular verb at once. A learner at stage X would be someone who already knows that *see* takes a direct object noun phrase, but does not yet know that it can also take a sentential complement. When this learner notices sentences like (2b), these provide positive evidence that an addition must be made to the lexical entry for *see*, to accommodate the fact that this verb takes both complements.[2] Once this information is entered, the learner has a different grammar, Y, which represents an addition to X.

(3)

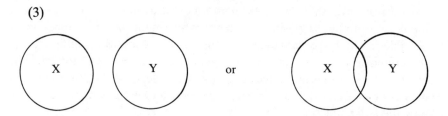

Another situation where positive evidence motivates change arises when something in grammar X has to be replaced by something else, as illustrated in (3).

Certain kinds of overgeneralization fall into this category. Suppose, for example, that the learner is forming all English past tenses totally regularly, by the addition of the morpheme /-ed/, resulting in overgeneralizations such as *bringed*, *runned*, etc. It might seem that negative evidence would be required to get rid of these overgeneralizations. However, they can be disconfirmed by positive evidence of the existence of the alternate forms: *brought*, *ran*, etc. That is, the positive evidence contains instances of the correct, irregular forms. The learner could change from grammar X (the one having an overgeneral past tense rule) to Y (the one that recognizes exceptional forms) with positive evidence only.

A potential problem in situations like (3) is that the learner might think that he is in a situation like (1). For instance, he might think that *brought* or *ran* represent additional past tense forms, as opposed to their being the only possible forms. We cannot assume that language learners regularly get explicit information that such and such a form replaces some other form, rather than complementing it. Many theorists therefore suggest that learners are guided by a uniqueness principle, which says that any particular semantic concept will have only one syntactic or morphological realization (Berwick 1985; Pinker 1984). Thus, for any particular verb, past tense can only be realized in one way. This means that when the learner notices forms like *brought* or *ran*, the uniqueness principle will force them to recognize these as replacements for *bringed* and *runned*.

The third potential situation pertaining between X and Y is where X contains forms or rules which are incorrect for the target grammar and which must be deleted without being replaced by an alternative, as shown in (4).

(4)

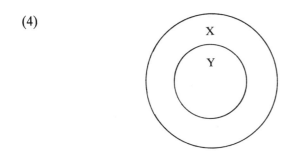

These are the situations which require negative evidence, that is, drawing the learner's attention to the fact that certain forms are non-occurring, or ungrammatical, in the target language. Such evidence is required when learners have adopted grammars which are overinclusive. A classic example (Baker 1979) involves the English dative alternation, as in (5):

(5) a. John told his problems to Mary
     b. John told Mary his problems
     c. John explained his problems to Mary
     d. *John explained Mary his problems

If the learner uses input like (5a) and (5b) to assume a rule-governed relationship between NP PP and NP NP complements to all dative verbs, the result will be a grammar with an overinclusive rule which will generate ungrammatical forms like (5d). If the overinclusive rule operates at stage X and is to be excluded from stage Y, a problem arises with the kind of evidence required to motivate the retreat. There is no positive evidence in the English input of the non-occurrence of (5d). In contrast to the previous examples, this is not a case of adding a form not yet noticed; nor does it involve replacing an incorrect form with a correct one. It requires the learner to drop something and replace it with nothing. On the face of it, it would appear that explicit negative evidence is required to draw to the learner's attention the fact that sentences like (5d) are not permitted in English.

2. Universal Grammar and the Subset Principle

Research in first language (L1) acquisition suggests that children either do not receive or do not take note of negative evidence (Braine 1971; Brown and Hanlon 1970) or that any available negative evidence is ineffective (Pinker 1989). Hence, any kind of grammar change in L1 acquisition must be achieved mainly or exclusively on the basis of positive evidence, and incorrect hypotheses must be disconfirmable on the basis of positive evidence. In other words, children must not get themselves into the kind of situation shown in (4).

In the L1 acquisition and learnability literature, there are a number of proposals which have the effect of preventing L1 learners from arriving at overinclusive grammars from which they could retreat only via negative evidence. Firstly, the *types* of hypotheses entertained by the child are constrained via Universal Grammar (UG). Secondly, the *order* of hypotheses is constrained by a learning principle known as the subset principle (Berwick 1985; Manzini and Wexler 1987; Wexler and Manzini 1987), which has the effect that the child's initial hypotheses are conservative.

Constraints on *wh* movement provide an example of the first kind, that is of UG limiting the types of hypotheses that language learners make. Children are exposed to data which indicate that questions can be formed by moving *wh* elements to the front of the sentence, as in (6):

(6)   What did Mary see _ ?

This can be extended to more complex sentences, as in (7):

(7)   a.   What did John think (that) Mary saw _ ?
       b.   What did Jane say (that) John thought (that) Mary saw _ ?

However, in certain cases the *wh* word cannot be extracted, as in (8):

(8)   a. *What did John believe the claim (that) Mary saw _ ?
       b. *What did John wonder whether Mary saw _ ?

How do children come to know the prohibitions on *wh* movement? One possibility is that they make errors like (8a,b) and are then told that such sentences are not possible, i.e. that they arrive at the correct facts on the basis of negative evidence. Two factors suggest that this cannot be the source of their knowledge. Firstly, as mentioned above, children are not reliably given negative evidence. Secondly, and more important, L1 learners unconsciously know a number of extremely subtle and complex phenomena, such as the constraints on *wh* movement, without making the relevant errors in the first place. If learners do not make the relevant errors, then no amount of negative evidence will be useful.

Instead, children are assumed to have built in knowledge of UG, including the subjacency principle which places constraints on *wh* movement, so that they never assume a grammar in which sentences like (8a,b) are possible. Thus, UG provides one way in which the child's approach to language is constrained: certain logical possibilities are never entertained and so the question of what kind of evidence might remove them does not even arise.

However, even granted such principles, L1 learners may still get themselves into situation (4) unless some means can be found to order their hypotheses. This is where the subset principle plays a role. In recent versions of generative grammar, it is assumed that many principles of UG are parameterized, varying in their effects from language to language (e.g. Chomsky 1981, 1986). Thus one cannot, in principle, rule out certain possibilities within UG, and yet one might need to guarantee that children try out the possibilities in one order rather than another because one ordering would result in the need for negative evidence whereas the other would not.

An illustration is provided by the null subject (or prodrop) parameter. There are a number of languages, such as Spanish and Italian, which allow sentences without overt subject pronouns, and a range of properties cluster with this phenomenon. Other languages, like English, require overt subjects and do not have the other properties. To account for this variation, UG is assumed to contain a parameter which can be set as either [+null subject] or [−null subject], allowing or excluding sentences without overt subjects (Chomsky 1981).

The problem for the language learner is as follows: there is some input which is consistent with both [+null subject] and [−null subject] languages, and which could mislead the learner into making the wrong choice. Both [+null subject] and [−null subject] languages allow lexical pronouns, but only [+null subject] languages allow subject pronouns to be omitted.[3] Suppose that the language learner, on hearing a sentence with a lexical pronoun, decides that he is learning a [+null subject] language and sets the parameter this way, generating sentences without overt pronoun subjects. This is problematic if the target language is a [−null subject] language, because it will result in sentences with missing subjects, which are not permitted; negative evidence will then be required to set the parameter to [−null subject].

If the language learner starts off with the most conservative hypothesis compatible with the input data, then a solution to this problem is achieved. This is effected by the subset principle, a learning principle which says that, given input which is compatible with more than one grammar, the learner will adopt the most restrictive grammar consistent with that data, i.e. the grammar which generates the narrowest language. A more general grammar will only be adopted when explicit evidence is available as to the appropriateness of that grammar. Thus the learner starts off with the grammar whose output is a subset of the sentences generated by the more general grammar. In other words, the learner will start off with a situation like (1), where, if necessary, positive evidence can motivate a change from the narrower grammar to a broader one, rather than (4), where negative evidence is required to go from a broader grammar to a narrower one. In the case of the above example, since the [−null subject] value of the parameter generates a subset of the sentences allowed by the [+null subject] setting, the learner will start off with the [−null subject] value and only change the value to [+null subject] when faced with explicit positive evidence, in the form of sentences without overt subjects.[4]

3.   A Potential Role for Negative Data in L2 Acquisition

We have seen that in L1 acquisition linguistic principles (UG) guarantee that the child's hypotheses about language are constrained in appropriate ways and the subset principle guarantees that hypotheses will be entertained in a particular order. Together these prevent learners from getting into situation (4) and they do away with the need for negative data.

In L2 acquisition, on the other hand, a number of situations arise where learners find themselves in situation (4). That is, the learner fails to start off with the narrowest grammar consistent with the L2 data, and instead internalizes a grammar which generates a superset of the sentences actually allowed by the L2, suggesting that the subset principle is not operating. In these circumstances, negative evidence may be required at some point if an L2-like grammar is to be achieved.

Certain cases of L1 transfer lead to exactly this situation. If the L2 learner transfers an L1 rule or parameter setting, or uses L1 data as input to the interlanguage grammar, and if this L1 rule generates language which is a superset of that actually found in the L2, then the result will be as shown in (9), i.e. a situation analogous to (4), in which negative evidence is required to retreat from the overinclusive hypothesis:[5]

(9)

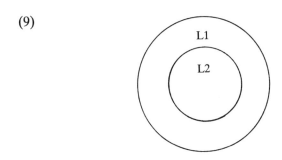

As an illustration, we can reconsider the null subject parameter. It has been suggested above that the [+] value of the parameter generates a superset of sentences allowed by the [−] value. Native speakers of Spanish (+null subject) learning English (−null subject) assume that the L1 value of the parameter is appropriate for L2 and that English allows sentences without overt subjects (Hilles 1986; Phinney 1987; White 1985, 1986a). They are, therefore, in the situation illustrated in (9).

What kind of evidence can disconfirm this incorrect hypothesis about the L2? Positive evidence alone appears to be insufficient: there is no positive evidence which says that English does not allow null subjects. The presence of explicit subject pronouns is, after all, consistent with both types of language. Here is a case, then, where we might be able to put L2 learners onto the right track by pointing out that certain things are *not* possible in the L2, i.e. by supplying them with negative evidence, evidence that sentences like (10) are ungrammatical in English:[6]

(10) *John eats too much. Is very fat.

Other cases are discussed by Bley-Vroman (1986), Rutherford (1987), White (1986b, 1987, 1989a), Zobl (1988). These include cases like the adjacency condition on case assignment, where French allows a superset of the sentences allowed by English, in that it allows adverbs to appear between verb and direct object as well as after the direct object, as can be seen in (11):

(11) a. John drinks his coffee quickly
     b. *John drinks quickly his coffee
     c. Jean boit le café rapidement
     d. Jean boit rapidement le café

French learners of English who assume that sentences like (11b) are grammatical will not encounter positive evidence to show that this is not the case. Other examples involve preposition stranding and the double object structure, where English allows a superset of the sentences found in French, as shown in (12) and (13). Here, potential problems arise for English learners of French who assume that (12d) and (13d) are grammatical.

(12) a. To whom did John give the book?
     b. Who did John give the book to?
     c. A qui Jean a-t-il donné le livre?
     d. *Qui Jean a-t-il donné le livre à?

(13) a. John gave the book to Mary
    b. John gave Mary the book
    c. Jean a donné le livre à Marie
    d. *Jean a donné Marie le livre

Such cases suggest that L2 acquisition sometimes involves the adoption of overinclusive grammars and, hence, that negative data may be required for disconfirmation, unlike the situation in L1 acquisition.

4. The Form of Negative Evidence

So far, it has been suggested that L2 learners get themselves into situations where negative data are necessary for disconfirmation. That is to say, if they are eventually to arrive at the narrower grammar which is appropriate for the L2, having postulated an overly general grammar on the basis of the L1, they will not be able to change from the overinclusive grammar to the narrower grammar unless someone indicates to them that certain sentences are ungrammatical in the target language. This does not mean, however, that L2 learners will necessarily be able to make use of such evidence: this is an empirical question. The point is that such evidence might be beneficial in just these circumstances.

There is, of course, the possibility that in some of the cases where over-inclusive grammars have been adopted, alternative sources of positive evidence in fact exist which could lead to grammar change. For example, in the cases where parameters of UG are involved, it is usually assumed that a parameter involves a cluster of related properties and it is possible that positive evidence from some other property within a cluster will eventually lead to change (in other words, some cases of situation (4) turn out to be cases of (3)). It is also possible that appropriate positive evidence is to be found in some other aspect of the grammar, with phonological evidence having effects on syntax, etc. Zobl (1988) points out that as learners become more proficient, parsing considerations force them to take additional data into consideration, leading them to replace a grammar which generates a superset with one which generates a subset. All of these proposals are reasonable, and, if pursued, can increase our understanding of how grammar change can be achieved without negative evidence. However, unless one can show that *every* case of situation (4) is amenable to disconfirmation via later sources of positive evidence, the learnability problem remains. That is, there will be cases where negative evidence is required for disconfirmation. Let us, therefore, consider the form that such disconfirming evidence might take.

Differences between the potential effectiveness of correction, explicit grammar teaching and other forms of consciousness raising (Rutherford 1987) will not be discussed here. The point at issue is the fact that in those cases where negative evidence is required on learnability grounds, this evidence has to be quite specific, in some way focussing the learner's attention on the relevant properties of the L2 input, on the ungrammaticality of certain sentence types.

There have been a number of proposals in the literature that certain types of negative data are available to both L1 and L2 learners in natural input, i.e. they do not depend on the presence of explicit instruction. However, such evidence is problematic as a means of eradicating overgeneral hypotheses, since it is often vague and its occurrence is unreliable. For example, Hirsh-Pasek *et al.* (1984) argue that mothers repeat (and in the process correct) young children's ungrammatical forms more often than their grammatical ones. Such repetitions are a questionable source of negative evidence unless the learner can be sure that every repetition signals an incorrect form, which is not the case, or can tell which repetitions are meant to count as corrections. Schachter (1984) suggests that various kinds of communication failure, such as failure to be understood, could serve as negative evidence but this suffers from the problem of not being specific enough. If a learner is misunderstood, there could be many bases for that misunderstanding: phonology, vocabulary choice, incorrect syntactic or morphological form, etc. Furthermore, it is not even clear that the kinds of cases I have been discussing will actually lead to misunderstanding anyway.

Another possible source of negative data from outside the classroom is so-called indirect negative evidence, the assumption that learners simply notice the non-occurrence of certain sentence types. The idea is that if the learner does not hear evidence of a particular form, he will conclude that the form is not allowed. Sometimes this works, particularly if the learner has some kind of expectancy that certain structures will show up. If a particular form is expected, its non-occurrence in that context could be taken as evidence as to its ungrammaticality. For example, a learner whose L1 is a null subject language like Spanish may expect null subjects when certain discourse conditions are fulfilled. Meeting these conditions in an L2 like English but hearing explicit pronoun subjects might be sufficient to indicate the non-occurrence of empty subjects in English.[7]

However, in many cases involving overinclusive grammars, there does not seem to be an appropriate expectation associated with only one of the possible forms, so that indirect negative evidence could not work. In addition, there are cases which suggest that learners do not make appropriate use of such evidence even when they notice non-occurrence. Bley-Vroman (1986) discusses learners who, on the basis of the situation in the L1, assume that the English word *hello* means both *hello* and *goodbye*. One of these learners reported that although he had noticed that Americans did not say *hello* when they meant *goodbye*, he nevertheless assumed it to be a possible variant. In other words, he did not change his incorrect lexical entry even though he had noticed the non-use of the term in question.

More problematical for the indirect negative evidence idea are cases where learners do not even notice the absence of the relevant forms. I know of no research which addresses this question directly; to do this it would be necessary to study learners who could be said to have completed the learning process, since it is always possible that noticing the non-occurrence of certain forms might occur at a late stage of L2 development, and who could be shown not to have received more explicit forms of negative evidence. However, any research which shows that L2 learners accept superset forms which are disallowed in the L2 (e.g. Bley-Vroman 1986; White 1989a; Zobl 1988) suggests that indirect negative evidence is not made use of, especially in the cases where learners are advanced or have been exposed to the L2 for a long time.

In any case, one needs to be very careful about this kind of proposal, since it could undo many things that learners actually achieve. Learners make many generalizations, both correct and incorrect, which go beyond the primary data, something that the indirect negative evidence proposal would preclude. It seems, then, that though alternative sources of negative data are sometimes available in the acquisition context, these sources are insufficiently reliable to guarantee that the L2 learner will be able to make use of them.

5.   Is L2 Acquisition Like L1 Acquisition?

Negative evidence is often associated with certain kinds of hypothesis testing models of acquisition, where the language learner is assumed to entertain a wide range of hypotheses about the target language, and to subject these hypotheses to confirmation and disconfirmation. In order to home in on the target, negative data play a crucial role. We have already seen that the assumption in the L1 learnability literature is that L1 acquisition cannot be of this type because (a) children do not get suitable negative evidence and (b) they don't make the full range of errors that would be predicted under this approach anyway.

Although arguing from opposite positions, Bley-Vroman (1989) and Schwartz (1987) both assume that the availability of negative data in L2 acquisition implies that L1 and L2 acquisition are not alike. Bley-Vroman argues that because L2 learners get negative evidence, their mode of learning must be essentially different from L1 learners, i.e. that they do in fact learn by hypothesis testing, rather than being constrained by UG.[8] In contrast, Schwartz assumes that L2 acquisition is guided by UG in exactly the same way as it operates in L1 acquisition and therefore she denies that negative data can serve any useful role in L2 acquisition. A similar assumption underlies Krashen's emphasis on comprehensible input, which consists only of positive evidence (e.g. Krashen 1985).

Both these assumptions involve a fundamental misconception. While it is true that hypothesis testing requires negative evidence and UG does not, the converse does not follow; the existence or use of negative evidence does not logically imply that UG has been replaced by hypothesis testing. Recall that the major argument in favour of UG is that L1 learners unconsciously know a number of extremely subtle and complex phenomena without making the relevant errors in the first place. This is also true in L2 acquisition. There are all sorts of errors that L2 learners do not make; they do not change into unconstrained hypothesis testers just because they happen to get negative data; they do not start making "wild" hypotheses in L2 acquisition but appear to be constrained by principles of UG such as subjacency (Ritchie 1978; White 1988).

The situations I have outlined above, where I have suggested a useful role for negative data in L2 acquisition, represent a quite restricted range of problems, relating to the ordering of hypotheses. Where learners have adopted grammars which generate a superset, these are nevertheless "possible" grammars, in the sense that they are found in the world's languages, and they do not represent cases of unconstrained hypothesis testing. The fact that L2 learners might find negative evidence, or other forms of consciousness raising, useful in these circumstances does not mean that their whole mode of learning is different.

However, I do not believe that L1 and L2 acquisition are totally identical, and one of the ways in which they are not identical appears to be that the subset principle does not operate successfully in L2 acquisition. Although many L2 learners do not achieve a state which is identical to that of a native speaker, they will nevertheless internalize a complex grammar which allows them to make effective use of the L2; superset errors do not, after all, lead to output which is incomprehensible.

6.   Conclusion

In conclusion, current theories of language learnability identify situations which seem to require negative evidence and these are avoided for L1 acquisition by the assumption that learning is guided by the subset principle. L2 learners do not observe this principle but adopt grammars which generate a superset of the structures actually allowed. This suggests that there are cases where negative evidence or grammar teaching will be of benefit in drawing the learner's attention to the actual properties of the L2 input. It does not mean that L2 learners approach language learning in a totally different way from L1 learners. The idea that negative evidence may be helpful is a testable hypothesis. One can identify situations where learners adopt overinclusive grammars: in such circumstances, learners who are given explicit instruction on the points in question should ultimately fare better than learners who only get positive evidence. (For recent experimental evidence supporting this claim, see Tomasello and Herron (1988), White (1989b).)

Notes

1.   I should like to thank Kevin Gregg for his comments and suggestions. This research was conducted with the aid of the following research grants: grant no. 410-87-1071 from the Social Sciences and Humanities Research Council of Canada and grant no. 88 EQ 3630 from the Government of Québec Formation de Chercheurs et l'Aide à la Recherche.

This paper was one of four presented at the Symposium of the AILA Scientific Commission on Second Language Acquisition on *The Role, in Second Language Acquisition, of Explicit Metalinguistic Knowledge or Instruction*, convened by Patsy Lightbown. The other presentations were by Birgit Harley on "Functional grammar in French immersion: a classroom experiment", Manfred Pienemann on "Determining the influence of instruction on L2 speech processing" and William Rutherford on "Learnability, second language acquisition and explicit metalinguistic knowledge".

2. This raises the issue of why learners often fail to notice positive evidence that has been present in the input all along, a question I will not address here.

3. In null subject languages, discourse constraints are involved in determining when pronouns are overtly present.

4. A number of authors have argued on learnability grounds that [−prodrop] is the narrower grammar, and hence must be the initial, unmarked assumption (e.g. Berwick 1985; White 1986b). See Hyams (1986) for arguments that [+prodrop] is in fact the unmarked case. (Note that her arguments do not depend on the subset principle.)

5. I do not wish to imply that the L1 is the only candidate source of superset hypotheses in L2 acquisition. See Bley-Vroman (1986) for examples that are not based on the learner's L1 and Zobl (1988) for cases where properties of the L2 input can mislead the learner into inappropriately choosing a grammar which generates a superset.

6. Kevin Gregg (personal communication) points out that negative evidence can be phrased in entirely positive terms; information such as "English sentences must have subjects" contains negative evidence. See Rutherford (1987) for related discussion, and various types of consciousness raising that could help draw the learner's attention to the fact that English is not a prodrop language.

7. I am indebted to Bill Littlewood for this example.

8. However, this is only one of his arguments in favour of L2 learning as a form of hypothesis testing.

References

Baker, C. 1979. "Syntactic Theory and the Projection Problem". *Linguistic Inquiry* 10. 533-581.

Berwick, R. 1985. *The Acquisition of Syntactic Knowledge*. Cambridge, MA: MIT Press.

Bley-Vroman, R. 1986. "Hypothesis Testing in Second-Language Acquisition Theory". *Language Learning* 36. 353-376.

———. 1989. "The Logical Problem of Foreign Language Learning". *Linguistic Perspectives on Second Language Acquisition* ed. by S. Gass & J. Schachter, 41-68. Cambridge, U.K.: Cambridge University Press.

Braine, M. 1971. "On Two Types of Models of the Internalization of Grammars". *The Ontogenesis of Grammar* ed. by D. Slobin, 153-186. New York: Academic Press.

Brown, R. & C. Hanlon. 1970. "Derivational Complexity and the Order of Acquisition of Child Speech". *Cognition and the Development of Language* ed. by J.R. Hayes, 11-53. New York: Wiley.

Chomsky, N. 1981. *Lectures on Government and Binding*. Dordrecht: Foris.

———. 1986. *Knowledge of Language: Its nature, origin and use*. New York: Praeger.

Hilles, S. 1986. "Interlanguage and the Pro-drop Parameter". *Second Language Research* 2. 33-52.

Hirsh-Pasek, K., R. Treiman & M. Schneiderman. 1984. "Brown and Hanlon Revisited: Mother's sensitivity to ungrammatical forms". *Journal of Child Language* 11. 81-88.

Hyams, N. 1986. *Language Acquisition and the Theory of Parameters.* Dordrecht: Reidel.

Krashen, S. 1985. *The Input Hypothesis: Issues and implications.* London: Longman.

Manzini, R. & K. Wexler. 1987. "Parameters, Binding Theory, and Learnability". *Linguistic Inquiry* 18. 413-444.

Phinney, M. 1987. "The Prodrop Parameter in Second Language Acquisition". *Parameter Setting* ed. by T. Roeper & E. Williams, 221-238. Dordrecht: Reidel.

Pinker, S. 1989. *Learnability and Cognition: The acquisition of argument structure.* Cambrdige, MA: MIT Press.

Ritchie, W. 1978. "The Right Roof Constraint in an Adult-Acquired Language". *Second Language Acquisition Research* ed. by W. Ritchie, 33-63. New York: Academic Press.

Rutherford, W. 1987. *Second Language Grammar: Learning and teaching.* London: Longman.

Schachter, J. 1984. "A Universal Input Condition". *Language Universals and Second Language Acquisition* ed. by W. Rutherford, 167-183. Amsterdam: John Benjamins.

Schwartz, B. 1987. "Ruling Out Negative Evidence in Second Language Acquisition". Paper presented at SLRF, Los Angeles, February.

Tomasello, M. & C. Herron. 1988. "Down the Garden Path: Inducing and correcting overgeneralizations in the foreign language classroom". *Applied Psycholinguistics* 9.237-246.

Wexler, K. & R. Manzini. 1987. "Parameters and Learnability in Binding Theory". *Parameter Setting* ed. by T. Roeper & E. Williams, 41-76. Dordrecht: Reidel.

White, L. 1985. "The 'Pro-drop' Parameter in Adult Second Language Acquisition". *Language Learning* 35. 47-62.

———. 1986a. "Implications of Parametric Variation for Adult Second Language Acquisition: An investigation of the pro-drop parameter". *Experimental Approaches to Second Language Learning* ed. by V. Cook, 55-72. Oxford: Pergamon.

———. 1986b. "Markedness and Parameter Setting: Some implications for a theory of adult second language acquisition". *Markedness* ed. by F. Eckman *et al.*, 309-327. New York: Plenum Press.

———. 1987. "Against Comprehensible Input: The input hypothesis and the development of L2 competence". *Applied Linguistics* 8. 95-110.

———. 1988. "Island Effects in Second Language Acquisition". *Linguistic Theory in Second Language Acquisition* ed. by S. Flynn & W. O'Neil, 144-172. Dordrecht: Reidel.

———. 1989a. "The Principle of Adjacency in Second Language Acquisition: Do L2 learners observe the subset principle?" *Linguistic Perspectives on Second Language Acquisition* ed. by S. Gass & J. Schachter, 134-158. Cambridge, U.K.: Cambridge University Press.

———. 1989b. "The Verb-Movement Parameter in Second Language Acquisition: Some effects of positive and negative evidence in the classroom". Paper presented at the Boston University Conference on Language Development, October.

Zobl, H. 1988. "Configurationality and the Subset Principle: The acquisition of V¹ by Japanese learners of English". *Learnability and Second Languages: A book of readings* ed. by J. Pankhurst, M. Sharwood Smith & P. Van Buren, 116-131. Dordrecht: Foris.

On the Acquisition of Word Order Rules in Swedish as a Second Language

Maria Bolander

Introduction

All four languages involved in this study are SVO- and subject-prominent languages, but the word order in the learners' mother tongues is more pragmatic than Swedish word order. Swedish has grammatical word order although the word order is not totally fixed. In certain contexts, Swedish has pragmatic options as well.

Swedish, like for example German, is often said to be a "verb-second" language, which means that when for pragmatic reasons an element other than the subject is placed in initial position the word order must be altered from S-V-X to X-V-S. This is a grammatical rule that is hard to acquire when learning Swedish as a second language (cf Hammarberg 1985).

The acquisition of the inversion rule for declarative main clauses has previously been studied by Klein and Dittmar (1979) and Clahsen, Meisel and Pienemann (1983) for German, and Hyltenstam (1978) and Dahlbäck (1981) for Swedish. In Hyltenstam's study on favourable contexts, the results, based on elicited data, did not indicate that any context is more favourable than any other. In Dahlbäck's study, on the other hand, which was also based on elicited data, it was found that the inversion rule was more often correctly applied in sentences with preposed objects than in those with preposed adverbials.

Against this background it is of interest to investigate whether spontaneous speech data might further elucidate the pattern of acquisition of the inversion rule.

Methods

This study is based on data from 60 adult learners of Swedish as a second language: 20 Finnish, 20 Polish, and 20 Spanish speaking learners. Each of these groups of 20 learners consists of 10 high level and 10 low level learners. Taking native language and proficiency level into account, we can thus distinguish 6 different learner groups: high Finnish, low Finnish, high Polish etc. The allocation of the subjects to the high level and low level groups, respectively, was done by a labour training center where the subjects were attending a course in Swedish during a 4 month period when the data was collected.

The present study is based on data of three different types: (1) free speech from a 15 minute interview conducted at the beginning and at the end of the course, (2) speech from a picture description task, and (3) an acceptability test, in which the learners were asked to judge and correct written sentences.

All declarative main clauses were divided into error-free clauses and clauses containing errors for each learner and for each of the learner groups. Furthermore, all declarative main clauses were coded with respect to (a) type of subject, (b) type of verb, (c) type of preposed element, (d) the data type (interview/picture description) and (e) the occasion for the recording.

Results and Discussion

As expected, the high level learners use more inversion structures, and show more correct applications of the inversion rule than the low level learners. No systematic differences were found between learners with different mother tongues.

An examination of the data from the two recording sessions for each individual learner and for each of the six groups showed few significant differences in the application of the inversion rule. Some of the learners produce slightly more error-free clauses at the end of the Swedish course, thereby indicating acquisition of the rule during the course, but for others the results are the opposite.

Thus, despite focussed instruction during the Swedish course, the rule seems to be acquired slowly over a long period of time, a finding that is in agreement with the results reported by Clahsen (1984) for the acquisition of the German inversion rule.

Likewise, a comparison between the interview data and data from the 'picture description task reveal only minor differences in how the rule was applied. Furthermore, the results of this study show that differences in the application of the inversion rule seem to be due to the type of constructions, and thus only indirectly to the type of task (see below on the discourse functions of the inversion clauses).

With regard to how inversion is executed, it would appear that there are no obvious and systematic differences between the native language groups, the different recording occasions and the different speech production tasks. Therefore, the present paper displays only the total numbers and relative frequencies for correct application in different contexts, i.e. the type of subject, verb, and the preposed elements, for the learners as a whole. In addition, the discourse functions of the clauses are considered.

Concerning the *subjects* of the inversion clauses, the categories examined are: (1) noun/NP:s; (2) the indefinite pronoun *man* "one"; (3) the first person pronouns *jag* "I" and *vi* "we"; (4) the second and the third person pronouns; and (5) the empty slot-filler *det* "it/there". The second and third person pronouns were grouped together as no systematic differences for these types of pronouns could be found.

The most frequent subjects in the data are the pronouns *jag/vi* "I/we", the other pronouns, and the nouns. The reason for the high number of *jag/vi* is of course the topics of the interviews: the learners do a lot of talking about their earlier lives, their home countries and so on. (It is noticeable that many of the learners are quite error-free at the very beginning of the interviews, but subsequently, when they become more involved in the conversation and focus more on their messages, they seem to forget the linguistic form.)

Thus, the first person pronouns are the most frequent, and they are

Table 1: Frequencies of inversion contexts for different types of subjects

jag/vi	"PRON"	N/NP	*det*	*man*	Total
1274	852	635	292	235	3288
0.43	0.22	0.56	0.33	0.50	0.40

Upper values — total numbers; lower values — relative frequencies of correct word order also more error-free than clauses with second and third person pronouns as subjects. However, the highest values for relative frequency of correctness are in fact obtained for nouns and the indefinite pronoun *man* "one".

As for the *verbs* in these inversion clauses the most frequent are: *vara* "be" 376; *komma* "come" 228; *kan/kunde* "can/could" 200; *tro* "think/ believe" 184; *måste* (+V) "must" (+V) 153; *gå* "go" 113; *ha* "have" + V 106; *ta* "take" 104; *finnas* "be/exist" 88; and *göra* "make/do" 72.

Ranked according to correctness, however, the order for verbs with at least 40 occurrences in inversion clauses is the following: *tycka* "think" 0.77; *komma* "come" 0.74; *tro* "think/believe" 0.59; *veta* "know" 0.54; *kan/ kunde* "can/could" 0.48; *ha* + V "have" + V 0.47; *bli* "become" 0.45; *ska/ skulle* "will/would" 0.43; *göra* "make/do" 0.41; and *finnas* "be/exist" 0.40. In this latter grouping, there are 3 verbs expressing opinion/belief and two modal auxiliaries. The high number for the verb *komma* "come" is caused by its high frequency of occurrence in the picture descriptions (cf. below).

Interestingly, the most frequent verb *vara* "be" is not among the "most correct" verbs, whereas we find verbs in this category that do not rank high in frequency, namely *veta* "know"; *bli* "become; and *ska/skulle* "will/ would". These results support similar findings from other studies (e.g. Dulay and Burt 1978; Chaudron 1985), that show that the frequency of a structure is not sufficient for successful acquisition. One explanation in this case may be differences in perceptual salience for different combinations of verbs and subjects.

The copula *vara* is very often combined with *det* "it/there". However, the relative frequency of correctness for the combination *är det* "it/there is" is 0.26, which is a rather low value compared to the similar combination *kommer det* 0.45. The semantically empty combination *är det* "is it/there" is very often pronounced very fast and unstressed, and the different sounds are often very hard to distinguish — even for native speakers (cf. Bolander and Hene 1982).

Another pronunciation of *är det*, and a more salient one, is *ä re* which is similar to a common pronunciation of *kommer det* as *komme re*. Evidence for the importance of input and pronunciation for the perception and acquisition of these combinations may be that some of the subjects use the form *re* instead of *det* in initial position too, e.g. *re tycke ja* "it think I".

Furthermore, it may also be possible that salient combinations such as *komme re* are memorized as formulas. An indication of this may be that some of the learners in this study make overgeneralizations with *komme re*, which is also the case for another frequent and very often correctly inverted combination, namely *kan man* "can one".

In order to clarify what combinations these most frequent verbs occur in, the inversion clauses were divided into three groups according to their *discourse functions*:

1. existentials/presentatives without *det* "it/there", e.g. *sen kommer ambulans* "then comes ambulance";
2. all clauses containing *det*, e.g. *så kommer de bil* "then comes there car";
3. narrative clauses with a "known" pronoun/noun as a subject, e.g. *då kom hon hit* "then came she here".

The narrative clauses are divided into two subgroups according to the type of subjects: (a) first person pronouns and (b) nouns, second/third person pronouns and the indefinite pronoun *man* "one".

For these learners, the results for correct application of the inversion

Table 2: Correctness in different types of clauses

Subjects	Existentials/ presentatives without *det*	Existentials/ narratives with *det*	Narratives	
	N/NP	*det*	*jag/vi*	N/Pron/*man*
finnas "be/exist"	1.	0.34	–	–
komma "come"	0.95	0.45	0.27	0.16
sitta "sit"	0.94	(0)	–	–
vara "be"	0.91	0.26	0.33	0.27
stå "stand"	0.83	(0.25)	–	(0)
flyga "fly"	0.78	(0.25)	(0)	(0)
gå "go"	(0.5)	0.43	0.31	0.20
ta "take"	–	(0)	0.13	0.20
klä av/på "undress/dress"	–	–	–	0.08

The values within brackets denote less than 5 occurrences.

rule show conspicuously higher values in the clauses consisting of existentials / presentatives without *det* "there", which indicates a preference to place new information towards the end of the clause. This is a tendency known from many languages, including the learners' mother tongues (cf. Givón 1983; Grzegorek 1984). Hence, an explanation of the findings in terms of transfer is also a possibility (cf. Zobi 1983).

As for the two subgroups of subject types in the narratives, the differences are small, with somewhat higher values for the first person pronouns. In clear contrast to the high values for the presentative verbs are the low values for the verbs *ta* "take" and *klä av/på* "undress/dress". One reason for the extraordinarily low value for *klä av/på* may be that many of the learners seem to have vocabulary problems in describing some of the pictures where this verb is used. Thus, the as yet unintegrated rule seems to be violated when the processing capacity is overloaded by searching for adequate lexical units. This tendency was found not only in the inversion study, but also in a study of negation (cf. Bolander 1988).

Also remarkably low are the values for the first person pronoun *jag* as subject in combination with *ta* "take". All but one of these occurrences contain frequent combinations, some of which are most formula-like, e.g. *ta tåget* "take the train" and *ta det lugnt* "take it easy". All of these combinations are frequently used in everyday speech and, perhaps, these occurrences might be seen as the result of some kind of fossilization. Very likely, such combinations are acquired early in order to handle situations in daily life. Thus, they are acquired at the SVO-stage where a great deal of effort is given to the explicit marking of the pronominal subjects, which are obligatory in Swedish, but not in the learners' mother tongues. Later, when the rule for inversion is being acquired, the combination of pronominal subject followed by verb may be highly integrated in interlanguage as S-V which restricts the syntactic inversion rule.

For these learners such a hypothesis is also supported by the results for other contexts, for example the verbs *prata* "speak" and *förstå* "understand". This formulaic patterning is the case for the inversion as well as for the negation study.

Further evidence for hypothesising an early bound S-V order for pronominal subjects may be the fact that several of these learners correct themselves in the following way: *sen går* "then goes" immediately corrected to *sen hon går* "then she goes". This may be interpreted as if the learner, when hearing his/her utterance, becomes conscious of the rule for obliga-

Table 3: Frequencies of inversion contexts for different types of proposed elements

Adverbs	PP	Objects	Subclauses	Pred	Total
1932	561	403	373	19	3288
0.36	0.35	0.82	0.19	0.35	0.40

Upper values — total numbers; lower values — relative frequencies of correct word order

tory pronominal subject, restarts and adds the subject with the dominant order S-V.

Thus, the most favourable context for the application of the inversion rule seems to be the existential or presentative constructions in which the inversion can be conceived as having a pragmatic function as well (cf. Pfaff 1986).

The results with regard to *preposed elements* are presented in Table 3.

The most frequently preposed elements are, as expected, the adverbs, followed by the prepositional phrases and the objects. The most frequent adverbs are *sen/då* "then" (967), *nu* "now" (164) and *här/där* "here/there" (164).

However, with regard to correct application of the inversion rule, clauses with preposed objects have the highest values and clauses with preposed subordinate clauses the lowest. Due to the higher degree of complexity, the results for the subordinate clauses may be said to be expected, but the high values for the objects may seem somewhat surprising. Preposed objects are often said to have low frequency in Swedish and in grammars for teaching Swedish as a second language recommendations can sometimes be found not to introduce this type of clause in the early stages of teaching.

A more detailed analysis of these clauses, however, provides some explanation for these results, since most of the object clauses are of the following type:

(1)   *de tror ja*
      "it/so think I"
(2)   *de kunde man gora*
      "it/so could one do"
(3)   *de har ja läst*
      "it have I read"
(4)   *de utnyttjade ja*
      "it made use of I"

We see that the clauses are very similar in their construction. Although all elements but *det* are varied, the clauses are very formulaic. The question is, then, whether they result from a creative rule or some kind of formulaic rule.

Inversion in this kind of clause also appears when the object is omitted:

(5) *Ø [det] kan man säja*
"Ø [it/so] can one say"

(6) *Ø [det] tycke ja*
"Ø [it/so] think I"

(7) *Ø [det] måste ja säja*
"Ø [it/so] must I say"

This "formula", then, seems to be rather well integrated in the inter-language of these learners, and appears in the Swedish of most of them.

Some kind of formulaic speech is most probably the case in the following tag-like type too:

(8) *han pratar bra spanska tycker ja*
"he speaks good Spanish think I"

(9) *de håller värme bättre menar ja*
"they keep warm better mean I"

The verbs used in this type of construction are verbs used to express personal points of view, and some of them are found among the verbs with the high values for correctness discussed earlier in the paper.

The most frequent and also most error-free of these two constructions are the clauses with preposed *det* "it/so". The most frequent subject is *jag* "I", and the correctness for this type is as high as 0.92.

To summarize so far, two tendencies are especially worth noting. Firstly, the inversion rule seems to be acquired earlier in combination with the first person pronouns than in combination with the other pronouns in nearly all contexts. This might, perhaps, be explained by some principle like the suggested "me-first-principle" or the "closeness-to-ego" principle for choosing perspective in language (see Bates and MacWhinney 1982). Another very favourable context is that of clauses containing a preposed object *det* "it/so".

For both contexts, early acquisition is highly probable due both to the learners' communicative need and frequency of input. Studies on spoken Swedish have shown that inversion-clauses preposed by the object *det* "it/ so" are highly frequent in spoken Swedish (Jörgensen 1976), and used by speakers to confirm their own or the interlocutor's utterances.

A question that remains, however, is whether there are any other error-free clauses with preposed objects except these formula-like ones. This is in fact the case; they contain different types of objects, verbs and subjects. The correctness for these clauses is 0.6, i.e. not as high as the values for the formulaic ones, but higher than for, e.g., clauses preposed by adverbs, with 0.36 (cf. Table 3).

This indicates that the rule for inversion in "object-clauses" is acquired earlier than in for example "adverb-clauses", which accords with the result of Dahlbäck's (1981) study on elicited data. One interpretation of these results may be that formula learning can be one way of acquiring abstract grammatical rules.

However, formula learning may also cause problems in the later acquisition of syntactic rules. One example of this is shown in the negation study based on the same data (Bolander 1988). In Swedish main clauses the negative particle *inte* has the marked position after the finite verb, and in the context of complex verbs this means that the particle is placed immediately before the non-finite verb. Yet, very often in early Swedish learner language the negative particle is placed before the finite verb. In fact, many of the learners in this study make very few errors in the placement of negation in main clauses, but those errors that do occur are found in the context of complex verbs and show an interesting pattern. In all but one of these occurrences, the negative particle is placed after the non-finite verb, which is a position very little discussed in earlier studies. In some of these cases the placement should probably be interpreted as constituent negation, mostly negating an object (cf. Clahsen *et al.* 1983), but many of these occurrences are of the following kind:

(10) *han kan säja inte så mycke*
      "he can say not very much"
(11) *de har blivi inte så mycke svårare*
      "it has become not very much more difficul*t*"
(12) *dom hade haft inte så många kompisar innan*
      "they had had not so many pals before"

It seems reasonable to suppose that the frequent and useful sequences *inte så mycket/många/*adjective "not very much/many/" with or without an adjective have been perceived as formulas and are used as such in processing. This pattern appears in subordinate clauses too, and, in the contexts where there is a need to split the sequence, the result is very often an error clause; even by learners who in other contexts are error-free.

Thus, the study of these 60 learners repeatedly indicates that frequent and needed sequences are learned and used as formulas and that formulaic speech is a common phenomenon (cf. Hatch 1973; Hakuta 1974). Furthermore, such sequences seem to be stored and processed as units, which sometimes prevents the application of syntactic rules which are being acquired in other contexts.

At least 10 of these 60 learners show tendencies towards what may be called "formulaic learning" in the sense that they show occurrences of all the mentioned examples of formulaic speech.

The main trends observed for the group of learners as a whole are also clearly reflected among the individual learners: the types with high values for correctness are the ones that are produced by learners with only a few correct inversion clauses, and the errors made by the advanced learners are those with low values for correctness.

As for the *awareness of the inversion rule*, there seems to be some variability among the learners. Some of them clearly indicate by correcting themselves that they are aware of the rule, and furthermore, the acceptability test indicates that, as a whole, their speech production is correlated to awareness of the rule.

Concluding Remarks

The results of this inversion study indicate that the errors observed are not totally random. There seems to be an interaction between the type of verb, the subject and the preposed elements, and moreover some contexts seem to be more favourable for the learners' application of the inversion rule.

Based on the data presented, the following generalizations can be made for order of acquisition for the inversion rule:

- FAVOURABLE CONTEXTS/EARLY ACQUIRED are: existentials/ presentatives without the empty slot-filler *det* "it/there" and clauses with preposed objects. Furthermore, clauses containing first person pronouns as subjects are more favourable than those containing second and third person pronoun subjects.
- UNFAVOURABLE CONTEXTS/LATE ACQUIRED are: clauses with preposed adverbs — especially *sen* "then/after that" —

and subordinate clauses. Also unfavourable are contexts where the speaker does not have access to adequate lexical units.

In summary, the main results of these studies on the acquisition of word order rules as interpreted here are the following:

- a functionally motivated rule is acquired earlier than a rule which is solely grammatically motivated;
- communicative needs govern acquisition and a common strategy in second language learning is to "tune in" and memorize frequent and needed sequences of words as formulas which later are sometimes hard to break for syntactic purposes.

Depending on personality and eagerness to communicate, such a strategy may more often be used by certain learners than by others.

Acknowledgements

This study is part of the project "Språkutveckling och undervisningsmodeller" (SUM), which has been financed by The Swedish National Board of Education. I would like to thank Kenneth Hyltenstam and Christopher Stroud for valuable comments on the manuscript, and Håkan Johansson for valuable and inspiring discussions around different hypotheses concerning the brain's processing of language.

References

Bates, E. & B. MacWhinney. 1982. "Functionalist Approaches to Grammar". *Language Acquisition: The state of the art* ed. by E. Wanner & L.R. Gleitman, 173-218. London: Cambridge University Press.

Bolander, M. 1988. "Is There Any Order? On word order in Swedish learner language". *Journal of Multilingual and Multicultural Development* 9(1&2). 97-113.

Bolander, M. & B. Hene. 1982. "'Hä gå bra dä!' Varianter till *det* i regionalt standardspråk i Arvidsjaur". *Nordsvenska* ed. by C.C. Elert & S. Fries. Umeå: Acta Universitatis Umensis.

Chaudron, C. 1985. "Comprehension, Comprehensibility, and Learning in the Second Language Classroom". *Studies in Second Language Acquisition* 7. 216-232.

Clahsen, H. 1984. The Acquisition of German Word Order: A test case for cognitive approaches to L2 development". *Second Languages: A cross-linguistic perspective* ed. by R.W. Andersen, 219-242. Rowley, Mass.: Newbury House Publishers.

Clahsen, H., J.M. Meisel & M. Pienemann. 1983. *Deutsch als Zweitsprache. Der spracherwerb ausländischer arbeiter*. Tübingen: Gunter Narr.

Dahlbäck, H. 1981. "Datatyp och interimspråkskompetens 1. En variationsanalys av olika slags testdata på inversion och rak ordföljd i invandrares svenska". University of Lund: Department of Linguistics.

Dulay, H. & M. Burt. 1978. "Some Remarks on Creativity in Language Acquisition". *Second Language Acquisition Research: Issues and implications* ed. by W.C. Ritchie, 65-89. New York: Academic Press, Inc.

Givón, T. (ed.). 1983. *Topic Continuity in Discourse. A quantitative cross-linguistic study*. Amsterdam/Philadelphia: John Benjamins Publishing Company.

Grzegorek, M. 1984. *Thematization in English and Polish. A study in word order*. Poznan: UAM.

Hakuta, K. 1974. "Prefabricated Patterns and the Emergence of Structure in Second Language Acquisition". *Language learning* 24. 287-297.

Hammarberg, B. 1985. "Learnability and Learner Strategies in Second Language Syntax and Phonology". *Modelling and Assessing Second Language Acquisition* ed. by K. Hyltenstam & M. Pienemann, 153-175. Avon: Multilingual Matters.

Hatch, E. 1973. "Second Language Learning — Universals?" *Working Papers on Bilingualism* 3. 1-18.

Hyltenstam, K. 1978. "Variation in Interlanguage Syntax". *Working Papers* 18. Lund: Department of General Linguistics.

Jörgensen, N. 1976. *Meningsbyggnaden i talad svenska*. Lund: Studentlitteratur.

Klein, W. & N. Dittmar. 1979. *Developing Grammars*. Berlin/Heidelberg: Springer-Verlag.

Pfaff, C.W. 1986. "Functional Approaches to Interlanguage". *First and Second Language Acquisition Processes* ed. by C.W. Pfaff, 81-102. Cambridge: Newbury House.

Zobl, H. 1983. "L1 Acquisition, Age of L2 Acquisition, and the Learning of Word Order". *Language Transfer in Language Learning* ed. by S. Gass & L. Selinker, 205-221. Rowley, Mass: Newbury House.

A Crossover Effect in Interlanguage: Learners' Use of English Predicate Complement Constructions

Helen Borland

Introduction

The application of variability analysis techniques to the study of learner's language has enabled us to achieve a much greater understanding of the process of second language acquisition (Dickerson 1975; Hyltenstam 1977, 1984; Borland 1985). By studying individual learners and groups of learners at different points in the process of learning second languages, it has been possible to determine sequences of development within discrete areas of the syntax of the language being learned (e.g. Hyltenstam 1977, 1984). By comparing the patterns obtained on various elicitation tasks, a greater understanding of one aspect of learners' variable application of second language rules, style shifting, has been achieved (Tarone 1983; Schmidt 1977). Using implicational techniques in preference to the more traditional morpheme order approach, more comprehensive insights have been gained into the learning of different grammatical morphemes in relation to each other (Andersen 1977; Borland 1983). All these aspects of variation and their explanation have been thoughtfully discussed in recent papers by Ellis (1985) and Schachter (1986).

The use of variability analysis techniques, however, needs to be reassessed in the light of our understanding of the developmental process, primarily gained through detailed longitudinal study of a relatively small number of learners (Cazden, Cancino, Rosansky and Schumann 1975; Hansen-Bede 1975; Pienemann 1980; Nicholas 1985). These studies have indicated that development is not always unidirectionally towards target forms. Learning appears to be a sophisticated type of sorting process in which the learner, starting from a simple grammar, acquires a rule of the second language, but applies the rule to a number of environments in which its application is not appropriate. At later stages the application of the rule is modified, until ideally its application conforms to that in the language of native speakers. Such observation of the acquisition process suggests that the relationship between the realisation of a form in a number of environments (for example, the copula), or of a number of related forms in their respective environments (for example, negation, in which the negator is placed after the appropriate form of the auxiliary) may not always be constant and, thus, will not show an invariant implicational hierarchy. If variability analysis is to be a valuable tool in the study of second language development in areas of the grammar where such phenomena may be manifest then it must be able to reveal the existence of such non-uniform relationships and be able to cope adequately with their description.

Recent work on the use of predicate complement constructions has brought to light such a case and the intention of this paper is to demonstrate that, when a number of interrelated, variability analysis techniques are carefully employed, such aspects of the SLA developmental process, far from being obscured, are actually able to be extremely clearly observed.

Predicate Complementation in English

All English predicate complement constructions share a common property, that of being marked by a unique set of complementisers (Rosenbaum 1967). The THAT complementiser is used to introduce *finite* predicate complement constructions (sentence 1), the FOR-TO complementiser to introduce the more common of the two non-finite predicate complement constructions (sentence 2), and the gerund complementiser, POSS-ING, to introduce the second non-finite predicate complement (sentence 3).

(1)   John knows that he is going to France this summer.
(2)   John wants to go to France this summer.
(3)   John will enjoy going to France this summer.

The choice of complementiser is largely dictated by the verb in the main clause under which the predicate complement is subordinated. Some verbs can take complements of all three types, for example *believe* or *like* (although usually one or two of the possible types are more common), whilst others require one particular means of complement formation obligatorily,

for example *enjoy*. In addition to complementing verbs, predicate complements can complement predicative adjectives (sentences 4, 5 and 6).[1]

(4)   Mary is glad (that) she went.
(5)   Her mother was happy to see her again.
(6)   I'm sad about leaving so soon.

In more colloquial language the THAT complementiser, and POSS in the
POSS-ING type are deleted.

The Subjects

Sixty-eight recently-arrived adolescent immigrants attending Melbourne
secondary schools were selected to undertake a task designed to elicit evidence of their use of predicate complement constructions. All were receiving specialised ESL instruction, although the amount offered varied to a
certain extent from school to school. The full range of predicate complement constructions are rarely taught systematically in such programmes.

At Time 1 the subjects' length of residence ranged from 1 to 27
months, with the average length of residence being 8.6 months. Age on
arrival in Australia ranged from 10.5 to 17.6 years, with the average age on
arrival being 13 years.

The 68 learners divided into three groups according to their native language. Twenty-one learners spoke Spanish as their native language, 22 Russian and 25 Vietnamese. The participation of three such subgroups enabled
the possibility of comparison of learning by learners from vastly different
native language backgrounds.

Predicate Complementation in the Subjects' First Languages

All three native languages have means of expressing predicate complementation.

Spanish has the equivalent of the THAT type finite complement construction, *que*, but unlike English this is generally restricted to use in cases
where the main clause subject is not the same as the subject in the subordinate clause. The non-finite infinitive complement, sometimes accompanied
by the preposition *de*, is generally used in cases where the main and subor-

dinate clause subjects are identical.

Russian, similarly, possesses the two basic means of expressing predicate complementation; using the finite complementiser *shto* "that", and the infinitive verbal suffix *-t'* for the non-finite complement. Whilst the non-finite means of forming predicate complement constructions can be used only when the subjects in the main and subordinate clauses are identical, the finite means can be used also when the subjects are not identical. The additional complementisers *shtoby* and *kak* are used to form finite complement constructions with certain verb types.

Finite complementation in Vietnamese is formed by use of the complementiser *rằng* or less commonly *là*. Such complement constructions are possible regardless of the relationship between the subjects in the main and subordinate clauses; the use of the means of complementation is dictated by the main clause verb. The non-finite means of complementation, since Vietnamese does not possess an equivalent to an infinitive marker, is the base verb form. As in English it can be used regardless of the relationship between the subjects in the main and subordinate clauses, the indicator of syntactic relationships within the sentence being word order. By using the time relationship particle, *dang*, to denote an incomplete action preceding the complement verb it is also possible in Vietnamese to express a complement not dissimilar to the English gerund complement.

The Task

A sentence correction task was used to elicit evidence of the learners' formation of predicate complement constructions. On each of four separate test occasions, at roughly two monthly intervals, the learners were asked to correct 27 sentences containing examples of incorrect predicate complement constructions. These 27 sentences, 9 each for each target means of complementation, formed part of a larger correction task containing 189 sentences with errors covering a large range of English syntax. This ensured that the learners' attention was not exclusively focussed on any one particular aspect of syntax and thus, that the task was not a discrete point one.

The learners were instructed (with written instructions provided in their native language) to read each sentence and decide if they thought it to be *good* English. If they considered it to be correct they were required to place a tick (√) beside the sentence. If they considered it not to be good

English they were required to correct it in the same way as the teacher corrects their work (i.e. by deleting from, adding to, and altering the sentence as necessary).

A controlled elicitation task was necessary in order to ensure that sufficient occurrences of each complement type were obtained to enable the analysis of the learners' knowledge of English predicate complement constructions. In spontaneous tasks the phenomenon of avoidance is well-documented (Schachter 1974; Kleinmann 1977). It appears to be particularly common in the case of complex constructions, since such constructions can always be expressed alternatively using simple sentences. In devising the sentences containing deviant predicate complements, care was taken to choose forms which were representative of the types of errors generally found in learners' language for these constructions. This information was obtained by analysis of the learners' written work and responses to pilot tests. In addition, as far as possible, an attempt was made to choose incorrect forms which would not overtly give the learner assistance in deciding what the correct form ought to be. In all sentences to be corrected the complementisers were deleted. This meant that for the non-finite complements the sentences contained uninflected verb forms, for example:

> Paul wants buy a bicycle (Time 1, A49)
> Jenny enjoys Karen visit her (Time 3, B67)

Devising suitable sentences for finite complementation proved much more difficult. The insertion of the THAT complementiser was not considered to be necessary, let alone obligatory, since in colloquial language it is generally not used. However, providing the uninflected verb or incorrect verb form gives some clue as to what is necessary and the responses tend to be more an indication of knowledge of verb morphology than of the appropriate means of complementation. For the THAT type the most satisfactory incorrect form was consequently to use the wrong means of complementation. This ensured that the learner could only correct to the appropriate form if he or she genuinely knew it. Many instances of sentences requiring THAT complementation were of this form with the remainder containing uninflected base verb forms.

Only simple, frequent main clause verbs were used in the task. This was to ensure that the learners' failure to choose the correct means of complementation was not merely a result of their lack of familiarity with the verb in the sentence. The verbs and predicative adjectives chosen for each complement type are listed in Appendix 1.

In assessing the learners' corrections, evidence of the correct choice of complementiser (where obligatory) and of means of complementation had to be provided by the learner's correction for it to be considered correct. In the case of non-finite complementation, either TO or ING, depending which was appropriate, had to be provided. The omission of the additional complementisers for these two types, FOR with TO and possessive with ING, both of which can be, or are always, optional in colloquial language, was not considered to make the correction unacceptable. In the case of the finite means of complementation it was not considered necessary for THAT to be provided, since this complementiser is optional and is normally omitted in less formal language. For the correction to be considered to provide evidence of the learner having made a choice to use this means of complementation there had to be clear evidence of the formation of a finite subordinate clause with a conjugated verb and, if necessary, the deletion of the infinitive, *to*.

The maximum score for each complement type was nine. Of the nine sentences for each means of complementation, six contained main clause verbs (three each for Equi and Non-Equi types) and three main clause predicative adjectives. It was possible for subjects to occasionally avoid the necessity to use the expected form or means of complementation. Such cases did not generally appear to involve the intentional avoidance of difficult aspects of complementation, but rather seemed to reflect the facility of some subjects and their ability to discern a number of alternative solutions yielding correct sentences. Such responses were excluded from the analysis and subjects' scores normalised from the other responses given.

The Results

In analysing the learner's corrections the preliminary analyses were carried out for each group as a whole.[2] A modified version of Andersen's group range method (Andersen 1977) was used with data from all four test times combined in order to be able to determine the overall pattern and to determine whether variability existed in the use of predicate complements dependent on the complement type required. For each of six score ranges, the number of subjects in that range for each complement type was calculated. These are displayed in Table 1. From this analysis the percentage of

Table 1: Group range analysis for predicate complementation

Score range	Complement type		
	THAT	TO	ING
1. *Spanish*			
0	6	19	44
1-2	15	10	15
3-4	13	9	4
4.5-6	16	8	4
7-8	17	13	3
9	5	13	2
TOTAL:	72	72	72
% ⩾ 7	30.6	36.1	6.9
% ⩾ 4.5	52.8	47.2	12.5
% ⩾ 3	70.8	59.7	18.1
2. *Russian*			
0	1	23	58
1-2	17	16	9
3-4	17	7	6
4.5-6	28	8	2
7-8	10	13	2
9	4	10	0
TOTAL:	77	77	77
% ⩾ 7	18.2	29.9	2.6
% ⩾ 4.5	54.6	40.3	5.2
% ⩾ 3	76.6	49.4	13.0
3. *Vietnamese*			
0	5	27	63
1-2	29	16	8
3-4	18	9	6
4.5-6	20	16	3
7-8	17	12	10
9	6	15	5
TOTAL:	95	95	95
% ⩾ 7	24.2	28.4	15.8
% ⩾ 4.5	45.3	45.3	19.0
% ⩾ 3	65.6	54.7	25.3

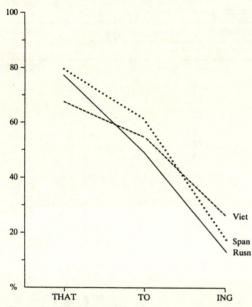

Figure 1a. Percentage of subjects in score ranges: scoring ≥ 3 for each complement type

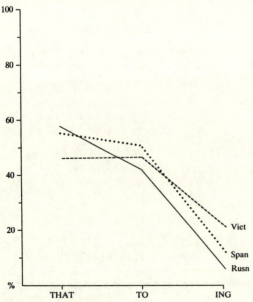

Figure 1b. Percentage of subjects in score ranges: scoring ≥ 4.5 (50%) for each complement type

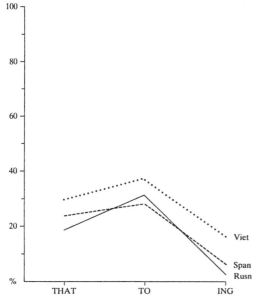

Figure 1c. Percentage of subjects in score ranges: scoring ≥ 7 for each complement type

learners in each cumulative score range can be calculated. In Table 1, in addition to the number of sets of scores in each range, the percentage of subjects scoring ≥ 7 (out of 9), ≥ 4.5 and ≥ 3 are given. These percentages are also shown in Figures 1a to 1c.

The analysis of the learners' distribution of scores across the possible score ranges reveals the following points:

1. For all groups for all sections of the group range ING is clearly the least favoured and thus most difficult of the complement types. In all cumulative score ranges the Vietnamese group has scored comparatively better on ING than the other two groups.

2. At the ≥ 3 score level all groups show a higher percentage of subjects attaining this score level for THAT than for TO.

3. At the ≥ 4.5 (50%) level the situation is the same for the Russian and Spanish groups, so that THAT is favoured over TO. In the Vietnamese group the percentage of subjects scoring ≥ 4.5 for these two types is identical.

4. For all groups for the higher score ranges (i.e. ≥ 7) there are a larger

number of subjects using TO correctly than using finite complementation with THAT correctly.

The clearly different order obtained for THAT and TO at different levels in the cumulative frequency analysis of the group range distribution for all groups suggests the possibility that the learning of these two complement types is occurring at different rates causing a reordering of the target realisation of the types in relation to each other dependent on the learners' overall accuracy level.

Scattergrams were produced which showed for each group the distribution of scores for each individual complement type against overall scores for predicate complementation (obtained by adding scores for all three types together). These scattergrams show more clearly group trends in the use of these three target means of forming predicate complement constructions in relation to each other throughout the whole range of overall scores. From the scattergram a curve was drawn which approximated the line of best fit for that group of learners for the realisation of that particular complement type in relation to complementation as a whole. By combining the three such curves obtained for each group, each representing the realisation of

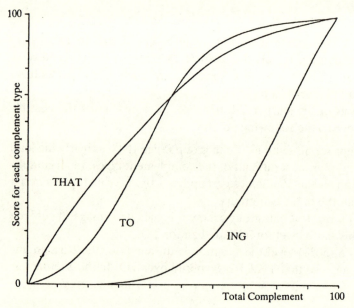

Figure 2a. Approximation curves for scores for the three types: Spanish subjects

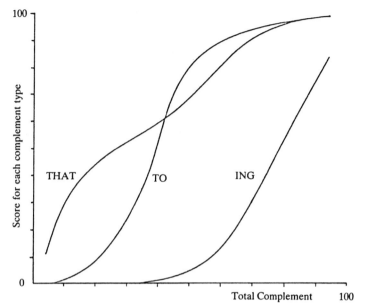

Figure 2b. Approximation curves for scores for the three types: Russian subjects

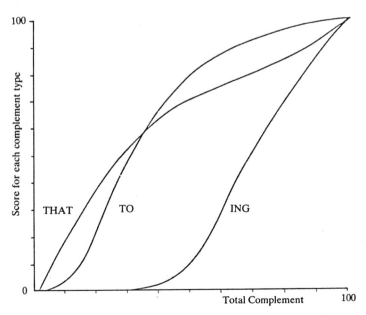

Figure 2c. Approximation curves for scores for the three types: Vietnamese subjects

one of the three types, it was possible to obtain a visual representation of the average relationships of the target realisations of three possible means of complementation. The sets of curves obtained for each group are shown in Figure 2a-2c.

These curves all show clear evidence of the crossover between the THAT and TO types which was suggested by the group range analysis. In all three groups of learners THAT appears to be the more favoured of the two types in the lower score ranges (until the total score reaches about 40%). Once the correction of the TO complement has commenced, having been less favoured initially, it appears to progress very rapidly and at total complement score 30-40% it becomes on average more favoured by learners in that score range than the THAT type. On average, the reordering appears from the curves to take place when the scores for the two individual types are each between 45% and 70%, precisely as the group range data suggested.

The results presented in previous sections indicate that, for all groups, clear trends are evident in the interrelationship of the use of the three predicate complementisers. A further important question is that of the extent to which individual learners in each group conform to such trends. To investigate this aspect of the data, implicational scaling was used.

Implicational scaling (Guttman 1944) allows the scaling of language varieties, in this case of individual learners, in terms of the accuracy of use of a number of related linguistic features, in this case the predicate complementisers THAT, TO and ING. In the simplest form of scale, each individual's responses (frequencies of occurrence) can be divided according to a binary distinction (0 or 1). The level considered to constitute a 1 can be set at any criterion from 1-100% according to what is appropriate to the purpose of the analysis. For the scale to be considered significant, individuals' responses have to conform to a high degree to stages in a theoretical implicational hierarchy, such as in Table 2 below. Such a non-random pattern, if it is evident, suggests a high degree of individual conformity with the results of the group taken as a whole. A statistic, the Coefficient of Reproducibility, enables assessment of the significance of a scale, a valid scale being indicated by a coefficient $\geq$ .90.

Using the SPSS Guttman Scale Program, data for individual subjects was scaled for each test time separately and for all four test times combined. To enable comparison with group trends, scaling was carried out for two division points (i.e. for allocating a 1 instead of a 0), $\geq$ 4 out of 9 (i.e.

Table 2: Theoretical model of bimodal scale

Variety/Speaker	Complement 1	Complement 2	Complement 3
1	1	1	1
2	1	1	0
3	1	0	0
4	0	0	0

Table 3: Values of R for complement types, using division points of 4 and 7

Group	Time	Division point - 4 Best order for all = That ≥ TO ≥ ING R	Division point - 7 Best order for all = TO ≥ THAT ≥ ING R
A: Spanish	1	.93	.93
	2	.96	.93
	3	.96	.92
	4	.92	.96
	1-4	.94	.94
B: Russian	1	1.00	.94
	2	1.00	1.00
	3	1.00	1.00
	4	1.00	.97
	1-4	1.00	.97
C: Vietnamese	1	.97	.95
	2	.97	.92
	3	.92	.97
	4	.91	.97
	1-4	.94	.95

44%) and ≥ 7 (78%). The coefficients obtained for the best implicational order of complementisers is summarised in Table 3.

These scaling coefficients indicate that the scales which produce the highest degree of reproducibility are the same for all groups at all test times considered separately and with results from all four times combined. Furthermore, the scales produced differ in the ordering of complement types dependent on the division point used. For all groups at the lower division

Table 4: Values of R for multi-valued scaling of complementation types

Group	THAT ≥ TO ≥ ING Time	R
A: Spanish	1	.97
	2	.93
	3	.92
	4	.92
	1-4	.94
B: Russian	1	.98
	2	.90
	3	.93
	4	.91
	1-4	.93
C: Vietnamese	1	.96
	2	.94
	3	.92
	4	.92
	1-4	.94

point (4) the favoured order for scaling individuals in that group is THAT ≥ TO ≥ ING, whereas at the higher division point (7) the favoured order is TO ≥ THAT ≥ ING. These results suggest a high degree of individual conformity to the group pattern, at least at this level of analysis.

This trend is further confirmed by analysis of the more sensitive multi-valued scales, in which actual scores rather than binary scores are scaled (see Table 4).

In assessing these scales, allowance was made for chance factors such as fluctuations in concentration whilst working through the large number of sentences (186 in total), so that only discrepancies in the numerical scale pattern greater than one item out of the total nine was considered a deviation from the implicational pattern. For all groups the overall best order for multi-valued scaling is THAT ≥ TO ≥ ING, reflecting the fact that a larger proportion of subjects in each group are in the lower scoring ranges, where this order is the favoured one. All Coefficients of Reproducibility are significant. However, for the Vietnamese group the order TO ≥ THAT ≥

ING produced higher coefficients at Time 3 (0.93) and Time 4 (0.96). For all groups virtually all deviations in the pattern in individuals' sets of scores arise from the ordering of THAT and TO (see Appendix 2 for actual scales).

Evidence from analyses of group trends and individuals within each group point to a clear pattern in learners' variable use of required complementisers in predicate complement constructions. In contrast to findings for some other aspects of variability in learners' language, in this case the ordering of constraints is not uniform throughout the full range of scores. All analyses indicate a crossover effect in the ordering of the THAT and TO complementisers; THAT is favoured over TO at lower overall score levels, and TO over THAT at higher overall scores (approximately > 50%).

All analyses, but in particular the multi-valued scaling, show that there are differences between groups and within each group between individuals concerning the point at which the crossover, or reordering, of the two more favoured complementisers takes place. For some subjects it appears to happen quite early in the course of the realisation of the two types (e.g. Span. 03(T2) or Rusn. 18(T1)), whereas for others it happens much later, or in a small number of cases not at all (e.g. Viet 18 and 24). All groups show an overall significant increase in average scores between Time 1 and Time 4. A closer look at the longitudinal data for individual learners indicates considerable variability in the amount and direction of their changes in scores over the four times. A small proportion actually appear to regress. Nevertheless, for each group there are subjects who make substantial progress and whose changes conform to the cross-sectionally suggested trend of the reordering of THAT and TO (e.g. Viet. 04, Span. 13, Rusn. 01). Whilst the phenomenon of reordering is well established as a trend in each of the groups, it appears that the precise point of the reordering is determined by the individuals' rate of realisation of the two types. It seems reasonable to suggest that this relates to the relative rate of acquisition of the two complementisers. Caution does need to be exercised in relating results of this type of study to the definition of acquisition sequences.

Discussion

The results reported in this study provide clear evidence of the use of related second language forms in a non-uniform implicational hierarchy. The variety of different, but related analytic techniques were able to highlight the complexities of the patterns in the use of the forms, and thus presumably in the process of development, much more accurately and revealingly than do more traditional static measurement techniques. For example, Anderson's (1978) study using a traditional accuracy order approach with an 80% criterion reported a hierarchy in which TO preceded THAT, and Simukoko's (1981) study using Guttman Scaling, but with only a 66% division point, reported a hierarchy in which THAT preceded TO, but with a number of discrepancies from the pattern. Clearly, if results of the present study are accurate, each of these studies has captured part of a much more complex picture. As the present study indicates, variability analysis techniques can capture these complexities, if they are used sensitively and exhaustively. They can be a valuable tool in the study of the use of second language forms in areas of grammar where non-uniform implicational relationships exist.

To conclude the discussion let us explore further the observed "crossover effect" and the reasons for its existence. Variationists, such as Wolfram (1973), Fasold (1973) and Bailey (1974), have discussed the phenomenon of the reordering of constraints. They consider it "a function of regular language change" (Wolfram 1973:7). According to their analyses reordering is only possible if constraints are not in their unmarked order, thus the reordering consists of a change from a marked to a less marked, or unmarked order. This type of explanation suggests that the infinitive complement is less marked than the finite complement. The gerund complement appears to be the most marked, something Mazurkewich (1987) argues for convincingly in her paper contrasting TO and ING complements.

Predicate complement constructions are syntactically necessary in the language of even quite elementary learners. Without some way of expressing such complements it is impossible to express basic needs and desires. Proto-forms of these complement constructions exist in the language of learners in early stages of learning. They are basically of two types, which roughly correspond to the two target types in English, THAT and TO. These two forms in English correspond to the two most basic means of predicate complementation exhibited in world languages, one being a finite sentential complement and the other the infinitive complement. In the early stages of a learner's language, the proto-THAT complement is formed by conjoining two sentences. Because the learner's grammar at this stage is also very primitive, the form of the verb in both main and embedded clause is likely to be the uninflected base verb form (e.g. *She want he come*). Similarly the proto-TO type also contains the uninflected base verb form (e.g. *He want buy bicycle*). It may be that of these two proto-types, one is actually the precursor of the other, or indeed that initially one is used in all Equi sentences (e.g. proto-TO) and the other in all Non-Equi sentences (e.g. proto-THAT). Unfortunately, this study could not provide the data necessary to trace the precise characteristics of these early stages of development, but it certainly suggests possible areas for further investigation. Thinking about the structure of these proto-types and of the initial pattern evident in our results, it is possible to suggest a tentative explanation for the initial favouring of THAT over TO. To produce correct THAT complementation, the learner is not required to learn any new element of grammar. In English the word 'that', which can mark the complement, is not obligatory and indeed would be inappropriate in informal language. Thus to produce a correct THAT complement the learner merely needs to produce a clause which is identical in form to those in main clauses. In contrast, to produce a correct TO complement from the sentences given for correction, not only did the learners have to decide that this form of complement was the appropriate one, but they also had to insert the infinitive marker 'to' in the appropriate position. In essence, to form a correct TO complement, the learner needs some new knowledge, whereas to form a correct THAT complement no new learning of linguistic forms is required. The cross-sectional and longitudinal data provided in the study suggest that once the learners have learned the use of the infinitive marker 'to' they progress very rapidly in extending its use, and thus the rate of acquisition of the correct form of this complement type, once started, is comparatively rapid (see for example the approximation curves). The slower progress in the THAT type in the later stages of development of the two types suggests a tendency to overgeneralise the use of the probably less marked TO type to contexts in which TO is unacceptable and THAT is obligatory. The tendency to overgeneralise the THAT type to TO contexts is much less common. These tendencies, which are observable in our subjects, have also been remarked on by Anderson (1978:101) and possibly reflect the inherent centrality of non-finite infinitive complementation in the grammar of language.

Notes

1.   All examples included here are the type in which there is identity of subjects in the main
      clause and predicate complement, the EQUI-type in Rosenbaum's (1967) analysis. For all
      examples similar sentences can be formed where there is a non-identity between subjects
      (Non-Equi-type).
      e.g.   (1)   John knows that Sue is leaving next week.
              (2)   John wants Sue to leave next week.
              (3)   John will celebrate Sue's leaving next week.
              (4)   John is glad that Sue is leaving.
              (5)   John was eager for Sue to stay longer.
              (6)   John is sad about her leaving so soon.

2.   In addition to the analyses reported here on the use of THAT, FOR-TO and POSS-ING,
      the effect of the identity or non-identity of subjects in the main clause and predicate com-
      plement was investigated. For all groups, use of the correct complementiser was more
      likely where the subject of the complement was identical to that of the main clause.
      Details of this part of the study are discussed in Borland (1983).

Appendix 1

Main clause verbs and predicative adjectives used in the complementation sentences

| | Complementiser | | |
VP Form	THAT	TO	ING
Verb	believe	want	give up
	think	ask	enjoy
	say	decide	like
	hope	expect	hate
	know	tell	stop
Predicative	sorry	angry	keen on
Adjective	unhappy	glad	sure of
	sure	happy	interested in

Appendix 2

Multi-valued implicational scales

A: SPANISH

A.1: Time 1 — Complementation Type

SUBJECT NUMBER	THAT	TO	ING
11	9	8	4.5
05	8	8	0
17	8	6	4.5
03	8	6	3
X21	7	7	2
04	3	7*	1
12	5	8*	0
13	6	2	0
16	5	1	0
02	4	1	0
X09	4	1	0
15	3	4	0
14	3	2	0
10	5	0	0
06	2	0	0
08	2	0	0
01	2	0	0
X20	2	0	0
07	0	0	0
X19	0	0	0

R = .97

A.2: Time 2 — Complementation Type

SUBJECT NUMBER	THAT	TO	ING
17	9	9	7.5
11	9	9	5
13	7	7	1
02	7	3	3
05	6	9*	1
03	4	6*	1
04	6	8*	0
12	3	7*	0
16	7	3	0
08	5	6	0
X09	4	1	0
15	2	3	0
14	2	2	0
10	4	0	0
X19	2	0	0
06	1	0	0
01	1	0	0
07	0	0	0

R = .93

A.3: Time 3 — Complementation Type

SUBJECT NUMBER	THAT	TO	ING
17	9	9	9
11	8	6	8
08	8	9	0
03	7	4	4
05	6	9*	1.5
13	6	7	1
02	6	4.5	1
16	5	4.5	1
04	7	9*	0
14	4.5	2	0
10	4	3	0
12	3	9*	0
15	3	2	0
X09	3	0	0
06	2	0	0
01	1	0	0
07	0	0	0

R = .92

A.4: Time 4 — Complementation Type

SUBJECT NUMBER	THAT	TO	ING
11	8	9	9
17	9	9	7.5
04	8	9	3
08	8	9	1
16	8	8	2
02	8	8	0
03	8	4	1
05	6	9*	6
14	6	3	1
10	6	3	1
13	5	8*	1
12	2	7*	0
15	2	5*	0
X22	3	0	0
06	1	0	0
01	0	1	0
07	0	0	0

R = .92

B: RUSSIAN

B.1: Time 1 SUBJECT NUMBER	Complementation Type		
	THAT	TO	ING
X19	9	9	7
15	8	9	3
14	8	4	6
X16	7	8	6
17	7	7	0
13	7	4	0
06	6	1	0
12	5	3	0
18	4.5	6*	0
10	4.5	2	0
09	4	2	0
22	3	2	0
02	3	1	0
01	3	1	0
03	2	2	0
04	5	0	0
X20	3	0	0
11	2	0	1
08	2	0	0
07	2	0	0
05	1	0	0

R = .98

B.2: Time 2 SUBJECT NUMBER	Complementation Type		
	THAT	TO	ING
X19	9	9	7
13	8	7	0
15	6	9*	4.5
17	6	9*	3
12	6	7	1
10	6	4.5	0
09	5	6	0
18	4.5	8*	0
14	4	6*	0
06	3	3	0
01	2	2	0
22	0	2	0
02	2	1	0
03	4.5	0	0
07	4	0	2
04	3	0	0
08	3	0	0
11	2	0	0
05	2	0	0

R = .90

B.3: Time 3 SUBJECT NUMBER	Complementation Type		
	THAT	TO	ING
13	8	9	2
17	8	8	4
15	6	9*	4
12	5	8*	1
09	4	7*	1
06	6	3	1
18	4.5	9*	0
03	6	4.5	0
01	5	4.5	0
10	4.5	3	0
22	2	1	0
14	5	0	0
08	3	0	0
04	3	0	0
02	2	0	0
05	2	0	0
07	1	0	0
11	1	0	0

R = .92

B.4: Time 4 SUBJECT NUMBER	Complementation Type		
	THAT	TO	ING
13	9	9	1
17	9	8	4
15	5	8*	3
14	4	4	1
12	7	9*	0
18	6	8*	0
01	5	8*	0
03	7	5	0
09	6	7	0
06	4.5	6*	0
10	6	2	0
07	6	1	0
05	5	1	0
08	4	1	0
X23	3	1	0
02	3	0	0
11	2	0	0
22	1	0	0
04	1	0	0

R = .91

C: VIETNAMESE

C.1: Time 1 — Complementation Type

SUBJECT NUMBER	THAT	TO	ING
20	9	9	9
02	8	9	7
11	8	9	4.5
22	8	8	3
24	9	5	7
18	9	6	0
14	6	3	2
12	2	0	2*
13	6	7	0
04	6	5	0
21	5	1	0
03	3	7*	0
19	3	3	0
23	3	1	0
X09	2	2	0
08	1	2	0
07	6	0	0
25	3	0	0
X05	3	0	0
15	2	0	0
16	2	0	0
06	2	0	0
01	2	0	0
17	1	0	0
X10	1	0	0

R = .99

C.2: Time 2 — Complementation Type

SUBJECT NUMBER	THAT	TO	ING
20	8	9	9
11	7*	9	8
24	9	6	7
18	8	5	3
02	7	8	7
22	4.5	9*	4.5
13	4	5	1
21	7	4	0
03	1	6*	0
04	4.5	4	0
14	4	4	0
06	4	1	0
07	3	2	0
19	2	2	0
23	2	1	2
01	2	1	0
X10	1	1	0
12	5	0	0
08	2	0	0
25	1	0	0
15	1	0	0
16	1	0	0
X09	0	2	0
17	0	0	0

R = .94

C.3: Time 3 — Complementation Type

SUBJECT NUMBER	THAT	TO	ING
20	8	9	9
11	8	8	9
24	8	8	8
02	5*	8	7
19	6	6	1
18	6	3	3
04	5	7*	1
13	5	6	1
22	4.5	9	4
21	7	7	0
03	2*	6	0
06	4	2	0
01	3	3	0
23	3	2	0
07	3	1	0
X09	1	4.5	0
08	1	2	0
12	3	0	0
10	1	0	0
25	1	0	0
15	1	0	0
16	1	0	0
14	0	6*	0
17	0	0	0

R = .92

C.4: Time 4 — Complementation Type

SUBJECT NUMBER	THAT	TO	ING
20	8	9	9
11	9	9	8
24	9	9	8
02	8	9	8
21	8	7	1
13	6	5	1
18	5	5	4
22	4.5	9	4.5
04	3	9*	3
06	4.5	9*	0
14	7	8	0
19	2	8*	0
01	7	1	0
03	6	6	0
07	5	3	0
23	4	3	0
08	3	4.5*	0
12	3	0	0
25	1	0	0
16	1	0	0
17	1	0	0
15	0	0	0

R = .92

References

Andersen, R.W. 1977. "The Impoverished State of Cross-Sectional Morpheme Acquisition/Accuracy Methodology". *Working Papers on Bilingualism* 14. 47-82.

Anderson, J. 1978. "Order of Difficulty in Adult Second Language Acquisition". *Second Language Research: Issues and implications* ed. by W. Ritchie, 91-108. New York: Academic Press.

Bailey, C.-J.N. 1974. *Variation and Linguistic Theory*. Washington, D.C.: Georgetown University Press.

Borland, H. 1983. "The Acquisition of Some Features of English Syntax by Four Groups of Adolescent Migrants to Australia". Unpublished PhD Thesis, University of Edinburgh.

———. 1985. "Constraints on Copula Realization in Learners' Language". *Australian Review of Applied Linguistics* 8(1). 87-104.

Cazden, C.B., H. Cancino, E. Rosansky & J. Schumann. 1975. *Second Language Acquisition Sequences in Children, Adolescents and Adults*. Final Report to National Institute of Education.

Dickerson, L.J. 1975. "The Learner's Interlanguage as a System of Variable Rules". *TESOL Quarterly* 9. 401-407.

Ellis, R. 1985. "Sources of Variability in Interlanguage". *Applied Linguistics* 6. 118-131.

Fasold, R.W. 1973. "The Concept of 'Earlier-Later': More or less correct". *New Ways of Analysing Variation in English* ed. by C.-J.N Bailey & R.W. Shuy, 183-197. Washington, D.C.: Georgetown University Press.

Guttman, L. 1944. "A Basis for Scaling Quantitative Data". *American Sociological Review* 9. 139-150.

Hansen-Bede, L. 1975. "A Child's Creation of a Second Language". *Working Papers on Bilingualism* 6. 103-123.

Hyltenstam, K. 1977. "Implicational Patterns in Interlanguage Syntax Variation". *Language Learning* 27. 383-411.

———. 1981. "The Use of Typological Markedness Conditions as Predictors in Second Language Acquisition: The case of pronominal copies in relative clauses". *Second Languages: A cross-linguistic perspective* ed. by R.W. Andersen, 39-58. Rowley, Mass.: Newbury House.

Kleinmann, H. 1977. "The Strategy of Avoidance in Adult Second Language Acquisition". *Second Language Research* ed. by W. Ritchie, 157-174. New York: Academic Press.

Mazurkewich, I. 1987. "The Role of Core Grammar in Second Language Acquisition". Paper presented at AILA '87, Sydney, 18 August.

Nicholas, H. 1985. "Individual Differences in Interlanguage Use". *Australian Review of Applied Linguistics* 8(1). 70-86.

Pienemann, M. 1980. "The Second Language Acquisition of Immigrant Children". *Second Language Development* ed. by S. Felix. Tubingen: Gunter Narr.

Rosenbaum, P. 1967. *The Grammar of English Predicate Complement Constructions*. Cambridge, Mass.: MIT Press.

Schachter, J. 1974. "An Error in Error Analysis". *Language Learning* 24. 205-214.

————. 1986. "In Search of Systematicity in Interlanguage Production". *Studies in Second Language Acquisition* 8. 119-134.

Schmidt, R.W. 1977. "Sociolingusitic Variation and Language Transfer in Phonology". *Working Papers on Bilingualism* 12. 79-95.

Simukoko, Y.T. 1981. "Some Aspects of the English of Bantu Speakers in Urban Primary Schools in Zambia". Unpublished PhD Thesis, University of Edinburgh.

Tarone, E. 1983. "On Variability in Interlanguage Systems". *Applied Linguistics* 4. 142-163.

Wolfram, W. 1973. "On What Basis Variable Rules?" *New Ways of Analysing Variation in English* ed. by C.-J.N. Bailey & R.W. Shuy, 1-12. New York: Academic Press.

A Comparison of Performance on Chinese and English Dichotic Listening Tasks by Bilingual Native Mandarin Speakers

Lee Thomas and Harry L. Gradman

The research we are reporting on investigated the processing of Mandarin Chinese and English by bilingual native speakers of Mandarin Chinese. Processing strategies were analyzed for laterality effects in order to address the question of whether the two languages elicited equal or different participation of the left and right cerebral hemispheres in the subjects tested. Mandarin Chinese-English bilingual speakers were chosen because of the physical characteristic of tone, which differs between the two languages. It was hypothesized that the acoustic realization of tone might affect the processing strategies employed in the perception of tonal versus nontonal languages.

Second language acquisition literature has largely ignored the intrinsic physical characteristics of the language. The majority of lateralization studies on language processing in speakers of more than one language have investigated variables other than the stimulus. This category includes age of the learner at the time of second language acquisition, proficiency stage in the second language, and manner of language acquisition. Studies have been inconclusive in their ability to demonstrate a difference in laterality (Genesee 1982), leading to the consideration of the stimulus as a factor affecting bilingual processing.

Current research accepts the assumption of cortical localization of function, with language functions normally associated with the left hemisphere of the brain (Lenneberg 1967; Kimura 1961b). There is recognition, however, that while there may be a significant advantage in the performance of one hemisphere, it may not be to the total exclusion of the other

(Kimura 1961b). The nondominant hemisphere normally appears to process a large proportion of the stimulus correctly, thus participating in some manner in the processing of language with a nonoverwhelming, though statistically significant margin of difference. Repp (1977) cautions the interpretation of laterality from previous studies.

Laterality research concerning bilinguals had utilized experimental techniques employing visual and acoustic stimuli, and results from these two modalities have been used indiscriminately in supporting various hypotheses. If one assumes a localization of function theory, it follows that on some level visual and acoustic stimuli should not be assumed to be identically processed. The focus has been so exclusively on learner-internal variables that the language stimulus has not been adequately investigated. Not only have visual and acoustic stimuli often been considered together; it has also been assumed that all languages produce equal stimuli.

Second language acquisition research has been constrained by an interpretation of the conclusions of those such as Lenneberg and Kimura that verbal stimuli are processed in the left hemisphere (in right-handed individuals). While this is taken to refer to first language acquisition, by extension second language acquisition is hypothesized to be processed either the same way (left laterally) or the opposite way (right laterally). As this may not be the most meaningful framework in which to analyze evoked laterality effects in language processing, we have adopted a "systems approach", drawn from Carol Fowler's "A Systems Approach to the Cerebral Hemispheres" (1975), for our perspective from which to review the data.

Briefly, "a system is a whole or a unit composed of hierarchically organized and functionally highly interdependent subunits that may themselves be systems" (1975:26). Common examples of systems include an atom, a person, and a society. Drawing from the work of Weiss (1969, 1971), she illustrates two important concepts of a systems approach, "microindeterminacy" and "equifinality". Microindeterminacy reflects the variation inherent in discrete stimuli which does not deter from the realization of the ultimate goal. Speech production used as an example illustrates that duration of individual acoustic segments is relatively controlled. The system of speech production "consistently reaches a (relatively) fixed goal, despite the microindeterminacy of its component subparts" (1975:26). It is the endpoint that a system is constrained to reach, but the route to this point can tolerate some variation.

> This tendency for a system to reach a constant endpoint from a variety of starting points and by a variety of routes is called "equifinality". It is characteristic of any organization that, as a whole, has functional properties that do not inhere in any of the subparts individually. (In the speech production system, for instance, word duration is not a functional property of any of the system subparts responsible for producing the different acoustic segments.) These functional properties or systems dynamics constitute an equilibrium state of the system. They define the configuration or endpoint toward which the system will tend; they do not, however, define the precise way in which it will attain that configuration. (1975:27)

Fowler adds to this interpretation the concept of "leading part," introduced by Bertalanffy (1968) with respect to biological systems. A leading part is a "subunit in a system whose activities are highly influential with respect to the state of the whole system" (1975:30). While a leading part is a subunit, it enjoys influence over other subparts. It appears to function as a coordinator of the system.

In summing up her presentation of a systems approach to lateralized functions, Fowler posits that

> such functions are whole-brain modes and the modifier "lateralized" simply means that the one hemisphere contributes more influentially than the other to the character of the processing. Since there are at least two differently lateralized processing modes, the term "dominance" can only be ascribed to a hemisphere with reference to a particular mode of functioning. (1975:31)

Thus developed, a systems model allows us to view lateralization results somewhat differently. The language system may utilize a "leading part" which in the normal human brain may be situated in the left hemisphere. It is plausible, however, that various subunits which feed into the leading part are outside of this anatomical region. It is even feasible that such subunits subserve other systems as well, a concept developed at length by Fodor (1983). Surely written symbols enter the language system by a route different than that of phonetic symbols. Acoustic cues may as well, depending upon their characteristics, require the activation of different subunits for their initial processing. In the case of the bilingual, various subunits may process incoming stimuli, depending on their intrinsic physical properties, before the language system has access to this information.

This study addresses two basic questions related to the processing of two languages which utilize properties previously shown to involve different participation of the cerebral hemispheres in native speakers of English. In dichotic listening studies, normal speakers of English demonstrate a right ear advantage indicating stronger left hemispheric participation in the processing of English (Bryden 1963; Curry 1966; Kimura 1967). Auditory tasks involving melodic stimuli produce a left ear advantage, indicating a stronger performance of the right hemisphere (Kimura 1964; Milner 1962). Since Mandarin Chinese, a tonal language, requires the perception of acoustic stimuli incorporating both verbal and melodic stimuli, what would be the hemispheric processing effect in a native speaker of Mandarin Chinese?

Several studies have demonstrated a stronger left hemispheric participation in the processing of English as a second language by learners above the beginning levels of proficiency (Galloway and Scarcella 1982; Shanon 1982; Silverberg, Bentin, Gaziel, Obler and Albert 1979; Sussman, Franklin and Simon 1982). The subjects of these studies, however, tend to be native speakers of Indo-European languages or Hebrew, languages which require far less tonal perception than Mandarin Chinese. Would native speakers of Mandarin Chinese who have acquired English as a second language also demonstrate a right ear advantage in the processing of English?

Three hypotheses were tested to provide some insight into the above questions:

1. Native speakers of Mandarin Chinese performing dichotic digit and monosyllabic word tasks in Mandarin Chinese will not demonstrate a significant right ear advantage in recalling input.
2. A right ear advantage will be demonstrated by the same group in performance on dichotic digit and monosyllabic word tasks in English.
3. An analysis of variance of English vs. Chinese tasks will lead to a rejection of the null hypothesis, thereby suggesting a difference in processing strategies of tonal and nontonal languages by bilingual speakers.

Replicating methodologies of Kimura (1961a) and Curry (1966), digits from one through ten were presented such that the subjects would hear a different digit in each ear simultaneously. After three pairs of digits were presented to the subjects, they were asked to recall what they heard, no matter the order. Thirty-two groups of six digits were presented. Similarly, six pairs of monosyllabic words were presented such that each ear received a different word at the same time. Twenty such sets were presented, with recall order not mattering. Both digit and monosyllabic word tasks were prepared in English and in Mandarin Chinese versions according to similar criteria. They were not translations of identical materials.

·   The tasks were recorded on dual channel tape so that simultaneous presentation of different stimuli to the two ears would be possible with stereophonic earphones. Subjects were presented with either the Mandarin or the English tasks first. Test procedures counterbalanced procedures across ears. After each set of stimuli, consisting of three pairs or six separate stimuli, the subjects reported as many of the stimuli as possible to a native speaker of the language, who was present to record the correct responses. Scores were based on the number of correct responses attributed to each ear.

The subjects who took part in this study consisted of twenty-six native speakers of dialects of Chinese, all of whom were proficient in Mandarin Chinese. While Mandarin was the native dialect of only 38% of the subjects, an analysis of variance (ANOVA) indicated no effect on the results of the Mandarin tasks due to dialect difference. All subjects were right-handed, and all demonstrated normal hearing in both ears. All subjects were graduate students at Indiana University, Bloomington, Indiana, U.S.A., where the study was carried out.

Table 1 presents mean recall scores for all tasks in this study. The scores demonstrate the directionality of ear advantage.

No significant ear advantage was demonstrated in performance of the Mandarin Chinese tasks. The analysis of variance on left-right ear difference in both the digit ($p=.29$) and monosyllabic word ($p=.45$) tasks failed to reach statistical significance at the $p<.05$ level.

On the English tasks, however, a right ear advantage was demonstrated. The analysis of variance on left-right ear difference in the digit task ($p=.0005$) indicated significance at the $p<.001$ level and in the monosyllabic word task ($p=.005$) indicated significance at the $p<.01$ level. Similar results were seen with a small control group of fourteen native speakers of English, who demonstrated a right ear advantage in the digit

Table 1: Mean recall scores by language, task, and ear (Percentage Correct)

Language	Monosyllabic task		Digit task	
	Left ear	Right ear	Left ear	Right ear
Mandarin	69.89	73.27	92.84	93.74
English	39.17	49.55	72.66	81.43

task significant at the p<.01 level and in the monosyllabic word task significant at the p<.001 level.

When the data were pooled by language, the ear advantage in Mandarin Chinese failed to demonstrate significance (p=.31). The right ear advantage in English demonstrated significance at the p<.001 level (p=.0004). In a further analysis of variance comparing performance on the English vs. Mandarin Chinese tasks, significance was demonstrated at the p<.05 level.

That bilingual speakers of Mandarin Chinese and English perform differently on dichotic listening tasks in Mandarin Chinese and English, as all hypotheses were supported, suggests that differences do exist at some level in their language processing strategies. Further, physical characteristics of the languages, the presence or absence of tone in this case, appear to be important in that processing difference. Assuming a "leading part" role for the left hemisphere in language processing, along with various processing subunits located in both hemispheres which feed initial information to the "leading part", the results of this study seem nicely viewed in the systems model of language processing.

References

Bertalanffy, L. von. 1968. *General Systems Theory*. Rev. ed. New York: Brazillier.

Bryden, M.P. 1963. "Ear Preference in Auditory Perception". *Journal of Experimental Psychology* 65. 103-105.

Curry, F.K. 1966. "A Comparison of Left-Handed and Right-Handed Subjects on Five Verbal and Non-Verbal Dichotic Listening Tasks". Unpublished dissertation. Northwestern University.

Fodor, J.A. 1983. *The Modularity of Mind*. Cambridge, Mass.: MIT Press.

Fowler, C. 1975. "A Systems Approach to the Cerebral Hemispheres". *Haskins Laboratories Status Report on Speech Research SR-44*. 17-35.

Galloway, L. & R. Scarcella. 1982. "Cerebral Organization in Adult Second Language Acquisition: Is the right hemisphere more involved?" *Brain and Language* 16. 56-60.

Genesee, F. 1982. "Experimental Neuropsychological Research on Second Language Processing". *TESOL Quarterly* 16. 315-322.

Kimura, D. 1961a. "Some Effects of Temporal-Lobe Damage on Auditory Perception". *Canadian Journal of Psychology* 15. 156-165.

——. 1961b. "Cerebral Dominance and the Perception of Verbal Stimuli". *Canadian Journal of Psychology* 15. 166-171.

——. 1964. "Left-Right Differences in the Perception of Melodies". *Quarterly Journal of Experimental Psychology* 16. 255-358.

Kimura, D. 1967. "Functional Asymmetry of the Brain in Dichotic Listening". *Cortex* 3. 163-168.

Lenneberg, E. 1967. *Biological Foundations of Language*. New York: John Wiley & Sons.

Milner, B. 1962. "Laterality Effects in Audition". *Interhemispheric Relations and Cerebral Dominance* ed. by V.B. Montcastle. Baltimore: The Johns Hopkins Press.

Repp, B.H. 1977. "Measuring Laterality Effects in Dichotic Listening". *Haskins Laboratories Status Report on Speech Research SR-49*, 149-185.

Shanon, R. 1982. "Lateralization Effects in the Perception of Hebrew and English Words". *Brain and Language* 17. 107-123.

Silverberg, R., S. Bentin, T. Gaziel, L.K. Obler & M.L. Albert. 1979. "Shift of Visual Field Preference for English Words in Native Hebrew Speakers". *Brain and Language* 8. 184-190.

Sussman, H.M., P. Franklin & T. Simon. 1982. "Bilingual Speech: Bilateral control?" *Brain and Language* 15. 125-142.

Weiss, P. 1969. "The Living System: Determinism stratified". *Beyond Reductionism* ed. by A. Koestler & J.R. Smythies, 3-55. Boston: Beacon Press.

Weiss, P. 1971. "The Basic Concept of Hierarchical Systems". *Hierarchically Organized Systems in Theory and Practice* ed. by P. Weiss, 1-43. New York: Hafne.

The Language of Neurolinguistics: Principles and Perspectives in the Application of Linguistic Theory to the Neuropsychology of Language

Gordon Bruce McKellar

Neurolinguistics emerged in this country in the 1960s as a multi- and inter-disciplinary field of inquiry designed to bring together studies concerning language and the representation of language and higher cortical functions in the human nervous system. Motivated by the growing body of information accruing from a century of aphasiological research, from studies in linguistic theory, from applied linguistics, from psycholinguistics, from speech pathology, from neuropsychology and from numerous related areas, neurolinguistics was established as a broad and relatively unstructured framework within which a wide range of questions, theoretical orientations, methods and goals could be pursued.

Despite the passage of nearly a quarter of a century, however, little serious discussion has been given to neurolinguistics as a discipline, or a sub-discipline, in its own right with its own clearly defined object of inquiry, its own assumptions and its own general theory. For the most part neurolinguistics has remained an atheoretical interdisciplinary hyphenate, failing to breed even a serious liaison among investigators from other disciplines much less an interdisciplinary focus within the single investigator. Without immediate corrective action of both a theoretical and an educational nature, neurolinguistics, as so many interdisciplinary efforts of past years, faces the very real danger of becoming a forum for disciplinary bias in the investigation of complex questions rather than a forum for interdisciplinary balance.

The roots of the problem are clear and can be found in the foundational papers upon which neurolinguistics has been built.

The first problem concerns the vagueness of the initial formulations of neurolinguistic inquiry. The charter of neurolinguistics, it was frequently noted, was the correlation of multi-disciplinary information from numerous fields concerned with human language, the synthesis of such information, or the inquiry into the relationship between language and the nervous system. The limitations of notions like "correlation", "synthesis" and "relationship", when applied to data and theoretical constructs from very unlike disciplinary orientations, were seldom discussed. Nor has there been sufficient discussion of the nature of the theoretical constructs necessary for hybrid disciplines either as a general problem (despite the recent emergence of other interface disciplines like biochemistry, molecular biology, genetic engineering, and so on) or in the particular case of neurolinguistics.

Secondly, there was an over-reliance on the mechanisms and clinical data of aphasia as effecting a major bridge between linguistics and the neurology of language. This too is flawed since aphasia is fundamentally a neuroanatomical level pathology. Both "neuroanatomical level" and "pathology" are significant here. First, the neuroanatomical level reveals little more than the sensory and motor aspects of language processing. It is the neurophysiological and neuropsychological levels that seem to be critical to the neurology of language in the broader sense of the term "language" that is more familiar to linguists, and these today remain poorly understood. Secondly, aphasia is not a pathology of language, but rather of the biological substrate of language. The two are very different matters and one should not make too much of the fact that "language" is somehow common in both cases. As a pathology of normal neural mechanisms, aphasia is ultimately unintelligible without a prior knowledge of these mechanisms and how it is that their disruption yields the clinical phenomena observed.

The vague initial formulations of neurolinguistic inquiry and the over-reliance on the mechanisms and clinical data of aphasia is apparent as far back as Edith Trager's 1960 "The Field of Neurolinguistics". There, setting what were to become enduring foundations, Trager wrote of neurolinguistics as:

> ... a field of interdisciplinary study which does not have a formal existence. Its subject matter is the relationship between the human nervous system and language ...
> [Though trained neurolinguists will not be ready for some time] neurolin-

guistic work has certainly been carried on under other names, by people who work with aphasia, by neurosurgeons and neurologists, and by experimental neuroanatomists, neurophysiologists and neuropsychologists ... Although the work on aphasics and other people with brain damage was done without a knowledge of modern linguistics or even of speech mechanisms, it is the chief source of how the central nervous system and the peripheral nerves operate to make language possible. (Trager 1960: 70-71)

By the 1970s similar accounts of neurolinguistic inquiry had become commonplace. Typically, neurolinguistics was being defined as an interdisciplinary 'correlational', 'interface' or 'borderline' field embracing participants from the disciplinary fields of linguistics, psychology, neurology, speech pathology and other allied disciplines. Typically the study of aphasia was seen as the central object of analysis, the binding and often the *raison d'être* for the entire interdisciplinary effort. A central figure in this early casting was Harry Whitaker. "The term 'neurolinguistics'," Whitaker wrote during this period:

... is in more common use in Russia and Europe than in the United States, although the general subject matter, aphasia, is studied everywhere. The basic premise and research methodology is analogous to that of physiological psychology and neuropsychology: studying the physiological correlates of behavior and studying abnormal behavior produced by known neurological deficits can both provide insights into the basis of normal behavior ... One assumption in neurolinguistics is that a proper and adequate understanding of language depends upon correlating information from a variety of fields concerned with the structure and function of both language and the brain, minimally neurology and linguistics. Such a synthesis is expected, among other things, to provide independent confirmation for hypotheses about linguistic structure, to provide a framework for a performance model of the speaker-hearer, and to provide additional insights into brain functioning. (Whitaker 1971: 137, 139)

A similar position was taken by Whitaker in the "Editorial Statement" of the first volume of his journal *Brain and Language*:

Two long-standing problems of science are elliptically represented by the name of this new journal, *Brain and Language*. Although studies of brain function have been generally the province of the medical and neural sciences and studies of language structure and function generally the province of the behavioral and social sciences, in the past century one may find clear precedent for interdisciplinary approaches to these problems. The nascence of such fields as physiological psychology or, more recently, neurolinguistics, is simple evidence that many recognize the value of an enlarged conceptual base and new analytical tools in the complex area of

> language, the brain and the interrelationships between them ... (Whitaker
> 1974a: iii)

In service of further research into the interrelationship between brain
and language, the journal *Brain and Language* went on to solicit papers:

> ... from a variety of disciplinary perspectives: neurology, linguistics,
> psychiatry, neurophysiology, psychology, neuroanatomy, speech pathol-
> ogy, neurosurgery, audiology, physiological psychology and related
> specialties. The unifying factor in these diverse approaches is that each
> paper is expected to consider some aspect of human language or communi-
> cation in a manner that can be related to the brain or brain function.
> (Whitaker 1974b)

Similar positions have been adopted by other writers and by the editors
of other journals concerned with brain and language. The editors of the
Journal of Neurolinguistics, for example, note in their editorial statement
that their journal "is concerned with the interface of neurology and linguistics, an interdisciplinary realm of specialization that takes upon itself the
exploration of brain function in language behavior and experience". (Peng
1985: 1). There are many such examples.

The benefits of these initiatives notwithstanding, there is a growing
awareness not only that these foundations have directed neurolinguistics
away from the task of developing its own theoretical framework, but also
that the built-in disciplinary bias, where it has not simply licensed interdisciplinary speculation on disciplinary data, has skewed neurolinguistic
research more toward the concerns of clinical neurology and speech pathology. In Lamendella's words:

> ... in spite of early efforts to outline a unified theoretical framework which
> merged linguistic theory and neurological facts, a tight association with lin-
> guistic theory has not been sustained. Focusing on language disorders as its
> principal object of study (with a strong secondary interest in brain laterali-
> zation), neurolinguistics proper has actually developed more as a branch of
> neurology than as a branch of linguistics. This divergence has perhaps been
> due in part to a tendency to gravitate toward the already well-established
> research interests of clinical neurologists and in part to the waning in
> importance within linguistics of transformational grammar and the sub-
> sequent absence of one generally accepted theoretical framework within
> linguistics. (Lamendella 1979: 373).

If this skewing is to be corrected, and if neurolinguistics is to claim a
position among the sciences as a discipline in its own right, it is essential
that we shift the foundations of neurolinguistic inquiry and take the con-

struction of a unified general theory merging linguistic theory and neuropsychology, first for normal systems and then for the normal systems disordered. And this in turn demands the identification, on principled grounds, of a compatible linguistic theory. The question, of course, is "compatible with what, and on what grounds?" Certainly not with a pre-existing and already given neurology of language. Rather, the issue is the identification of a general linguistic theory and a general neurological theory compatible with respect to a higher and still more general theoretical frame of reference, embodying the common mediational principles and relationships.

This is to say that neurolinguistics must first have a clear object of inquiry yet more general than the sum of its linguistic and its neurological theories, and a relatively explicit general theoretical framework of this object defining the central explanatory concepts and relations, before neurolinguistic research is possible. Then and only then will the neurolinguistic consumer know what to require of other disciplines to fulfill his theoretical needs. This is most important in the case of linguistic theory.

I have argued elsewhere and at some length (McKellar 1985, forthcoming a) that the more general object of inquiry at issue here, far from being an arbitrary characterization, is the legacy of a nearly century long period of transition in the human sciences stretching from Darwin, Durkheim and Saussure onward through the termination of the period in the 1960s.[1] The object of inquiry that has emerged from this transition period cases man as an evolutionary 'social man', thus casting the corresponding general theory as an evolutionary socio-neuropsychological theory.

It is with our notion of evolutionary social man and within our socio-neuropsychological theory then that we are able to establish neurolinguistics as a special discipline. The reason for this is a simple one: language is paramount in the life of man and pervades all areas of the socio-biological spectrum. And it is only after we are familiar with the socio-biological system that we can properly ask after the nature of language (i.e. its underlying organizational principles) and of the appropriate neural systems. Thatcher hit at the heart of the matter when he wrote of neurolinguistics as:

> ... multidisciplinary, involving such diverse areas as psychology, anthropology, biology, and neuroscience. Anthropology is especially important since speech is among the few truly species-specific behaviors of *homo sapiens*. The study of the evolutionary pressures that evolved specialized anatomical and biochemical structures which subserve speech in the left cerebral hemisphere are subsumed under the disciplines of anthropology, paleontology, and biology. The fundamental physiological

processes by which speech is received and expressed are under the domin-
ion of neuroscience and biology. Finally, psychology, the study of
behavior, is among the most integrative of the disciplines since language is
best understood in terms of its social, perceptual, and cognitive processes.
Thus, Neurolinguistics ... is a comprehensive scientific field of study concerned with explaining and integrating the biological and neurophysiological foundations of language on the one hand with the cultural and
psychological context in which language operates on the other. (Thatcher
1980: 235)

Whatever else we may say about the object and the theory of neurolinguistic inquiry, it is clear that our formulation cannot stand apart from the
still wider context of the dynamic, evolutionary-functional and socio-
interactional mechanisms of which it is a special case. Thus a first step will
be to remove language theory and the supporting neurolinguistic systems
from the static and lifeless structural formulations of the past and replace
them in the evolutionary-functional and socio-interactional systems of
which they have always been a part.

Thus the question of the nature and the boundaries of neurolinguistic
inquiry give way to the prior, independent and still deeper questions of the
nature of man. The issue however is not whether we accept or reject this
added burden to neurolinguistic theory. The question rather is whether we
commit ourselves to making these assumptions explicit, showing them to be
independently and scientifically justifiable, or whether, leaving them
implicit, we silently carry over the metaphysics, and the disconnected,
incomplete and arbitrary assumptions of the past. A few comments on the
emerging picture of evolutionary social man, and of the emerging socio-
biological theory, are in order here.

Since roughly the mid-point of the nineteenth century, in the work of
many diverse thinkers, there has been emerging a radical and far-reaching
transformation in the scientific conception of human nature. It is, as the his-
torical record clearly shows, a transformation born not by independent individual men but by a continuity of men carried by the movement of centuries
of scientific progress. If we take the broad view, leading aspects of this
movement, and thus the nature of this transformation, can be brought into
bold relief.

Until the mid-nineteenth century, philosophical and scientific inquiry
conceived of man as independent of other men (a social autonomy), man as
distinct from other forms of life (a biological autonomy), the "real self" —
first on supernatural and then on introspective grounds — as a conscious

mind, subjective self or "ego", man as the passive processor of a given world "out there", and language as a simple symbolic representational mechanism for an objective, external world passively perceived.

The cumulative effects of scientific inquiry, however, have yielded a quite different and vastly more coherent picture — one recasting man as an evolved biological organism developing, acting and adapting in meaningful socio-interpersonal contexts, and recasting language as a dynamic semiotic system with a primary and pluri-functional role in both the socio-interpersonal and biological processes.

Paradoxically it has been this movement on one hand toward socio-semiotic description and a sociology of knowledge, and on the other toward natural (i.e. evolutionary, biological, neurophysiological, chemical and so on) explanation that has provided the foundational cornerstones of psychological research. Apart from these boundary conditions there is no independent psychology. The human world is not simply the physical environment of sensory, perceptual and motor systems but is rather a social environment constituted of other people, of organized meanings and meaning systems, and of complex non-automatic adaptive demands. The human being is a biological being constituted fundamentally of organized biological mechanisms — neuroanatomical mechanisms, neurophysiological mechanisms and neuropsychological mechanisms evolutionally constituted from lesser to greater degrees of plasticity, complexity and so on — that have in part evolved in service of the adaptive demands made by this human environment.

On this interpretation the psychological level of analysis thus becomes essentially a functional inter-level with its structures, processes and mechanisms determined by the need for an optimal equilibrium between external environmental forces and internal biological (i.e. neuroanatomical and neurophysiological) potential. All psychological level structures, processes and mechanisms are as they are because of the functions that they evolved to serve. Thus the intimate relationship between this level and the — unconscious — mechanisms of the also functional physiological level.

This recasting of psychology — for centuries, on supernatural and introspective foundations the definitive basis of human self-perception — is not however in any way contingent upon the particulars of the socio-biological model being outlined here. It is, rather, prior, having been demonstrated with greater and greater precision in the work of numerous investigators throughout the last century in fields ranging from clinical neurology and psychiatry to psychology itself. Among numerous others we might cite Angell and Mead, Freud, Piaget, and Hughlings Jackson. For these all, and for many others, consciousness, intelligence, "volition" (i.e. "less automatic" mechanisms) and similar mechanisms are all explainable in principle on evolutionary-functional and biological grounds. Consciousness and intelligence are functional and adaptive mechanisms; mind is not a state of system separate from organic structure and biological law; consciousness in man is very limited with most biological activity not accompanied by awareness; free will is not so free but is determined by unconscious, social and mechanical processes over which we have little direct control; our shared phylogenetic and unique ontogenetic pasts determine much of our actions at any given time and thus history becomes crucial for biological systems; higher cortical mechanisms are not passive receivers of an absolute and singularly ordered universe but rather, given fragments of information, fill in gaps while constructing and creating our reality; dynamic and relational processes of living and dialectical systems replace prior theories of static psychological structure; and so on.

Our interest in the mechanisms of a functional psychology however is itself a functional one, i.e. we are interested in its role as a functional inter-level in a comprehensive socio-neuropsychological theory rich enough to recast and to mirror the complex processes attending "social man". Thus it is one of a system of interdependent levels, each with its own language, the totality of which provides the basis of a working model of human development, higher cortical functions, language and socio-cultural processes. In so doing we are rejecting the arbitrary boundaries of the skin, and the arbitrary boundaries of the "ego" (indeed we are rejecting many notions of the ego all together) in the analysis of intra-organism processes. Hence a unitary, ultimately indivisible and irreduceable, object of inquiry.

Here, in our rejection of these arbitrary boundaries, two quotations serve us well. One, from the socio-semiotic side, is from Halliday; the other, from the biological side, is from Lewontin, Rose and Kamin. The commonality is both clear and striking.

First, writing of the formulation popular in many quarters of the "language and culture" complex as an "information system", Halliday observes that:

> ... If information is to be located somewhere, no doubt it will have to be at
> the interface where the organism joins with its environment; but why do
> we need to localize it by reference to the skin? Meaning inheres in the sys-

tem: in the information system that constitutes the culture, and in the various semiotic modes (of which language is one) that serve to realize the culture. The system is more general than its representation either as knowledge or as behavior ... (Halliday 1977b: 21)

Hence an approach to the biological from the social and socio-semiotic point of view.[2] Complementing this is the position of Lewontin, Rose and Kamin who approach the issue from the other way around, though observing the importance in our age to begin to:

> ... point the way toward an integrated understanding of the relationship between the biological and social. We describe such an understanding as dialectical, in contrast to reductionist. Reductionist explanation attempts to derive the properties of wholes from intrinsic properties of parts, properties that exist apart from and before the parts are assembled into complex structures.
>
> ... About the only sensible thing to say about human nature is that it is "in" that nature to construct its own history ... At every instant the developing mind, which is a consequence of the sequence of past experiences and of internal biological conditions, is engaged in a recreation of the world with which it interacts. There is a mental world, the world of perceptions, to which the mind reacts, which at the same time is a world created by the mind. It is obvious to all of us that our behavior is in reaction to our own interpretations of reality, whatever that reality may be ... Any theory of psychic development must include not only how a given biological individual develops psychically in a given sequence of environments, but how the developing individual in turn interpenetrates with the objective and subjective worlds to recreate its own environments (Lewontin *et al.* 1984: 10-11, 276).

Both Halliday and Lewontin *et al.*, among numerous other researchers (McKellar forthcoming a), perceive the pressing need in the human sciences for an expanded frame of reference, though neither have the resources at their disposal for constructing the outlines of the required system. In part this is a function of the continuing disciplinary residue of the university system. Each, despite considerable vision, have ultimately remained disciplinary.

The problem of education and interdisciplinary thinking in the creation of a comprehensive interdisciplinary science has been reflected in the writings of many over the course of the past quarter century. One of the best statements, however, came in the early 1960s from Milton Miller, M.D., then Chairman and Professor of the Department of Psychiatry, and Director of the Wisconsin Psychiatric Institute at the University of Wisconsin

Medical Center. Speaking at an interdisciplinary research conference of biological and social scientists from all parts of the continent, and looking forward to a day that has unfortunately not yet come, Dr. Miller noted the growing appreciation of many investigators from differing fields of the "growing appreciation of the unity of [their] diverse efforts," noting that this:

> ... is to be credited in part to those few who pass knowledgeably between us, thereby forming the rudimentary shape of the bridge, or bridges, to come. In the decade ahead these bridges will be much better traveled, and, hopefully, such travel will be in both directions. It is not enough to say that everything psychological has a biochemical basis or that biochemistry is a necessary step in understanding the phenomenon of experiencing. Rather, an adequate understanding of either psychology or biology requires an appreciation of the unifying closed circle of events which encompasses both ...
>
> The task of building bridges, as in all construction work, is vigorous labor ... [and] there are not many good institutional models. Many of the "interdisciplinary" efforts of the last decade proved disappointing for, in the normal course of things, we tend to associate with individuals whose training and experience is most like our own, people able to understand and appreciate our efforts. This is not surprising ...
>
> Nevertheless, the growing magnitude of our knowledge and of our awareness of the complexity of many phenomena which have hitherto been studied only in part has begun to disrupt hierarchical barriers separating psychology, psychiatry, the social and analytic biological sciences. We need to be more attuned to the question "What can this co-worker do?" — rather than to the question "What degree has he?"
>
> The scaffolding of tomorrow's bridges can be visualized if we look closely. The architecture is on the drawing boards. An interdisciplinary awareness within the single investigator rather than an interdisciplinary liaison among investigators may become a more prevalent model (Miller 1963: 3, 7-9).

With the applied potential of socio-biological theory and of its subordinated theories of psychiatry, psychology, speech pathology, clinical neurology, sociology, linguistics and neurolinguistic inquiry, and so on, we can no longer wait for the university system and for complacent disciplinarians to lead the way. The outlines of a comprehensive general theory are within reach now — indeed they have been for quite some time. To delay construction further, it seems to me, is inconsistent with scientific responsibility.

Since I have discussed the particulars of socio-neuropsychological theory in some detail elsewhere, only a few comments on the nature of socio-biological theory are necessary here.

First, socio-neuropsychological theory (the MATRIX paradigm, see McKellar forthcoming c) is a relational theory consisting of a specifiable number of interrelating and interdependent levels, each with mechanisms, concepts and relations cast in terms appropriate to the nature of that level. These levels are further organized within two fairly autonomous though interpenetrating components: a socio-semiotic component specifying the theory of language and higher semiotic structure, mechanisms of cultural transmission, and so on; and a neuropsychological component consisting of a hierarchical arrangement of neuroanatomical, neurophysiological level mechanisms. These components mirror the mechanisms of the biological organism and the socio-semiotic systems in which it develops, to which it continually adapts, and so on.

Secondly, the mechanisms of each level are necessary for the normal functioning of the levels above and below it, and thus necessitate the normal functioning of the levels below it. Moreover, and most importantly, the properties of the parts and wholes of the system codetermine each other. As Lewontin *et al.* have noted, the properties of human beings:

> ... do not exist in isolation but arise as a consequence of social life, yet the nature of that social life is a consequence of our being human. It follows, then, that dialectical explanation contrasts with cultural or dualistic modes of explanation that separate the world into different types of phenomena — culture and biology, mind and body — which are to be explained in quite different and nonoverlapping ways ...
>
> Wholes are composed of units whose properties may be described, but the interaction of these units in the construction of the wholes generates complexities that result in products qualitatively different from the component parts (Lewontin *et al.* 1984: 11).

Thirdly, given the mediation of common, fundamental and all embracing principles in the structure and functioning of the mechanisms of each component — principles of the scope and generality of evolutionary theory and the derivative functional nature of the mechanisms, the fundamental goal of optimal biological adaptation in the socio-cultural as well as the physical world, the centrality of semiotics and of meaning in the life of man, the necessary emphasis on dynamic mechanisms of system and process rather than static structural mechanisms alone, the focus upon (phylogenetic and ontogenetic) history in the life of the organism, and the demand for order, control and organization throughout the system — the stamp of these principles should be easily visible at all higher cortical and social levels.

Lastly, given the principle of the codetermination of parts and wholes throughout the system, given unity of the system as a whole in normal circumstances, and given the pervasiveness of the common, fundamental and all embracing principles just enumerated, it would seem in principle that the mechanisms at each level imply something about the kind of mechanisms to be found at other levels, and, given a knowledge of the mechanisms at various levels or of the common and fundamental system-wide principles, features of missing mechanisms at particular levels might be predictable.

It is precisely this latter condition that faces us as socio-neuro-psychological and now neurolinguistic consumers in our selection of linguistic theory for our socio-semiotic component. The parameters are clear: it must be evolutionary in nature and pluri-functional in design; it must be compatible not just with semiotic theory but more must itself be interpretable as a social semiotic; it must be structured as a dynamic mechanism foregrounding system and process; it must be structured as a tool of adaptation in the socio-cultural world of people and meanings as well as in the physical world semiotically interpreted; and lastly it thus must be a descriptive linguistic theory rather than an explanatory theory. The linguistic level alone is not an explanatory level. Explanation is a function of the rest of the system.

While these are broad parameters of the most general kind, compatibility at this level is all that one can expect of a linguistic theory. This is because no existing linguistic theory has yet been developed from such a broadly interdisciplinary foundation, and for such interdisciplinary purposes, as is being developed here. Thus the theory chosen will entail variable degrees of reinterpretation, redefinition and recasting.

Given this proviso, the most compatible theory, and thus a preliminary though potentially useful base for solving the pressing problem of linguistic theory for neurolinguistic science noted earlier by Lamendella, is that of M.A.K. Halliday.

While many linguists, most focally Chomsky, have stressed the explanatory autonomy and self-containedness of linguistic theory — i.e. the sufficiency of internal, formal logico-linguistic constructs alone for the foundations of a relevant explanatory linguistic theory — Halliday's work assumes the inverse view: the necessity of infusing non-formal foundational elements and central scientific concepts taken from the fruits of scientific inquiry external to linguistics as the basis of a principled, descriptive and comprehensive linguistic theory sufficient to the needs of specific linguistic "consumers". (Halliday 1964). On Halliday's interpretation, formal linguistic mechanisms are simply representational devices with no intended psychological, neuropsychological, philosophical or metaphysical status.

Critical then is Halliday's focus upon the systemic-functional analysis of language structure, the social (interpersonal, interactional) interpretation of man as developing and acting within a social and a physical environment, the primacy of intersubjective, semiotic meaning systems — hence of "meaning" itself — as definitive of human nature and of social man, the mechanisms of cultural and educational transmission, the primacy of spoken, living language texts as basic to the construction of a dynamic linguistic theory, and the consequent importance of building 'system and process' into linguistic theory, and not simply object and product.

For Halliday the notion "social man" reflects "not simply man in relation to an abstract entity like 'society as a whole' but rather man in relation to other men". (Halliday 1971: 165). Thus the shift of emphasis from the physical to the human environment, and with this to language, meaning and dynamic, symbolic intersubjectivity. Hence the study of social man "presupposes the study of language and social man" Halliday 1971: 165). Thus:

> Linguistics is a necessary part of the study of people in their environment, and their environment consists, first and foremost, of other people. Man's ecology is primarily a social ecology, one which defines him as "social man"; and we cannot understand about social man if we do not understand about language ... [What is needed is an] integrated picture of the relation of language to other social phenomena, a general framework expressing the social meaning of language ... the terminal direction of which will be towards integration — towards eliminating boundaries rather than imposing them, and towards a unifying conception of language as a form of social semiotic (Halliday 1975: 19).

For Halliday, the effect of this social, semiotic intersubjectivity is twofold. First there is the preeminence of meaning throughout the system, and secondly there is the social construction of reality. Social man is effectively 'sociosemiotic man', a repository for social meanings. The individual is not situated in a fixed external reality which is merely represented by language, but rather constructs his reality socio-symbolically. Hence the recasting of the linguist as a sociosemiotician and linguistics as sociosemiotics. "A distinctive feature of the past decade", Halliday writes:

> ... has been the development of semiotics as a mode of thinking, not just about language, but about all aspects of culture. From the semiotic

standpoint culture is ... 'a body of knowledge which members use to interpret experience and to structure behavior ...' Semiotics is not a discipline
defined by subject matter. It is a way of interpreting things. In
Pyatygorsky's words, "when I analyze anything from the point of view of
what it means, this is a 'semiotic situation' ..."
Once the semiotic perspective develops an intellectual stance, it can, so to
speak, turn back on [the system of] language, so that language is thought
of as one among many semiotic systems [a social semiotic] that constitute
the culture ... Halliday 1977a: 47).

Here we return, now with new eyes, to the essence of Halliday's
sociosemiotic inquiry: the investigation, though focusing on language, of
the interrelation of systems of meaning — the investigation of the underlying system if you will — at once constituting the symbolic universe and symbolic resources of man as realized through individual experiences. With
respect to language itself, this is to interpret the entirety of the linguistic
system as constituting a system of heterogeneous mechanisms of meaning:
(1) stratal systems of semantic meaning, lexicogrammatical (lexical and
grammatical) meaning, and phonological meaning; (2) structural meaning;
(3) functional meaning (for example the categories of actor, theme, past,
given, and so on which define the functional meaning of lexical items, etc.,
in grammatical use); and (4) an underlying, so to speak, macrofunctional
meaning axis of ideational[3] (experiential and logical), interpersonal[4] and
textual[5] semantic organization. And these, together constituting the linguistic system as a whole, in turn realize the other semiotic systems of culture
(Halliday 1977a: 47), the behavioral or sociosemantics of the social system
(Halliday 1973), and the semiotic structure of contexts of situation (Halliday 1978).

Such heterogeneous mechanisms of meaning however do not arise
arbitrarily, randomly or by chance. If the analysis is to be scientifically viable, they must arise on a principled basis yielding principled and motivated
criteria, and in Halliday's thinking they do. They arise on a functional basis,
and with the introduction of this axis we simultaneously put forward a second of Halliday's primary foundations.

As with the first of his primary foundations, we can again associate
Halliday's general theory with a scientific construct of independent origin
and with independent confirmation external to linguistics: the theory of
evolution — the "greatest unifying theory in all biology" (Mayr 1963: 3) —
and the dynamic relationship between structure and function that this
implies. For though Halliday himself does not incorporate this, it is a funda-

mental law of biology as well as linguistics that all structures, whatever their nature, are as they are because of the functions that they evolved, in specific environmental context, to serve. As principled bases of wide scope, such external criteria of relevance serve as a means of insuring a far reaching interdisciplinary validity.

In part, support for the functional view of language has been cited earlier in our discussion of the general and pervasive distribution of meaning, through varied and heterogeneous sociosemiotic mechanisms in the language and in the life of man. Here we move still further into the essence of human nature by placing these sociosemiotic mechanisms themselves, and meaning itself as the most general of human functions, within the wider — causal — mechanisms of biological evolution. Halliday's question, and his answer, are crucial here:

> Why is language as it is? The nature of language is closely related to the demands that we make of it, the functions it has to serve. In the most concrete terms, these functions are specific to a culture ... But underlying such specific instances of language use, are more general functions which are common to all cultures. We do not all go on fishing expeditions; however, we all use language as a means of organizing other people, and directing their behaviour ... The particular form taken by the grammatical system of language is closely related to the social and personal needs that language is required to serve. But in order to bring this out it is necessary to look at both the system of language and its functions at the same time; otherwise we will lack any theoretical basis for generalizations about how language is used (Halliday 1970: 31).

Halliday's point is that if we consider what language is required to do in the life of man, what functions it must fulfill in all human cultures regardless of differences in the physical environment, then we have a basis for understanding why language is as it is (1974: 19). "There is", Halliday notes, "no *a priori* reason why human language should have taken just the evolutionary path that it has and no other" (1974: 19), and that, were it not for a set of universal demands made upon language by the social intersubjective environment of man during the course of his evolution, "our brains could have produced a symbolic system of quite a different kind" (1974: 19).

For linguistics this is a critical step, and for socio-neuropsychology, particularly for neurolinguistics, it is equally so. In one giant step we have moved well beyond the static associationistic view of language and localization put forward in the last century toward a principled dynamic process model, one now related to (social) environmental demands and through this to the structure of living language, of complex, emergent, and evolutionary-functional neuropsychological systems much more compatible with the conclusions of Jackson, Lashley and Luria.[6]

As outlined by Halliday, the general functions that language has had to evolve to serve in the life of social man are three.

First, language has to interpret the whole of our experience, and reduce in the process the indefinitely varied phenomena of the world around us, and of the world inside us, to a manageable number of classes of phenomena representing types of processes, events and actions, classes of objects, persons, institutions, qualities, states, abstractions and so on.[7] Additionally language must represent basic logical relations like 'and', 'or' and 'if' as well as those relations that are themselves created by language as 'namely', 'says' and 'means'. Together the mechanisms of the experiential and logical functions constitute the ideational component of the linguistic system.[8]

Secondly, language has to express the speaker's participation in the speech situation in the form of the roles that the speaker himself takes on and those that he imposes on others, as well as the speaker's expression of his feelings, attitudes and judgments. In this we find the categories and systems of the interpersonal linguistic roles (the interpersonal component) of the linguistic system defining speech functions like statement, question and answer, command and exclamation, the speaker's comment on probabilities, degree of relevance, etc., of the message, and his attitude about it as, for example, confirmation, reservation and contradiction.

Lastly, language must provide mechanisms for the creation of 'texture' in human language by which text is distinguishable from non-text. This is the function of the textual component of language and in this we find categories and systems of theme, information and cohesion which organize the clause as a message in and through time. Thus the difference, for example, between: (1) *She would marry Horatio. She loved him*; and (2) *She would marry Horatio. It was Horatio she loved* (Halliday 1970: 14) — or again, holding constant the experiential meaning, while rendering complementary sentences nonsensical through manipulation of the information system, between: (1) *No one else had known where the entrance to the cave was situated. The one who discovered the cave was John*; and (2) *No one else had known where the entrance to the cave was situated. What John discovered was the cave* (Halliday 1968: 210).[9]

"It is the demands posed by the service of these functions", Halliday thus writes, "which:

> ... have moulded the shape of language and fixed the course of its evolution. These functions are built into the semantic system of language, and they form the basis of the grammatical organization, since the task of grammar is to encode the meanings deriving from these various functions into articulated structures. Not only are these functions served by all languages, at least in their adult form; they have also determined the way human language has evolved (1974: 20).

But it is not only the ideational, interpersonal and textual mechanisms of language that have evolved from the demands made by widely varying environmental contexts. All aspects of language have evolved in this way.

Since I have reworked and reinterpreted Halliday's work to sociobiological ends elsewhere,[10] further discussion here is unnecessary. Given the context of the present paper it is sufficient to underscore Halliday's sociosemiotic and systemic-functional theory of language as an important though still preliminary linguistic contribution to both evolutionary socioneuropsychological and subordinated neurolinguistic theory.

With respect to the MATRIX paradigm discussed earlier, the mechanisms of systemic-functional grammar thus define the linguistic level of the sociosemiotic component and are congruent with (though not identical with, for reasons stated earlier) (McKellar forthcoming c) the higher level semiotic mechanisms of that component. Moreover they are congruent in principle with a number of the fundamental principles underlying the organization of the higher level aspects of the tri-stratal neuropsychological component. This being the case, and since there is a codetermination to some degree between levels of the system taken as a whole, something more of the parameters of the neurolinguistic mechanisms per se of this tri-stratal system should be made clear. And of course the reverse is also true.

The point here however is neither to outline in detail the MATRIX paradigm nor to explore in detail the nature of the neurolinguistic mechanisms proposed. That certainly would take us too far afield. It is, rather, to reinforce that a 'multidisciplinary discipline' of neurolinguistics is indeed possible and that linguistic theory, if it is carefully chosen by a 'neurolinguistic consumer' clear on his theoretical needs, can and must play a central role.

Linguistics has produced many theories of language and each, by its assumptions and by its structure, implies a corresponding neurolinguistic

theory and theory of the nature of man. Whitaker's 'correlation' of transformational linguistic theory with neuroanatomical structures, for example,
when made explicit, resulted in the confusion of levels of analysis and, in
many cases, the deduction of normal mechanisms from anatomico-
pathological ones.[11] It is not enough that linguistic hypothesis simply be
compatible with hypotheses about the structure and function of the human
brain. This is far too general. It is a principled selection of linguistic theory
within the context of a principled theory of the nature of language and man
that is at issue here. It is this that has been missing from neurolinguistic
theory now for nearly three decades.

Earlier, from his vantage point in the 1960s, Dr. Miller wrote of being
able to visualize the scaffolding of the kind of interdisciplinary bridges that
would lead to precisely the kind of unified general theory that today is possible. "The architecture is on the drawing boards", he wrote. "An interdisciplinary awareness within the single investigator rather than an interdisciplinary liaison among many may become a more prevalent model".

Extending this metaphor, we might say today that plans are off the
drawing board, the foundations are in and the general superstructure is up.
It is now up to like minded investigators, and to the educational systems, to
take down their disciplinary boundaries and to help in what cannot fail to
be the most far-reaching of scientific initiatives.[12]

Notes

1. Though the boundaries marking any period of intellectual movement are in the final
   analysis arbitrary, the boundaries set for this transition period (1860-1960) nonetheless
   reflect a clear period of significant change in the human sciences of a particular character
   and embodying coherent and specifiable conclusions.

2. Halliday however never takes this step and this is not without cost to his theory. See
   McKellar (Forthcoming b).

3. In the ideational function, language has to interpret the whole of our experience, and
   reduce in the process the indefinitely varied phenomena of the world around us, and of
   the world inside us, to a manageable number of classes of phenomena representing types
   of processes, events and actions, classes of objects, persons, institutions, qualities, states,
   abstractions and so on.

4. In the interpersonal function, language has to express the speaker's participation in the
   speech situation in the form of the roles that the speaker himself takes on and those that
   he imposes on others, as well as the speaker's expression of his feelings, attitudes and
   judgments.

5.   In the textual function, language must provide mechanisms for the creation of "texture" in human language by which text is distinguished from non-text.

6.   Thus we move toward a functional, evolutionary process model of the brain acknowledging though subsuming the localizationist associationist model within a wider, all encompassing one.

7.   The functions expressed here are taken from Halliday, 1968: 209 and 1974: 19-20.

8.   Halliday notes further that "The three terms 'semantic', 'representational' and 'logical' refer to different aspects of this combined function: 'semantic' suggests its place in the total linguistic system, 'representational' emphasizes its relation to extralinguistic factors, while 'logical' implies an underlying structure that is independent of syntax and may be opposed merely to 'grammatical' as meaning to 'form' (1968: 209)." M.A.K. Halliday. "Notes on Transitivity and Theme. Part 3", op.cit. p.209.

9.   We note here also the evolutional demand for the more situationally definable mechanisms underlying the transmission of those aspects of the culture which are to constitute an individual's experience of the world, of social roles and of social positioning, and underlying the variable, socially defined registers through which so much human interaction takes place. These however are not part of the 'linguistic system' as such now under discussion.

10.   Some confusion has arisen from my 1987 paper. A number of readers have — wrongly — gotten the impression that my reworking and reinterpretation of Halliday's work within a broader set of social and biological constructs actually was derived from Halliday's work itself, i.e. that Halliday had built his linguistic theory upon biological, evolutionary, neuropsychological, etc. principles or that Halliday himself was interested in pursuing a broadly interdisciplinary theory in the multidisciplinary sense therein outlined. This however was not and is not the case.

     The confusion was my fault. Although at the end of the first section I clearly noted that:

> Halliday himself, and those working within his paradigm, failed to provide broad foundations, interpretations and contexts for his work ... even major internal issues as Margaret Berry and Christopher Butler have pointed out, have gone without serious attention from systemicists, leaving serious gaps, inconsistencies and even contradictions in the theory that are sure to put off many readers.

And further (in footnote 22) that:

> Halliday himself does not reduce his work to, or discuss his work in biological [evolutionary, etc.] terms. But such a reduction, if his work is correct, must in principle be possible. If possible, then it must be done; if not, then the theory must be re-evaluated.

I did go on to overinterpret Halliday when I later wrote that:

> In his writings Halliday has tended to view the social and biological perspectives as "*complementary*, though with *shifts of emphasis* between them" (my italics). Thus Halliday's explicit acceptance in principle of the socio-biological frame and his rejection in principle of cultural and biological determinism.
>
>   Some caution must be exercized here, for a superficial reading of Halliday's papers might yield the impression that it is a psychological rather than a biological (neuropsychological, etc.) basis that he has in mind for the internal mechanisms of the individual. Halliday's writings sometimes do tend to blur the line between a

psychological or psycholinguistic basis (i.e. language as 'knowledge') and one more biological (i.e. more mechanistic language where notions like knowledge are of little relevance), but this is more of an artefact of the contexts in which he is writing than to a commitment to psychological explanation. Taken on balance, however, there is little question of Halliday's evolutionary, biological foundations. (987: 537-538).

And that

... there is an explicit dialectical relationship between the social and the biological componenents underlying Halliday's thinking. Analytically however it is, as was implicit in the evolutionary-functional parts of his writing, the functional study of the social and semiotic phenomena of man ... that can shed light upon biological phenomena (McKellar 1987: 538).

In point of fact, one must go a considerable distance to get this from Halliday's writings. His references to biology are few and far between, and when they do occur are done only in passing. Halliday's continuing alliance with psychological theories — theories of language and mind as narrow and as falsifiable as the stratificational psycholinguistics of Sidney Lamb or the systemic psycholinguistics of Robin Fawcett make this clear. It is also clear from these alliances that 'interdisciplinary' for Halliday does not mean 'multidisciplinary' where points of contact or points of synthesis between constructs *independently derived*, but rather 'unidisciplinary' where linguistic theory is *imposed* upon other disciplines. Hence, in one step, systemic or stratificational linguistic theory can become 'psychologically real'. That Halliday has continued to take this road is to my deep disappointment.

11.   This has caused considerable confusion in neuropsychological research. See McKellar 1985 (Vol.II) and Forthcoming c.

12.   I would like to express my deep appreciation and gratitude to Kathy Sortor, Sandra Carter and Joe Collins for their continuing support and encouragement.

References

Halliday, M.A.K. 1964. "Syntax and the Consumer". *Report of the XV (First International) Round Table Meeting on Linguistics and Language Study*, ed. by C.I.J.M. Stuart, 11-24. Washington D.C.: Georgetown University Press. (= Monograph Series in Languages and Linguistics 17).

——. 1968. "Notes on Transitivity and Theme in English." Part 3." *Journal of Linguistics* 4.179-215.

——. 1970. "Language Structure and Language Function". *New Horizons in Linguistics*, ed. by J. Lyons, 140-165. New York: Penguin.

——. 1971. "Language in a Social Perspective". *Educational Review* 23. 165-188.

——. 1973. "Towards a Sociological Semantics." *Explorations in the Functions of Language* ed. by M.A.K. Halliday, 72-101. London: Edward Arnold.

——. 1974. *Language and Social Man*. London: Longmans. (= Schools Council Programme in Linguistics and English Teaching: Papers Series II, Vol. 3).

———. 1975. "Language as Social Semiotic: Towards a general sociolinguistic theory". *The First LACUS Forum* ed. by A. Makkai and V.B. Makkai, 17-46. Columbia, South Carolina: Hornbeam Press.

———. 1977a. "Ideas about Language". *Aims and Perspectives in Linguistics*, 32-49. (= Applied Linguistics Association of Australia Occasional Papers 1).

———. 1977b. M.A.K. 1977b. "The Context of Linguistics". *Aims and Perspectives in Linguistics*, 19-31. (= Applied Linguistics Association of Australia Occasional Papers 1).

———. 1978. "An Interpretation of the Functional Relationship between Language and Social Structure". *Language as Social Semiotic* ed. by M.A.K. Halliday, 183-192. London: Edward Arnold.

Lamendella, John T. 1979. "Neurolinguistics". *Annual Review of Anthropology* 8.373-391.

Lewontin, R.C., Steven Rose & J. Kamin. 1984. *Not in Our Genes: Biology, ideology and human nature.* New York: Pantheon Books.

Mayr, Ernst. 1963. *Animal Species and Evolution.* Cambridge, Mass.: Harvard University Press.

McKellar, Gordon Bruce. 1985. *Social Man: The Grand System. On the foundations of a constructive neuropsychology*, 3 vols. Ph.D. dissertation, University of Sydney.

———. McKellar, Gordon Bruce. 1987. "The Place of Sociosemiotics in Contemporary Thought." *Language Topics*, ed. by Ross Steele and Terry Threadgold, 523-548. Amsterdam/Philadelphia: John Benjamins.

———. Forthcoming a. "Models and Methods in the Human Sciences. Part 1. The Self-destructing Semiotics of Structuralism and Structuralist Critical Theory". To appear in *Toronto Semiotic Circle Working Papers* (= Papers of the IX International Summer Institute for Semiotic and Structural Studies, Australian Symposium, 1988).

———. Forthcoming b. "Models and Methods in the Human Sciences. Part III. Language as Social Semiotic: A critical discussion of the systemic-functional structuralist grammar of M.A.K. Halliday". To appear.

———. Forthcoming c. "Models and Methods in the Human Sciences. Part IV. The MATRIX of Social Man: Semiotic systems, constructional Socio-neuropsychology, unconscious processes and the dialectical explanation of human nature." To appear.

Miller, Milton. 1963. "On building Bridges". *Psychoanalysis and Current Biological Thought*, 3-8. Madison: University of Wisconsin Press.

Peng, Fred. 1985. "Editorial Statement". *Journal of Neurolinguistics* 1.1-6.

Thatcher, Robert W. 1980. "Neurolinguistics: Theoretical and evolutionary perspectives". *Brain and Language* 2. 235-260.

Trager, Edith. 1960. "The Field of Neurolinguistics". *Studies in Linguistics* 15. 70-71.

Whitaker, Harry. 1971. "Neurolinguistics". *A Survey of Linguistic Science* ed. by W.O. Dingwall, 136-251. College Park: University of Maryland.

———. 1974a. "Editorial Statement". *Brain and Language* 1.iii-iv.

———. 1974b. "Editorial Policy". *Brain and Language* 1.

Orthographic Complexity and Orthography Acquisition

Philip A. Luelsdorff

0. Introduction

A frequent finding of first and second language acquisition research is that some linguistic structures are acquired after others. Efforts to explain such differential orders of learning, and the forces that drive them, appeal to notions like perceptual salience, frequency, negative transfer, overgeneralization, simplification, regularity, typological markedness, parameter (re)setting, and rule complexity, each with varying degrees of clarity and success (cf. Rutherford 1982).

A virtually uncharted terrain of L2 acquisitional research is developmental orthography. We have some understanding of preliterate spellers' creative spelling (Ferreiro 1983; Read 1986), several theories of the development of English (Ehri 1986; Gentry 1982; Frith 1986) and German (Günther 1986) spelling, and several theories of the processing of English orthography by dyslexic and normal adult readers and spellers (cf. Ellis 1984). What we lack is a theory of second orthography acquisition in reading and spelling by learners literate or quasi-literate in their mother tongue: a theory of developmental biliteracy (Luelsdorff 1986, 1987a; Philips 1984). Sorely lacking is a universal theory of orthographic complexity to explain the facts of differential orders of acquisition in spelling and reading in first and second language acquisition, different degrees of processing difficulties in mature readers and spellers, and different kinds of orthography loss in the reading impaired (Coltheart, Patterson and Marshall 1981).

Our present purpose is to partially articulate a general theory of orthographic complexity and use it to predict the facts of the acquisition of English orthography by German school children. In particular, we are interested in establishing and explaining differential orders of acquisition of L2-English developmental orthography in the domain of the orthography of inflection and contraction.

The orthography of inflection and contraction appears to be a promising area of developmental inquiry because the allomorphs of the inflectional morphemes may be spelled quasi taxonomic-phonemically, as in the plural and third singular, morphophonemically, as in the regular past and past participle, quasi morphophonemically and morphemically, as in the possessive singular, and purely morphemically, as in the possessive plural. Complicating matters are the contracted forms of third singular auxiliary and main verb *is* and *has*, which sound like the plural and third singular and possessive singular, but look only like the possessive singular.

There are also several inflection-dependent orthographic phenomena, such as $<y> \rightarrow <ie>$ in the plural and third singular and the doubling of consonants after stressed, short vowels in the progressive, past, and past participle, and comparative and superlative of the adjective. To the extent that such metaorthographic processes are determined by inflection, they belong to the orthography of inflection.

Our thesis is that the various normative spellings of the inflected and contracted allomorphs of English exhibit various degrees of complexity depending upon the kind and amount of linguistic information needed to relate their sound to their spelling. Further, we propose that this differential complexity determines the order in which the orthography of inflection and contraction is acquired in first and second language acquisition.

In order to test this hypothesis, we adopted and extended a partial theory of orthographic complexity and elicited pupils' written responses to the relevant variables on a sentence dictation test (reproduced in Appendix I). Sentence dictations were essential to the task at hand, since many of the items would have otherwise been morphologically and syntactically ambiguous. The sample tested consisted of intact classes of German pupils in English as a foreign language in grades 6 (N = 32), 7 (N = 26), 8 (N = 18), and 9 (N = 14) of the Gymnasium. Gymnasium pupils have been exposed to the normative spelling of inflection and contraction by their second year of English in grade 6.

Since this is a pilot investigation, we had no way of knowing in advance which orders of acquisition to expect in which grades. Consequently, we adopted a design which was both cross-sectional and longitudinal, with the same dictation administered to all the pupils in all the grades on three separate occasions at roughly two-month intervals beginning in September, the start of the school year. The results reported here are restricted to the analysis of the first and third testings in grade 9 (N = 14), where the pupils, with an average age of 15;3-7, are in their fifth year of English.

Orders of acquisition were determined by applying a modified version of the ordering-theoretic method (Dulay, Burt and Krashen 1982:222-225) according to which a structure A is acquired before a structure B if the percentage of disconfirming cases (where B is right and A is wrong) is "sufficiently small" (5% to 7%). Furthermore, structures form an unordered pair (are acquired at the same time) if they exhibit a small percentage of disconfirming cases in *both* directions (7% in one direction and not more than 14% in the other).

We adopted the more conservative criterion of grouping features together if the difference in both directions was 7% or less and the more liberal criterion of otherwise placing A before B if the percentage of disconfirming cases was less than that of B before A.

1. Orthographic Complexity

Systemic deviation from grapheme-phoneme biuniqueness is the major source of error in the acquisition of a native or foreign alphabetic script. Therefore, a reasoned typology of such deviations may be used as the basis for a theory of orthographic complexity.

A first step in the direction of such a typology was recently taken by Sgall (1987). According to Sgall's proposal, the deviations from one-to-one correspondence between grapheme and phoneme may be ranked along two scales, a scale of complexness and a scale of univocality.

The scale of complexness is as follows:

   i.   protographeme — a grapheme no variant of which contains a diacritic sign: Czech <b, f, g, k, l, m, p, r, v>;

   ii.   complex grapheme with regular subgrapheme (diacritic): Czech <á, é, í, ó, ú; š, ž, č>;

  iii. complex grapheme with irregular subgrapheme: Czech <ř>;

  iv. protographeme string: Czech '<ti>:/t'i/, <di>:/d'i/, <ni>:/n'i/; <ty>:/ti/, <dy>:/di/, <ny>:/ni/;

   v.   string with some complex elements, but no irregular subgraphemes (no examples in Czech);

vi.   string, some of whose elements have an irregular subgrapheme: Czech <dě>:/d'ɛ/, <tě>:/t'ɛ/, <ně>:/n'ɛ/;

vii.   as in (vi), with the irregular subgrapheme corresponding to more than one phoneme in the pronunciation (or with some other difference between the number of phonemes and the number of graphemes): Czech <pě>:/pjɛ/, <město>:/mnɛsto/.

The logic underlying the scale of complexness appears compelling:

1.   simplex grapheme (protographeme) before complex grapheme;
2.   protographeme string before complex grapheme string;
3.   regular subgrapheme before irregular subgrapheme;
4.   one-to-one before one-to-many;
5.   one-to-one before many-to-one.

The second axis, the scale of univocality, specifies the kinds and degrees of ambiguity of the operations of (oral) reading (pronunciation) and spelling. For spelling, the more complex of the two, the scale of univocality is as follows:

a.   absolute biuniqueness: Czech <b, f, g, ...>;
b.   relative biuniqueness: Czech <a, c, d, e, ...>;
c.   regular deviations: different graphemes are used for a single phoneme with different morphemes, the choice being given by a general rule and corroborated by phonemic alternations in the given morphemic position (with a different phonemic context): Czech <psy>;
d.   as in (c), without the corroborating alternations (no Czech examples);
e.   irregular deviations, the choice being given by a difference between lexical morphemes: Czech <byl>;
f.   irregular deviations, the choice being given by a morpheme whose single graphemic shape is thus ensured: Czech derivational affix <-yne>;
g.   irregular deviations with the choice given idiosyncratically (traditionally, without a functional justification): Czech <jazyk>.

A deviation from biuniqueness is graphemically ambiguous if the relation between grapheme and phoneme is many-to-one and phonemically ambiguous if the relation between grapheme and phoneme is one-to-many. The above scale of univocality for spelling thus specifies a hierarchy of graphemic ambiguity.

Like the scale of complexness, the scale of univocality has great intui-tive appeal. In essence, it states that the degree of complexity of an ambiguous orthographic representation is directly related to the kind and amount of linguistic information needed for its resolution. Such information ranges from context-free phoneme-grapheme correspondences to phoneme-grapheme correspondences whose context is sensitive to phonology, inflectional morphology, derivational morphology, semantics, and lexis.

Sgall's theory of orthographic complexity could be further developed using information derived from studies of orthographic universals (Justeson 1977; Volkov 1981) and profitably used for formulating hypotheses in the areas of developmental and acquired reading disorders, developmental psycholinguistics, and the psychology of reading and spelling. Rather than dwell on such extensions and applications, we turn to orthographic complexity and the orthography of inflection and contraction in an acquisitional setting.

2.   Orthographic Complexity and the Orthography of Inflection

The theory of linguistic complexity delivers universal categories of linguistic complexity ranked from least to most complex. Under the complexity hypothesis on language acquisition, more complex categories are acquired later than those which are less complex. We tested this hypothesis in the area of the orthography of English inflection and contraction, where the details of the phonology of English inflection and contraction are given in Luelsdorff (1969, 1987b) and Luelsdorff and Norrick (1987).

Knowledge of the boundaries and identities of the inflected and contracted morphemes of English is a necessary prerequisite for their correct spelling. Failure to recognize that <whacks> and <tacks> are in the third singular or plural might result in their being spelled <wax> and <tax>. Failure to recognize that <passed> and <packed> are in the preterite or are past participles might result in their being spelled <past> and <pact>. Failure to recognize that <boy's> is in the possessive singular might lead to its being spelled as either the plural <boys> or the possessive plural <boys'>, or as a contracted main verb or auxiliary <is> or <has>, i.e. correctly, but for the wrong reason.

Assuming that the boundaries and identities of the inflected and contracted morphemes are known, the orthography/phonology/morphology

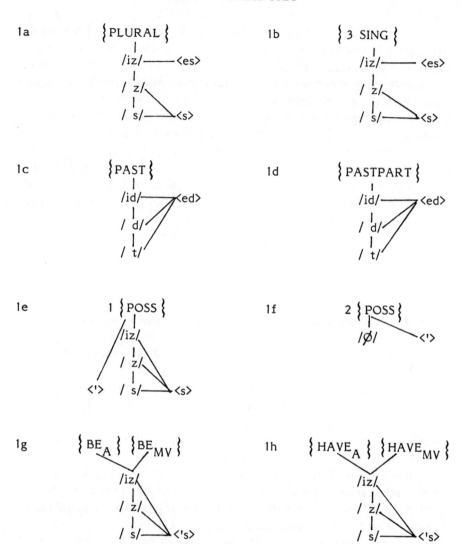

Figure 1: Phonology and orthography of inflection and contraction

interface exhibits the relations displayed in Figure 1.

The simplest cases are those of the plural, third singular, and the syllabic preterite and past participle. In such instances, either the same letter stands for either of two sounds, or two letters stand for two sounds. This complexity we represent in (1):

(1) a. $\begin{Bmatrix} /s/ \\ /z/ \end{Bmatrix} \rightarrow <s>$ b. $/d/ \rightarrow <d>$

    c. $/i/ \quad \rightarrow <e>$

(1a.-c.) rank 1 on the scale of complexness, (1b.-c.) 1 on the scale of univocality. (1a.) ranks 2 on the scale of univocality, since /s/ and /z/, with major correspondences in <s> in word-final position, are relatively biunique.

Consonant singling and doubling, which are stem-finally implicated by the spelling of the preterite, past participle, and progressive, are more complicated than the plural and third singular, because they are more context sensitive. A stem-final consonant sound is spelled singly if it either follows a tense vowel or occurs in a consonant cluster, as in <dined> and <dented>. In consonant doubling, a single, stem-final consonant sound is spelled doubly if it follows a stressed lax vowel and precedes a vowel-spelling, as in <wagged> and <bragged>. Of the two, consonant doubling appears the more complex, since it is sensitive to information in both the preceding and following context for its proper operation and operates on letters, rather than sounds. This relative complexity we represent in (2):

(2) a. $/C/ \rightarrow <C> /X\_\_$
    b. $<C> \rightarrow <CC> /Y\_Z$

What is their relative complexity measurement? We propose treating "vowel 'digraph' + single consonant" sequences as strings with the consonant letter a protographeme and the vowel 'digraph' a complex grapheme; the latter usually consisting of a protographeme followed by a regular subgrapheme (diacritic), as in <ea, oa; aa, ee, ie, oe, ue; ai, ei, oi, ui; eu, ou>. These complex graphemes have a left-handed head and a right-handed specifier, where the specifier is an instruction to pronounce the head by means of letter naming as a spelling strategy (cf. Luelsdorff 1986). That this singled consonant letter encodes the tenseness of the preceding vowel becomes evident in the orthography of inflection and derivation, where the weight of encoding tenseness is shifted from the vowel complex to the following singled consonant, as in <waged> vs. <wagged>, <bi*d*ing> vs. <bidding>, and <deri*s*ive> vs. <permissive>. Similarly, "simplex vowel + doubled consonant" sequences are protographeme strings in which the vowel laxness is encoded in the first of the following two consonants before an inflectional suffix beginning with a vowel spelling. On this view, both singled and doubled consonants are constituents of strings with complex elements: singled consonants after doubled vowels and doubled consonants after singled vowels. Doubled consonants are more complex than singled because they are complex graphemes with regular subgraphemes (the doubled letter functioning as a diacritic) rather than protographemes. Therefore, on Sgall's scales of complexness and univocality we assign consonant singling and consonant doubling the ranks of 5 and 2, singling with complexity in the vowel, and doubling with complexity in the consonants.

The voiced and voiceless preterite and past participle are sound-letter structures which are both (1) zero-to-one and (2) one-to-one, comprising jointly a relationship which is one-to-many, as in (3):

(3)   a. $/\emptyset/ \rightarrow$ <e>   b. $\begin{Bmatrix} /d/ \\ /t/ \end{Bmatrix} \rightarrow$ <d>

In either case, there is one phoneme spelled by two graphemes. Hence, the voiced and voiceless preterite and past participle occupy rank 7 on the scale of complexness and rank 6 on the scale of univocality, since <ed> stands sometimes for /t/, sometimes for /d/, and sometimes for /i/, i.e. the relationship is one of irregular deviation, the choice given by a morpheme whose single graphemic shape is thus ensured.

In the voiced and voiceless non-syllabic possessive singular and the non-syllabic contractions, a diacritic <'> is followed by <s> and stands for either /s/ or /z/, i.e. further sound-letter relationships which are one-to-many. These we depict as in (4):

(4)   a. $/\emptyset/ \rightarrow$ <'>   b. $\begin{Bmatrix} /s/ \\ /z/ \end{Bmatrix} \rightarrow$ <s>

In each case there is one phoneme spelled by a diacritic and a grapheme. Since <'> has no sound value, it cannot be a subgrapheme. Furthermore, since it stands mainly for either possession or contraction, it cannot be regular. For these reasons, we assign <'s> to rank 8 on the scale of complexness, and, on the scale of univocality, rank 6.

In the possessive plural, the diacritic $<$'$>$ bears a direct, unmediated relationship to the grammatical category of possession. It differs from the possessive singular in that neither sound nor letter are involved. The possessive plural we represent as in (5):

(5) $/\emptyset/ \rightarrow <$'$>$

Due to the absence of both letter and sound, we assign the possessive plural to rank 9 on the scale of complexness, and, on the scale of univocality, rank 8.

In the syllabic possessive singular and the syllabic contractions of the main verb and auxiliary $<$has$>$ and $<$is$>$, syllabic $/\text{ɨz}/$ is uniformly spelled $<$'s$>$. This we represent as in (6):

(6) a. $/\emptyset/ \rightarrow <$'$>$ b. $/\text{ɨ}/ <\emptyset>$ c. $/\text{z}/ \rightarrow <$s$>$.

In view of the fact that (6) includes (5), which we assigned rank 9 on the scale of complexness, we assign (6) the rank of at least 9 on the scale of complexness and at least 8 on the scale of univocality.

Evidently, the relations among orthography, phonology, morphology and contraction depicted in Figure 1, and the relations among orthography, phonology, and morphology in consonant singling and doubling, may be reduced to the rules presented in (1-6). As it happens, the rules (1-6) may themselves be reduced to three groups: those which are one-to-one (1), those which are one-to-many (2, 3, 4), and those which are none-to-one or one-to-none (5, 6). If it is normal for a sound signifié to have a letter signifiant, it must be less normal for a sound signifié to have several letter signifiants, and even less normal for no sound signifié to have a letter signifiant or a sound signifié to have no letter signifiant. Accordingly, our hypothesis on the acquisition of the orthography of inflection and contraction is as follows:

> one-to-one correspondences are acquired before those which are one-to-many, and one-to-many correspondences are acquired before those which are none-to-one or one-to-none.

We indicated above that knowledge of the orthography of inflection necessarily depended upon knowledge of phonology and morphology. Now, since recognition of the morphology depends upon the syntax and the syntax interacts with the semantics, knowledge of the orthography of inflection and contraction depends upon knowledge of syntax and semantics.

Since our learners possess imperfect knowledge of the syntax and semantics of English, it is to be supposed that this imperfect knowledge will adversely influence their performance on the orthography of inflection and contraction, quite independently of their knowledge of the principles of English orthography themselves. For example, if a possessive is incorrectly categorized as a plural, it will be spelled as a plural, irrespective of whether the speller knows how to spell the possessive. Consequently, some errors cannot be understood without reference to a hierarchy of morphemic complexity.

Brown (1973) provides us with the acquisition order and complexity order of 13 "morphemes" of English. Categories common to both our studies are: (1) plural, (2) past regular, (3) third person regular, (4) contractable copula, and (5) contractable auxiliary. To these we add: (6) contractable main verb *has*, and (7) contractable *has* as an auxiliary. Comparison of the scale of grammatical complexity with the scale of orthographic complexity reveals the interesting fact that the two do not coincide. The third singular and the plural, for example, differ in morphemic complexity but are orthographically equally complex, and the syllabic and non-syllabic preterite differ in orthographic complexity but are morphemically equally complex. Were these two scales, the orthographic and the morphological, the same, one might expect the observed acquisition hierarchy to be a function of one or the other. The fact that these parameters are different, however, induces a systemic dynamism or disequilibrium (Vachek 1983), and this dynamism is responsible for the production of classes of errors which cannot be understood on the basis of the scale of orthographic complexity alone.

3.   Acquisition of the Orthography of Inflection and Contraction

Applying the above-mentioned methodological procedures to the data from the first dictation, we obtained the results depicted in Table 1. Here, the Roman numerals in the first column represent the acquisitional groups, the Arabic numbers in the second column the number of structures the items in each acquisitional group precede, and the Arabic numerals in the third column the individual structures comprising the acquisitional groups (defined in Appendix II).

In order that the acquisitional groups are not merely an artifact of the

Table 1: Acquisition hierarchy at t_1

Group		Precedes	Structures
I	I	26	3.3, 11.2, 11.3, 11.4, 4.1, 4.2, 4.3, 4.4, 6.1, 6.3, 9.2, 12.2, 6.2
II		20	8.2, 12.1
III	II	15	5.2, 5.3, 12,3, 3.1, 1.1, 7.2, 9.1, 10.1
IV		11	1.2, 7.1, 11.1, 5.1
V		10	8.1
VI		8	3.2, 10.2
VII	III	3	2.2, 2.1, 7.3, 8.3, 9.3
VIII		0	1.3, 2.3, 10.3

method used for determining them, it appears essential to ask whether the structures within the groups are the products of a *common* set of processing strategies and whether the structures within different groups are the products of a *different* set of processing strategies. Only then can we be relatively sure that our method-derived acquisitional groups correspond to something other than the method.

Acquisitional group I, from this perspective, contains structures which bear a one-to-one relationship between letter and sound: the plural, the syllabic past participle, and the syllabic third singular (but see below).

Groups II, III, IV, V, and VI contain the environmentally conditioned spellings of consonant singling after long vowels, consonant doubling after short vowels, structures with a one-to-many relationship between sound and letter, as in the voiced and voiceless preterite and the voiced past participle, or diacritic and sound, as in the voiced and voiceless non-syllabic possessive singular, and a whole array of non-syllabic contractions (voiceless main verb and auxiliary <is> and <has>). These groups are distinguished from group I by the greater complexity of their sound-letter mapping and the greater complexity of their underlying semantics, syntax, and phonology (cf. Brown 1973:308-309).

Groups VII and VIII consist of either structures where something, an apostrophe, is used to spell nothing sensible, a zero allomorph, or structures where nothing is used to spell something, namely the vowel in the syllabic possessive singular and the vowels in the contracted syllabic main verb and auxiliary <is> and <has>. These last acquired groups thus consist of signs with either a zero signifiant or a zero signifié and occupy the highest rank on both Sgall's scale of orthographic complexness and Brown's scale of grammatical morphemic complexity.

There is no unambiguous evidence countering the claim that observed order of acquisition does not differ from the order of acquisition predicted by the order of orthographic complexity. Apparent counterexamples include third singular /s/ and /z/ and the syllabic preterite /id/. According to the complexity hypothesis presented above, these three structures are among the simplest, yet the first appears in acquisition group III, the second in acquisition group VI, and the third in acquisition group II. Typical errors include <jumpes, jumped> for <jumps>, <rubbes, robbes> for <rubs>, <wages> for <wags>, and <dentied> for <dented>. If one regards the extraneous vowels as constituents of the endings, i.e. <jump + es, rubb + es, wag + es, dent +ied>, then the observed acquisitional orders contradict the ones predicted. If, however, one treats the extraneous vowels as constituents of the stems, i.e. <jumpe + s, rubbe + s, wage + s, denti + ed>, then the acquisition orders observed correspond to the acquisition orders predicted, and there are no counterexamples to the claim that acquisition order = complexity order. In fact, the evidence in support of this hypothesis is so strong that it appears that the complexity order itself may be used to resolve the analytical ambiguity of the errors in question. Moreover, there is independent evidence for the existence of overgeneralizations and long vowel spellings for short in both first (Ehri 1986) and second language acquisition (Luelsdorff 1986).

In sum, the application of a mechanical procedure for partitioning the data into acquisitional groups results in eight major groupings and eight minor groupings of structures in adjacent major groupings. The structures in adjacent major groupings differ from one another by at least two errors, and the structures within major groups and within minor groups differ from one another by at most one. Insistence on unifying principles underlying groupings results in the reduction of the initial eight groups to three. In the first of these, the relationship between letter and sound is one-to-one. In the second, the relationship is either context-sensitive or one-to-many. In the third, either a diacritic stands for no sound or some sound is not represented by a letter. Differences in semiotic principles, rather than rules, thus underlie the differentiation into groups. Inasmuch as the acquisitional groups observed correspond to the acquisitional groups predicted, we conclude that the acquisitional order of the orthography of inflection and contraction supports the theory that complexity explains acquisition.

4. Acquisitional Stages

Ehri (1986:141) distinguishes three stages in the development of orthographic knowledge of English according to the type of regularity evident in the spellings invented by children in the course of learning to read and spell: (1) the semiphonetic; (2) the phonetic; (3) the morphemic. In the semiphonetic stage children use their knowledge of alphabet letter names to create partial spellings of words, for example, spelling <dress> as <S> or <elevator> as <L>. The phonetic stage emerges when short vowel spellings are learned in the first grade and lasts until spellings break away from a one-to-one relationship between letter and sound. The morphemic stage may begin in the second grade when spellers shift from an exclusive reliance on one-to-one relations to the use of word-based spelling patterns as well. Ehri stresses that phonetic spellings are not abandoned in the morphemic stage, but supplemented by morphemic patterns.

The analysis of the errors in the spellings of the inflections and contractions provides very strong confirmation of a *mixed* stage of phonetic and morphemic spelling in the acquisition of L2-English orthography by German school children. For example, the most frequent error on the syllabic possessive singular and the contractions of syllabic main verb and auxiliary

<has> and <is> is the addition of a spurious letter to represent the vowel. Syllabic possessive singular <Rich's> is most frequently misspelled <Richie's> (7x), <Richi's> (2x), <Richy's> (1x), <Richies> (1x), <Rigia's> (1x), and <Bridge's> (1x), where the vowel letter is phonetic and the apostrophe is morphemic. Syllabic auxiliary <has> in <Ross's> is misspelled <Ross is> (8x) and with a syllabic <e> (4x), and <Rich's> is misspelled <Rich is> (5x) and with a syllabic stem vowel (7x). Contracted syllabic main verb <has> is written with an extraneous stem-final vowel in 11/14 cases. Since most of these examples of phonetic spelling also contain the required morphemic <'s>, they persuasively demonstrate the coexistence of phonetic and morphemic spelling. Further, uncited examples point in the same direction.

It would be misguided, however, to construe the morphemic stage as consisting of spelling patterns which are solely word-based, because, as repeatedly emphasized above, the very recognition of the inflected and contracted allomorphy presupposes syntactic and semantic categorization beyond the word. Failure to syntactically categorize or categorize correctly results in errors even if one does know the correct inflected and contracted spellings. Such miscategorizations typically involve spelling the possessive as though it were the plural, main-verb <has> contractions as though they were the possessive, and auxiliary <has>-contractions as though they were uncontracted auxiliary <is>, i.e. rank-downshifting along the scale of grammatical complexity (see above). One major example must suffice. Contracted syllabic main verb <has> in <Mitch's> was misspelled <Mitche's> on 8/14 occasions. At first sight, <Mitche's>, with an <e>, for <Mitch's>, appears to be just another example of phonetic spelling, with the vowel letter <e> used to spell the vowel sound /iz/. However, <has> as the contracted syllabic auxiliary in <Ross's> was misspelled <Ross is> on 8/14 occasions, not <Rosse's>, as one would expect if auxiliary <has> were being processed like main verb <has>. We suggest that this difference in error types for the same standard language phonetic and orthographic form is correlated with a difference in syntactic processing strategies resulting in a difference in morpheme recognition: <Mitche's> as the *possessive* constituent of the spurious NP [[[Mitche]'s] [photos]] in the dictated sentence *Mitch's photos of America's buffalos* and <Ross is> as the spurious constituent $[_?[_N$ Ross] $[_{AUX}$ is]] in the dictated sentence *Ross's often cheated on his hardest tests*. This example at once illustrates that the spellings of the English inflections and contractions are not word-based in their entirety and that the constraints on their misrepresentation can consequently not be fully understood without recourse to a syntactically or semantically-based scale of morphemic complexity.

5. Individual Variation

The above remarks are generalizations about structures, not the individuals responsible for the production of those structures. Aspects of individual similarities and differences are presented in Table 2. Here, the columns contain the numbers of the structures studied, the rows contain the numbers of the individual subjects, and the cells contain either a 1 or a 0, depending upon whether the subject's performance was normative or non-normative. The Roman numerals I, II, and III stand for the semiotically and psycholinguistically motivated groups, where the asterisked structures 3.2, 3.1, and 5.3 in group II, if the above reanalysis is accepted, belong to acquisitional group I.

All subjects performed uniformly correctly on group I, but considerable interindividual variation appears in groups II and III, with some implicational patterning within each of these groups. Within group III, for example, if an individual performs normatively on 2.1, then s/he will perform normatively on 2.2. Within group II, to take another example, if an individual performs normatively on 10.1, then s/he will perform normatively on 8.2. The most important single generalization, however, is that each individual's performance is better on structures of group I than on structures of group II, and better on structures of group II than on structures of group III, a distribution which follows from the complexity theory of orthography acquisition. Note that this theory constrains the class of individual variants, permitting I > II > III, but prohibiting I > III > II, II > III > I, II > I > III, III > II > I, and III > I > II. Within each acquisitional group, individuals are free to vary outside the confines of the implicational constraints, whatever they may be. Within acquisitional group III, for example, it would be strange to find an individual who could spell the possessive plural after /s/, but not the possessive plural after /z/. Thus viewed, implicational relations follow from orthographic universals and establish and constrain the parameters along which individuals may vary.

Table 2: Implicational scale at t_1

Structure \ Subject	7	2	3	9	11	10	13	1	6	4	14	5	12	8	
2.3	o	o	o	o	o	o	o	o	o	o	o	o			III
10.3	o	o	o	o	o	o	o	o	o	o	o	o			
1.3	o	o	o	o	o	o	o	o	o	o	o	o		1	
8.3	o	o	o	o	o	o	o	1	o	o	o	o	1	o	
2.1	o	o	o	o	o	1	o	o	o	o	1	o	1	o	
7.3	o	o	o	o	o	o	o	o	o	1	o	1	o	o	
9.3	o	o	o	o	o	1	o	o	o	o	o	o	1	1	
2.2	o	o	o	o	o	1	o	o	o	1	o	1	o	1	
3.2	o	o	o	1	o	o	1	o	o	1	1	o	o	1	II
10.2	o	1	o	1	o	o	o	o	o	o	1	o	1	1	
8.1	o	1	o	o	o	o	1	1	o	o	1	1	o	1	
1.2	o	o	1	o	1	o	1	1	1	1	1	1	1	1	
7.1	o	1	o	1	o	1	1	o	1	1	1	1	1	1	
3.1	1	o	1	o	1	o	1	1	1	o	1	o	1	1	
11.1	1	1	1	o	1	o	o	1	1	1	1	o	1	1	
5.1	1	1	1	o	1	o	1	o	1	1	1	1	o	o	
1.1	1	o	1	o	1	o	1	1	1	1	1	1	1	1	
7.2	o	1	o	1	1	1	1	1	1	1	1	1	1	1	
9.1	o	1	o	1	o	1	1	1	1	1	1	1	1	1	
10.1	o	1	o	1	o	1	1	1	1	1	1	1	1	1	
5.3	1	o	1	o	1	1	1	1	1	1	1	1	1	1	
12.3	1	o	1	o	1	o	1	1	1	1	1	1	1	1	
6.2	1	1	1	1	1	1	1	1	1	1	1	1	1	o	
8.2	o	1	1	1	1	1	1	1	1	1	1	1	1	1	
12.1	1	1	o	1	1	1	1	1	1	1	1	1	1	1	
5.2	1	1	1	o	1	1	1	1	1	1	1	1	1	1	
3.3	1	1	1	1	1	1	1	1	1	1	1	1	1	1	I
11.2	1	1	1	1	1	1	1	1	1	1	1	1	1	1	
11.3	1	1	1	1	1	1	1	1	1	1	1	1	1	1	
11.4	1	1	1	1	1	1	1	1	1	1	1	1	1	1	
4.1	1	1	1	1	1	1	1	1	1	1	1	1	1	1	
4.2	1	1	1	1	1	1	1	1	1	1	1	1	1	1	
4.3	1	1	1	1	1	1	1	1	1	1	1	1	1	1	
4.4	1	1	1	1	1	1	1	1	1	1	1	1	1	1	
6.1	1	1	1	1	1	1	1	1	1	1	1	1	1	1	
6.3	1	1	1	1	1	1	1	1	1	1	1	1	1	1	
9.2	1	1	1	1	1	1	1	1	1	1	1	1	1	1	
12.2	1	1	1	1	1	1	1	1	1	1	1	1	1	1	

6. Developmental Orthography

The conclusions drawn thus far have been based on cross-sectional data elicited from one group of subjects at one point in time. The acquisition orders observed were found to flow from universal scales of orthographic complexity and the errors made from the directed interaction of scales of complexity both orthographic and morphemic. Moreover, individual variation was found to be constrained by the relationship between adjacent complexity groups such that the quality of performance in a more complex group directly predicts the quality of performance in an adjacent group that is less complex. The resultant model of language acquisition is thus constrained by both *adjacency* and *directionality* and, requiring the interaction of different scales of complexity, is *interactive* and modular.

What remains to be shown is the development of the orthography of inflection and contraction and the variation that this development exhibits. To this end, we duplicated the above experiments with the same group of subjects four months later, with the results presented in Table 3.

If it is true that acquisition groups I, II, and III are increasingly more complex, as stipulated by the universal hierarchy of orthographic complexity, and the universal hierarchy of orthographic complexity controls the order of orthography acquisition, as shown above, then (1) the members of *adjacent* acquisitional groups ought to be acquired before the members of non-adjacent acquisitional groups, i.e. II to I, and III to II, rather than III to I, and (2) different acquisitional groups with forgotten members ought to be *adjacent* and forgetting should proceed from less to more complex. Call (1) the Adjacency and Directionality Conditions on Acquisition and (2) the Adjacency and Directionality Conditions on Attrition. Taken together, (1) and (2) constrain linguistic mental movement up and down the scales of linguistic complexity, hence language learnability and teachability (cf. Pienemann 1986).

Are the actual observations consistent with these predictions? Comparison of Tables 1 and 3 reveals the fact that structures 2.2, 7.3, 8.3 of acquisition group III in hierarchy I have entered acquisition group II in hierarchy II and that none have entered acquisition group I. Furthermore, structures 1.1, 5.2, 5.3, 7.1, 7.2, 8.2, 9.1, 10.1 of acquisition group II in hierarchy I have entered acquisition group I in hierarchy II. Since members of III have entered II and members of II have entered I, while no members of III have entered I directly, the experimental results are consistent with

Table 3: Acquisition hierarchy at t_2

Group		Precedes	Structure
I	I	18	3.3, 11.2, 11.3, 11.4, 4.1, 4.2, 4.3, 6.1, 6.3, 7.2, 8.2, 10.1
			1.1, 5.2, 5.3, 7.1, 9.1, 9.2, 12.2, 4.4
II		12	12.3, 6.2
			11.1, 3.1, 10.2, 12.1
III	II	9	5.1, 7.3, 1.2
IV		7	8.1 8.3
V		5	3.2 2.2
VI		2	10.3, 2.1, 9.3
VII	III	0	2.3, 1.3

Table 4: Transition matrix from t_1 to t_2

Subject	1.1	1.2	1.3	3.1	3.2	3.3	11.1	11.2	11.3	11.4	4.1	4.2	4.3	4.4	2.3	2.1	2.2	5.1	5.2	5.3	6.1	6.2	6.3	7.1	7.2	7.3	8.1	8.2	8.3	9.1	9.2	9.3	10.1	10.2	10.3	12.1	12.2	12.3	0→1	1→0	Total
1	1	1	0	1	0	1	1	1	1	1	1	1	1	1	0	0	0	1	1	1	1	1	1	0	1	1	1	1	1	1	1	0	1	1	0	1	1	1	4	0	4
2	1	0	0	0	0	1	1	1	1	1	1	1	1	1	0	0	1	1	1	1	1	1	1	1	1	1	1	1	1	1	1	1	1	1	0	1	0	1	4	2	6
3	0	0	0	1	1	1	1	1	1	1	1	1	1	1	0	0	1	0	1	1	1	0	1	1	1	1	1	1	1	1	1	1	0	1	1	1	0	0	5	5	10
4	1	1	0	1	1	1	1	1	1	1	1	1	1	1	0	1	1	1	1	1	0	1	1	0	1	1	1	1	0	1	0	1	0	1	1	1	1	1	3	1	4
5	1	1	0	1	1	1	1	1	1	1	1	1	1	1	1	0	0	1	1	1	1	1	1	1	1	1	0	1	1	1	1	1	1	0	1	1	1	1	4	1	5
6	1	1	0	1	1	1	1	1	1	1	1	1	1	1	0	0	0	0	1	1	1	1	1	1	1	0	0	1	1	0	1	1	0	0	1	1	1	1	4	0	4
7	1	0	0	1	0	1	1	1	1	1	1	1	1	1	0	0	1	1	1	1	1	0	1	1	1	1	0	1	0	1	1	1	1	0	1	1	1	1	8	2	10
8	1	1	0	1	0	1	1	0	1	1	0	1	0	1	0	0	1	1	1	1	1	1	1	1	1	0	1	0	1	1	0	1	1	1	1	1	1	1	2	3	5
9	1	0	0	1	0	1	1	1	1	1	1	1	1	1	0	0	1	1	1	0	1	1	1	1	0	1	1	1	1	1	1	0	1	1	1	1	1	0	5	1	6
10	1	0	0	1	0	1	1	1	1	1	1	1	1	1	0	1	0	0	1	1	1	0	1	1	0	1	0	1	1	0	0	1	1	1	0	1	1	1	5	2	7
11	1	0	0	1	0	1	1	1	1	1	1	1	1	1	0	0	0	1	0	1	1	1	1	1	1	0	0	1	1	1	1	0	1	1	0	1	1	1	6	0	6
12	1	0	0	1	0	1	1	1	1	1	1	1	1	1	0	1	0	0	1	1	1	1	1	1	1	0	1	0	0	1	1	0	0	1	0	1	0	1	1	2	3
13	1	1	0	1	1	1	1	1	1	1	1	1	1	1	0	0	0	0	1	1	1	1	1	1	0	1	0	1	1	0	1	0	0	1	0	1	1	1	5	0	5
14	1	0	0	0	0	1	1	1	1	1	1	1	1	1	0	0	1	1	1	1	1	1	1	0	1	1	0	1	0	1	1	0	1	1	0	1	1	1	0	3	3
0→1	3	2	1	2	3	0	2	0	0	0	0	0	0	1	1	1	1	0	0	1	0	0	0	4	3	5	3	1	6	2	0	0	3	7	4	0	0	1			
1→0	1	2	0	1	2	0	1	0	0	0	0	0	0	0	0	1	0	1	0	0	0	2	0	0	0	0	3	0	0	2	1	0	0	1	0	3	1	1			
Total	4	4	1	3	5	0	3	0	0	0	0	0	0	1	1	2	1	1	0	1	0	2	0	4	3	5	6	1	6	2	1	0	3	8	4	4	1	1			

the Adjacency and Directionality Conditions on Acquisition. Moreover, 1/ 30 structures, namely the <-ed> in past participle <bragged>, suffers attrition to the extent that it falls to a different acquisitional group. Since this attritional movement is from group I to group II, these experimental results (cf. also below) are consistent with the Adjacency and Directionality Conditions on Attrition.

The Complexity Theory of Orthography Acquisition, including a Hierarchy of Complexity, and Adjacency and Directionality Conditions on Acquisition and Attrition, strongly constrains language learning and language forgetting. If the theory of complexity stipulates that III is more complex than II, and that II is more complex than I, then I is learned before II and II before III. This means that III is more error-prone than II, and that II is more error-prone than I. Furthermore, in acquisition, the members of III will enter II and the members of II will enter I and, in attrition, a lost member of I implies a lost member of II, and a lost member of II implies a lost member of III.

Aspects of the orthographic development of the sample from time t_1 to time t_2 (four months) are given in the transition matrix in Table 4. The structures are in the columns, the subjects in the rows. 1 in the cells stands for acquired, 0 stands for not acquired, an underlined 1 stands for a structure acquired between t_1 and t_2, and an underlined 0 for a structure forgotten between t_1 and t_2. $0 \rightarrow 1$ and $1 \rightarrow 0$ stand for the numbers of subjects learning and forgetting and the numbers of structures learned and forgotten. The totals stand for the total number of changes the subjects and structures underwent.

For any given transition period, the easiest structure is the structure with the most learning and the least forgetting. By the Adjacency·and Directionality Conditions on Attrition, a forgotten member of a less complex group implies a forgotten member of a more complex group (directionality) and the two groups must be adjacent. For example, if an individual forgets a structure in group I, then another forgotten structure belongs to group II. Similarly, if an individual forgets a structure in group II, then another forgotten structure will belong to group III. Examples include subjects 14, 10, and 8 in Table 4. Subject 14 forgot the non-syllabic third singular (group I), then non-syllabic auxiliary <is>-contraction (group II) and the possessive singular <'s> (group II). Subject 10 forgot the plural with stem change (group I) and the non-syllabic past participle <ed> (group II). Subject 8 forgot the non-syllabic third singular (group I), non-syllabic auxiliary <is>-contraction (group II), and the possessive plural <'> (group III). The fact that there are no subjects who forgot structures in groups I and III, while at the same time not forgetting structures in group II, must mean that language attrition, like language acquisition, is subject to law. This law, we suggest, is the Law of Complexity.

7. Conclusion

A core concern of studies in both first and second language acquisition is the discovery and explanation of differential orders of language learning, including orthography in its use in spelling and reading. In work in progress (Luelsdorff and Eyland 1989) we report that input frequency, in the sense of both relative and absolute type frequency, plays a negligible role in determining the order of acquisition of the spellings of the English short and long vowels.

A more promising approach to the explanation of acquisition order is to attempt to significantly correlate orders of acquisition with orders of complexity. In this paper we present and extend Sgall's universal scales of orthographic complexity and use them to assign complexity to the orthography of inflection and contraction and the entailed areas of consonant singling and doubling. Since the correct spellings of the inflections and contractions crucially depend upon morpheme recognition, and morpheme recognition in turn depends upon disambiguation by the syntactic and semantic context, the correct spellings of the inflections and contractions also depend upon syntactic and semantic recognition beyond the word.

We hypothesized that the order of orthography acquisition is a function of the order of orthographic complexity and tested this hypothesis for 38 orthographic structures on a sample of 14 fifth-year German learners of English as a foreign language. Disconfirming evidence could only come from simpler structures on the hierarchy of orthographic complexity being acquired after structures that are more complex. The data was found to be consistent with the hypothesis, and apparently disconfirming evidence led to an independently motivated reanalysis.

Moreover, the existence of different types of errors corresponding to morphologically different forms with the same normative surface phonology and orthography suggested the interaction of the scale of orthographic complexity with the scale of morphemic complexity. Other things being equal, misspelled higher ranking morphemes are spelled as morphemes of lower ranks.

The resultant notion of L2-orthography development is not one of stages defined in terms of *rules* appearing in a predictable order (Meisel, Clahsen and Pienemann 1981:110), but of stages defined in terms of successively more complex inclusive *semiotic schemata* defined on relations like one-to-one, one-to-many, none-to-one, one-to-none, and their combinations, upon whose prior, general presence the emergence of particular rules depends.

The complexity theory of orthography acquisition not only explains the order of orthography acquisition, but also constrains the class of possible interpersonal variations, such that the implicational relations among and within the complexity schema provided by the complexity theory must not be violated.

Developmentally, the members of adjacent acquisitional groups are acquired before the members of acquisitional groups that are non-adjacent, and attrition in a less complex acquisitional group implies attrition in an acquisitional group that is adjacent and more complex. These constraints on learning and forgetting were also seen to follow from the theory of orthographic complexity.

The explanatory potential of complexity linguistics invites further exploration and testing in this and other areas of developmental psycholinguistics, language processing, and language pathology.

Appendix I: Dictation exercise

Please read each of the following sentences aloud to your pupils twice, stopping each time for a pause at the place marked /. During the second reading have your pupils write the sentences to dictation. Do not explain any unfamiliar words. Tell your pupils to use *contracted forms (Kurzformen) whenever possible*. After the dictation is over, read through the sentences aloud once again. Pupils may make corrections whenever they wish by writing the form they think to be correct over the form they think to be wrong.

1. Rich's father/ teaches swimming/ and horseback riding.
2. Kit's mother/ pushes her/ to try harder.
3. Yesterday/ the Whites' children/ dented their parents' sports car.
4. John's already raked up/ the bigger leaves.
5. Last week/ Jack's brother/ stabbed a bank robber.
6. Susan's three valuable radios.
7. Ross's fattest cat/ rubs its front paws together.

8. Fritz's absolutely reliable.
9. The two boys' uncle/ speaks five languages.
10. Mitch's photos of America's buffalos.
11. Last year/ John's teacher/ cramped all his pupils' progress.
12. Jack's a lot of peaches and potatoes.
13. John's dining on/ fresh oranges.
14. Hank's an expert/ on pianos.
15. The Joneses' Jack's/ humming happier songs/ these days.
16. John's one of/ the country's heroes.
17. Rich's already striped/ his bike white.
18. Mary's often bragged/ about her highest marks.
19. The two judges' horse/ jumps over higher fences.
20. The children's puppy/ wags its tail/ fastest when happiest.
21. Jack's already flopped/ into the biggest bed.
22. Ross's wading/ in the deepest water.
23. Yesterday/ Mary's oldest sister/ trimmed the biggest bushes.
24. Ross's often cheated/ on his hardest tests.

Appendix II: Test words

The numbers in parentheses are the numbers of the sentences in which the test words occur.

1.1 Possessive singular /s/:<'s>
Kit's (2), Jack's (5)
1.2 Possessive singular /z/:<'s>
America's (10), John's (11), country's (16), Mary's (23)
1.3 Possessive singular /iz/:<'s>
Rich's (1), Ross's (7)
2.1 Possessive plural after /s/:<'>
Whites' (3), parents' (3)
2.2 Possessive plural after /z/:<'>
boys' (9), pupils' (11)
2.3 Possessive plural after syllabic /iz/:<'>
Joneses' (15), judges' (19)
3.1 Third singular /s/:<s>
speaks (9), jumps (19)
3.2 Third singular /z/:<s>
rubs (7), wags (20)
3.3 Third singular /iz/:<es>
teaches (1), pushes (2)
4.1 Plural /s/:<s>
sports (3), Whites' (3), parents' (3), marks (18), tests (24)
4.2 Plural /z/:<s>

paws (15), songs (15), days (15), boys' (9), pupils' (11)

4.3 Plural /iz/:<es>
languages (9), peaches (12), oranges (13), Jones's (15), judges' (19), fences (19), bushes (23)

4.4 Plural with possible stem change
radios (6), photos (10), buffalo(e)s (10), potatoes (12), pianos (14), heroes (16)

5.1 Preterite /t/:<ed>
cramped (11)

5.2 Preterite /d/:<ed>
stabbed (5), trimmed (23)

5.3 Preterite /id/:<ed>
dented (3)

6.1 Past participle /t/:<ed>
raked (4), striped (17), flopped (21)

6.2 Past participle /d/:<ed>
bragged (18)

6.3 Past participle /id/:<ed>
cheated (24)

7.1 <is> contraction: main verb /s/:<'s>
Hank's (14)

7.2 <is> contraction: main verb /z/:<'s>
John's (16)

7.3 <is> contraction: main verb /iz/:<'s>
Fritz's (8)

8.1 <is> contraction: auxiliary /s/:<'s>
Jack's (15)

8.2 <is> contraction: auxiliary /z/:<'s>
John's (13)

8.3 <is> contraction: auxiliary /iz/:<'s>
Ross's (22)

9.1 <has> contraction: main verb /s/:<'s>
Jack's (12)

9.2 <has> contraction: main verb /z/:<'s>
Susan's (6)

9.3 <has> contraction: main verb /iz/:<'s>
Mitch's (10)

10.1 <has> contraction: auxiliary /s/:<'s>
Jack's (21)

10.2 <has> contraction: auxiliary /z/:<'s>
John's (4), Mary's (18)

10.3 <has> contraction: auxiliary /iz/:<'s>
Rich's (17), Ross's (24)

11.1 Consonant doubling: verbs
swimming (1), stabbed (5), humming (15), bragged (18), flopped (21), trimmed (23)

11.2 Consonant doubling: comparative
  bigger (4), happier (25)
11.3 Consonant doubling: superlative
  fattest (7), biggest (21, 23), happiest (20)
11.4 Consonant doubling: nouns
  horseback (1), Jack (5), robber (5), Ross (7), buffalos (10), progress (11), puppy (20)
12.1 Consonant singling: third singular
  rubs (7), speaks (9), wags (20)
12.2 Consonant singling: progressive
  riding (1), dining (13), wading (22)
12.3 Consonant singling: preterite
  raked (4), striped (17), cheated (24)

References

Brown, Roger. 1973. *A First Language. The early stages*. Cambridge, Mass.: Harvard University Press.

Coltheart, Max, Karalyn Patterson & John C. Marshall. 1980. *Deep Dyslexia*. London: Routledge & Kegan Paul.

Dulay, Heidi, Marina Burt & Stephen Krashen. 1982. *Language Two*. New York: Oxford University Press.

Ehri, Linnea C. 1986. "Sources of Difficulty in Learning to Spell and Read". *Advances in Developmental and Behavioral Pediatrics* ed. by M.L. Wolraich & D.K. Routh, Vol. 7, 121-195. Greenwich, Connecticut: JAI Press.

Ellis, Andrew W. 1984. *Reading, Writing, and Dyslexia: A cognitive analysis*. London: Lawrence Erlbaum.

Ferreiro, Emilia. 1983. "The Development of Literacy: A complex psychological problem". *Writing in Focus* ed. by Florian Coulmas & Konrad Ehlich, 277-290. Berlin: Mouton.

Frith, Uta. 1986. "Psychologische Aspekte des orthographischen Wissens: Entwicklung und Entwicklungsstörung". *New Trends in Graphemics and Orthography* ed. by Gerhard Augst, 218-233. Berlin: Walter de Gruyter.

Gentry, J. Richard. 1982. "An Analysis of Developmental Spelling in *GNYS AT WRK*". *The Reading Teacher* 36 (2). 192-199.

Günther, Klaus B. 1986. "Entwicklungs- und sprachpsychologische Begründung der Notwendigkeit spezifischer Methoden für den Erwerb der Schriftsprache bei sprachentwicklungsgestörten, lernbehinderten und hörgeschädigten Kindern". *New Trends in Graphemics and Orthography* ed. by Gerhard Augst, 354-382. Berlin: Walter de Gruyter.

Justeson, John S. 1976. "Universals of Language and Universals of Writing". *Linguistic Studies Offered to Joseph Greenberg* ed. by Alphonse Juilland, 57-94. Saratoga, Calif.: ANMA Libri.

Luelsdorff, Philip A. 1969. "On the Phonology of English Inflection". *Glossa* 3. 39-48.

————. 1986. *Constraints on Error Variables in Grammar: Bilingual misspelling orthographies*. Amsterdam: John Benjamins.

————. 1987a. "The Abstractness Hypothesis and Morphemic Spelling". *Second Language Research* 3(1). 76-87.

————. 1987b. "On Contraction in English. *Orbis* 26.

Luelsdorff, Philip A. & Ann Eyland. 1989. "Psycholinguistic Determinants of Orthography Acquisition". *IRAL* 27(2). 145-158.

Luelsdorff, Philip A. and Neal R. Norrick. 1987. "On *Have*-Contraction". *Orbis* 27.

Meisel, Jürgen M., Harald Clahsen & Manfred Pienemann. 1981. "On Determining Developmental Stages in Natural Second Language Acquisition". *Studies in Second Language Acquisition* 3(2). 109-135.

Ortmann, Wolf Dieter. 1976. *Beispielwörter für deutsche Leseübungen*. München: Goethe Institut.

Philips, Donald J. 1984. "A Prototypical Procedure Used for Designing Specific Teaching Alphabets to Enable L2 Learners to Read English More Effectively". *Australian Review of Applied Linguistics* 7. 179-192.

Pienemann, Manfred. 1986. "Is Language Teachable? Psycholinguistic experiments and hypotheses". *Australian Working Papers in Language Development* 1(3). 41.

Read, Charles. 1986. *Children's Creative Spelling*. London: Routledge & Kegan Paul.

Rutherford, William E. 1982. "Markedness in Second Language Acquisition". *Language Learning* 32(1). 85-108.

Sgall, Petr. 1987. "Towards a Theory of Phonemic Orthography". *Orthography and Phonology* ed. by Philip A. Luelsdorff. Amsterdam: John Benjamins.

Vachek, Josef. 1961. "Some Less Familiar Aspects of the Analytical Trend of English". *Brno Studies in English* 3. 9-71.

————. 1983. "Remarks on the Dynamism of the System of Language". *Praguiana: Some basic and less known aspects of the Prague Linguistic School* ed. by Josef Vachek, 241-254. Amsterdam: John Benjamins.

Volkov, Alexandr A. 1982. *Grammatologija: Semiotika pis'mennoj reči (Grammatology: The semiotics of written speech)*. Moscow: Izdatel'stvo moskovskogo universiteta.

Zwicky, Arnold M. 1987. "Suppressing the Zs". *Journal of Linguistics* 23. 133-148.

"Process" vs. "Product" or Down with the Opposition!

Helen Moore

The Impact of Process Approaches in Australia

For language educators in Australia, the 1980s will be marked as the decade in which "process" was discovered or, more accurately, brought to our shores.

The process movement has come to Australia from the U.S.A. and Britain with somewhat different forms and emphases. American ideas, most notably those of Donald Graves (e.g. 1983), have had a significant impact on the teaching of writing in both English mother tongue and E.S.L. contexts (see, for example, Walshe 1981; Hornsby *et al.* 1986). British applied linguists, such as Widdowson, Breen and Candlin (the latter now at Macquarie University, Sydney) are contributing to E.S.L. curriculum guidelines and discussions, to date largely in the Adult Migrant Education Program and the National Curriculum Development Project (Widdowson 1983; Brumfit 1984; Candlin and Murphy 1987). The Australian Language Levels (ALL) project for schools has been greatly influenced by John Clark and his work as a consultant to the project team (1986, 1987).

Like almost everything in language education that preceded it, the process movement was engendered and continues to exist in an atmosphere of conflict and debate. Advocates of a process orientation to writing and second/foreign language teaching entered the arena overtly criticizing other approaches to teaching and research methodologies. Likewise, process approaches have not gone unchallenged, in Australia or elsewhere. Considerable vigour, not to say ferocity, seems to characterize much of the debate that the process writing approach has generated.

For example, the Australian genre theorists have been unrelenting in their critique of the process approach to writing. Their views now have extensive circulation through Sydney University's *Working Papers in Linguistics*, various articles (e.g. Christie 1985; Hammond 1987), the "Writing to Mean" conference papers (Painter and Martin 1986) and the Deakin University series in Language and Education (see also Reid 1987).

The Australian genre theorists are not the only ones to challenge the process approach to writing. On the E.S.L. front, a survey of back issues of *TESOL Quarterly* reveals a clash of views in E.S.L. circles in North America. Horowitz (1986:796) writes, as he later admitted, "out of anger — at the arrogance ... encountered among process advocates at TESOL '85", that:

> The phrase "process, not product" has now risen to the heights, or perhaps sunk to the depths, of the great buzzwords of TESOL's past: it is the "communicative competence" of the mid-1980s. (1986:141-144)

To my knowledge, the process perspective on second/foreign language teaching has not been challenged in the same way as process writing (see, however, Moore 1987). Within British applied linguistics circles, some disagreement and differences of perspective appear to be emerging within an overall orientation to process (Widdowson 1987). However, in so far as process approaches to writing and language teaching share similar perspectives and appeal to similar grounds for justification, some of the arguments directed at process writing, although not intended as such, have application to process approaches in general.

This paper considers the controversy surrounding the process movement, particularly as it is being experienced here in Australia. It attempts to discover whether the debates have any substance, and if so, what the substantive points of difference might be.

Argument by Dichotomy

Although certainly not unique in this, the process movement has proliferated arguments set in terms of dichotomies or words placed in opposition to each other. The most obvious of these is the injunction that "process" rather than "product" should be the concern of teaching. Along with the process/product distinction, numerous other dichotomies are also in play.

For example, Candlin and Breen advocate syllabus design which emphasizes *means* rather than *ends. Abilities and skills for "communicating and learning"* should be prioritized ahead of *imparting knowledge of the target language* (Breen 1984:53). Breen prioritizes *process* in preference to *content* and argues for syllabus planning that focusses on *how the classroom functions* rather than on *subject matter*.

The form of argument is frequently to pose choices in pedagogy and to argue for one alternative in preference to the other. Thus, Candlin argues for a syllabus that:

> is personal, intrinsic and ... one of "reality" in process

as against one that:

> is extrinsic, idealistic, and presents a picture of static "reality".
>
> (1984:30)

He poses a choice between:

> the syllabus premised upon a pre-packaging of knowledge seen-as-items, orientated as it is to the teacher as agent

and a syllabus "orientated to the learner". The function of the latter, which is Candlin's preferred model, is:

> one of facilitating the exploration by that learner of his or her own values and ways of "cutting up the world". Such ways, moreover, will frequently be at odds with those identified externally, in advance and on his or her behalf. (1984:32)

These choices are presented by Candlin as competing and mutually exclusive, while Breen (1984:53) proposes his dichotomies as representing a "significant change of emphasis".

Widdowson's characteristic style of argument is similarly developed through sets of distinctions, most notably the posing of *use* against *usage*, and *discourse* against *text* (1978). The focus on *usage* and *discourse* has been central to the development of communicative language teaching in the last twenty or so years. More recently, and in the context of a concern with "process", Widdowson has distinguished *capacity* from *competence* and *education* from *training* (1983).

The way in which these dichotomies are set up is, however, somewhat different from the oppositions used by Candlin and the Australian genre theorists. Widdowson's dichotomies, at least as they are initially presented, do not always necessitate mutually exclusive choices for pedagogy. Thus *capacity* is defined in a way that necessitates the *existence* of *competence* not its *exclusion*. Capacity is:

> the ability to make meanings by interpreting a particular instance (an
> event, an expression), as related to some formula, thereby assimilating the
> instance into a pre-existing pattern of knowledge, or, when necessary, by
> modifying the available formulae so that the instance can be accommo-
> dated within them. In this way, capacity works both to exploit existing
> competence and also to extend that competence for creativity and change.
> (1983:106)

Widdowson's style of argument demonstrates that a dichotomous distinction does not necessarily represent opposing positions or choices. In the
same way, the *mind/body* distinction or the Chinese notion of *yin* and *yang*
do not require us to choose to explain the human condition solely in terms
of one or the other. They can be used to draw our attention to the necessity
to take account of both sides of the distinction. Dichotomies used in this
way are *heuristic devices*, that is, they alert us to the different facets of reality that need to be accounted for.

   In fact, Widdowson seems to hover uneasily between using
dichotomies as heuristic devices and to indicate preferred choices between
competing alternatives. *Education* and *training* are distinguished along a
continuum whose polar oppositions are, respectively, *creativity* and *conformity*, *procedures for problem-solving* and *established patterns of knowledge*,
self-realization and *adherence to social demands*, *divergence from established practices* and *reliance upon them*. On this argument, Widdowson
(1983:16-23) suggests that neither "pure" education nor training are possible or desirable.

   The distinction between education and training seems to have a heuristic quality in implying that teaching always contains elements of both education and training. But the overall line of argument, expressed in the
metaphor of a continuum along which programs might be identified, is
against the interpretation of these dichotomies as complementing each
other and is more in the style of Breen's priorities for emphasis.

   Moreover, Widdowson (1983:107) proposes that the "central task of
teaching" is to "activate" capacity and (1983:26) that capacity is "the natural language analogue of the educational process". This proposal would
seem to be a *de facto* argument for education in preference to training,
together with creativity, problem-solving, self-realization and divergence.
At least as far as language teaching is concerned, established patterns of
knowledge, adherence to social demands and the other features identified
with training seem to have no preferred place. Interestingly, a later paper
(Widdowson 1987) seems to move closer to a view of teaching that incorpo-

rates knowledge and social demands.

Widdowson's ambivalence in regard to the distinctions he draws illustrates how, once dichotomous distinctions are created for heuristic purposes, they are very liable to generate opposing explanations and choices for practice. In the same way, although the *mind/body* distinction can be used to remind us of different facets of reality that we seek to explain, it has also become the basis of the opposing explanations of learning given by cognitivists and behaviourists.

Creating dichotomies is, as Christie (1985:25) points out, a fundamental human tendency. She is, however, doubtful of their ultimate usefulness:

> ... dichotomies certainly have some heuristic value: that is to say, they
> have served to assist investigation and enquiry into many matters, includ-
> ing complex elements of human behaviour. But to acknowledge that such
> dichotomies have a heuristic value is not to claim, for the purposes of real
> practice, that the distinctions created by them actually exist.

Christie dismisses the usefulness of the individual/social dichotomy as a reminder of two aspects of learning, i.e. as a heuristic device. She argues (1985:25) that the distinction between cognitive growth and social development does not "actually exist". The distinction "between the individual and society, between the inner being and the outer world" cannot be sustained. Hence social not cognitive explanations of learning are to be preferred.

In their attacks on process writing, Christie and the other genre theorists have set up their arguments in terms of oppositions. This is a similar style of argument to Candlin's in that it poses mutually exclusive choices, this time at the level of explanation. For example, Martin (1985:56) describes nine beliefs about children that characterize the process approach. He challenges these with explanations "from the point of view of linguistics", by which is meant systemic linguistics. Martin (1985:54-61) asserts that children are not *individuals* but rather *social beings*; they are not *spontaneous learners* but learn language from *models*. He poses the virtues of *factual writing* against *creative writing* and accuses process approaches of *reproducing social difference* rather than *promoting democratic values*.

Candlin does not, however, deny the existence of the positions he opposes: both types of syllabus are possible, even though one is undesirable. The genre theorists deny the power of alternative explanations: cognitivist explanations of learning, in their view, are no explanation at all. Neither are other models of linguistics. In using a socially based explanation to account for the totality of learning, the genre theorists obliterate the distinction between the individual and society. Their explanations seek to do away with dichotomies.

Immediately prior to writing this paper, I completed reading the end-of-semester essays written by practising teachers in further training in our courses. A worrying number seem to be reacting to the dichotomies surrounding the process movement in the same way as politicians are described as doing by that well-known British civil "servant", Sir Humphrey Appleby from the T.V. series *Yes Minister*:

> They don't want to understand what's going on. They just want to know who the goodies and baddies are, so they can know what to say. (freely quoted)

"Goodies" and "baddies" are another possibility in the process of argument by dichotomy. They represent clear-cut and self-evident choices between the ultimate opposition of Good and Evil.

This paper seeks to clear some of the ground in the arguments by dichotomy that surround the process movement. It explores the extent to which these dichotomies truly represent opposing explanations and clear-cut choices about what should guide teachers in their practice. It also considers how heuristically useful these dichotomies might be as reminders of important facets of the reality we face in language education.

Since some well-known "goodies" and "baddies" appear to offer the most clear-cut choices, it seems reasonable to consider these first.

Goodies and Baddies

In the literature engendered by process approaches to writing and language teaching, the Goodies and Baddies are distinguished by some descriptions which are as old as education itself and some which, although not the unique property of the process movement, seem to have gained particular salience. Oppositions used to identify a necessarily preferred position include:

GOODIES VS. BADDIES
Describing the curriculum/teacher:
- democratic *not* authoritarian
- empowering *not* power-depriving

- flexible *not* rigid
- respecting student values *not* imposing teachers' values
- giving learners what they really want/need *not* working from a misguided teacher viewpoint

Describing students:
- autonomous *not* dependent
- active *not* passive

Describing theories/views of language and learning:
- dynamic *not* static
- classroom-centred *not* academic/linguistic

Describing ways of teaching:
- effective *not* ineffective

These dichotomous oppositions appear to offer a clear-cut guide to the choices educators should make. It goes without saying that an effective approach to teaching is preferable to an ineffective one, as is likewise a dynamic view of language in comparison to a static one. To be relevant to teachers, classroom-centred theories would seem advisable. Faced with a choice, only the most eccentric teachers might support authoritarian approaches that encourage dependency in students in preference to those which are democratic and promote student autonomy.

But, having decided in favour of democracy, for example, we encounter a problem. Avowedly opposing approaches to language education lay claim to this same ground. Candlin (1984) argues that teaching is intrinsically authoritarian and that teachers must redefine their role in the classroom. But Martin (1985:61) claims that the "refusal to teach" is anti-democratic because it "helps reinforce the success of ruling class children in education". Clearly, Candlin would oppose exactly the sorts of carefully targetted teaching and planning described by the genre theorists (e.g. Martin 1986).

This difficulty in actually identifying which approaches should be accepted or rejected on the grounds of adherence to self-evident values repeats itself with each of the descriptors listed above. Martin (1985:60) argues that process writing withholds "the kinds of writing that would allow children to understand and challenge the system in which they live". In contrast, Giroux (1987:179) praises Graves for *empowering* both teachers and students. He claims that Graves does exactly what Martin accuses him of failing to do:

> Graves raises questions about how learning can provide the grounds for
> students to be critical and self-determined thinkers. (1987:175)

Likewise, Graves (1983) proposes that teacher-imposed topics take
away student control but Horowitz (1986:143) thinks that telling students to
choose their own topics is an unwarranted teacher imposition on students'
values.

All this is rather confusing for the seeker of Goodies and Baddies. It
seems difficult to know where these dichotomies are taking us. Although
the dichotomies clearly indicate what should be chosen, they don't seem to
provide any guidance as to which practices fall into what category. If
everyone is searching for ways of promoting democracy, why do they end
up with opposing proposals for classrooms?

One possible conclusion is that the differences between supposedly
opposing positions are trivial; simply matters of slight emphasis. If
everyone supports democracy and is trying to promote active learning
which empowers learners and gives them autonomy, there may be no real
differences between process approaches and the others they criticize or who
criticize them. Are some slight differences being blown out of all proportion?

If we consider some of the classroom practices that are in debate, the
differences between process writing and genre theorists may well be simply
a product of the sorts of simplifications that go on when complex expositions in books and articles are recycled into one page inservice handouts.
To counteract this sort of simplification into rigid prescriptions for practice,
Graves has found it necessary to write a paper entitled "The Enemy is
Orthodoxy" in which he lists what he calls the extreme orthodoxies which
bother him the most (1984:185). Some of these are:

> children should only write in personal narrative ... Children should own
> their own writing and never be directed to do anything with their writing
> ... Children should choose all their topics ... Spelling, grammar, and punc-
> tuation are unimportant.

These prescriptions *disclaimed* by Graves are precisely some of the
pedagogic points on which the genre theorists and others criticize process
writing.

Graves (1984:185) claims that these orthodoxies are "the result of early
problems in research (my own included) ... [and] people who try to take
shortcuts with very complex processes". So are the attacks on process writing really just misled by these shortcuts? Or perhaps, in order to score

points, have they even contributed to unwarranted over-simplifications?

From much of the current rhetoric, it is difficult to determine whether we are facing opposing practices, opposing principles, both or neither. It seems that pitting one practice against another is to simplify the issue too much. But if we return to matters of underlying philosophy, everyone rests their appeal on commonly accepted notions such as democratic values. Where, if at all, do the real oppositions lie?

Dichotomies that appeal to self-evident values are not particularly helpful. Sometimes they obscure more than they reveal. Used to designate a given position, the oppositions listed above will not even reveal who is different from whom, much less where any Goodies and Baddies might be found.

In fact, what is indicated is the moral and ideological ground that is being fought over. Everyone wants possession of democracy, autonomy, active learning and so on. These words suggest where contemporary language education, at least in the West, is *agreed*, for better or worse, that it should be heading.

The true oppositions in contemporary Western language education (and other fields of endeavour) will not be found by seeking out those who do or don't adhere to such goals as democracy, theorizing that captures the dynamics of the theorized, or even effectiveness. If oppositions and choices exist, they will be found in the theoretical and pedagogical *content* that is given to both principle and practice, not in the ideological labels that various positions assign to themselves or others.

A starting point for discovering this content in the process debate may be to consider the principles and practices claimed as distinctive by process approaches.

Process Vs Product

As has been noted above, the process movement claims its distinctiveness in terms of an orientation to process in preference to product, along with other related oppositions, such as means rather than ends. The dichotomies used to describe the process approach are couched in terms of alternatives for pedagogic principle and practice, with the process alternative argued as the preferred choice.

This argument is essentially that the teachers and researchers should invest what goes on *in the course of learning* with some integrity: the teacher's or researcher's view of desirable outcomes should not cloud their capacity to understand and value what happens *as* learners learn. What actually happens in classrooms is not just as a pale shadow of some ultimate goal or annoying deviation from it. Rather, the classroom experience is the day-to-day embodiment of the real learning that is effected. As Candlin says,

> ... the content of any experience is necessarily bound up with the process of the experience itself. (1984:33)

This same point is made in different form by Breen:

> The genuine priority for the participants in the classroom is that knowledge be worked upon in ways which facilitate its teaching and learning. (1984:53)

Thus each step along the path of learning must itself be of value. Each step also has a potential importance in relation to the steps that have preceded it and those that will follow.

From this starting point, the "process not product" catch-cry has commonly been used to deplore the simplistic view that what should happen in classrooms day-by-day or minute-by-minute is discoverable by taking desirable end-products to pieces (Murray 1980; Widdowson 1983:52-54; Candlin 1984:39; Clark 1986:24).

For example, although we may aim for learners to write tightly organized essays, they may not actually achieve this by analysing model essays or by writing to models and the formulae that they appear to employ. Research into how such desirable end-products actually come into being indicates that a first draft may have few of its final product characteristics, such as a clear plan of argument or good paragraphing (Zamel 1982).

It is claimed that the procedures practised in "process writing" classrooms come closer to what has been discovered by case study research to be the actual process by which good writing takes shape. "Process writing" classrooms for English as a mother tongue or a second language generally have in common practices that encourage students to:

- take responsibility for and hence make choices about the direction of their work, for example, topics for writing, the kinds of revisions, presentation;
- focus on subject matter first and then formal features, usually through a series of drafts;

- consult with teacher and peers in various sorts of "conferences";
- know what their achievements are and take pride in them;
- bring their best work to a level that can be made public, for example, by reading it aloud or publishing it in book or magazine form.

Underlying the advocacy of these and other practices is a view that texts emerge from a process that involves changes. These changes are accompanied by different sorts of activity by the writer at different stages in the text's emergence. The teacher's task is to prompt those activities:

> At the beginning of the composing process there is only a blank paper. At the end of the composing process there is a piece of writing which has detached itself from the writer and found its own meaning, a meaning the writer probably did not intend ...

> If we stand back to look at the writing process, we see the writer following the writing through three stages of rehearsing, drafting and revising as the piece of work ... moves through its own meaning. These stages blend and overlap, but they are also distinct. Significant things happen within them. They require certain attitudes and skills on the writer's and the writing teacher's part. (Murray, 1980:17)

In regard to second/foreign language teaching, the argument also focusses on the idea that long-term goals (for example, the study of English in order to gain entry to an electrical engineering course) do not necessarily indicate what will promote learning. Language learning is claimed to be dependent on activities that engage learners' interests to the extent that they feel an *immediate need* to make sense with the target language. Such activities must therefore be relevant to learners in the process of learning and not simply as long-term goals (Widdowson 1983; Hughes *et al.* 1987). Candlin and Breen argue that what is most relevant to learners is the learning process itself, hence the syllabus should be focussed around decision-making about how learning shall proceed (Candlin 1984; Breen 1984).

Unlike proposals for process writing (where, if anything, the reverse is the case), the practices proposed by those who advocate a process perspective for second/foreign language teaching are less unified in direction than are their statements of principle. Where there is consensus of opinion, there is considerable vagueness in implications for a distinctive practice. Thus the idea of a syllabus realized through "tasks" or activities has gained sway. In the descriptions and definitions so far available in the literature, it seems that anything from grammar analysis, structure practice, reading comprehension, role play or information gap exercises may constitute a task (Brumfit 1984b; Candlin and Murphy 1987). Conversely, where distinctive practices are advocated, for example, Candlin and Breen's syllabus as a *post hoc* description of rather than a plan for teaching, there is no consensus that this is a reasonable interpretation of what constitutes a process approach (Widdowson 1987).

In its most constructive forms of principle and practice, the process movement addresses our attention to two important matters. Firstly, it asks teachers to consider the value of the here-and-now in learning and teaching, and to be able to justify what goes on at each point in time. Secondly, it recognizes that learning involves growth and change. Hence teachers must take account of the fact that the product of the moment may look different from but still be *en route* to desired outcomes.

However, in setting process against product, the process movement is, in fact, blind to the significance of its own argument. In enjoining teachers to attend to what happens in classrooms on a day-to-day and minute-by-minute basis, the process movement does not dispense with an orientation to product. Rather, it directs our attention to *products that may otherwise be disregarded*. The products of the here-and-now have been elevated to greater importance than they previously may have had. The process argument *necessitates greater attention to product*.

If the products of the "here and now" are to be valued, it can only be because they are seen in terms of some wider framework of values than the "here and now". Our culture does not value scribble on a page or poorly organized writing in themselves. Such things may, however, be valued if they are interpreted as signs of creativity, intelligence or a step towards some desired outcome. Likewise, we do not value students making decisions or talking to each other except in so far as we see these activities as embodying democratic practices, personal responsibility or using English in some desirable way. In other words, to value the "here and now" requires us to place the product of the moment into some wider context beyond the "here and now". This context may be a superordinate set of values that the product is seen either to embody or to be on the way to achieving.

In education, one important reason for valuing the product of the moment is because of its significance as part of a pattern of change and growth towards desired goals. In arguing, for example, that drafts are significant to developing good writing, the process argument is, in fact, an injunction to take account of *products over time* and their changing relationship to each other. Taking account of products set in relation to each other cannot provide grounds for abdicating an interest in and responsibility for the cumulative effect of what is done over a given time frame. In fact, the reverse is the case: the product of the moment is to be understood and valued because, despite its possible difference from desired outcomes (such as writing well-structured essays or using English fluently, accurately and appropriately), it constitutes evidence about how these desired outcomes are in process of being realized.

The logic of the process argument should lead to a more complete view of products or outcomes in both long- and short-term contexts. The notion of process cannot exist independent of product or outcome. Precisely because we are asked to consider each step on the path of learning in relation to what has gone before and will or should follow, a view of what might and should constitute long-term products or outcomes is essential: it is impossible to trace patterns of growth without knowing where something is supposedly going.

For teachers, their view of possible long-term goals derives from an understanding of the content of what they are teaching. For language teachers or teachers of writing, this view is of *effective language use* both in general terms and in relation to what is feasible and appropriate in a particular teaching context. That is to say, teachers can have no view of what their students do in their classrooms on a day-to-day basis without a view of syllabus goals, what it means to know the language (i.e. competence) and what a desired repertoire of communication might be (i.e. purposes).

The notions of process and product do not represent competing choices or priorities for classroom or research practice. And, on the same argument, we can demolish the spurious choices posed by the ends/means and the goals/ methodology dichotomies. Likewise, we can reject as nonsensical the idea that a capacity for communication can be prioritized ahead of a repertoire of communciation. It is impossible to conceptualize one without a clear view of the other.

Teachers cannot focus on means rather than ends. They cannot foster language learning "strategies" or "capacity" in preference to language knowledge or competence. Each is entirely dependent on the other. Advocating that teachers turn their attention from syllabus outcomes to methodology is to simply encourage them to refuse to be explicit about the goals their program is pursuing or to take responsibility for them. Research projects and teachers are in danger of considerable confusion when they attempt to chart language or writing development without end-product criteria by which to gauge the directions in which specific cases under observation are going. In encouraging a focus on means in preference to ends, or strategies in preference to knowledge, process approaches disguise rather than obviate the ends they endorse and the plans to which they work.

Seen as representing choices or competing priorities, the process/product opposition offers teachers confusion. As a heuristic device to draw attention to two facets of teaching, the process/product dichotomy has potential. It can bring into sharper focus what has often been ignored, namely, what teachers and students actually do in the fulfilment of their goals for teaching and learning.

Understanding the significance of the here and now necessitates, as we have seen, a view of how the product of the moment reflects growth and change towards effective language use. A view of how language is learned and the purposes for its use is required. The question therefore arises as to what view of language and language learning is given or implied by process approaches. It is at this level of argument that real debate is clearly evident.

Language Learning

For the process movement, explanations of the dynamics and purpose of learning are not proposed in terms of dichotomies or alternatives to an opposing viewpoint. Rather, as Christie (1985:26) points out, they assume a "universal commitment to the view that the prime object of education ... is to develop individuals". In the process view, learning is motivated by individuals realizing their own intentions and capabilities. The purpose of learning is personal fulfilment. The teacher's role is to assist this.

In writing, Graves sees "voice" as the "dynamo" for development:

> The writing process has a driving force called voice ... it underlies every part of the process. To ignore voice is to present the process as a lifeless, mechanical act ...

> Take the voice away and the writing collapses of its own weight. There is no writing, just words following words ... The voice shows how I choose information, organize it, select the words, all in relation to what I want to say and how I want to say it ...

> Not only is it the dynamo for the writing, but it contributes most to the development of the writer. It pushes the writer into confronting new problems through interesting topics, gives energy to persist in their solution, then carries the writer onto a new set of issues. (1983:227-229)

"Voice" is, by definition, personal. It is the "ego-force" behind a person's intentions (Graves 1983:238):

> Voice is the imprint of ourselves on our writing. It is that part of the self that pushes the writing ahead ... (Graves 1983:227)

The skilled teacher works to both encourage the development of the writing process, i.e. to help learners to face up to the problems writing imposes, and at the same time maintain the "driving force" of personal voice:

> The unchecked voice-ego ... can be a hungry undiscriminating wolf. It has a ravenous appetite for praise from self and others, so much so that the writer is blind to personal biases about content and quality. The trick for the writer and teacher is to keep the wolf-voice fed while still asking tough decentering questions. The writer then sees the problem afresh in light of living up to internal demands of excellence and the original reason for writing in the first place. Thus, the wolf is fed and the writer still maintains control, while improving the piece. (Graves 1983:244-245)

The classroom procedures used in process writing aim to assist learners to stay in touch with the energy and direction their own voice provides, while at the same time pushing writing development forward. Voice is firstly an expression of personal meaning, hence it is crucial that learners be encouraged to choose their own topics for writing and make decisions about how to write. The learner must be encouraged to take personal responsibility. Drafting and revision are generally necessary to allow the writer to attend to the various aspects of gaining control over his/her text "in relation to what I want to say and how I want to say it". Interaction with others through conferences and publication helps to make clear one's purposes and the power and limitations of what one has said. Motivation to learn derives from a sense of ownership of one's ideas in writing and from others' recognition of what one has communicated in writing.

Candlin and Breen have a similar, though less metaphorically expressed, explanation of the dynamic for learning:

> any learning outcome will be significantly shaped by the learners' own ... assumptions about what they themselves should contribute; their view of the nature and demands of the task itself; and their personal definitions of the task situation. In other words, any learning task will be reinterpreted by a learner in his or her own terms. (Breen 1987:24)

Because learners see learning tasks from their own points of view, plans for teaching, for example syllabuses or course books, are exercises in teacher self-deception (Breen 1984:58). The focus of Breen and Candlin's pedagogy is an attempt to utilize and make explicit learner reinterpretations or "contributions" (Breen 1987). Procedures which utilize the learner's contribution give learners choices about what they do in classrooms and have them reflect on those choices. Thus Breen and Candlin are similar to Graves in seeing the dynamic for learning best activated by offering the learner conscious choices. Decision-making is proposed as the essential "subject-matter of learning a language" (Breen 1984:52). Decision-making prevents both learners and teachers becoming "alienated and incapacitated servants of a set of requirements at odds with their individuality and the realities of the classroom" (Candlin 1984:32). The syllabus secures its "continuing relevance for the learner" through allowing for the realization of the "vested and mutual interest in personal objectives" of learners and teacher (Candlin 1984:33).

Unlike Graves, Candlin lacks faith that the teacher can work at the "optimal learning moments" (1984:40-42). He argues that we lack sufficient information as to what these may be and, even if we had such information, it would not be practical for teachers to work individually with learners to assist them to capitalize on these moments. This problem is solved if the syllabus is formulated around learner decision-making or if it is a *post hoc* account of decisions taken (Candlin 1984:42; Breen 1984).

For ideological, as well as practical reasons, the teacher's and course designer's attempts to plan for learning are undesirable. Prescribing directions or intervening in the learning process is to take control from the learner and to subvert the course and purpose of learning. Similarly to Graves, Breen and Candlin see the only pedagogically and ideologically acceptable role for the teacher as a resource person and as a facilitator for learner decision-making.

The genre theorists attack the notion of individual intention, creativity or decision-making as being at the centre of learning. They attribute to Graves, and by inference to Candlin and Breen, a naive view of learning. According to the genre theorists, this naive view sees learning as a process of "natural" growth which mysteriously unfolds in each individual: how learning proceeds is unknowable by others and hence can only be tainted by social process (Christie 1984:89, 1985:27).

The genre theorists propose a truly alternative explanation of how learning occurs and what its purposes are. Unlike the process movement, they do not see social context as inherently repressive. Rather, they argue that individuality cannot be expressed or understood except as a result of and through social processes:

> Like all other aspects of social experience, individuality is itself created, negotiated and sustained in social experience.
>
> (Christie 1987:29-30)

> ... persons achieve individuality through active participation in social processes, by learning to engage more fully in the various ways of meaning characteristic of their social context ... It is out of manipulation of one's own culturally created ways of making meaning that one learns to express one's own individuality, and, ultimately, to develop new ways of making meaning.
>
> (Christie 1985:26)

The dynamic for writing and all learning is social context, not personal intention or choice:

> it is social context, not individual choice, that has the greatest influence on what people say and write. (Martin *et al.* 1987:77)

This is echoed by the American, Horowitz (1986:143), who claims that, rather than focussing on students' capacity to write on topics of their choice, it is more important to teach "students to write intelligently on topics they do not care about".

Context provides the learner with models and with interaction that necessitates attention to and utilization of those models:

> In learning to speak one is learning the discourse structures of a particular culture.
> ...
> Children construct texts (including stories) JOINTLY with adult partners. Children are able to internalize models of language and of genres which have been provided through repeated conversational interaction.
> ...
> The adult provides models of language and genres in the processes of:
> − responding to the child's meanings, which shared experience puts him/ her in the best position to do;
> − "scaffolding" the child's own text-extensions by means of questioning probes and interpretative acknowledgements;
> − highlighting for the child the salient characteristics of a genre's structural and functional requirements, whether this latter is done implicitly, as in the early years, or explicitly, later on.
>
> (Painter 1986:81-82)

These opposing views on the place of personal intention, decision-making and social context in the learning process reflect a fundamental disagreement over the purpose of education. As we have seen above, for Candlin the proper goal of education is to assist the individual to challenge the social order (1984:30,32). Widdowson, as we have seen, aligns education with creativity, self-realization and divergence from established practices. In direct contrast, Christie sees the purpose of education as a process of initiation into social life:

> An educational process in an important sense is a process of initiation: an initiation, that is, into the ways of working, or of behaving, or of thinking (the terms all mean similar things to me) particular to one's cultural traditions. (1987:30)

These opposing explanations of the learning process and its desired purpose make clear the content of what each side sees as education's contribution to democracy. For Candlin (1984:30), democracy rests on the capacity of the individual to question and challenge the established order. For Giroux, process writing contributes to democracy by valuing individual experience. If individuals know their experiences are legitimate and valued, they have a basis of power from which to ask questions. Process writing assists in:

> developing a critically affirmative language that works both *with* and *on* the experiences that students bring to the classroom. This means not only taking seriously and confirming the language forms, modes of reasoning, dispositions, and histories that give students an active voice in defining the world, it also means working on the experiences of such students in order for them to examine both their strengths and weaknesses. (Giroux 1987:177)

For the genre theorists, democracy is an issue of who does and does not have access to and participation in social life. Education can work to include or exclude individuals and groups from this life. Empowerment is therefore argued in terms of access. Notions of individual creativity and intention are seen to be potentially disempowering:

> overly strong emphasis on individual creativity quite overlooks the fact that children come to school with very different linguistic/ generic preparation from home. To the child from the literate middle-class home the teacher's exhortation to express him/herself is no threat — she or he will implement the generic forms acquired at home. A child from the inner-city slums of Sydney cannot respond in the same way. If the possibility of generic creativity is thought to reside in individuals, then success or failure equally can be laid at the door of the individual — entirely inappropriately. Our society already produces too many instances of "blaming the victim for the crime" ... (Kress 1987:43)

These opposing explanations of the learning process and the purpose of education as either *an induction into social life* or *a liberation of the individual* constitute the true oppositions that surround the process movement in language education. These explanations provide the motivation for the classroom practices that each side has generated, whether these practices are themselves similar or different. These explanations confront the teacher with real alternatives in the principles which can guide their teaching.

Before rushing in to make a choice, we may, however, pause to ask whether this is indeed the choice we want to make. Each side of the argument seems to contain within it the weaknesses, as well as the strengths, of the position it adopts.

On examination, it seems that the process movement has, in fact, remarkably little to say about how language is learned. At a superficial level, it may seem paradoxical that an emphasis on the learning process should be so unclear in explaining how language learning proceeds, but, in fact, this is the logical as well as the practical outcome of posing process as an alternative rather than complementary to product and outcome.

In process approaches, because products and goals are unaccounted for, the learning process remains mysteriously described in terms of metaphors such as voice, the unknowable in-built syllabus and personal engagement. Because it is unexplained, it is also open to re-interpretation in purely ideological terms, such as found in Candlin and Breen's justification for decision-making as the basis for syllabus design. If the purpose of education is personal fulfilment, which is indeed idiosyncratic and unknowable, there is no necessity for the process to be publicly accounted for in either language learning theory or in pedagogic practice. In both writing and language teaching, what constitutes forward development or good decision-making is, therefore, left up to the individual and thereby inexplicit.

Because the path of learning and teaching is inexplicit, the teacher's role is essentially reactive:

> The child must lead, the teacher intelligently react.
>
> (Graves 1983:127)

The questions left unanswered by process approaches to both writing and language teaching are: on what basis must the teacher react? how should the teacher interpret the learner's "leadership"? what are we looking for and why?

In contrast, the genre theorists offer us a view of language development which clearly defines outcomes in terms of text types or genres. The means by which these outcomes are achieved is through modelling and interpersonal interactions. The role of the teacher is to provide the desired interactions.

But, in redefining learning as entirely socially constructed, the genre theorists also leave some important questions unanswered. In dismissing notions of cognitive development, they fail to explain why language development takes time and is, in many respects, sequential no matter what the context (Pienemann and Johnston 1987). If what people learn is simply the outcome of what they are exposed to, we have an insufficient basis to explain how change and transformation systematically occur in the spoken and written language people are capable of understanding and producing. And, despite Christie's (1987:29) disclaimer to the contrary, the genre theorists provide us with no explanation of how learners move from conformity to creativity.

In ascribing failure to learn as simply dependent on an absence of or failure in interaction, genre theorists also leave teachers with insufficient explanation of why the same interactions have different effects on different learners. If it is important that teachers do not shirk responsibility for how students respond to their teaching, then the principles they espouse must explain the necessity of seeking the individual learner's engagement in and personal responsibility for the work at hand. The process by which products come into existence is not entirely explained by a theory that gives no place to individual interest and responsibility. Teachers find themselves faced by individuals in their classrooms, no matter whether or not their importance is defined out of existence by theory.

Heuristic Device or Opposing Explanation?

The dichotomies of *process/product*, *means/ends*, *capacity/competence* and *methodology/syllabus goals* proposed by the process movement are at best heuristic devices. The process movement has confused language educators by putting forward mutually exclusive choices and priorities which seem to require the rejection of one side of the distinctions they propose in favour of the other. But attention to the learning process necessitates a view of product, ends, competence, and syllabus goals. Without this, the learning process itself remains unexplained.

The genre theorists have attacked the process movement on the grounds of its mysterious and personal notions of learning. They have proposed explanations of the learning process that focus on social context, product (i.e. texts) and goals. While the process movement has constructed the debate in terms of oppositions that cannot truly be argued as such, the genre theorists have identified the true sources of disagreement between themselves and the process movement. The opposition is between socially and individually motivated explanations of learning.

The process movement and the genre approach represent genuinely alternative explanations and practices, and hence a choice for teachers. But each side ignores a crucial part of the reality of the classroom. The process approach is individualistic and offers no explanation of knowledge and social context. The genre theorists are deterministic and collapse individuality into social process.

While these explanations of the learning process may be truly opposing, choosing between them does not, however, provide a solution. The Chinese explanation of *yin* and *yang* supposes two opposing forces at work in the universe. However, each is necessary to and relies on the other. The challenge is to find an explanation that does justice to both. We await a theory and a practice that not only uses *the social* and *the individual* as a heuristic device but also sets them in relation to each other without distorting the reality that this dichotomy seeks to explain.

References

Breen, M. 1984. "Process Syllabuses for the Language Classroom". *General English Syllabus Design* ed. by C. Brumfit, 47-60. Oxford: Pergamon.

Brumfit, C. ed. 1984a. *General English Syllabus Design*. Oxford: Pergamon.

———. 1984b. "The Bangalore Procedural Syllabus". *ELT Journal* 38(4). 233-241.

Candlin, C.N. 1983. "Syllabus Design as Critical Process". *General English Syllabus Design* ed. by C. Brumfit, 29-46. Oxford: Pergamon.

———. 1987. "Towards Task-Based Language Learning". *Language Learning Tasks*. Lancaster Practical Papers in English Language Education No. 7 ed. by Candlin, C.N. & D.F. Murphy, 5-22. London: Prentice-Hall International.

Candlin, C.N. & D.F. Murphy. eds. 1987. *Language Learning Tasks*. Lancaster Practical Papers in English Language Education No. 7. London: Prentice-Hall International.

Christie, Frances. 1985. *Language Education*. Geelong: Deakin University Press.

Clark, J.L. 1986. "Curriculum Renewal in School Foreign Language Teaching: An overview". *Australian Review of Applied Linguistics* 9(1). 14-42.

———. 1987. *Curriculum Renewal in School Foreign Language Learning*. Oxford:

Oxford University Press.

Giroux, H.R. 1987. "Critical Literacy and Student Experience: Donald Graves' approach to literacy". *Language Arts* 64(2). 175-181.

Graves, Donald H. 1983. *Writing: Teachers and children at work*. New Hampshire: Heinemann.

———. 1984a. "The Enemy is Orthodoxy". *A Researcher Learns to Write: Selected articles and monographs* ed. by Donald H. Graves, 184-193. New Hampshire: Heinemann.

———. 1984b. *A Researcher Learns to Write: Selected articles and monographs*. New Hampshire: Heinemann.

Hammond, Jennifer. 1987. "An Overview of the Genre-Based Approach to the Teaching of Writing in Australia". *Australian Review of Applied Linguistics* 10(2). 163-181.

Hornsby, D., D. Sukarna & J. Parry. 1986. *Read On: A conference approach to reading*. Sydney: Martin Educational.

Horowitz, Daniel. 1986. "Process, Not Product: Less than meets the eye". *TESOL Quarterly* 20(1). 141-144.

———. 1986. "The Author Responds to Hamp-Lyons". *TESOL Quarterly* 20(4). 796-797.

Hughes, C., R. Barthel & D. Slade. 1987. "Needs-Based Programming and the Provision of English Tuition in the Adult Migrant Education Program". *Prospect* 2(2). 183-199.

Kress, Gunther. 1987. "Genre in a Social Theory of Language: A reply to John Dixon". *The Place of Genres in Learning: Current debates*. Typereader Publications No. 1 ed. by Ian Reid, 35-45. Deakin University: Centre for Studies in Literary Education.

Martin, J.R. 1985. *Factual Writing: Exploring and challenging social reality*. Geelong: Deakin University Press.

———. 1986. "Intervening in the Process of Writing Development". *Writing to Mean: Teaching genres across the curriculum*, Occasional Papers No. 9 ed. by Clare Painter & J.R. Martin, 11-43. Sydney: Applied Linguistics Association of Australia.

Martin, J.R., F. Christie & J. Rothery. 1987. "Social Processes in Education: A reply to Sawyer and Watson (and others). *The Place of Genres in Learning: Current debates*, Typereader Publications No. 1 ed. by Ian Reid, 58-82. Deakin University: Centre for Studies in Literary Education.

Moore, Helen. 1987. "Process, Outcome and Education: A discussion". *Australian Review of Applied Linguistics* 10(2). 128-162.

Murray, Donald. 1980. "Writing as Process: How writing finds its own meaning". *Learning by Teaching* ed. by Donald Murray, 17-31. Montclair, N.J.: Boynton Cook.

———. ed. 1982. *Learning by Teaching*. Montclair, N.J.: Boynton Book.

Nunan, D. ed. 1987. *Applying Second Language Acquisition Research*. Adelaide: National Curriculum Resource Centre.

Painter, Clare. 1986. "The Role of Interaction in Learning to Speak and Write". *Writing to Mean: Teaching genres across the curriculum*. Occasional Papers No. 9 ed. by Clare Painter & J.R. Martin, 62-97. Sydney: Applied Linguistics Association of Australia.

Painter, Clare & J.R. Martin. eds. 1986. *Writing to Mean: Teaching genres across the curriculum.* Occasional Papers No. 9. Sydney: Applied Linguistics Association of Australia.

Pienemann, M. & M. Johnston. 1987. "Factors Influencing the Development of Language Proficiency". *Applying Second Language Acquisition Research* ed. by D. Nunan, 45-141. Adelaide: National Curriculum Resource Centre.

Raimes, Ann. 1983. "Tradition and Revolution in ESL Teaching". *TESOL Quarterly* 17(4). 535-552.

Reid, Ian. ed. 1987. *The Place of Genres in Learning: Current debates.* Typereader Publications No. 1. Deakin University: Centre for Studies in Literary Education.

Tickoo, Makhan L. ed. 1987. *Language Syllabuses: State of the art.* Anthology Series 18. Singapore: SEAMEO Regional Language Centre.

Walshe, R.D. ed. 1981. *Donald Graves in Australia.* Sydney: Primary English Teachers Association.

Widdowson, H.G. 1979. *Teaching Language as Communication.* Oxford: Oxford University Press.

——. 1983. *Learning Purpose and Language Use.* Oxford: Oxford University Press.

——. 1987. "Aspects of Syllabus Design". *Language Syllabuses: State of the art.* Anthology Series 18 ed. by Makhan L. Tickoo, 65-89. Singapore: SEAMEO Regional Language Centre.

Zamel, Vivian. 1982. "Writing: The process of discovering meaning". *TESOL Quarterly* 16(2). 195-209.

Towards an Alternative Curriculum for Acquisition-Poor Environments

Makhan Lal Tickoo

0. The main points of my presentation are the following: EF(S)L syllabuses in state-level systems all over India have, in their essential framework, remained unchanged for more than a quarter century. Two major events of the last few years suggest however that alternative models developed in the West, especially Western Europe and more particularly the United Kingdom, are being imported into or promoted for use in some of these systems. These reforms have not produced the hoped for results even in their countries of origin or in situations that are comparable to theirs. And there are other, more compelling reasons that make such importation wrong. What is needed is curriculum design and development based on a different set of criteria and a different understanding of what is involved in language teaching in such settings and environments. Some thoughts on these developments and on a possible design for such an alternative curriculum are presented.

1.1 Exactly 35 years ago the Structural Syllabus (SS) was introduced into the national systems of EFL in India (Smith 1962). It spread fast and became strongly entrenched in the next decade. Although its failures, both apparent and real, began to surface soon after, it has not been replaced. In their essential framework the English-language curricula used in most state-level systems and many tertiary-level institutions continue to depend on it.

1.2 Syllabus reform has been a major preoccupation in the field of applied linguistics since some time in the mid-sixties. A main reason as pointed out by Stern (1984) has been the growing dissatisfaction with the methodology-based answers that had emerged in the 40s and 50s. But whatever the reasons powerful alternatives have emerged. In the mid-seventies the Council of Europe's work began to bear fruit (Van Ek 1976). David Wilkins' *Notional Syllabuses* (Wilkins 1976) was an important offshoot which stood out at the time of its publication. For some time it in fact represented the communicative alternative that was meant to replace the form-focussed linguistic syllabuses.

But not for long. Doubts arose about almost everything that it claimed. It was seen to lack a basis in linguistic theory (Paulston 1981). It was found much less economical and far less efficient than what it sought to replace (Brumfit 1981). It was judged to be as cumulative and as item-and-unit based as SS (Widdowson 1979; Crombie 1985). And very soon it became known that many of the systems where such a syllabus had been introduced had found it unworkable. Brumfit, for example, found in 1984 that several national educational systems that had "gone notional-functional" or "gone communicative" had retreated after a brief trial period to whatever they had before (Brumfit 1984). What in fact came about can perhaps be best summed up by saying that the seven wise fathers of the communicative syllabus movement soon found themselves disowning it. Widdowson expressed this dissatisfaction most explicitly in 1983 when he wrote "There is no such thing as a communicative syllabus: there can only be a methodology that stimulates communicative learning". He has further defended his stand on this in 1987 (Widdowson 1987).

1.3 At the beginning of the 1980s and at a time when disillusionment with this type of communicative syllabuses and more particularly Notional-Functional syllabuses (NFs) was growing and becoming more and more pronounced in the country of their origin several Asian countries adopted such a syllabus. In India too one state-level system (viz. that of West Bengal) adopted NFs in its schools and began work on producing instructional materials for it. That work is still on and textual materials that foreground notions and functions are replacing those that enveloped structures inside situations.

1.4 In the first half of this decade realisation that the notional-functional alternative had failed to provide what it promised led to work on a few more radical alternatives. Most prospective syllabuses, it was argued, are restrictive and all of them become redundant in the classroom (Candlin 1984; Breen 1984). Such syllabuses also mainly require the learner to bank received knowledge rather than to explore new ways of acquiring it. The truly communicative syllabus has to provide for teacher freedom as much as learner initiative and creativity. And only a syllabus which gives up the fetters of pre-selection based on either linguistic or semantic considerations can do all this. Retrospective syllabuses that can serve as record of work in the classroom or as accounts of what gets done rather than as guide-maps to what should be done following a prespecified plan of action have been proposed. Breen's Process Syllabus (Breen 1984/1985) and Candlin's Retrospective Syllabus (Candlin 1984) are two such and they claim to be truly communicative alternatives to both SS and NFs. Both also utilize some of the seminal findings in language acquisition besides seeking to align syllabus design and implementation with innovative ideas on classroom organisation and learning- or learner-centred pedagogy.

1.5 A five-year-long school-based experiment has brought this type of syllabus to at least one part of India. N.S. Prabhu's Procedural Syllabus (Prabhu 1983/ 1984) which, in his own words, is "the cumulative outcome of the major ideas and insights that have emerged in the last fifteen years or so, as a reaction to the structural approach" shares much of the radicalism of retrospective syllabuses although it differs from them in that it draws some of its pedagogic strengths from actual teaching done in Indian schoolrooms. Much like Breen and Candlin, Prabhu also finds the language syllabus "detrimental to desired forms of teaching" and even the semantic syllabus "a needless distraction". All forms of pre-selection are in fact unacceptable as is every activity which is seen to pay deliberate attention to teaching language forms.

1.6 Elsewhere I have examined this type of what I call "scholars' syllabus" for what it offers or fails to give the user systems that need change (Tickoo 1986a, b, 1987). Although such syllabuses profess a basic reform they in fact deny the very object they seek to improve. In their extremism they deprive the ordinary teacher of the fruits of collective wisdom and at the same time deny the language systems the tool that helps them to relate to practitioners on the one hand and to remain open to parents and taxpayers on the other.

1.7 The Procedural Syllabus has a definite edge over both the Process Syllabus and the Retrospective Syllabus in that it has a respectable stockpile of over four hundred tested tasks and a number of usable insights from ordinary schoolrooms. On the other hand it makes large claims that need proof rather than proclamation. Prabhu's basic belief that grammatical competence comes about without any provision being made for it in actual teaching appears to promise a lot for very little input especially in the acquisition-poor, one hour a day English classrooms that he and the select band of teachers taught in South India. Even in the far richer and much more intensive Canadian immersion programmes grammatical competence that emerged was found to be far from native-like. Grammatical competence, as we learn from Cummins' and Swain's recent studies of the Canadian experience, is "strongly dependent on the amount and type of input received by the individual" (e.g. Cummins and Swain 1986; also see Clark 1986). Proof rather than assertion is also needed to support the belief that even the "zero level" learner inside an ordinary English classroom where the teacher herself is often an indifferent communicator in English is capable of entering into communicational activities that engage his mind.

1.8 The main point of the brief outline presented so far has been to show that far from being the best models for export the two major syllabus alternatives that have evolved in Western Europe/United Kingdom and got promoted for use elsewhere have not come anywhere near to solving the problems that confront the relatively small-scale EFL operations that face the pioneers in their countries. Their importation into entirely dissimilar linguistic settings and teacher-learning situations and to serve aims and objectives that are incomparably different appears to be unwise if not also in some ways indefensible.

1.9 In moving next towards some thoughts on an alternative model that, in my view, should prove useful for state-level EFL systems in countries like India I shall first say a brief word on what may have gone wrong in this long search for alternative syllabuses which are said to incorporate several seminal socio- and psycho-linguistic ideas on language and language acquisition.

A study of the developments in language curriculum design during this period suggests that the main preoccupation in it has been to react to what existed before. NFs grew in reaction to SS; it stood for the reversal of much that was found as being wrong with such a syllabus — its synthetic base, its form focus, its incrementalism and linearity, its support for accumulation rather than integration and so on. That it is now seen as having failed in all this is perhaps not so important as the fact that it mainly aimed at displacement. The retrospective syllabuses have in turn reacted to the excesses and limitations of NFs most of which it is now seen as sharing in common with SS. The preoccupation all along has also been primarily, even puristically, linguistic. The elements of language that have received attention and assumed centrality may have changed — from the smallest to the largest and in a few cases back to the smaller (see, for example, D. and J. Willis 1987 on lexical syllabuses; Carter 1987) but the design of the curriculum has been seen as little more than an offshoot of a type of applied linguistics.

Space does not allow the detailing of even the larger problems that this lopsided preoccupation has fathered. What I do need to point out however is the attitudinal change that has recently begun to surface as a result. I shall use two short quotes to illustrate it. Writing on language syllabuses in 1987 Keith Morrow makes an honest admission: "Generally valid language-teaching syllabuses do not exist" but he goes on to add that this is because of "the nature of language and the nature of learners". Elsewhere in the same paper he explains the reason:

> One of the paradoxes of progress is that the more sophisticated our analyses of language and language use become, the more variables there are to take into account in formulating a syllabus, and the less able we are to chart anything like a coherent path through the jungle. (Morrow 1987)

Translated into the layman's language this amounts to saying that the applied linguist knows much more than he can use, so the user systems must remain content with unusable products. What a price to pay for progress in a field which, among other things, is meant to improve language teaching! A similar view but with much greater authority came two years earlier. Speaking of the problems he had had in South India in getting his Procedural Syllabus accepted Prabhu lamented the fact that he had not succeeded "in persuading teachers and administrators that an indirect attempt to promote acquisition is all we can usefully make in language pedagogy" (Prabhu 1985). And once again like Morrow he found support in "the nature of language and its acquisition" for his certainties about how best the EFL systems in India should go about this business of language teaching. What perhaps gets conveniently forgotten in all this is the fact that some of the beliefs that underpin such syllabuses and have been accepted as axiomatic truths (e.g. a total separation of the paths to acquisition as opposed to learning) and the rejection of several established practices in the teaching system (e.g. the work done to build a firm basis in the language's grammatical structure) may in reality have made them unacceptable as alternatives.

2.1 Towards the Alternative

Work on the design and development of alternative EFL/ESL syllabuses has thus, in my understanding, failed to produce much of what it set out to achieve and the reasons for it lie in a failure to provide for many essentials that could not be fitted inside the chosen theories on language and language use. But something makes such syllabuses even less useful for the EFL systems in countries like India. That something is that in these systems English serves entirely different objectives, operates in a measurably different type of multilingual setting and inside it confronts different sets of crosslinguistic influences, gets taught in a learning environment which is characterised by highly dissimilar ways of interaction and behaviour and remains in the hands of teachers who often bring with them strongly entrenched beliefs and practices on what works in schoolrooms and what may not.

Understanding these basic differences and working out their implications has to become the first preliminary to the design and development of a usable language curriculum. But there is one other thing whose neglect has largely contributed to the more than three decades of non-progress/stagnation in India's EFL curricula that I referred to at the beginning of my presentation. It is the need to prioritize, to decide what should come before what and how the major goals can receive the time and resources they deserve. The why and what of this needs a word of explanation.

2.2 The making of a usable state-level curriculum is a shared responsibility between professionals and policy-makers. It is not a task that is or should be left to the specialists alone because any exercise in curriculum renewal must be informed by factors that go way beyond the subject (in this case English) and its teaching. Placed as he often is, the planner aims at what can be done rather than what ought to be done. For him, as Bruner very aptly puts it, curriculum renewal is "a patient pursuit of the possible". The professional has a different perspective. He is informed by current thinking on his subject and how it can best be taught. He seeks what ought to be rather than what can be achieved. The two do not always see eye to eye with each other and there is some tension between their world-views at the best of times.

The professional scholar's search for alternative TEFL syllabuses in India has taken place in a kind of self-defeating isolation. He has found excitement in the study of innovative curriculum designs in the West and not kept in touch with the changing goals and priorities on the national scene. In his scheme of things there is no place for the partialness of India's EFL objectives, for the differentness of the interlanguage phenomena that operate in it or for the far more complicated and challenging multilingualism that envelopes all these. There is also no place in it for the networks of interdependent and interanimating factors, linguistic and non-linguistic, that operate in state-level systems of schooling. The reforms proposed therefore focus on a different set of objectives and are best suited to work within other linguistic settings and teaching-learning situations. What has to come first is a willingness on his part to allow such seemingly extraneous factors to inform the processes of curriculum reform and renewal. In what follows I shall briefly refer to the main ones and relate them to my present concern.

3.1 By far the most important factor to explore is the type of multilingualism that surrounds TEFL in India, and inside it to understand the primary roles this language is meant to perform. The dominant pattern here is of those state systems where English is taught after the first 4-5 years of schooling through the medium of one or two Indian languages. Minority patterns exist and vary from state to state but I shall say no more of these here. Within the dominant pattern English becomes a second or third language which is usually taught for one class-hour each working day. English continues to be taught thus for 5 to 7 school years. For a majority of those who enter the university or find places in technological institutions, English thus serves either as the main second language or may, in a percentage of cases, assume the place of the sole language of learning.

English thus enters the education system after one or two Indian languages have been taught and used for interpersonal, affective and cognitive roles. It comes in to serve as an additional tool whose primary objective is to provide a link to the world of knowledge or, what comes to much the same, to serve as the main "library language" (Education Commission 1964-66). The study group that advised the Government of India on the changed roles of English from the mid-sixties expressed the implications of its changed status thus:

> There will be a shift of emphasis from expression to comprehension. The main aim of teaching will then be to develop the ability of students to read and understand books and journals and reference materials in English ... The main emphasis will be on reading and comprehension. (MOE 1967)

That was exactly twenty years ago but it remains equally true today.

Meaningful curriculum renewal must therefore begin in recognition of the fact that the primary role of English is as an additional instrument of cognitive growth. It is true that for large numbers English will continue to serve as a main tool for interpersonal interaction or even of social survival among people who speak another language. It is also true that English is the main vehicle used by the businessman and banker, the politician or pundit part of whose professional interests may lie outside the country. But though the number of such users is large and their work may be of great significance to the growth and development of the nation, such uses of English which demand high levels of oral competency ought not to be taken as the central concerns of TEFL in the state-level systems. For the vast majority of those who enter schools English is primarily meant to provide access to the world of learning and scientific scholarship.

What implications does such a view of English — its status and roles — have for curriculum design in state-level systems? The following points should constitute part of an answer.

3.2 If it is true that in the vast majority of cases English comes to the child after he learns one or two Indian languages at least one of which is also used as the vehicle of school instruction, then the most important task before the curriculum designer ought to be to explore ways in which English can serve as an aid to conceptualization and the expression of abstract relations. Depending on how far and with what success the Indian language that precedes it has or has not been used to serve such a role, English must step in to enhance the possibilities of such learners being able to use language to perform the higher-order skills of reading and written language in academic/scientific domains. Use of language in performing such cognitively demanding and context-reduced tasks will require a lot of effort on the part of teachers of both languages. What will help best however is work on a type of additive bilingualism where the second language supports and strengthens what the first may have built. As it is taught now English does not enhance such abilities nor provide such support towards the shared responsibility of serving as a basic tool for cognitive growth and academic achievement. Even where they matriculate with distinction, tertiary-level students are found to "fail generally to understand their P.U.C. or higher secondary texts or the lectures delivered in English in the P.U.C. classes. As for expression, it is almost non-existent in the large majority of cases"

(Report 1967). What makes it worse is the understanding backed up by some recent research (see Eapen 1987; Das 1978) that in most such cases the deficiencies that surface in their use of English are equally true in such students' reading/ writing in L1. A majority of such students are thus not just poor readers in English; they also lack the abilities of mature reading in the language that is meant to serve as the main instrument of their personal and professional lives. The reverse phenomenon appears to be at work in those cases where a select minority of students succeeds fully in learning English for all the purposes that it is taught today. In their efforts to make this prestige language the sole medium of all aspects of life rather than of just academic learning, such learners may find that success in English which leads to a neglect of the earlier language(s) is accompanied by first language loss or loss of at least part of their ability to function creatively in it. If true such subtractive bilingualism and the processes of reverse transfer that it generates may be doing more harm than good.

To make English serve its role as a useful tool of truly additive bilingualism it will become necessary most of all to invest in strategies and materials that bring together the common concerns of the two or more languages that are used for cognitive growth and academic achievement. How this can be achieved as part of long-term programmes is a task that requires both deep enquiry and careful implementation. There is however some support for such work in language-teaching history. Long years ago Michael West working in British India found out for example that reading is a general ability whose main skills are transferable from language to language (West 1926). He provided experimental support for it by showing how work done in a relatively short period of time to improve reading abilities in English brought about an unexpectedly high degree of improvement in the learner's reading abilities in his first language. That some of this is both possible and capable of producing the hoped-for results appears to have ample support in recent language teaching experiment and experience. Studies done on the French immersion programmes have, for instance, extended the possibilities of such transfer in that they show that "once one has learned how to use language as a tool for conceptualizing, drawing abstract relations or expressing complex relationships in one language, then these processes, or language functions, are applicable to any language context" (Cummins and Swain 1986:103). They show too that: "first language literacy-related instruction is associated with improved second language performance in literacy-related tasks" (ibid.:105). All this is based on research-supported understanding that "L1 and L2 cognitive/academic proficiency are interdependent as a result of the fact that both are, to a significant extent, manifestations of the same underlying cognitive proficiency" (*ibid.*:212). Curriculum renewal in English must primarily address itself to the tasks of exploring this common territory where two literate languages can work together and share the responsibility that belongs to both. Syllabuses that work towards communicative tactics and skills that are useful for meeting social needs or goals are not the best means towards it since as Saville-Troike found out (1984) there is a qualitative difference between these and the strategies demanded by academic achievement.

3.3 Being informed by and responsive to the challenges and responsibilities of India's multilingualism is thus the first prerequisite of planned curriculum renewal. A second is equally fundamental and it has suffered equal neglect. It is the understanding of the setting in which English or any other language gets taught in the subcontinent. Classrooms vary greatly — from those in large metropolises to those in small and distant villages, from schoolrooms in richly endowed "public" schools to those in ordinary state-supported schools. Those who teach in them must differ too — as much in their qualifications and training as in their competence in English or their commitment and creativity. So must the learners. At this stage we also lack adequate research support for at least two essentials — one, the nature and characteristics of a language classroom in India and two, the dominant patterns of behaviour and interaction among the learners of English and other languages in the sub-continent. Work done in both these areas in recent years (e.g. Young and Lee 1985; Young 1987; Wong 1984, 1988 on the Chinese classroom and the Chinese learner of English respectively) have begun to provide much-needed support for the design and development of language curricula that can become truly sensitive to the delicate balance of the behaviours, beliefs and expectations that make up the culture of such a classroom.

But major variations and lack of research support notwithstanding there are basic similarities which form part of any such system which is heir to a long tradition of learning and scholarship. The Indian classroom and its pedagogic conventions are largely shaped by established ways of teaching and learning. Teacher and learner attitudes and expectations form part thereof, so do the norms of good classroom organisation and management, of preferred ways of behaviour and interpersonal interaction. Established tradition and long use have also bestowed two other things with a special status — the ubiquitous textbook and the all-important examination. Such a classroom can thus be said to be dominated by three Ts: the prescribed textbook, the teacher and the unchanging system of tests and examinations. This in fact underscores its acquisition-poor environment much more than the fact that the contact with English may usually be limited to one class-hour per day.

To explain what happens when curriculum change is imposed in disregard of this setting I must briefly go back to what I said a little while ago. I said that SS continues to dominate the language teaching system in India. This now needs to be qualified. Although SS is the only document that guides the writers of textual materials and the setters of examinations and although it also serves as the administrator's public statement on what gets done at what stage in the school, such a document far from influencing the methodology of ordinary classrooms hardly ever gets consulted by such a teacher. If there is today one area of almost total mismatch in Indian TEFL it is that between curricular expectations and classroom practice.

That SS does not interest or influence the teacher of English came to light from a questionnaire-based study on syllabus use that I conducted over a three-year period (1981-1984) using trained graduate teachers of English in Hyderabad as my subjects (also see Tickoo 1986a). The study showed that about half of them had never found it either necessary or possible to study their syllabus. The vast majority saw no need to use it and a small percentage had either not seen one in print or not felt the slightest need to think of such a document as having any relevance to their professional work. That the methodology that accompanied SS has not found favour with ordinary teachers has been widely known for at least twenty of the thirty odd years of its adoption in Indian schools. Here, for example, is what two different national committees on the study and teaching of English wrote about the methodology that pervades. "In the majority of cases", the first report observed,

> there is a great gulf between the avowed approach and the actual practice. The aural/oral approach ... has not found its way into the ordinary classroom. Most teachers make free and often unsystematic use of the pupils' mother tongue on the lines of the old grammar-translation method. (Report 1969)

The second one found most teachers translating "each lesson and every sentence in it into the regional language" (Report 1967:46).

The important point however is not what has been happening but why. The main reason is that the methodology that SS brought to the sub-continent had been trial-tested in an entirely different teaching-learning environment. It called for a different type of teacher involvement, a different kind of classroom organisation and a different pattern of human interaction. Especially in the earlier stages of teaching it mainly depended on the teacher's ability to sustain long periods of oral-aural drills and pattern practice which neither appealed to her sense of good teaching nor fitted with the established patterns of pedagogy.

The methodology that accompanies the communicative or communicational alternatives is different. Ideally it works best in an environment in which as Candlin sees it "learners in company of their peers and their teachers chart their own paths to acquisition on the basis of negotiated interaction with input contained within a range of problem-solving tasks" (Candlin 1984). In theory at least being what Widdowson calls "person oriented" (Widdowson 1984) it also seeks only minimal intervention from the teacher. In reality as he rightly points out it makes assumptions about classroom organisation, human behaviour and interpersonal relationships which are totally at variance with what makes a good "position oriented" classroom.

For its success in the state-level systems the alternative curriculum must build upon what exists and invest in strengthening the same in ways that are affordable and user friendly. The well-known constraints include the large size of the class, the absence of teaching aids other than perhaps a blackboard, and the furniture that makes some forms of innovative activity, including group and peer work, difficult to undertake. Within it stands a teacher who feels happy in performing certain front-of-the-classroom roles and may not all at once accept a position of backstage manager. The student too believes that he learns best through a process of preparation, repetition and revision and may not readily welcome a wholesale adoption of discovery methods. What may therefore work is slow change which utilizes the strengths of teachers and pupils rather than one that upsets too many favoured apple carts.

But since the primary role of this language in the alternative curriculum will be to serve as a base for cognitive growth and development, and the main objective is thus to build maturity in reading related skills and abilities, revolutionary changes in methodology or classroom organisation may in any case be unnecessary. Where comprehension rather than production is the primary goal the system's constraints may be more apparent than real.

The materials and methodology to be used will vary with the ages and levels of learners, and especially in the early stages it pays to build oral foundations. The most important strategy will however be the one that most effectively paves the way into self reliance in reading. Some recent successes achieved in comparable circumstances (viz. the village schools in South Fiji; see Elley and Mangubhai 1979, 1983) using "a book-based approach to enrich children's exposure to English" appear to suggest however that sizeable gains become possible within relatively short periods of time. The book flood programme as it is called appears not only to produce better reading skills but also to improve the pupils' writing and grammatical structures. That it does so through greater dependence on better books rather than on higher levels of teacher proficiency and performance makes it an even more suitable model for adoption in ordinary Indian schools. An additional factor in favour of such an approach may be that it does not exclude other types of work that are more suited to building a multi-skills strength among the learners. There should therefore be no reason to believe that the adoption of a programme that accepts the primacy of reading and comprehension will lead to a Michael West-type exclusiveness or a reversion to grammar grind and translation. What such a methodology should aim at in the earlier stages is adequate provision for both intensive and extensive reading and the growth of learner self reliance.

Similar but much more powerful means will become necessary to help the learner grapple with the challenges of academic reading at the secondary and more so the tertiary level. Once again however a good deal of successful effort exists both in the current literature on language across the curriculum and in some recent works in genre-related ESP (see, for example, Swales 1985/1987 and Mohan 1985).

3.4 A fuller implementation of the alternative will also necessitate the harnessing of several types of reading-related resources and technologies. School libraries and graded class libraries and book corners will become a basic ingredient to its success. And since the material resources will continue as a major constraint ways will have to be found to help the teacher utilize less expensive ways of providing additional reading materials. Newspapers in English and the regional languages can, for example, be turned into a rich resource.

3.5 An almost totally unexplored area is that of interlingual cooperation. Where two or three unequal languages serve the same broad objective it will become necessary to define the realms in which each can best contribute to the shared responsibility. Where an Indian language has yet to reach a stage where it can be or is being used as a language of advanced learning English must singly serve as the medium for such development and use. But where the first/second language is capable of serving as a strong base for academic work the partnership will have to be defined with greater specificity. In all this it may pay to heed two major conclusions of research based on the Canadian immersion programme. One, that in literacy-related tasks time spent on L1 results in high dividends. Two, that subtractive bilingualism that in this case may be caused by the lower status of one of the two languages should never be allowed to come into operation. The most important thing however is to ensure that the two mediums both supplement and complement each other.

Successful curriculum renewal depends on a lot more than a clearer definition of the goals, a studied understanding of the linguistic scene and a lively responsiveness to the settings in which the language operates. Both in its design and implementation it must, for example, provide for the best means of dependable evaluation and efficient feedback. What I have attempted in this presentation is a mere outline of only part of a much larger framework for any such renewal. I did so to demonstrate why in language teaching for acquisition-poor national systems like those of TEFL in India such renewal must remain informed by changing national needs, responsive to the crosslinguistic influences and dependent on the strengths of the schoolrooms where it will be taught. Such a view may have some relevance to other similar situations in TEFL or for the teaching of other second/foreign languages. That however is something beyond the scope of this presentation, whose main aim was to suggest the need for alternatives to some of today's narrowly linguistic curricula that are being adopted for such systems.

References*

Breen, M.P. 1984. "Process Syllabuses for the Language Classroom". *General English Syllabus Design: ELT Documents 118* ed. by C.J. Brumfit, 47-60. Pergamon Press.
———. 1985. "Alternative Priorities and Criteria for the Design of Language Syllabuses for Adult Learners" (unpublished: mimeographed).

Brumfit, C.J. 1981. "Teaching the General Student". *Communication in the Classroom* ed. by K. Johnson & K. Morrow, 46-51. Longman. Also see D.A. Wilkins, C.J. Brumfit & C.B. Paulston. 1981. "Notional Syllabuses Revisited". *Applied Linguistics* II(1). 83-100.

——. ed. 1984. *General English Syllabus Design: ELT Documents 118.* Pergamon Press.

Candlin, C. 1984. "Syllabus Design as a Critical Process". *General English Syllabus Design* ed. by C.J. Brumfit, 29-46. Pergamon Press.

Carter, R. 1987. *Vocabulary: Applied Linguistic Perspectives.* Allen & Unwin.

Clark, J.L. 1986. "Curriculum Renewal in School Foreign Language Learning: An overview". *Australian Review of Applied Linguistics* 9(1). 14-42.

Clark, J.L. 1987. *Curriculum Renewal in School Foreign Language Learning.* Oxford University Press.

Crombie, W. 1985. *Discourse and Language Learning: A relational approach to syllabus design.* Oxford University Press.

Cummins, J. & M. Swain. 1986. *Bilingualism in Education.* Longman.

Das, B.K. 1978. "Written English in Functional Communication: An investigation". Ph.D. Dissertation, Sambalpur University, India (unpublished).

Eapen, L. 1987. "Extensive Reading at the Tertiary Level for the Low Achievers". Ph.D. Dissertation, CIEFL Hyderabad, India (unpublished).

Elley, W.B. & F. Mangubhai. 1979. "A Research Report on Reading in Fiji". *Fiji English Teachers Journal* 15. 1-7.

——. 1983. "The Impact of Reading on Second Language Learning". *Reading Research Quarterly* 19(1). 53-67.

Government of India, Ministry of Education. 1966. *Education and National Policy: Report of the Education Commission* (1964-1966).

——. 1967. *The Study of English in India: Report of the Study Group Appointed by the Ministry of Education.*

Mohan, B.A. 1986. *Language and Content.* Addison-Wesley.

Morrow, K. 1987. "Language Teaching Syllabuses: Fact or fiction?" *Language Syllabuses: State of the art anthology series 18* ed. by Makhan L. Tickoo, 33-38. RELC Singapore.

Paulston, C.B. 1981. "Notional Syllabuses Revisited: Some comments". *Applied Linguistics* 11(1). 93-95.

Prabhu, N.S. 1983. "Procedural Syllabuses, RELC Seminar 1983". *Trends in Language Syllabus Design* ed. by J. Read. Singapore University Press.

——. 1984. "Communicative Teaching: 'Communicative' in what sense?" RELC Seminar 1984. *Communicative Language Teaching* ed. by B.K. Das, 32-40. Singapore University Press.

——. 1985. "Coping with the Unknown in Language Pedagogy". *English in the World* ed. by R. Quirk & H.G. Widdowson, 164-173. Cambridge University Press.

Saville-Troike, M. 1984. "What Really Matters in Second Language Learning for Academic Achievement?" *TESOL Quarterly* 18. 199-219.

Smith, D.A. 1962. "The Madras Snowball: An attempt to retrain 27,000 teachers of English to beginners". *English Language Teaching* 17(1). 3-8.

Stern, H.H. 1984. "Review and Discussion". *General English Syllabus Design: ELT Documents 118* ed. by C.J. Brumfit, 5-12. Pergamon Press.

Swales, J. 1985. *Episodes in ESP*. Pergamon Press.

————. 1986. *English for Specifiable Purposes: Occasional Papers No. 42*. RELC Singapore.

Tickoo, M.L. 1986a. "Syllabuses, Scholars, and Schooling Systems". *Socio-linguistic Aspects of Language Learning and Teaching: Occasional Papers No. 41* ed. by R. Noss & T. Llamzon, 43-60. RELC Singapore.

————. 1986b. "Scholars Syllabuses: User friendly or utopian?" *Rajasthan University Studies in English*, Special Number on English Language Teaching, XVIII. 9-23.

————. 1987. "Ideas and Practice in State-Level Syllabuses: An Indian perspective". *Language Syllabuses: State of the art anthology series 18* ed. by M.L. Tickoo, 110-146. RELC Singapore.

Van Ek, J.A. 1976. *The Threshold Level for Modern Language Learning in Schools*. Longman.

Widdowson, H.G. 1979. *Explorations in Applied Linguistics*. Oxford University Press.

————. 1983. *Learning Purpose and Language Use*. Oxford University Press.

————. 1984. "Educational and Pedagogic Factors in Syllabus Design". *General English Syllabus Design: ELT Documents 118* ed. by C.J. Brumfit, 23-28. Pergamon Press.

————. 1987. "Aspects of Syllabus Design". *Language Syllabuses: State of the art anthology series 18* ed. by M.L. Tickoo, 65-89. RELC Singapore.

Wilkins, D. 1976. *Notional Syllabuses*. Oxford University Press.

Willis, D. & J. Willis. 1987. "Varied Activities for Variable Language". *ELT Journal* 41(1). 12-18.

Wong, Sau-ling S. 1988. "What We Do and Don't Know about Chinese Learners of English: A critical review of selected research". *RELC Journal* 19(1). 1-20.

Young, R. 1987. "The Cultural Context of TESOL — A review of research in Chinese classrooms". *RELC Journal* 18(2). 15-30.

Young, R. & Lee Sue. 1985. "EFL Curriculum Innovation and Teachers' Attitudes". *On Tesol 1984* ed. by Penny Larson et al., 183-194. TESOL Washington, D.C.

Interactive Discourse in the L2 Classroom

Robert J. Di Pietro

The Context

One of the trends observable at present in the field of L2 instruction is toward the promotion of discourse skills among learners. This trend is associated with another, longer standing trend toward the development of "communicative competence" as a preferred goal of language instruction. Communication must certainly involve interaction, either between the teacher and the students or among the students without the overt intervention of the teacher. Interactive discourse can be generated from such commonly understood classroom activities as information-gap games and staged sociodramas. Demands placed on the students may range from filling in lacunae in blocks of information to solving problems based on data of various sorts supplied to them (see Pica 1986 ms.). Simulations, as a rather intricate kind of communication activity, can involve the entire class in performing roles with prescribed agendas to be articulated (Jones 1982).

All of the above-mentioned classroom activities appear to derive from a common opinion about the purpose of human language, namely that people speak to each other primarily to exchange, negotiate, or clarify meanings. This opinion is also evident in the widely held conception of communication strategies as particular ways of making one's self understood while understanding others (see, for example, Canale and Swain 1979; Tarone 1981). On the other hand, there is reason to question such a view of communication strategy. Lantolf and Frawley (1985), for example, reject the so-called "conduit" metaphor of communication whereby ideas are "sent across" from speaker to hearer. Their preference is to interpret communication from a Vygotskyan perspective in which communication strategies are seen as efforts made by speakers to achieve self-regulation in the "presence of other speakers" (Lantolf and Frawley 1985:150). The notion of "regulatory agencies" has the potential for explaining much behavior evident in the performance of L2 learners. According to Vygotsky, there are three kinds of regulation: object, other and self (see Vygotsky 1978). A speaker who is overly object-regulated is one whose discourse is strongly conditioned by a struggle with the rules and conventions of the language. Other regulation is of two types: regulated and regulating. To be excessively other-regulated is to have one's verbal performance dictated by another person. Other-regulating activity is where one attempts to dictate the verbal performance of another individual. Finally, self-regulation occurs when the speaker feels unconstrained in expressing personal thoughts, positions or feelings. It is not difficult to find examples of discourse in the FL classroom that typifies all three kinds of regulation. Object-regulation is manifested in the discourse of those students who are forced to adhere to exercises and grammatical drills. Other-regulation occurs between the teacher and the students, with the former usually regulating the latter through contrived questions of various sorts. The student who is asked to speak freely on any subject has been given the invitation to exercise self-regulation. It is well to point out that all authentic discourse whether in the classroom or outside it has elements of all three types of regulation. The speaker who does not heed elements of the grammar or "artifact" of the language is not likely to be coherent. Certainly, participatory discourse requires a degree of other-regulation. Discourse without a modicum of self-regulation is usually nothing more than an exchange of ritualized protocols such as greetings and leave-takings.

If regulation is necessarily part of all interactive discourse then what special effects, if any, does it have on discourse in a second language, how should it be treated pedagogically and how should its results be interpreted? To find the answers to these three questions, a study was conducted of the discourse generated in the execution of scenarios in the classroom. The scenario is an activity that places learners in a situation in which they are free to choose among diverse goals and develop their own agendas for interaction as they work toward these goals (see Di Pietro 1987:41). The intention is to allow students to exercise self-regulation in the target language while acquiring the necessary knowledge of target language rules and target language conversational management skills. The scenario appears to be ideally suited for the promotion of interactive discourse in L2. Unlike role-plays or simulations, the students are not constrained to assume a prespecified attitude or goal. They choose their own goals and prepare their own plans for how to arrive at their goals.

The scenario typically consists of two roles, sometimes more. Each role contains the description of a situation in which the role player finds him/herself. For example:

Role A: You have been hospitalized after a rather serious heart attack. So far, no one has given you any indication as to your chances for recovery. Your doctor is about to visit you. Work out a plan to get this information from him.

A certain amount of tension is built into the role in order to make it more than a reason to solicit information from the other party. The player of Role A must wonder why no information has been forthcoming about the consequences of the heart attack, e.g. patients who are seriously ill are sometimes kept in the dark about their chances for recovery. The tension is increased by investing the counter-role, that of the doctor, with another, situationally related task:

Role B: You are a doctor. Your patient has had a rather serious heart attack and is in the hospital. He/she does not know it yet but he/she has just won the national lottery. You must pass this news on to your patient. How will you do it without causing so much excitement that he/she will have another heart attack?

Classroom performances of this scenario have revealed that the tension can build between the two role players as the patient tends to interpret anything the doctor might say about "taking it easy" or "going on a long vacation" as indications that his/her life on earth will be short. More significantly, the interplay of the two roles fosters self-regulation as both players attempt to fulfill their agendas. They also engage in other-regulation, being both regulating and regulated. Object regulation is mitigated by the fact that each role player goes through a rehearsal phase during which other students share in the preparation of the agenda for the role. During rehearsal, students may ask any kind of questions they wish about the grammar, the appropriate vocabulary, pronunciation, verbal strategies, and any other matter pertaining to the agenda being prepared. These questions may be directed to other members of the group or to the teacher. In this way, the collective knowledge of the group is brought to bear on the learning task at hand. It is to be presumed that the extent to which learners are regulated by the object (in the form of target language grammar, vocabulary, and con-

versational mechanisms) depends upon the level of proficiency attained in
target language discourse. The higher the level of proficiency, the more
native-like the discourse becomes in its reflection of the regulatory agencies
during the performance phase. Only the discourse of the students in performance has been assessed in this study. Discourse generated during rehearsal, as well as during the debriefing phase that normally follows performance in the strategic interaction (SI) approach, is primarily pedagogical in
nature and may be significantly different from what learners are likely to
say in environments outside the instructional frame. The interplay of regulatory agencies in the rehearsal and debriefing phases will become the subject of future studies. For the time being it is not unreasonable to assume
that other-regulation would predominate in both rehearsal and debriefing,
but it is not clear at this point how the central role of the teacher during
debriefing affects the dynamics of interaction. It is clear as the result of the
current study that performance discourse can serve as a stimulator for
learning about the target language and gaining confidence in using it.

Goals of the Study

The study has two related goals: to determine (1) the extent to which the
performance of a scenario in the target language promoted self-regulation;
and (2) how the opportunity to self-regulate contributed to increased proficiency in the target language.

Description of the Study

The study was conducted with a class of first-year students enrolled in the
English Language Institute of the University of Delaware during the second
and third week of January, 1986. The class of thirty-five students coming
from countries in Europe, Asia, and Latin America were broken down into
rehearsal groups of five to six students.[1] As in standard SI procedure, each
group was not allowed to know more about the coming interaction than
what was written on their role card. Two scenarios were prepared, with A
and B roles distributed to six rehearsal groups. After a period of approximately twenty-five minutes, single representatives from each group were
chosen to perform the role assigned to that group. The non-performing stu-

dents in each group were told that they should provide advice and help to their representative at any time he or she needed it during the performance. Due to limitations of time, only two performances took place, one each for the two scenarios assigned to the class. While both performances were videotaped, only the second one (of the scenario entitled "Journey to the Past"[2]) is the subject of the current analysis. This choice was made purely out of technical considerations: the students involved in the other scenario spoke very softly with the result that their voices were not clearly picked up by the recording equipment.

The roles of "Journey to the Past" were stated as follows:

Role A: You work as a traveling salesperson and you are riding on a train. The person sitting next to you is very well dressed. Since you sell clothing, this person may be interested in buying something from you. What will you say to him?

Role B: You are traveling on a train and are sitting next to someone who looks familiar to you. You realize that this person is the one who once sold you an expensive TV set that stopped working after one week. It cost you much money to have it fixed and you did not have the chance to tell this person about your problem because she was no longer at the store when you returned. What will you say now?

The roles could have been performed by either males or females. As it turned out, a female played role A and a male, role B.

A transcription was made of the dialog that took place between the two role players. In making the transcription, special care was taken to indicate all features of discourse that may have had some bearing on the interpretation of the interaction and the functioning of the regulatory agencies. An edited version of the dialog was then prepared from the transcription and given to the students at a class meeting held one week later. In making this edited version, the only changes were to correct grammatical errors, replace inappropriate or incorrect vocabulary where needed, and smooth out the style wherever it was overtly clumsy. Excluded from the edited dialog were all phenomena that related to conversational management such as overlaps, hesitations, and self/other repairs. No changes were made to the sense or intent of what was said by the performers.

The two original performers of roles A and B were given an opportunity to look over the edited script at the outset of the second class meeting.

They were told that the purpose of this script was to refresh their memories about what they had said in their first performance of the scenario. After approximately ten minutes, the script was taken away and the two were asked to re-perform their scenario. This second performance was videotaped and transcribed with the same care to record all features of discourse that have relevance to the analysis. The two performances were then compared and conclusions were drawn about the function of the regulatory agencies and the manifest signs of changes in the students' target language discourse skills from the first meeting to the second.

The Texts

Briefly put, three texts form the core of this study: a transcription of an initial performance of the scenario, an edited script of that performance which was shown to the students, and a transcription of the performance that occurred after the students had had a chance to review what they said initially.

Key to symbols used in transcriptions

▬▬	overloud speech	( )	compressed speech, with overfast delivery;
...	hesitation; each dot represents about .5 seconds of silence;	[ ]	segments of speech delivered simultaneously by both speakers
uh, uhhh	hesitation filler delivered with mid central vowel; additional h's indicate lengthened vowel;	⌐	rapid onset of speech by second party.
hmmm	bilabial nasal hesitation filler;		
↑	syllable following symbol is delivered on overhigh pitch;		

First Performance

A: ↑ Where're <u>you</u> going?

B: Oh, I going to New York City (How about you?)

A: First, good, I have to pass in . in the New New York because I . I just returned to the country.
You're ↑ <u>pretty</u> today! Where you buy your clothes?

B: Let me . let me . *oh!* . I remember that *uhhh* me meet .. in another time.

A: O, I don't think .

B: Oh yes! You sold me a (TV) a television set in a ... once .. time.

A: <u>No</u> ... I don't ⌈think so⌉

B: ⌊(you) ⌋ you remember in the last year ...

more or less in July ... I went to the ... *uhh* .. Radio Shack store ... you worked there?

A: Minute, please, just a minute.
                    A goes to her group for consultation.

A   Sir, I think you're wrong because I . I . my job is⌉
B: ⌊I am sure

A: No, no
B: ⌈because ⌉
A: ⌊ You you⌋ make a mistake you make a mistake because I,
         I'm traveling sales . sales . ⌈only sport⌉
Teacher: ⌊clothing ⌋
A: *Huh?*
Teacher: clothing.
A: only sales clothing .. OK? I I think you're you're .. y you're you're
         you're ⌉
              ⌊ I am sure because *uh* . *uh* . for your bad sold . I lost . so much ..
              money.
A: No, no .. You're crazy . you are crazy .. you are very crazy.
B: Tell me . I . I tell about ... I I told you about . my *uh* problem. When I bought
         the TV .. *uh* .. I lost . so much money because . the *uh* apparate ... apparatus
         .. *uh uh* was very ⌈very⌉ .. *uh* .. bad.
                           ⌊ohh⌋   It's terrible. But I I sell only clothes.
         ⌈I don't understand   ⌉
B: ⌊When I I send you ..⌋
A: ↑ anything on TV, radios, I don't understand anything ⌉
B: ⌊ I I ...
A: I sell ↑ only beautiful clothes .. OK?
B: I am sure .. youuuu ..⌉
A: ⌊No.
B: You send .. *uh uh* .. you sold me this apparatus.
A: No, no. I I don't sell ... I ↑ never sold (any) TVs and radios.
         I don't understand ↑ anything about ... ⌉
B: ⌊ Really?
A: Really. I am special. I understand only the special ... OK?
         I know, I know what's what's the man dress now, OK? What the women *uh*
         can dress ⌈now⌉ but TV, radio, I don't know.
B: ⌊ohh⌋
B: Maybe you are a twins?
                    (laughter from class)
B: You have a sis(ter) ...
Teacher: You have a sister? You have a sister? What do you say to him. Tell him tell
         him ⌉
A: ⌊ OK OK! *uhhh* I I my, my my I have a store, a big store, and *mmm*
         uhhh I (sell) only beautiful clothes for men ... you understand?
B: But *uh* my question for you ... (there) is a sister, someone similar to you?

A: I don't think so ... I am I am different for the other parents.
        I am Brazilian.
B: Are you sure?
A: Yeah ...

Edited Script
A: Where are you going?
B: To New York City. How about you?
A: I'm going to New York first. I need to stop off there because I've just returned
        to this country. You look handsome today! Where do you buy your clothes?
B: I seem to remember that we've met before.
A: I don't think so.
B: Oh, yes. You sold me a television set once.
A: No, I don't think so.
B: Do you remember last year, around July, I came to the Radio Shack store
        where you worked?
A: I think you're wrong because my job is selling clothes.
B: I am sure.
A: No, no. You're making a mistake because I'm a traveling salesperson. I only
        sell sport clothing.
B: I am sure because I lost a lot of money on account of you.
A: No, no. You're very mistaken.
B: Let me tell you about my problem. I lost a lot of money when I bought the TV
        because it was very defective.
A: Oh, that's terrible, but I sell only clothes. I don't know anything about TVs or
        radios.
B: But you sold me the TV.
A: I sell only beautiful clothes. I know what men are wearing now. I know what
        women are wearing. But I don't know anything about TVs and radios.
B: Maybe you are a twin? Do you have a sister somewhere who looks just like
        you?
A: No, I look quite different from my relatives. I'm from Brazil.
B: Are you certain?
A: Yes. There is no one like me in New York or anywhere else. Only in Brazil.

Second performance
A: Good morning. How are you?
B: Fine, fine.
A: I'm fine! Where're you going?
B: To New York City, *uhh hmmm* how about you?
A: *Ohhh* at first I'm going to New York because I .. just .. I've just *uhh*
        (re)turned to this country *uhhh* but you're very handsome todayyyy ..
        where're you buying your clothes?
B: *Ohhh* let me .. *hmmm* I seemed to remember *uhhh* we've meet before.
A: Nooo . I don't think so.
B: I am sure.

A: No, I don't think so.

B: Do you remember ll last year . around July . I . came to (the) Radio Shack where you work-ed?

A: I think you making . made a mistake because I oonl .. I sell only clothes. I am a traveling *uhhh* traveling person woman.

B: I am sure because I .. lost a lot of money account of you.

A: No, I don't accept anything about TVs or radios I am only a sale .. some clothes . sport clothes.

B: Let me tell you *uhh* when I *uh* bought the (TV) I losss *uhhh* lot of money because the TV was *uhhh* defective.

A: It's terrible I know but . I'm never sell .. TVs or I only sells clothes. Look at (your) shoes . I think you need to change your shoes.

These ⌈shoes are   ⌉ the last year's styles .

B: ⌊(These are nice shoes)⌋

A: the winter style.

B: *uh* but *uh* right now, I (don't need) any .. clothes .

A: ahhh but if . you , see . my . clothes .. it's wonnnnderful. I think you're . you need . to buy some thing.

B: But I suppose *uhhh* your ... store is (very ex)pense.

A: No, don't worry about the price. Its very very cheap. It

⌈ have a lot ⌉ of kind of fashions.

B: ⌊ *uhhhh*   ⌋   That's too bad because .. right now I only need a . a . recuper . recup . (my) money.

The Analysis of the Data

It is immediately apparent from a review of the first performance that each role player is intent on fulfilling their individual goals. Player A makes the first overt move in her role as clothing salesperson by complimenting player B ("You're pretty today") and then asking him to tell her where he buys his clothes. Rather than answer her, player B initiates his own agenda as "injured buyer" by suggesting that they already know each other from an earlier encounter ("I remember that *uhhh* we meet .. in another time"). Player A refuses to admit to having met player B and when player B insists by stating a specific date and place, she calls for time out in order to consult with her rehearsal group. When she returns to the interaction, she tells B that he is mistaken. The interaction becomes more heated after player B informs A that she was responsible for having sold him an inferior TV. She tells B that he is "crazy", a remarkably abrupt change from the politeness she displayed toward him just a few minutes earlier. Player B's counter move is to recount the details of the transaction that presumably occurred between them. A's defense is to insist that she knows nothing about TVs or radios and that she is in the clothing business. B changes his strategy to suggest that she may have a twin sister. A does not pick up this opening which would have allowed her a way out. Instead, she firmly states that she is quite distinctive in her family.

It is to be kept in mind that all of the content of the interaction was made up by the two interlocutors themselves. The only two attempts at other regulation by the teacher occurred when he supplied the appropriate lexical term "clothing" when player A was struggling to identify her assumed occupation and when he attempted to make her respond to B's suggestion that she had a sister. Neither attempt was successful, as A persisted in pursuing her own strategies in both instances. There is ample evidence from the discourse that each player attempts to regulate the other but neither is especially successful. The interaction ends with neither having given ground to the other. It is also clear that both players are having difficulty with the elements that make up the object-regulating agency, namely the pronunciation, grammar and vocabulary of English. Some examples can be found in the problems both A and B have with verb tense and in B's overslow and hesitant delivery at various points. Yet, it is not possible to conclude that object-regulation was a factor in shaping the discourse because there are no points at which concern for accuracy in pronunciation, grammar or vocabulary hindered the players from attempting to attain their personal goals. The interplay of strategies evident in the discourse leads to the conclusion that the overriding regulating agency was the self. B is clearly on the offensive in trying to get A to admit to engaging in an earlier transaction but A does not acquiesce. Instead, A counterattacks by telling B that he is wrong and/or crazy and extolling her own competence as a specialist in clothing. In general, the interaction has a distribution of object-, other-, and self-regulation which would be characteristic of an authentic discourse involving two individuals in a similar altercation in real life. What is special about this particular discourse is that it took place between two learners of English functioning in a formal classroom setting. The two players are obviously not fluent in their command of English, even though they found ways to defend their positions in the interaction. The question to be answered next is: what progress toward fluency, as well as accuracy, in the target language can be gained in this kind of pedagogical activity?

To answer that question, an investigation of the second performance is necessary. As pointed out above, the two role-players were given the chance to look over a corrected transcript of their conversation before performing it a second time. There is indication that the two role players were influenced by this review. The first three-quarters of their second performance is considerably more accurate in grammar and vocabulary than their first one. For example, A remembers to call B "handsome" rather than "pretty," and B replaces his fragmentary sentence, "I went to the Radio Shack / you worked there?" with one connected by a relative pronoun, "I came to the Radio Shack where you worked." An example of B's increase in fluency can be found by comparing his statements about how he lost money from the first and second performances: "... for your bad sold, I lost so much money" (first performance) and "... I lost a lot of money account of you".

The two performances differ in yet another, critical way. There are no overlaps in the major part of the second one. In the first performance, the overlaps, as well as the rapid onsets of speech, reflected the authentically polemical nature of the discourse. In contrast, the second performance appears to be almost a "textbook-perfect" dialogue being played out by students who have dutifully learned their roles. There is no need for overlap or rapid onsets because each player knows what is coming. In Vygotskyan terms, they are attending to the object and being regulated by it. However, at a point late in the interaction, player A decides to try a new strategy, one that she did not use in the first interaction. She draws attention to B's shoes, calling them "last year's styles" and suggesting that he purchase new ones. At this point, B overlaps with a hasty defense ("these are nice shoes") and the interaction becomes a new one, with the participants departing from what they said originally in the first performance and disregarding the corrected script that was prepared for them. B tells A that he does not need any new clothes, to which A retorts that her line of clothing is "wonnnnder-ful". B then supposes that her store is expensive, but A dispels his concern about prices, claiming that the store is "very, very cheap." B ends the interaction by expressing his regret about not recouping his money.

What inspired A to make her departure from the first performance and the script based on that performance? There are several possible answers to this question: the corrected script gave her the confidence in her grammatical ability needed to try a new approach or the desire to regain self-regulation was sufficiently compelling to lead her to abandon the safety of the predictable script. Perhaps both answers are the right ones. In any event, if we are to look for improvements in grammatical accuracy and fluency in the target language, it is necessary to examine *not* what was said in the first part of the second performance but in the part that begins with A's remark about B's shoes. It is in that portion of the discourse that the two players reassume their full roles as interlocutors in the scenario that formed the first performance. They resort to the same conversational style, with overlaps, hesitations and compressed speech. They also make some grammatical errors. Nevertheless, they produce some utterances that are very native-like, not only in form but in delivery as well. B's quick defense ("These are nice shoes") and A's reassurance about the cost of items in her store ("Don't worry about the price, it's very, very cheap") are indications that both students have made progress in their use of English in a realistic context.

The absence of native-like accuracy in the first performance of the scenario conforms to a finding by Lantolf and Khanji (1983) who noted an increase in parataxis in the discourse of an ESL student as he moved from performing in a structured interview to speaking freely on a topic of his own choice. Lantolf and Khanji also found, however, that syntactic accuracy decreased as the paratactic fluency of their subject became more dominant. The combination of accuracy and fluency in the speech of players A and B in the latter portion of the second performance of the present study suggests that a development toward greater control of the target language had occurred since the first encounter with the scenario a week earlier.

If this greater control is a manifestation of increasing proficiency in the target language, to what is it owed? The author would prefer to attribute it fully to the activity of the scenario, including the planning allowed by the rehearsal phase and the model of well-formed speech provided by the corrected script. However, since the students were studying the language in a country where it is also the language of the surrounding community, the potential effect of factors outside the classroom cannot be dismissed. It seems reasonable, at the very least, to conclude that the scenario, with its built-in interactional tension, served to focus the attention of the learners on tasks to be carried out in earnest: A was directed to sell clothing to B and B was charged with determining the culpability of A in an unfortunate past transaction. The suggestion being made here is that such a focus would lead the learner to process input from what is heard in the surrounding speech community and apply it meaningfully to gaining control over strategic discourse functions and critical vocabulary and grammar. In simpler words, the scenario has the potential to serve as a stimulator of second-language acquisition. A part of its success in doing so must derive from the encouragement it gives students to engage in self-regulation through interactive discourse on problematic issues.

With regard to application in the classroom, the scenario should be taken through its three phases of rehearsal, performance and debriefing (see Di Pietro 1987 for details). While the subjects in the present study were not put through a formal debriefing, they were allowed to review the corrected script of their own performances. This review served the function of a debriefing. Finally, promoting truly interactive discourse in the second-language classroom places new demands on the teacher and methodologist. Effective scenarios must be prepared and students must be free to find their own solutions to them. Issues must be chosen that are challenging and roles must be drawn up in a manner that does not force the players to work toward pre-determined ends. Above all, the teacher should not insist that a certain conclusion is to be preferred.

The scenario technique can easily serve as a bridge between elementary levels of instruction and more advanced ones. Some scenarios can function satisfactorily at any level of instruction. In anticipation of further research on the subject of interactive discourse in the context of second-language instruction, scenarios provide a unique framework for experimentation because they extend the paradigm beyond elements of language artifact to how learners utilize language in the service of their own egos.

Notes

1.   The author wishes to thank Mr. Scott Stevens, Director of the English Language Institute of the University of Delaware, and Ms. Sandra McCollum, ESL instructor at the University, for providing the opportunity to conduct this study in Ms. McCollum's class.

2.   The scenario "Journey to the Past" is the invention of Ms. Julie Docker, instructor of Italian at the Australian National University in Canberra.

References

Canale, M. & M. Swain. 1980. "Theoretical Bases of Communicative Approaches to Second Language Teaching and Testing". *Applied Linguistics* 1. 1-47.

Di Pietro, R. 1987. *Strategic Interaction: Learning languages through scenarios*. New York: Cambridge University Press.

Jones, K. 1982. *Simulations in Language Teaching*. New York: Cambridge Univeristy Press.

Lantolf, J. & W. Frawley. 1985. "On Communication Strategies: A functional perspective". *Rassegna Italiana di Linguistica Applicata* 2-3. 143-157.

Lantolf, J. & R. Khanji. 1983. "Non-Linguistic Parameters of Interlanguage Performance and Vygotskyan Psycholinguistics: Implications for L2 instruction". *The 10th LACUS Forum*, 425-440. Columbia, S.C.: Hornbeam Press.

Pica, T. 1986 ms. "Interlanguage Adjustments as an Outcome of NS-NNS Negotiated Interaction". Paper presented at the annual meeting of the Linguistic Society of America. New York, December.

Tarone, E. 1981. "Some Thoughts on the Notion of Communication Strategy". *TESOL Quarterly* 15. 285-295.

Vygotsky, L. 1978. *Mind in Society*. Cambridge, Mass.: Harvard University Press.

The Notion of Synchrony in Second Language Learning

June Gassin

Introduction

Synchrony refers to the discovery made by Condon and Ogston (1966) that in normal behaviour, speech and body motions are precisely and rhythmically coordinated. It has taken the better part of the past twenty years for the full import of this discovery to be felt, but Condon is now widely cited by specialists in many disciplines ranging from experimental psychology (Argyle 1975) to social anthropology (Kendon 1980) and linguistics (Von Raffler-Engel 1980; Menot 1982).

Traditionally, and until very recently, studies in human communicational behaviour have concentrated almost exclusively on either the verbal or on the nonverbal aspects of communication, and studies in nonverbal behaviour have often focused on the individual rather than on the individual in interaction. Condon's work has given an impetus to a new attempt at understanding some of the fundamental principles which underlie and regulate human behaviour at the interface of verbal and nonverbal behaviour both within and between individuals (cf. anthologies by Key 1980; Davis 1982).

It is the object of this paper to present Condon's major findings concerning synchrony and to emphasize their relevance with respect to second language learning. Some theoretical implications for second language acquisition (SLA) will be proposed as well as a description of one pedagogical approach congruent with the notion of synchrony.

Research Findings

Inspired by the early work of Birdwhistell (1952) and Scheflen (1964) in the field of micro kinesics, Condon and Ogston determined to search for "pervasive, recurrent and predictable regularities in normal behaviour" (Condon and Ogston 1966:342). A sound film of "normal" subjects conversing was taken at 48 frames per second. It was then scanned intensively using a time motion analyzing projector and the speech component segmented and transcribed accurate to 1/48th of a second.

> Intensive analysis revealed harmonious or synchronous organizations of change between body motion and speech in *both* intra-individual and interactional behaviour. Thus the body of the speaker dances in time with his speech. Further, the body of the listener dances in rhythm with that of the speaker! (Condon and Ogston 1966:338)

These two discoveries were termed self-synchrony and interactional synchrony.

The researchers subsequently analyzed approximately 30 other films of normal interaction including one of seven people listening to an eighth person speaking and found such self- and interactional synchrony to occur systematically (Condon and Ogston 1966:342).

By contrast, micro analysis of aphasic and schizophrenic patients revealed instances of self-dyssynchrony. The presence or absence of synchrony, therefore, appeared to have a correlation with the psychological well-being of the individual. Subsequent micro analyses conducted by Condon supported this view: "People with severe psychopathology or communication disorders are self-asynchronous and also interactionally asynchronous" (Condon 1982:61).

A study conducted by Condon and Sander (1974) involving neonates from 12 hours to 14 days old, revealed that alert infants synchronized their movements with the articulatory rhythm of adult speech, but they did not synchronize to isolated vowel sounds or tapping noises. Furthermore, American neonates synchronized as well to Chinese as to American English. The findings of this research prompted Condon and Sander to raise profound questions about the nature of language acquisition and of human interaction:

> If the infant, from the beginning, moves in precise, shared rhythm with the organization of the speech structure of his culture, then he participates developmentally through complex, sociobiological entrainment processes

in millions of repetitions of linguistic forms long before he later uses them in speaking and communicating. By the time he begins to speak, he may have already laid down within himself the form and structure of the language system of his culture. This would encompass a multiplicity of interlocking aspects: rhythmic and syntactic 'hierarchies', suprasegmental features, and paralinguistic nuances, not to mention body motion styles and rhythms. (Condon and Sander 1974:101)

The infant lives itself into language and culture: into the forms which surround and support it. It does not 'acquire' them as if from a separate system existing apart. (Condon 1980:57-58)

More recently, Condon has suggested that each culture may have its own peculiar micro rhythms, "it may be that those having different cultural rhythms are unable really to 'synch-in' fully with each other" (Condon 1982:66). He cites as an example of this the syncopated rhythms of black American behaviour which contrast with the more even 4/4 rhythms of white American behaviour.

Implications for SLA Theory

Condon's findings appear to have important implications with respect to SLA theory. Interactional synchrony implies that there could be fundamental perceptual and emotional differences between first and second language learners. If, as Condon suggests, the form and structure of the individual's language system are being laid down from the first moments of life through the medium of the rhythmic structure of adult speech, then the greatest difference between a first language learner (LL1) and a second language learner (LL2) is that the LL2 is lacking in a very basic perceptual and organizational framework in the L2, that of rhythm. The speech rhythms of the L2 would have to be "acquired" *along with* all the other forms of the new language instead of being integrated beforehand.

Consequently, not only will the adult LL2 have some difficulty in perceiving the new rhythms, given that he already possesses a native rhythmic structure, but he will also lack the essential rhythmic framework into which to slot the new lexical, syntactic, phonological, semantic and paralinguistic forms of the L2. The forms of the L2 will be perceived in accordance with the existing L1 rhythmic structure which will result in distortion at various levels. The body motions of the LL2 will be in synchrony with his L1 rhythms, but not with those of the L2. He may in this way be excluded from interactional synchrony with L2 speakers which could have negative psychological consequences resulting in feelings of isolation and rejection.

A secondary difference between the LL1 and the LL2 would be emotional. Although the LL2 may have developed many cognitive structures which are of help to him in learning a new language, he will not have been "socialized" into the L2 through repeated participation in rhythmic interaction with the surround. Emotional involvement on an unconscious level may involve participation in shared forms of rhythmic order (Condon 1980).

Condon's work also raises some interesting questions about children learning a second language. Can young children as well as infants automatically or more easily synchronize with foreign speech? Such a hypothesis might provide a valuable insight into why young children appear to acquire second languages more easily than adults. It is also interesting to speculate on whether this ability to entrain (synchronize body motions to within 50 milliseconds to incoming speech) is developmental and can, therefore, be lost or whether it can be reactivated.

Implications for Second Language Learning and Teaching

The behavioural unity of speech and body motions reveals the necessity for language learners and teachers to embrace a view of human communication which encompasses verbal, nonverbal and paralinguistic behaviours (Menot 1982; Von Raffler-Engel 1980a; Pennycook 1985). Body motions such as gesture, posture, eye contact and facial expressions can no longer be viewed as separate expressive systems existing apart from the verbal system, but rather as rhythmically integrated, co-occurring components of total speech behaviour. Menot (1987) has carried out careful analyses of French speech behaviour including rhythmic, intonational and gestural parameters.

> The prosodic organization of discourse in French is inscribed in the movements of the whole body. In other words, the body including the eyes speak the native language ... (Menot 1987:15; translation by present author)

Menot holds the view that inasmuch as body motions necessarily accompany any speech act, the body itself can be used as a pedagogical tool in establishing new rhythms in the LLs. Practice in moving the whole body or parts of the body in synchrony with the speech rhythms of the L2 forms one of the bases of her approach to corrective phonetics.

In the light of the important role that rhythm plays in the perception and production of speech (cf. Wenk 1985) as well as in social interaction, rhythm needs to be considered of central rather than of peripheral concern in language learning and teaching. Exclusive emphasis on the understanding and production of verbal behaviour without concomitant attention to rhythm can amount to denying language learners a means of psychological as well as physiological integration. Second language speakers whose speech is grossly out of synchrony with the rhythm of the target language can be seen as living a dual or even pathological reality, the body operating on one system and speech on another. This may be one of the profound although unconscious reasons for many of the acute discomforts experienced by L2 learners and speakers. It may contribute in a significant way to the lack of motivation in learners. Participating in activities which make them feel "uncoordinated" can only be demotivating for many.

Interacting effectively in a second language, therefore, presupposes a reasonable integration and production of the rhythmic properties of the new language. The closer one can approximate the new rhythms and coordinate one's speech and body rhythms to those of the native speaker of the L2, the closer one will come to being able to communicate effectively.

Von Raffler-Engel (1980b) has established a list of psychological factors affecting intercultural communication. She ranks body rhythms as the least conscious element among them and hypothesizes that "interactional difficulties increase as consciousness decreases" (1980b:127). For this reason as well as for that of promoting a feeling of psychological integration, there is a need to make explicit to the language learner that relationship between speech rhythms and communicative possibilities.

It must not be forgotten, however, that speech rhythms as well as interaction rhythms (discourse length, turn taking etc.) are extraordinarily complex. "Each of us has a *repertoire* of them — a repertoire that is contingent upon ethnicity, region, class, and probably occupation" (Scheflen 1982:17). Further, speech, body and interaction rhythms can and do change according to context and situation and are sometimes changed wilfully (Scheflen 1982:17). This last point is important in understanding dominance/subordinate relationships in conversation behaviour (Myllyniemi 1986) and has implications with respect to accommodation theory which are yet to be explored. It offers a further explanation of why second language speakers who do not have a mastery of second language rhythmic structures are often obliged to take a subordinate role in interactions with native speakers and must suffer the psychological consequences. Rhythm, then, can be a means of attaining and maintaining control in interaction.

Language teachers are, therefore, engaged in a most delicate and perilous endeavour, for to offer language without attention to rhythm is to a certain degree to offer language without power, power in and over oneself and power over others. At the same time, the language teacher needs to remember that "to adjust to another's body rhythm or to force someone else to conform to one's own is the utmost invasion of privacy" (Von Raffler-Engel 1980b:128). Such being the case, the language teacher needs to develop strategies which allow the student to discover and participate in the new rhythms in a natural and non-threatening way.

Pedagogical Applications

There are many different ways of helping students achieve a better perception and production of rhythm in a second language (cf. Menot 1982; Wenk and Wioland 1986; Pegalo 1985). The approach ultimately adopted by a given teacher will depend not only on the total pedagogical situation, but on the teacher's personality and teaching philosophy.

One approach which has been used for intermediate and advanced level ESL students at the University of Melbourne is drama (Gassin 1986). The drama workshop, whether or not theatrical works are used as a basis of instruction, provides a physical, emotional and intellectual atmosphere which is conducive to the task: that of freeing the mind from concentration on grammar, syntax and lexis so that the learner's perception of rhythm and its relationship to body, breath, voice and interaction can be heightened.

In a typical drama workshop, students engage in a variety of activities: breathing and relaxation exercises, voice production exercises, nonverbal activities, role play and improvisation. In each type of exercise students focus on rhythm in a different way.

For example, one of the aims of breathing and relaxation exercises is to help students become aware of the rhythm of their breath and the role of breath in speech production. Voice production exercises are conducted in rhythmic unison before students are asked to experiment with pitch, intonation, and volume contours. Gesture and posture are explored through synchronization with music as well as with speech. The appropriate and natural use of gesture becomes a means of developing rhythm in the whole body.

Nonverbal activities which focus on perception through experiential rather than cognitive means can provide interesting insights into the need for appropriate interaction rhythms. One such exercise involves jumping rope. Students take turns jumping and turning the rope. This exercise consistently elicits precise comments on the role of rhythm and tempo in speech and the need to know when to "get in" as well as to "get out" of a conversation. The students' comments show that they are instinctively aware of the importance of interaction rhythms and their variability across cultures.

Dramatic activities provide many occasions for intense verbal interaction among participants as they negotiate how they are going to carry out a given activity or while preparing and performing role plays and improvisations. Students are encouraged to explore stress, intonation, tempo, pause and silence for their semantic effects. Increased ability to manipulate meaning through timing at whatever level, syllabic, phrasal or interactional, can provide students with a new sense of control in the L2 and contribute to their overall communicative performance.

In order to test the hypothesis that rhythm and the corresponding synchronization of body motions could be improved through participation in a drama workshop (15 hours of instruction given in one week), three students were randomly selected and asked to give a short talk on a topic of their choice before and after the workshop. The talks were videotaped in a room with which the students were very familiar, and in which the students had all been videotaped on previous occasions. All three students demonstrated perceptible amelioration in their communicative performance including rhythm and gesture. An informal analysis of one student's performance is provided below as an illustration of the results obtained by the experiment.

Because a complete analysis of all the rhythmic features of the following speech samples is beyond the scope of this paper, one aspect of rhythmic patterning was chosen for investigation: the unfilled pause. While it is recognized that pausing is a natural occurrence in all speech (Goldman-Eisler 1968) the patterning and frequency of pauses contribute significantly to the perception of breaking or keeping the rhythm to the native ear.

In the transcripts below all unfilled pauses are marked by a double slash. Those which seemed "unnatural" and which seemed to break with an expected rhythmic grouping are additionally marked by an asterisk. The bracketed numbers represent types of "unnatural" breaks; the types are defined and exemplified after the transcripts. The speaker is a middle-aged male, formerly a lawyer from El Salvador.

Before

I am talking about* (2)//El Salvador//El Salvador is a country* (3)//in the middle of America//eh//El Salvador now is a* (1)//trob social trouble// because eh fighting* (3)//est and west//eh//the country* (4)// is eh rich in natural resource// the* (1)//minerals//gold//silver//manganeso etc//eh//the country eh was beginning* (3)//for Espaniard* (1)//conquestors//hasta eh* (2)//80's//hasta late 80's//when some eh* (1)//Indian people* (4)//was eh independent//the independence* (4)//was in 80's//23-24//eh but from independence//to today//everyday fighting//

After

Now I talk about* (2)//my country//my country is a small one in Latin America//it's El Salvador//El Salvador was a* (1)//colony from Spain//eh// that independence was in 1924//from 1924//to 1986-87//every year*//the government and people fighting//eh the fight is eh government with people//the government with eh religious people//and professional people//eh//the government thinking too much eh//is everybody a communist//he is afraid at communism//today//eh El Salvador have now 53 universities//in that universities//everyone is communist//

There were 12 unfilled pauses which were identified as "unnatural" in the first passage (73 words), but only 3 in the second passage (83 words). The number of filled pauses also decreased from 13 in the first passage to 8 in the second. The overall effect of these changes in pausing patterns was to produce a smoother flow of discourse, and to make the discourse more understandable.

How might the relationship between the change in pausing placement and listener comprehension be explained? A grammatical analysis of the points of rupture in the discourse can help us understand this more clearly. In the first passage we can identify four different levels of "unnatural" breaks in boundary constituents; (1) breaks within lower order noun phrases; (2) breaks within a preposition phrase, falling between the preposition and its object noun phrase; (3) breaks within a higher order noun phrase constituent falling between noun phrases and/or preposition phrases; (4) breaks between subject and predicate. Because speech is hierarchically organized at both syntactic and discourse levels, breaks at the boundaries of lower order constituents such as line 4 "the//minerals" (type 1) or line 5 "espaniard//conquestors" (type 1) are potentially more disruptive than those which occur at the boundary of higher order constituents such as line 3 "country//is" (type 4) or line 7 "independence//was" (type 4). All of the pauses identified as "unnatural" in the first passage conformed to one of these four types, while all of the "natural" pauses were of a higher order (e.g. pauses between clauses or after adverbial phrases within the clause).

In the first passage there are 4 instances of breaks within lower order noun phrases; 2 instances of breaks between preposition and object noun phrase; 3 instances of a break within a higher order noun phrase, falling between lower order noun phrases and/or preposition phrases; and 3 instances of subject predicate disruption.

In the second passage there is only one instance of a break within a lower order noun phrase, one instance of a break between a preposition and its object within a preposition phrase. One break perceived as "unnatural" was between an adverbial phrase 'every year' and the subject noun phrase which followed it.

The point being made here is not so much that there were fewer pauses, although there were, but that the placement of the pauses in the second passage coincided more with higher order syntactic discontinuities and hence comprehension was facilitated. It seems reasonable to postulate that an increased perception and production of rhythmic features in English was responsible for the shifts indicated.

Moreover, in view of the synchronization of body motions and speech, we could expect that the improvement in the speaker's rhythmic patterns would be kinetically expressed. This indeed seemed to be the case. The speaker's use of gesture in the two presentations was remarkably different. In the first one, the student held his hands behind his back throughout. His most visible body motions were a forward bending on several occasions and the shifting of his weight from one foot to the other. In the second presentation, the arms and hands were used freely, in most cases moving together in a parallel fashion. The use of hand gestures for emphasis gave the whole performance a more natural and rhythmic flow, and it seemed that this made it easier to follow.

It is evident that much more research needs to be carried out before any firm conclusions as to the efficacy of drama techniques on the development of rhythm in L2 learners can be drawn. It does seem clear, however, that there is a demonstrable connection between speech rhythms, body motions and communicative effectiveness.

Conclusion

The notion of synchrony brings new and complex perspectives to the study of second language learning and teaching. These perspectives involve physiological, psychological, emotional and cognitive parameters all of which merit further investigation. The basic concept of the behavioural unity of speech and body motions should not be forgotten in the fray, however, and language teachers should be encouraged to use and discover techniques which help their students "live into language".

References

Argyle, M. 1975. *Bodily Communication*. London: Methuen.
Birdwhistell, R.L. 1952 [1974]. *Introduction to Kinesics* (Photo Offset). Foreign Service Institute. Louisville: University of Louisville Press.
Condon, W.S. 1980. "The Relation of Interactional Synchrony to Cognitive and Emotional Processes". *The Relationship of Verbal and Nonverbal Communication* ed. by Mary Ritchie Key. The Hague: Mouton.
———. 1982. "Cultural Microrhythms". *Interaction Rhythms* ed. by Martha Davis. New York: Human Sciences Press.
Condon, W.S. & W.D. Ogston. 1966. "Sound Film Analysis of Normal and Pathological Behaviour Patterns". *Journal of Nervous and Mental Disease* 143(4). 338-347.
Condon, W.S. & L.W. Sander. 1974. "Neonate Movement is Synchronized with Adult Speech: Interactional participation and language acquisition". *Science* 183(4120). 99-101.
Davis, M. ed. 1982. *Interaction Rhythms*. New York: Human Sciences Press.
Gassin, J. 1986. "Drama and the Advanced ESL Learner: An integrated approach to communication skills". *ARAL Series S* 3. 57-68.
Goldman-Eisler, F. 1968. *Psycholinguistics. Experiments in spontaneous speech*. London: Academic Press.
Kendon, A. 1980. "Gesticulation and Speech: Two aspects of the process of utterance". *The Relationship of Verbal and Nonverbal Communication* ed. by Mary Ritchie Key. The Hague: Mouton.
Key, M.R. ed. 1980. *The Relationship of Verbal and Nonverbal Communication*. The Hague: Mouton.
Menot, O.L. 1982. "Visual Behaviour and the Teacher". *SGAV Newsletter* 6. 21-36.

————. 1987. "Les Rapports 'Gestes-Parole' et les Montagnes Video comme Outils de Recherche et de Formation". *Geste et Image* 6. Paris. CNRS.

Myllyniemi, R. 1986. "Conversation as a System of Social Interaction". *Language and Communication* 6(3). 147-169.

Pegalo, C. 1985. "The Role of Rhythm and Intonation in the Silent Reading of French as a Foreign Language". *Reading in a Foreign Language* 3(1). 313-327.

Pennycook, A. 1985. "Actions Speak Louder than Words: Paralanguage, communication, and education". *TESOL Quarterly* 19(2). 259-282.

Scheflen, A.E. 1964. "The Significance of Posture in Communication Systems". *Psychiatry* 27(4). 316-331.

Scheflen, A.E. 1982. "Comments on the Significance of Interaction Rhythms". *Interaction Rhythms* ed. by Martha Davis. New York: Human Sciences Press.

Von Raffler-Engel, W. 1980a. "Kinesics and Paralinguistics: A neglected factor in second language research and teaching". *Canadian Modern Language Review* 36(2). 225-237.

————. 1980b. "The Unconscious Element in Intercultural Communication". *The Social and Psychological Contexts of Language* ed. by R.N. St. Clair & H. Giles. Hillsdale, N.J.: Lawrence Erlbaum Associates.

Wenk, B.J. 1985. "Speech Rhythms in Second Language Acquisition". *Language and Speech* 28(2). 157-175.

Wenk, B.J. & F. Wioland. 1986. "Phonetic Training for Migrant Worker Pupils". *I.T.L. Revue of Applied Linguistics* 73. 27-50.

Towards Discourse-Sensitive Cloze Procedures: The Role of Lexis

Ronald Carter

Introduction

Cloze procedure has been with us for some time now and it is probably fair to say that it is the most recognisable of the many techniques encountered by students of English and Modern languages. Most familiarly, and not altogether pleasantly, it is recognized and remembered as a testing device. Traditionally, the deletion rates are every seventh or eighth word and the test is of a student's ability to insert the grammatically correct item. The most significant observation is, however, that cloze procedure is normally targetted towards measuring grammatical competence and in any case the regularity of the deletion rate ensures a systematic encounter with the grammatical words of a text. A good example is the following extracted from a widely used book of cloze exercises (Moller and Whiteson 1981).

> *Libra (September 23-October 22)*
> Family members may grumble ____ a change in routine, but eventually they adjust to liking ____. Try to co-operate more with ____ at work and get better results. Avoid one who is ____ time waster.
>
> *Scorpio (October 23-November 21)*
> Start early on business matters so ____ have more time for recreation. Be willing to try new procedures. ____ honest with mate, or spouse about expectations and hopes. Avoid unnecessary spending of ____.

It can be seen here that there is little evidence to be gathered concerning a student's lexical competence; there are some substitutions involving common collocation but the main emphasis is on grammatical words, mostly prepositions and deictics. It is one of the aims of this paper to explore the extension of cloze procedure into the domain of lexis and to examine some

uses of cloze not so much for vocabulary testing as for vocabulary development. In particular, I want to argue that this general orientation is at its
most effective if attention is given to the role of lexical words in *discourse*.
Vocabulary development should not just be a matter of adding more words
to a lexical store or of simply knowing words as discrete items; instead, students also need to know how words are used and how to use them across
sentence boundaries, that is, as part of connected discourse and particularly
in so far as such words contribute to the cohesion and coherence of a text.
Although what I want to explore is of relevance to spoken as well as to written discourse and can be adapted for writing in a first language, the focus
here is on second language writing development.

Theoretical and Descriptive Frameworks

Interest in the relationship between lexis and discourse is burgeoning (see
Carter 1987:ch.4) and there is much recent applied linguistic research that
might be drawn on for purposes of extending cloze procedure, in particular
Deyes's (1984) work on discourse cloze. Limitations on space enforce a
relatively narrow focus and this will be on what I want to term text-organizing vocabulary. What are the most relevant recent developments in theory
and in the building of descriptive frameworks?

Most work takes its inspiration from Halliday and Hasan's *Cohesion in
English* and, most directly, from their embryonic analysis of lexical cohesion (Halliday and Hasan 1976:ch.6). Halliday and Hasan show how *lexical
cohesion* can be realized by various forms of reiteration across sentence
boundaries such as repetition of the same word or of a morphologically
related item or by the construction of a network between words through
structural semantic relations such as synonymy and antonymy. Another
means they describe is that of collocational cohesion, but it is only when
access is available to large corpora of naturally occurring text that such relations can be described in a systematic and predictive way. However, a particularly interesting text-organizing category is that of what Halliday and
Hasan term *general words*. These can be illustrated by the following sentences:

> The child is climbing the tree.
> The *idiot's* going to fall.

> My granny is eighty. But the old *girl's* going deaf.

Here the general word literally does general service by creating a semantic net into which more specific items can be trawled.

Closely related to the category of general word is that of *anaphoric nouns* which has been developed in text-based work by Francis (1986). Examples of anaphoric nouns would be:

> position, argument, point, question, problem, fact

It can be seen that such words can operate as text-organizers by summarizing whole chunks of preceding discourse with a single word. For example: "This whole *argument* has failed to carry conviction." Anaphoric nouns are not limited exclusively to single items or indeed to nouns. Phrases such as "line of reasoning" or "way of putting it" can operate equally effectively. However, especially in academic and in argumentative discourse, such items allow an economic mode of reference across discoursal boundaries.

Another important development in written discourse analysis has been the provision by Winter and Hoey (see, in particular, Hoey 1983; Winter 1977) of descriptive frameworks for analyzing how certain kinds of texts are organized into textual macrostructures such as problem-solution, general-particular, hypothesis-real and so on. The general analysis has revealed the importance of microstructural relations which operate as *lexical signals* signposting, as it were, the direction readers are to take through a text. Such lexical signals include items which operate both prospectively as well as anaphorically i.e. retrospectively. The term used to describe such items by Winter and Hoey is *Vocabulary 3* (Vocabulary 1 and 2 being reserved for the kind of grammatically cohesive items such as subordinators, anaphoric pronouns and the like charted in the major chapters of Halliday and Hasan (1976)). Here are some examples of Vocabulary 3 items in action:

1. One *condition* for the success of the team is obvious.
2. There is a distinct *difference* between their two characters.
3. The *reason* for this problem *hinges on two* aspects of the situation.

Here the underlined items clearly operate to anticipate ensuing information and to project the reader forward. In the case of the third example, which is a made-up example and would probably not occur in real texts, it will be seen that verbs and enumeratives (viz. *hinges, two*) also play a part alongside the more usual Vocabulary 3 nouns. One interesting feature of anaphoric and Vocabulary 3 nouns is that they allow adjectival modification; this in turn leads to the kind of lexical signalling which involves weighting or evaluating the development of an argument (e.g. "a crucial point"; "a central problem"; "a minor step"). This is a further feature of the role of vocabulary in discourse and underlines once again the importance of seeing (and teaching and learning) lexical items not as single decontextualised units but as discourse sensitive intersentential markers which are of crucial importance for the links between words which they establish. Cloze procedure can be a useful tool for bringing about enhanced sensitivity to the role of such lexis.

Recent and ongoing research at the University of Nottingham (see Carter 1988) demonstrates that discourse-based cloze, targetted at text-organizing vocabulary, plays a part in our perception of effective textual organization. Control groups of mother-tongue and ESL/EFL undergraduate students of economics were given cloze exercises, some discourse cloze and some standard cloze. It is clear from initial results that the ability to use text organizing vocabulary is one factor in tutor/informants' judgements of students' ability to write effective arguments; it is also clear that the use of effective text-organizers is a distinguishing mark between mother-tongue and ESL students, though it may be incautious to draw any conclusions from such results except to perhaps underline the need for greater practice in discourse organization on the part of all students, particularly second or foreign language learners.

However, one more obvious and important point does emerge; it is that text-organizing vocabulary functions on the surface of texts. Such items are important signals, but they are only surface signals. On their own they cannot make for effective discourse-specific writing, though they are, of course, an essential element of the product. Text-organizers are, in other words, necessary but not sufficient for discourse organization. The following sentences illustrate the same point: what is lexically cohesive is not necessarily equivalent to the construction of a coherent text.

> This morning I had a toothache
> I went to the dentist
> The dentist has a big car
> The car was bought in New York
> New York has financial troubles.

Hasan (1984, 1985) has pointed out that in such examples as this there is no sustained or "multiple" interaction between chains of lexical items which all have the same referent (identity chains) and those which form a chain because the items are connected with each other by synonymy, membership of the same lexical set, lexical association etc. (similarity chains). There is cohesion between the sentences taken in pairs but no cohesion between the sentences as a composite text. There are too many thematic switches for there to be multiple interaction between the respective chains. Discourse cloze activities need to be developed which encourage sensitivity to such patterning, particularly in the production of appropriately coherent patterning in students' own writing.

Classroom Examples

Space precludes detailed exemplification but the following examples — drawn from an excellent TEFL textbook (McCarthy *et al.* 1985) — may illustrate general principles from which more specific instances can be drawn:

> *Exercises*:
>
> A
> 1. The sofa is covered in leather
> 2. Lilac is very nice
> 3. The footstool is too
> 4. Cloth is not half as nice
> 5. There's one in bloom over the porch
> 6. The scent is heavenly
> 7. The suite is very plush.
>
> B
> process, aspect, situation, issue, decision, question, feature, argument, view, debate, move.
> One ____ that always raises a lot of tempers is whether the government has the right to exercise a monopoly in education.
> The ____ is in some ways a false one, since the government will itself decide whether it has that right.
>
> C
> | background | Railways decline because of growth in car ownership. |
> | problem | Government investment low. |
> | issue | Should we go on building more roads or |
> | question | revive the railways? |
> | move | The government has set up a committee to |
> | decision | decide on transport policy. |
> | features | |
> | aspects | |
> | view/conclusion | |

In example A students have to unscramble *two* coherent texts from the seven sentences. To do this requires the creation of semantic links across the sentences. An extension of the example would be to leave gaps in one or two places for insertion by, probably, more advanced groups. Example B is a standard "maze" activity involving choice of substitutable text-organizing vocabulary from a list of various possibilities. Example C involves the provision of a skeleton of information which has to be constructed into a meaningful and coherent text by using the designated text-organizers. Example D below is an attempt to sensitize to the role of lexis in different genres by inviting substitution of items relative to the kind of goal-directed language functions of each text. Further discussion of such relations is undertaken in Carter (1988) but a principal aim is to promote the lexical production of discoursal coherence.

D

Explanation
You take a strip of metal. Half the strip is brass and half the strip is iron. Then you heat it. The bar gets longer and then bends. The curve outside, which is brass, is longer. This shows that brass expands more quickly than iron.

Report
A bimetal bar is taken. The bar ____ two layers of metal. There is brass on the outer layer and iron on the inner. When ____, the brass layer bends the iron over. This ____ that brass expands at a faster rate than iron.

demonstrates; shows; you heat it; heat is applied; has; is composed of.

Finally, it is worth exploring the relations of vocabulary in literary texts. Discussions in Carter (1986) and specific text-book illustrations in Carter and Long (1987) may provide starting points, in particular for the following of theme(s) in poetry through the multiple branching and semantically dense interactions which are typically enacted in such contexts. The following discourse-cloze based exercises are, however, targetted rather more to discourse in a Foucauldian definition of the term. The passage is taken from George Eliot's *Middlemarch*. Here all explicit references to gender are removed and (advanced) students invited to insert appropriate lexical items marked: (1) for gender, (2) as pronouns, (3) as reflexives, (4) for names. The exercise teaches much about how men and women are "positioned" in respect of the "society" of the nineteenth century novel and this in turn reveals insights into authorial and societal ideologies. More fundamentally, however, discourse cloze exercises such as this serve to activate knowledge structures or socio-cultural schemata, which in turn underlines that simply knowledge of the language or of its cohesive properties, however linguistically thorough, is never entire enough to allow the appropriate insertions.

> Two hours later, _____ was seated in an inner room or boudoir of a handsome apartment in the Via Sistina.

> I am sorry to add that _____ was sobbing bitterly, with such abandonment to this relief of an oppressed heart as a _____ habitually controlled by pride on _____ own account and thoughtfulness for others will sometimes allow _____ __ when _____ feels securely alone. And _____ Casaubon was certain to remain away for some time at the Vatican.

> Yet _____ had no distinctly shapen grievance that _____ could state even to _____ and in the midst of _____ confused thought and passion, the mental act that was struggling forth into clearness was a self-accusing cry that _____ feeling of desolation was the fault of _____ own spiritual poverty.

> _____ had married the _____ of _____ choice, and with the advantage over most that had contemplated _____ marriage chiefly as the beginning of new duties: from the very first _____ had thought of _____ Casaubon as having a mind so much above _____ own, that _____ must often be claimed by studies which _____ could not entirely share; moreover, after the brief narrow experience of _____ girlhood _____ was beholding Rome, the city of visible history, where the past of a whole hemisphere seems moving in funeral procession with strange ancestral images and trophies gathered from afar.

> But this stupendous fragmentariness heightened the dreamlike strangeness of _____ bridal life. _____ had now been five weeks in Rome, and in the kindly mornings when autumn and winter seemed to go hand in hand like a happy aged couple one of whom would presently survive in chiller loneliness, _____ had driven about at first with Casaubon, but of late chiefly with Tantripp and their experienced courier. _____ had been led through the best galleries, had been taken to the chief points of view, had been shown the greatest ruins and the most glorious churches, and _____ had ended by oftenest choosing to drive out to the Campagna where _____ could feel alone with the earth and sky, away from the oppressive masquerade of ages, in which _____ own life too seemed to become a masque with enigmatical costumes.

Conclusions and Questions

1. Cloze procedures, with a variety of discoursally sensitive gaps, should continue to be exploited and experimented with. Clearly, in discourse cloze, exact recovery of an item used in the original or total reliance on

single word substitution would be inappropriate and students may have to be taught a new set of procedural norms for doing cloze.

2. For this reason it may be worth undertaking L1 discourse cloze before L2 discourse cloze, though we know very little about whether such skills transfer.

3. Text-organising vocabulary and other lexical signalling devices have an important role to play in discourse and should be targetted accordingly for cloze procedures. They are the scaffolding supporting different text-types and discourse-genres, competence in which is a recognized goal of many L1 and L2 teaching projects.

But

4. Further theoretical work on models of coherence in text and of the role of lexis in such coherence is needed. Such work is currently at embryonic stages and we must, therefore, proceed cautiously in applied linguistic development.

5. In terms of pedagogic and discourse theory further empiricial studies of the following questions are needed:
   a. Are certain kinds of text-organizers easier to predict than others?
   b. Are text-organizers easier to predict than non text-organizers?
   c. Does too-closely targetted a focus on discourse properties inhibit the skills of guessing or inference?
   d. What kind of a test of linguistic competence is revealed by discourse cloze compared with other cloze procedures?

In spite of the above general conclusions and reservations, I hope I have nonetheless succeeded in the course of this paper in opening up cloze a little.

Acknowledgement

Many of the ideas in this paper have drawn direct inspiration from discussions with and textbooks written by Dr. Mike McCarthy, English Language Research, University of Birmingham. Further explorations on many fronts continue in Carter and McCarthy (1988).

References

Carter, R.A. 1986. "Linguistic Models, Language and Literariness". *Literature and Language Teaching* ed. by C.J. Brumfit & R.A. Carter, 110-132. London: Oxford University Press.

———. 1987. *Vocabulary: Applied linguistic perspectives.* London: Allen & Unwin.

———. 1988. "Vocabulary, Cloze and Discourse". *Vocabulary and Language Teaching* ed. by R.A. Carter & M.J. McCarthy, 161-180. London: Longman.

Carter, R.A. & M.N. Long. 1987. *The Web of Words.* Cambridge: Cambridge University Press.

Carter, R.A. & M.J. McCarthy. 1988. *Vocabulary and Language Teaching.* London: Longman.

Deyes, A. 1984. "Towards an Authentic Discourse Cloze". *Applied Linguistics* 5(2). 128-137.

Francis, G. 1986. *Anaphoric Nouns.* ELR Monographs, University of Birmingham.

Halliday, M.A.K. & R. Hasan. 1976. *Cohesion in English.* London: Longman.

Hasan, R. 1984. "Coherence and Cohesive Harmony". *Understanding Reading Comprehension* ed. by J. Flood, 181-219. Newark, Delaware: IRA.

———. 1985. *Language, Context and Text: Aspects of language in a social semiotic perspective, part B.* Geelong, Victoria: Deakin University Press, with M.A.K. Halliday.

Hoey, M. 1983. *On the Surface of Discourse.* London: Allen & Unwin.

McCarthy, M.J., A. McLean & P. O'Malley. 1985. *Proficiency Plus: Grammar, lexis, discourse.* Oxford: Basil Blackwell.

Moller, A. & V. Whiteson. 1981. *Cloze in Class: Exercises in developing reading and comprehension skills.* Oxford: Pergamon.

Winter, E.O. 1977. "A Clause-Relational Approach to English Texts: A study of some predictive lexical items in written discourse". *Instructional Science* 6. 1-92.

The Analysis of Sales Encounters on the Island of St. Croix: An Ethnographic Approach

Alma Simounet de Géigel

Background Information and Rationale for the Study

The United States Virgin Islands are a small group of islands in the Caribbean archipelago which consist of three main islands — St. Croix, St. Thomas, and St. John — along with a number of islets and cays. Virgin Islanders are United States citizens as a result of the congressional enactment of 1927 following the United States purchase of these territories from Denmark in 1917 for the sum of twenty-five million dollars.

Saint Croix is the largest of the three main islands. Throughout the history of its colonization, seven flags have flown over this small territory: the flags of Spain, Holland, England, France, Knights of Malta, Denmark, and the United States of America. Despite this history and the presence of elements in the population with various linguistic backgrounds, English has been the predominant language in Saint Croix (Dookhan 1973; Boyer 1983).

It is estimated that Puerto Ricans represent 35 to 40% of the total Crucian population (Lewis 1972). At present, migration to St. Croix from Puerto Rico appears to be increasing in numbers. The economic boom reported in the local newspapers by the U.S.V.I. Department of Labor Statistics, the Department of Tourism and the St. Croix Real Estate Association (Di Meo 1986) may become a significant incentive for a greater influx of Puerto Ricans into Crucian society.

As a result of the influx of such large numbers of Spanish-speaking individuals into an English-speaking society, the U.S.V.I. Department of Education has been faced with a challenging linguistic and cultural problem. It was not until 1969 that plans were made for the first bilingual educa-

tion program in St. Croix. This initial step was followed by the establishment of a bilingual program. At first this program benefited only three
schools, but then in 1978 it was institutionalized in all the public schools of
the islands. Since English is the medium of instruction, the purpose of the
program was to develop English language facility in the non-English-speaking child and to maintain a dual or parallel course of study in both English
and Spanish in the case of Puerto Ricans. Under Fishman and Lovas' classification of bilingual education programs this program for Puerto Ricans
would fall in the category of partial bilingualism. This kind of program
seeks fluency and literacy in both languages.

Unfortunately, the initial program was not successful in eradicating
two serious problems still prevalent in the Puerto Rican student population:
one, a low level of achievement, and second, a high percentage of school
attrition. In order to tackle these two major problems the V.I. Government
invited the Social Science Research Center (SSRC) from the University of
Puerto Rico to conduct a study which would hopefully point out possible
ways of solving these two problems. Upon completion of the study, the
researchers who composed the investigative team filed a written report with
the V.I. Government in which they stated that the source of the two problems lay "in a deficiency which rests in two basic areas: language policy and
curriculum" (University of Puerto Rico 1970:9). It was the understanding of
this group of researchers that a revision in both areas would eliminate the
problems to a great extent.

After the institutionalization of the bilingual program in all the public
schools of the Virgin Islands Territory, however, the same two problems
have continued to plague the Puerto Rican student population (U.S.V.I.
Department of Education 1982). Upon examining some of the materials
utilized in the classroom and the social values reflected in them, the researchers from SSRC found a marked contradiction between the view of life
presented in school and the reality of the students' lives.

An examination of the textbooks being utilized at this very moment in
the ESL classes at the intermediate school level demonstrates that the problem still exists.

Little of the material examined provides the Puerto Rican students
with the language tools they need to function effectively in their Crucian
social interactions. The books are commercially prepared in the United
States. They are the U.S. mainland-based texts whose values, realities, and
language standards are alien to the reality of life as experienced by these

Hispanic students. No room is made for Crucian English, the variety of English spoken in St. Croix. Moreover, for those terminating their formal schooling in twelfth grade, the ESL objectives and materials do not bridge the gap between the world of school and the reality of their future work situations on the island. Thus the malaise prevalent in the Puerto Rican student population, attributed to inconsistencies in the school curriculum and language policy by the SSRC investigative group, is aggravated rather than healed by the present irrelevant ESL program for these particular students. The Spanish-speaking students have an additional difficulty in their language training besides the social problems of living in a new cultural context; namely, the language of the contexts of situation presented in their classroom has no relation to the English language contexts in which they would engage in the jobs available to them, jobs with no college requirements. Such jobs in St. Croix would involve positions such as office clerk or salesperson at retail stores, especially tourist-oriented ones, a business which accounts for over half of the entire Virgin Islands workforce (Di Meo 1986).

In order to plan an effective language program that would provide these Puerto Rican students with an experience that is transitional in nature between school and work, it is necessary to first look at some real working situations from a sociolinguistic perspective so as to extract the knowledge which is essential for the students to possess in order to function effectively therein. This knowledge would then have to be incorporated into the language syllabus. The inclusion of this material in a language program is of great importance in terms of the impact on the learner and his or her future social roles in the second language. This point was emphasized by Corder when he stated that "a speaker's freedom of social action is dependent upon the range of his repertoire. His lack of a command of some code or style will seriously limit his freedom in certain directions" (1973:64).

In order for the language syllabus to contain a more realistic picture of the linguistic repertoire that the Puerto Rican students in St. Croix must command in the work situations, it is imperative to examine the social interactions in which they will become involved within the context of natural conversation (cf. Hatch and Long 1980; Wolfson 1976; Brown and Yule 1983). Modern sociolinguistic thought is the basis of a conceptual framework within which such an analysis is made possible. This framework views the study of language in relation to society, restores to language the importance of its communicative role, and provides a unit of analysis of social interaction, that is, the speech event (Hymes 1974). It is this particular unit of analysis in the contexts of work situation in St. Croix which is the subject of inquiry in the present study.

Aim of the Study

This study was concerned with the identification and description of speech events in sales interaction in which employees with a high school education participated, and which occurred within the contexts of work situations in St. Croix. The goal was to provide the relevant information necessary for the initial development of language programs in the secondary school. Specifically, the study attempted to answer the following questions:

1. What characterizes the speech events of sales interaction in work situations in St. Croix in terms of the following components originally proposed by Hymes (1974) and later modified by Saville-Troike (1982):
    a.   the genre or type of event;
    b.   the topic of referential focus;
    c.   the purpose or function of the event in general and in terms of the interaction goals of the participants;
    d.   the setting (location, time of day, season of year, and physical aspects of the situation);
    e.   the participants (age, sex, ethnicity, role);
    f.   the message form, including the verbal and nonverbal channels, and the nature of the code used;
    g.   the message content;
    h.   the act sequence, or ordering of speech acts, including turn-taking and overlap phenomena;
    i.   the rules for interaction;
    j.   the norms of interpretation
2. What is the relationship among the components?
3. Which strategies of interaction such as politeness formulas characterize these encounters?
4. What are the cross-cultural and educational implications of the findings in terms of the cultural and linguistic background of the Puerto Rican students?

This study was delimited to the ethnographic and interactional analysis of three speech events of sales encounter in three stores in St. Croix. These three stores were a furniture store, a jewelry and china store, and a liquor store. The first store was located in a shopping mall on the outskirts of the town of Christiansted and the other two stores were located on the two main streets in the heart of town. Even though five events were video recorded at each store — twelve video plus two audio recordings for the jewelry store — only one event per store was selected for purposes of analysis. The writer felt the selection was representative of the recurring sales events at the contexts of situation.

Although the analysis took into consideration those nonverbal factors which had a bearing on the analysis such as gestures and facial expressions, these factors were not considered as thoroughly as their importance in the process and meaning of interaction merits.

Methodology

The investigative and analytical process in this study consisted of six major activities: (a) the identification of some contexts which had job opportunities for high school graduates in St. Croix; (b) the selection of the actual contexts or stores as the setting for the study; (c) the interviewing of different segments of the population to gather cultural information about the community, and the interviewing of owners, managers, and salespersons of various other stores, and the salespersons involved in the speech events under study; (d) the gathering of the data on sales encounters with the use of an audio-cassette recorder and a video-cassette recorder; (e) the distribution and collection of questionnaires to salespersons and customers; and (f) the analysis and interpretation of the data.

The study used the descriptive method of research framed within the ethnographic approach for language study proposed by Hymes (1974) and Saville-Troike (1982).

All notations used were taken and adapted from Schenkein (1980:xi-xvi) and are explained below. No phonological variation was marked.

[[	utterance starting up simultaneously
[	overlapping utterances which do not start up simultaneously
]	the point where overlapping utterances stop
(3)	number of seconds in a pause

!	animated tone of voices
me	stressed words in the interaction
(( ))	some phenomenon observed such as ((cough)), ((telephone ring)), ((whispered))
( )	inaudible item or items in doubt e.g. (book)
**	features of interest within the interaction.

The following are notations and abbreviations from the events analyzed:

(132)	= number of move	store J	=	jewelry store
SP	= salesperson	store F	=	furniture store
C	= customer	store L	=	liquor store

The transcript for the three events is available upon request from the author.

In order to present and analyze the data, the following units of analysis were selected from a discussion of conversational units by Owen (1981:105). In her analysis of natural conversation she utilized a "four-level hierarchy of units" which she enumerated from the largest to the smallest:

Section	Ex. topic section (functional), closing section (structural)
Interchange	Ex. an adjacency pair (structural), remedial interchanges (functional)
Turn	(a structural unit)
Move	(a functional unit)

Two types of analysis were used for each speech event: (a) an ethnographic analysis based on Saville-Troike's adaptation of Hymes' framework presented above, and (b) a conversational or interactional analysis of each encounter taking into consideration the different sections into which an encounter may be divided for the purpose of analysis. Within the conversational analysis, strategies of politeness were also analyzed utilizing Brown and Levinson's (1978) paradigm for the study of politeness formulas in interaction. Although the aim of the study was not crosscultural in nature, the implications of the findings were analyzed from a crosscultural perspective based on Nine-Curt's (1984) analysis of Puerto Rican communication patterns and the researcher's own introspective insights about her Puerto Rican culture.

Findings

The purpose of this section is two-fold: to examine the findings of the componential analysis of the three speech events recorded in terms of the most salient points and to take a closer look at the phenomenon of politeness within the parameters established by interactional or conversational analysis.

The three encounters analyzed displayed features characteristic of informal talk such as:

Ellipsis
(138) SP: Nine to five. (store J)
(113) C: Price like the other one? (store L)
(47)   SP: Understand what I say? (store F)

Every day expressions (casual talk)
(46)   SP: Wanna try it? (store J)
(25)   SP: Oh, oh, too bad. (store L)
(77)   SP: Should be but don't bet your life on this ... (store F)

Frequent occurrence of "okay" with eleven different functions.

These findings confirmed those of Tsuda (1980) in her analysis of sales encounters in the USA. Frake (1972) utilized the people's own categories to classify their behavior. On the basis of this approach, salespersons and customers identified two types of events which could occur in a store: the sales encounter and the "dropping-by-to-say-hello" encounter. The latter is a very common occurrence in St. Croix because of the small size of the shopping districts in town and outside of town and because of the relatively limited activity on the island. The former event, the focus of the present study, could have different manifestations depending on the purpose or function of the event itself and on the interaction goals of the participants. These manifestations would be:

1. Buying — According to salespersons, this involves customers whose intention is to purchase something.
2. Shopping — Customers who engage in this are only interested in spending the day by walking in and out of stores as a form of entertainment. It is also referred to as browsing. In the case of tourists, salespersons in store J added that many visitors on cruise ships came into the store only to compare prices with those of St.

Thomas, the ship's first stop and the historically-recognized rival of St. Croix. This point in particular irritated salespersons who were obliged to engage in sales talk knowing the intent of the customer. Various observations confirmed the occurrence of this matter.

3. Exchanging merchandise — This manifestation was made evident in the third speech event analyzed.
4. Returning merchandise.
5. Picking-up merchandise.
6. Selecting items for a bridal or anniversary registry.
7. Requesting information.

The purpose of the participants also affected two other aspects of the encounter: the number of moves utilized by participants and the number and kind of strategies of persuasion employed by the salesperson. In regard to the first aspect it was noted that the customer in store J did not seem to have the intention of buying the earrings — thus her turns during negotiation were characterized by few moves. The customer in store F did show a strong interest in paying the difference for the new executive desk. His turns were thus characterized by many moves. The aspect of intent in both cases was confirmed later on when salespersons reported that the customer in store J never returned to buy the earrings and the one in store F obtained the new desk in exchange for the one he had bought previously.

By the same token, the salesperson in store J was obliged to employ various strategies to convince the customer to buy and her turns were thus characterized by multiple moves. On the other hand, the salesperson in store F merely assented or briefly commented on the customer's words for he did not have to be convinced to buy. Thus this salesperson's turns were characterized by single moves.

The same observation was true of the event at the liquor store though the majority of turns displayed a tendency towards the single-move turn. Here the first customer's clear intention to buy was made evident immediately after the greeting. Her turns were characterized more frequently by multiple moves than those of the salesperson.

In relation to the number of moves per turn as was presented in the discussion above, the notions of topic and setting must also be brought into play. While the speech event in store J showed a tendency towards the multiple-move turn, the event in store L displayed a tendency towards the single-move turn. This difference in interaction is perhaps related to basic differences in context, that is, the type of store, the merchandise sold, the display of merchandise and the resulting sales approach. Store J is an attractive place to visit because of its decoration, its air-conditioned rooms and the comfort offered by the stools which invite the customers to sit, relax, and look at an array of beautifully arranged items. Whether the customer intends to buy or simply wants to browse, the salesperson will still show the customer a variety of items. This last condition by its very nature creates a situation in which the salesperson must engage in "more talk" in order to describe the items of interest. Store L, on the other hand, is not air-conditioned, and as a result of its open doors and uncarpeted floors, the noise level is very high. In addition to this, all the hard liquor is displayed in shelves built against the wall so that in order to buy, the customer is obliged to walk up and down the counter area.

One more fact which discourages the type of interaction observed in store J is that with liquor a customer does not come to see a great variety, but to buy items in particular such as Frangelico or Kahlúa as the dialogue clearly illustrated. Purchasing in store L then becomes an "I'll have a Stolichnaya" rather than an "I'm interested in vodka" encounter. This results in sales talk with a limited number of multiple-move turns and a more staccato-like flow of interaction. This type of encounter in store L, where customers order in cafeteria-like fashion, tends to instill a faster pace in the interaction because of the numerous single-move turns.

Besides the effect that topic and setting seem to have on the pace and nature of the interaction, these two components may also influence the roles of the participants. While the seller of jewelry in store J could be categorized as the leading figure of the interaction from beginning to end, the seller of liquor in store L undertook a more passive role at the start of a cafeteria-like encounter until the possibility of a bigger sale brought him out more forcefully. Thus he first took orders from the customer and when this was over, he proceeded to make direct offers of new and local products. The researcher had the opportunity to observe these same customers from store L in an encounter at store J earlier in the afternoon. There, both sat on the stools before the showcase, asked to see more pearl items, and sat quite passively listening to the salesperson while she gave information about the merchandise. However, in store L, the first customer made the initial approach, and continued to take the lead in the interaction, physically moving up and down the counter, placing requests, asking for information, making decisions, and getting her intended purchase out of the way. The second customer merely made suggestions and comments, and asked a few questions.

In store F both salesperson and customer were engaged in talk about a piece of furniture, a desk. As a matter of practicality, the sales talk occurred at the desk itself so that no physical obstacles — a counter, for example — separated the two participants. One, the customer, sat on the executive chair; the other, the salesperson, sat on top of the desk and moved to the side or behind the customer whenever she wished to show him the various assets which the desk had to offer. The physical proximity between both participants and the actual positioning of their bodies created an atmosphere closely associated with a conversation between two friends.

Thus the setting, the type of merchandise, the topic of the event, its purpose, the role of the participants, and the interaction of all these elements produce one unifying whole, the encounter, whose very nature may be affected by the slightest change in any of the components of its framework.

Besides the physical aspects of the context other aspects of the setting also played an important role. The ethnographic data collected showed that the season of the year produced a different group of customers and a different business pace. The hot summer months brought into the store the local residents and a limited number of tourists — the "not so wealthy" as labeled by one of the informants. The winter season brought the town of Christiansted back to life with an influx of a great number of tourists — the affluent or "wealthy" — and the so-called "snowbirds" or island residents during the winter months.

One final aspect must be mentioned concerning setting: the time of the day constraints on the ritual expressions of greeting and parting in the community. Table 1 indicates these constraints. It should be pointed out that the use of the expression "Good night" as a greeting is not shared by the speakers of Standard American English. Items in brackets are used only with visitors to the island. The hours shown may vary by minutes. Although most stores close at 5:00 P.M., complete time constraints were included.

Upon turning to the component of participants, three points deserve special consideration: the role of the salesperson, the notion of self-identity in the salesperson, and the role that ethnicity may play on the outcome of the interaction.

The three events analyzed and the additional sales encounters observed provide sufficient evidence to state that the salesperson is the pivotal participant in the interaction. Even though all events analyzed pro-

Table 1: Time constraints on the use of ritual expressions of greeting and parting

Time of day		Greeting	Parting
12:00 AM	11:59 PM	Good morning	Good bye. Bye..
			Have a good day.
			[Enjoy your stay.]
12:00 PM	4:49 PM	Good afternoon	Good bye. Bye..
			[Enjoy your stay.]
5:00 PM	6:59 PM	Good evening	Good bye. Bye.
			Good night.
			[Have a good evening.]
7:00 PM	11:59 PM	Good night	Good night.
			Good bye. Bye.

duced a balanced number of turns, the salespersons injected the conversation with a constant influx of utterances, either to verbalize physical moves, to repeat customers' requests or comments, or to subtly persuade the customer into buying a particular item. Observation of other salespersons and interviews with store managers revealed that although good salespersonship varied from individual to individual, some more successful than others, there was a constant "keeping in touch" and attending to customers' needs in a relaxed, non-threatening ambience which made many visitors return to the stores.

The second point concerns the salesperson's notion of self-identity. Data analyzed in the events indicated the occurrence of first person singular and plural pronouns in the turns of salespersons in each of the speech events analyzed. This interchange of pronoun use and referent indicates a flexibility in the salesperson to identify himself or herself with various persons and roles. In the case of store J, the salesperson identified herself as an individual, as a member of the community, as a participant in the dyad with a fellow employee, and as an integral part of the store. Figure 1 illustrates this expanded or multiple identity.

In the case of store L, even though the pronoun *we* was employed together with *I*, it was the latter use which outnumbered the first. Perhaps the fact that the salesperson was also the owner of the store influenced greatly his marked choice of the first person singular. Figure 2 illustrates the pronoun juxtaposition and multiple identity.

In the case of store F, the salesperson was also the manager of the

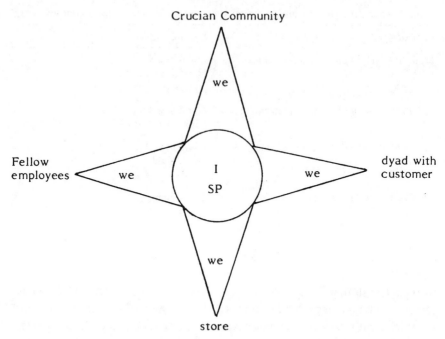

Figure 1: Multiple identity of SP in store J

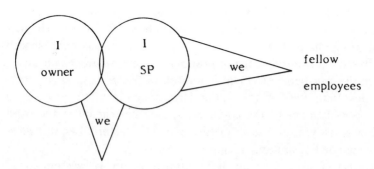

Figure 2: Multiple identity of SP in Speech Event II

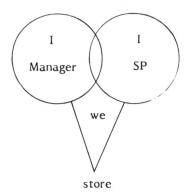

Figure 3: Multiple identity of SP in Speech Event III

store. She fluctuated in pronouns but utilized *we* only to refer to the store. Figure 3 illustrates the multiple identity.

The third point of interest and perhaps the one with the most serious implications is the role that ethnicity seems to play in the outcome of the communicative event.

Interviews held in the course of this study provided information concerning interviewees' complaints about bad experiences that they had had on various occasions in stores on the island. These same informants also provided their own interpretation of the reasons for the bad experience. It seems that the real problem stemmed from the multicultural nature of the community and the multiplicity of rules of speaking and norms of interpretation which were operating simultaneously. This co-occurrence of rules and norms was the cause of frequent communication breakdown which the writer observed and about which members of the community complained.

Before this part of the discussion on the componential analysis is brought to a close there are three general observations that should be made. The first one is related to the overlap phenomena observed in the act sequence. Although occurrences of overlapping in conversation are common but brief (Sacks *et al.* 1980), the sales encounter seemed to show even less overlapping. This is probably due to the relatively set pattern that it has in terms of its turn-taking (to be discussed in the next section). Still, five types of occurrences were found in the data:

1. Speaker A is able to answer a question or to complete a statement before speaker B is finished with the turn.

Example: Store L
(180)   C2:   Do you sell Don Q [here,] Bacardi?
**(181)   SP: [Sure.]

Store F
(2)   C: Hi' [Fine, thank you.
**(3)   SP: [Anything I can help you ...]

2. Speaker A confirms to speaker B that he or she is listening and accepts what B is saying. This is also referred to as "back channeling" (Sacks *et al.* 1980).

Example: Store J
(34)   SP: [... We do carry] them, ...
**(35) C: [Okay....]

3. Speaker A answers a question which was intended to have an alternative.

Example: Store J
(50)   SP: Are you visting the island
[or you live here?]
[**(51) C: I came]   ...

4. Speaker A's excitement gives free rein to the expression of that feeling before speaker B is finished.

Example: Store J
(42)   SP: Uh-huh. [This is nice,]
**(43) C: [Oh!]

5. Overlapping that is common in everyday conversation. This occurrence was found between the two customers in the event at store L.

Example: Store L
(122)   C2:   [You got the Kahlúa.]
**(123) C1:   [I got the Kahlúa ...]

The second observation refers to the form of the message in the encounters analyzed. Although the nonverbal mode of expression was employed, it usually reinforced rather than substituted for the message channeled through the verbal mode. Greetings ("Good morning", "Hi"), approaches ("Need some help?"), acknowledgements ("Yes, what can I do for you today?"), moves ("Let's see if we have any in this case here", "Just a moment; I'll be right back."), and leave-takings ("Goodbye. Have a nice day.") were all encoded verbally.

Different varieties of English were heard — Standard American, Crucian, Lucian, Kittian, Arubian, Puerto Rican. Still the variation at the phonological and syntactic levels did not seem to cause misunderstanding.

Finally, the componential analysis revealed a wealth of information concerning the use of rhetorical strategies by salespersons. Both salespersons and customers refused to acknowledge the use of persuasion in the performance of their job. For example, many of the salespersons interviewed for this investigation expressed their belief that their own personal opinions should be kept to a minimum. Yet the analysis of various sales encounters proved the opposite. Salespersons did formulate opinions which they communicated to their prospective buyers and they employed these opinions to persuade customers to purchase those items in which salespersons felt the customer had shown special interest. Therefore, the convergence of various types of data (natural language data, questionnaires, interviews) proved to be a system of checks and balances necessary for the discovery of what really is occurring.

Notwithstanding the implications of the results discussed above for language teaching, the additional ethnographic data collected pointed to the necessity of carrying out an additional analysis of the data. The most recurrent theme in the questionnaires and interviews was that of politeness, an attribute which according to the interviewees, both salespersons and customers, was the basis of what they termed good salespersonship and which seemed to account for the successful management of this type of interaction. This feeling was also evident in information gathered from letters to the editor (*The Daily News*, May 17, 1986; *The San Juan Star*, June 1, 1986; *The San Juan Star*, July 2, 1986).

In order to study politeness and its role in the communicative process, it was deemed necessary to perform an interactional analysis of the data. Saville-Troike (1982) underscored the importance of joining the strengths of ethnographic analysis and interactional analysis in the understanding of communication when she stated the following:

> While the foci and procedures of traditional ethnography and various models of interaction analysis differ, they are in a necessary complementary relationship to one another if an understanding of communication is to be reached. Ethnographic methods of observation and interview are most useful for a macro-description of community structure, and for determining the nature and significance of contextual features and the patterns and functions of language in the society; interactional micro-analyses build on this input information, and feed back into an ethnogrpahy of communication clearer understandings of the processes by which members of a speech

> community actually use and interpret language, especially in everyday interaction — a vital aspect of their communicative competence. (1982:132)

The theoretical work of Brown and Levinson on politeness (1978) provided the conceptual framework for the interactional analysis. A review of this stance is first made followed by its application to the data in question. Although Brown and Levinson's study identifies politeness as a universal phenomenon, the framework proposed by the authors provides room for cultural variation within the components of the model.

A concept which is central to this study is that of face, a notion derived in part from Goffman who defined face as "an image of self delineated in terms of approved social attributes" (1967:5). According to Brown and Levinson two components of faces are distinguished: negative face and positive face. Negative face refers to "the want of every competent adult member that his actions be unimpeded by others" (1967:67). It may be referred to also as the desire for freedom of action. Positive face is defined as "the want of every member·that his wants be desirable to at least some others" (1967:67). This may be referred to also as the desire for approval and belonging. Since there are various instances of conversational interaction in which face may be threatened or in danger of being lost by a face-threatening act (FTA) or what is verbally or nonverbally intended, then strategies must be called upon to manage the interaction successfully so as to achieve the speaker's goals. It is appropriate polite behavior which according to Brown and Levinson is then called into play. This behavior is classified as positive or negative politeness on the basis of the aspect of face to which it addresses itself.

These two types of politeness vary depending on the nature of the act and on three sociological variables, components of the model, which Brown and Levinson identify as: the social distance (D), the relative power (P), and the absolute ranking of impositions in a particular culture (R).

On the basis of the model, Brown and Levinson provided a categorization of the realizations of positive and negative face politeness strategies in language. These strategies appear in Appendixes A and B respectively in the form of a chart as published in the original study. They provide the framework for the analysis of the data.

Analysis of the Data

The analysis of the data is presented according to the three phases of conversational interaction: initial, medial, and final. The initial and final phases are taken together because they both entail the use of linguistic routines for the opening and closing sections of conversation. According to Firth (1972) language routines in everyday conversation have a ceremonial function. He stated:

> Greeting and parting is often treated as if it were the spontaneous emotional reaction to the coming together or separation of people, carrying overtly its own social message. But sociological observation suggests ... that for the most part it is highly conventionalized ... In a broad sense greeting and parting behavior may be termed RITUAL since it follows PATTERNED ROUTINES; it is a system of SIGNS that convey other than overt messages: ... and it has ADAPTIVE VALUE in facilitating social relations. (1972:29-30)

"Ritual" in this sense refers to "formal procedures of a communicative but arbitrary kind, having the effect of controlling or regularizing a social situation" (Firth 1972:3). Thus the discussion of these marginal phases of conversational interaction enters into a consideration of the messages through which participants negotiate and control social relationships. Laver (1981) posited that social factors of politeness play a dominant part in these routines because the social relationship between the participants is under negotiation; therefore, their social identity and recognition are at stake. Thus face is at great risk and appropriate polite behavior is called upon to minimize such risk.

The discussion then proceeds to an examination of the medial phase where the largest portion of the interaction usually occurs and where various language functions are employed by the speakers relative to the purpose of the encounter.

Because of the importance that first impressions have in the opening moments of any interaction, the initial phase of the sales encounter is crucial to the successful outcome of this smaller scale business venture. Here the responsibility for success or failure falls on the shoulders of the salespersons whose expertise is called upon to make use of all strategies known to them to manage the encounter successfully. In the initial phase of the encounter, language routines such as greetings are an intrinsic element of social negotiation.

The data from the Crucian speech community revealed that the greeting routines were usually present in the opening statements. Usage varied from the informal "Hi" or "Hello" to the more formal "Good morning" or "Good afternoon". The former was closely associated with speakers of Standard American English and the latter with black salespersons and customers from St. Croix and other English-speaking Caribbean islands where more formal greetings still prevail. Ethnographic data collected showed the importance that rituals such as greetings hold in the local community.

Together with greetings, routine approaches of the "May-I-help-you" type or "merchandise" type were employed as interaction openers. Observations at stores J, L and F revealed that salespersons were usually attentive to the needs of incoming customers and manifested this disposition by acknowledging the customers' presence through greetings and approaches. Thus the first strategy of politeness to be employed in the sales encounter was the first one for positive politeness: "attend to hearer's wants".

These findings differed markedly from those reported by Nine-Curt (1984) and Simounet de Géigel (1986). In a study on Puerto Rican politeness, Simounet de Géigel confirmed Nine-Curt's findings that Puerto Ricans channel most of their greetings, acknowledgments, and approaches through the nonverbal mode — a smile and other face gestures.

The final phase of the sales encounter is also considered an important section of the business interaction for, even though the sale has been completed, any "faux pas" may render the transaction void. That is to say, if the salesperson uses additional strategies which the customer interprets as rudeness or "pushiness", the latter may close the encounter before any sale is achieved. Schegloff and Sacks (1973) believe that conversational openings are not as difficult to accomplish as closings because the former employ a common starting point such as greetings while closings, on the other hand, must cut the flow of interaction and converge a variety of exchanges into a common closure such as "Goodbye". In order to arrive at this point of convergence, the final phase of the interaction must be preceded by a section called a "pre-closing" which occurs at the end of a topic and which serves as a transitional exchange to initiate the closing section.

Some of the markers of pre-closings as identified by Schegloff and Sacks are "we-ell", "okay", and "so" with a downward intonation contour. The data clearly demonstrate the use of polite pre-closing markers. In the following interaction from store J, notice in (107) the sudden and apparent change in topic which is in fact a "topic shading" which Schegloff and Sacks describe as a procedure through which differently focused but related talk to the previous utterance is fitted in (1973:305). The customer has finally decided on a pair of earrings, but she does not intend to buy them at the moment. Thus she initiates a polite extended apology (see Appendix B: strategy 6) for not completing the sales transaction. The salesperson then introduces the pre-closing in (110) which the customer accepts in (115). It is here, though, that more talk related to a previous topic is provided by the customer, a normal event according to Schegloff and Sacks. After extended talk about the earrings, the salesperson brings the conversation back (134) to the first pre-closing topic, but minimizes the sudden interruption in the flow of speech by employing the in-group identity marker of "dear" (Appendix A: strategy 4). This change in topic is ratified by the speaker (136) and the flow of conversation then takes a clear path towards the closing which occurs in (143) and (144).

(105)	C:	Those are pretty.
(106)	SP:	But for the money, this is *really* nice, sixty-seven fifty; it's a *lovely* earring.
(107)	C:	I have a friend that came yesterday from Washington, so we were going to come back over tomorrow.
(108)	SP:	Uh-huh.
(109)	C:	I want to go home and see her. I will be back tomorrow.
(110)	SP:	Well, if you'd like, we can always put those aside and hold them for you.
(111)	C:	Could you?
(112)	SP:	Yes, we'd be happy to, because we get a lot of people come in, they may, as soon as you walk out, somebody might just buy them.
(113)	C:	Yeah, uh-huh.
(114)	SP:	I will hold them for you.
(115)	C:	All right. ( ) not in my price range, but I like that.

(turns 116-128 have been omitted)

(129)	•C:	Well, I like this one.
(130)	SP:	Uh-huh.
(131)	C:	Something for work.
(132)	SP:	Yeah, you can dress this one up or down, which is nice.
(133)	C:	Yeah, uh-huh.
(134)	SP:	What is your name, dear and I'll put ...
(135)	C:	Brenda Balton, B-A-L-T-O-N.
(136)	SP:	Okay, Balton. Sure I'll be happy to put them away for you.
(137)	C:	Okay, tomorrow, at ten, nine?
(138)	SP:	Nine to five.
(139)	C:	Okay.
(140)	C:	Okay.

(141)   SP: Uh-huh. And, if I should not be here, just ask one of the girls; we will
              have the box here for you.
(142)   C: And your name?
(143)   SP: Dolores.
(144)   C: Dolores. Okay. All right. Thank you.
(145)   SP: *Yes*! You're welcome.

Once the initial phase of opening the social interaction is completed the action progresses to the phase that contains the language functions which give meaning to the sales encounter — the medial phase. Even though Laver believes that in this phase the "propositionally-relevant maxims [reference to Grice's maxims] exercise their major influence, with social factors of politeness playing a less dominant part" (1981:296) because of the nature of the sales encounter, polite behavior is still not only relevant but imperative. This can be readily seen by examining the conversational strategies of politeness used throughout this phase in the data.

Tables 2 and 3 present examples of the strategies of positive and negative politeness found in the data from stores J, L, and F. A second column incorporates data from the Puerto Rican speech community as reported by Simounet de Géigel (1986). The end in view is to have the opportunity to compare the data from the two speech communities so as to assess the cross-cultural and educational implications of the findings from a more solid perspective. Each table thus enumerates the strategy so as to correspond with Appendixes A and B and supplies a brief description of it.

On the basis of the data presented in these tables it is evident that there is close parallelism in the strategies utilized in both speech communities, thus giving support to Brown and Levinson's contention of the universality of politeness phenomena. Both data abound in examples of strategies of positive and negative politeness: however, a closer look at the content of some of these strategies brings out a variation that is shrouded under the veil of parallel forms.

In the discussion of some of the examples from Tables 2 and 3, the data from the Crucian speech community will be referred to as CSC and those from the Puerto Rican speech community as PRSC.

In the data from Puerto Rican Spanish for positive politeness, example 2 in Table 2 contains an expression, "Ave Maria" or "Holy Mary", which is not only considered socially unacceptable but may be classified as a profanity by many members in the English-speaking Crucian community Yet this expression, far from being rude, is a frequently-used interjection in Puerto Rican Spanish.

Because of the nature of strategy 4, an ingroup identity marker, cultural variation is expected in its use. The PRSC data for this strategy, example 4, is an interesting illustration of the change that is taking place in Puerto Rican social interaction, that is, the increasing tendency to eliminate the Tu-Vous pronoun distinction. This preference for the "tu" pronoun is evident in many San Juan stores where customers are also addressed with terms of endearment usually associated with more intimate relationships: "mija" (dear), "amor" (love), and "corazon" (my heart). A new term of address, "amiga" (friend) has also been observed to occur more frequently.

This more frequent use of "dear" in Puerto Rican Spanish is also evident in the Crucian context where it is more common among the local black individuals from St. Croix or other islands than among the speakers of Standard American English who now live on the island. One point should be made clear. In Speech Event I "honey" and "dear" are utilized by the salesperson in turns (134) and (62, 74) respectively. While *honey* in (74) is utilized affectionately by SP to greet a child, its use in (62) and the use of *dear* in (134) to address C are associated with two moves made by SP whose nature requires a communicative strategy to minimize the impact of the speech act in each instance. Specifically in (62) SP cannot please C with the information C is requesting and in (134) SP must minimize two things: the rupture of the anonymity of the customer in the encounter and the use of a speech act, the request, which English speakers sense as one of strong social impact according to House and Kasper (1981:177) and Ervin-Tripp (1976).

The use of safe topics for strategy 15 is another source of cultural variation. Examples six and seven in the PRSC data (Table 2) are good illustrations of actual topics for conversational exchange which may occur in the Puerto Rican context between strangers. Examples of safe topics from the American sales context, though, revealed the exclusion of private, personal matters in the sales encounter. Only the salesperson in store J indicated any questioning of customers about personal matters, but she added that she did so without the customer's awareness that it was taking place. Nine-Curt notes the problem of cultural variability and the misunderstandings it may breed (personal communication) in a Puerto Rican-English crosscultural interaction. The same situation may arise in the application of strategies 7 and 8 in particular where the object of joking is a matter of cultural norm so that what is permissible in one group may not be in the other.

Joking, an aspect of the Puerto Rican concept of "relajo", is an impor-

Table 2: Strategies of Positive Politeness in the Crucian and Puerto Rican data

Strategy	Description	Crucian speech community data	Puerto Rican speech community data
1	S notices and attends to H's needs, wants, interest	1. SP: Well, if you'd like, we can always put those aside and hold them for you. (110) J	1. SP: Sí es para la graduación de su hija, hay que empacarlo bonito. (If it's for your daughter's graduation it has to be wrapped nicely.)
		2. SP: So how does it feel? Sit down on it. (11) F	
		3. C: Do you have packages of three… bottles? (51) L SP: We can make one here. (52)	
2	Exaggerate interest, approval with H	4. SP: Now, that's pretty! That's pretty! (58) L	2. SP: ¡Ave María, que contenta está con la graduación de su hija! (Oh boy, you're really happy about you daughter's graduation!)
3	Intensify interest to H. Use of expression "you know" which draws H as a participant	5. SP: … we can really work out a good deal for you … (7) F	3. SP: Los precios han subido, usted sabe. (Prices have gone up, you know)
		6. SP: Well, they used to come in four different sizes, you know.	
		7. SP: Well you know, I suppose that could go just as great with the piña coladas … (67) L	
4	Use in-group identity marker (address form, dialect, ellipsis, diminutives)	8. C: Do you expect to get the ram heads at any time? (61) J SP: That, I don't know, honey … (62)	4. SP: ¿Qué color vas a usar? C: Voy de negro. SP: Fíjate, una cosa así iría bien.

Table 2: Continued

Strategy	Description	Crucian speech community data	Puerto Rican speech community data
			(What colour are you wearing?)
			(Black.)
			(You know, something like this would look nice.)
			5.C: ¿Tienes una libretita? (Do you have a small notebook?)
5	Seek agreement through use of safe topics and repetition	9. SP: Should be but don't bet your life on this. Not that easy. (77) F 10. SP: Are you visiting the island or you live here? (50) J 11. C: I want to start with Scotch. (4) L SP: Scotch, okay... (5)	6. SP: ¿Y cuándo es la graduación de su hija? (When is your daughter's graduation?) ¿Usted va? (Are you going?) 7. SP: ¿Y usted tiene muchas hijas? (And do you have a lot of daughters?)
6	Avoid disagreement by pretending to agree	12. C: That's something like the design, you know. (89) J SP: Yes, it has that effect, but a little larger (90) 13. C: Not really ... (47)	8. C: ¡Esas! (Those!) SP: Sí, pero no creo que sean su tamaño (Yes, but I don't think they're your size.)
7	Presuppose, assert common ground; S may presuppose familiarity	14. SP: You sound like me, ... (29) F 15. SP: That I don't know, honey ... (62) J	9. SP: Estas to irían muy bien. ¿Tu no crees? (These would look very nice. Don't you think?) 10. SP: Dime mija. (Tell me, dearie.)
8	Joke	16. C: That's too big for me to handle in my apartment .. (41) L SP: Very small apartment. ((laughter)) (42)	11. SP: Ah, pero usted es una "teenager". Le queda muy bien. ((laughter)) C: (But you're a teenager. It looks nice.)

Table 2: Continued

Strategy	Description	Crucian speech community data	Puerto Rican speech community data
9	Assert or presuppose S's knowledge of and concern for H's wants	17. C: And in a reasonable price range (8) J SP: Real ones. (9) C: ((laughter)) Right. (10) 18. C: What's this? (111) L SP: That's another local product also. I could probably give you a taste of it. (112) 19. SP: You sound like me, I have to be almost under the desk to be able to work with it. (29) F	12. SP: Estos no son los que me pediste pero los traje para que los vieras. (These are not the ones you asked for, but I brought them any way for you to see.)
10	Offer, promise; S chooses to stress his cooperation with H	20. C: ... How much was the other one; do you remember? (8) F SP: Not off hand, but I can find out for you and we can work out, ah ... how much we can give you ... back on it. (9)	13. SP: Déjeme ver si se las puedo conseguir en el suyo. (Let me see if I can get them in yours.)
11	Be optimistic	21. SP: That's one possibility, right? (60) J 22. C: You can make a package of three? (53) L SP: Sure. (54) 23. SP: I can probably give you most of the, of your money back; (45) F	14. SP: Esperese un segundito. (Wait a second.)

Table 2: Continued

Strategy	Description	Crucian speech community data	Puerto Rican speech community data
12	Include both S and H in activity (we, let's)	24. SP: Let's see what we have. We have some here too. (11) J	15. SP: Tenemos en rosa y azul. (We have them in pink and blue.)
13	Give (ask for) reason	25. C: Do you expect to get the heads…? 26. C2: Let me ask you a question. If we get … (194) L SP: No, because … (195)	16. C: ¿Y por qué non tienen? SP: Se ordenaron pero no han llegado todavía. (And why don't you have any?) (They were ordered, but they haven't arrived yet.)
14	Assume reciprocity	none observed	none observed
15	Give gifts to H (goods, sympathy, understanding, co-operation.)	27. SP: … Sure, I'll be happy to put them for you. (136) J	On two occasions, customers were heard to speak for a long time about personal matters.

Table 3: Strategies of Negative Politeness in the Crucian and Puerto Rican data

Strategy	Description	Crucian speech community data	Puerto Rican speech community data
1	Be conventionally indirect	1. SP: Do you want to take back anything you probably haven't had, you know, something new? What about ... (62) L	none observed
2	Hedge (want not to coerce H)	2. SP: ... These are rather nice ... 3. SP: ... Something like this is ninety-seven fifty, which is very nice ... (24) J 4. C: We are going to get one package. (32) L SP: So, just one package this time, okay. (33) 5. SP: So let me just get the information for you, and I'll be right back. (35) F	1. C: ¿Es lavable? SP: Bueno. Tiene que lavarlo a mano. (C: Is it washable?) (SP: Well, it has to be hand washed.)
3	Be pessimistic	6. SP: Why don't you take this over to the cash register while I pack it up. (275) L	none observed
4	Minimize imposition; use diminutives	7. SP: ... And if I should not be here just ask one of the 8. SP: Let me offer you ( ).	2. C: Hazme un favorcito. (Do me a little favor.)
5	Give deference	Formal forms of address were absent	3. SP: Señora, pase por aquí. (Ma'am, this way.)

Table 3: Continued

Strategy	Description	Crucian speech community data	Puerto Rican speech community data
6	Apologize through admission, reluctance, overwhelming reasons, begging forgiveness	See Speech Event I (62,64,70,72) II (139) III (47)	4. C: ¿Tienes jabones Guerlain? SP: No. (prosodics for regret) (C: Do you carry Guerlain soap?) (SP: No.)
7	Impersonalize S and H through impersonal verbs (it is necessary), passive voice, "we" (This is the business "we" which the study of Brown and Levinson refer to on p.207.)	9. SP: … I cannot even assure you if we're going to reorder it. (70) J	5. C: ¡Qué poca selección! SP: Se van a ordenar más. (C: What a limited selection!) (SP: More will be ordered.)
8	State the FTA as a general rule	none observed	none observed
9	Nominalize	none observed	none observed
10	Go on record as incurring a debt	none observed	none observed

(1) J = Turn 1, store J   S = Speaker   SP = Salesperson
                           H = hearer   C = customer

tant component of social interaction in Puerto Rico (Lauria 1964). It is not limited to friends but is readily achieved even in encounters where the participants are total strangers. Not that Puerto Ricans are disrespectful to each other through the use of jokes, but that a joking game may be quickly initiated as a "fail-safe" technique to enter into topics which could touch upon the respect and dignity of the participants. Example 11 presents a middle-aged woman who is buying costume jewelry, a type of merchandise which is usually associated with adolescents. She tries it on and complains that it has been made for a teenager, not for her. The salesperson remarks in a joking manner that the lady is a teenager and that the piece of jewelry is very becoming to her. The female customer laughs too and the interaction continues in the same joking mood until the customer leaves (Simounet de Géigel 1986).

The data for strategies of negative politeness also display an apparent similarity which may cause serious misunderstanding in a crosscultural communicative situation.

In their discussion of strategy 2 on the use of verbal hedges, Brown and Levinson explain that "perhaps most of the verbal hedges can be replaced by (or emphasized by) prosodic or kinesic means of indicating tentativeness or emphasis" (1978:177). In the case of PRSC, replacement and/or emphasis occur not only in this particular strategy but in practically all other strategies of positive and negative politeness. Nonverbal communication is such an impressive component of interpersonal communication among Puerto Ricans that, in her investigation, Nine-Curt re-constructed in verbal form dialogues which she herself had observed and recorded in Puerto Rico. This writer had a similar opportunity of observing and recording a short encounter at a Puerto Rican bank in St. Croix where a speaker of Standard American English approached a young female teller of Puerto Rican descent and engaged in the following conversation:

Client: Good morning.
Teller: (smiles)
Client: I'd like this in tens and twenties, please.
Teller: (Smiles. Looking at the client, she takes a check from the client and proceeds to cash it. After a minute or two, teller hands cash to client.)
Client: Thanks.
Teller: Have a good day.

Puerto Ricans' use of prosodics and nonverbal communication in the employment of strategy 6 of negative politeness is also a source of possible communication breakdown. While the Crucian data revealed the use of overwhelming reasons in performing an apology, the PRSC data reported in the Simounet de Géigel study stood out for its limited use of the verbal channel and its heavy reliance on paralinguistic features. Thus when examined closely, from the parallelism of both data included in Tables 2 and 3, there emerges a quality or flavor which is distinct for each cultural context.

Before concluding, there is one final point to be made. The general tone of all the speech events recorded could be described as cordial and friendly. Smiles and laughter were observed in an atmosphere of informality which was marked, however, by a seriousness of purpose. In an interview held immediately after the recording, the customers involved in the

Table 4: Comparison of Strategies of Persuasion employed in the sales encounters with Brown and Levinson's Strategies of Politeness

Strategies of persuasion	Strategies of politeness
1. Continuous acknowledgment of customer's requests and needs	1, 9 PP
2. Invitation to C to try on earrings, taste liquor and try desk	1 PP
3. Long explanations to dissuade or clarify	13 NP
4. Frequent use of business "we"	7 NP
5. Frequent use of "let's"	12 PP
6. Statement of SP's opinion on terms of C's	1, 2 PP
7. Frequent use of repetition	5 PP
8. Frequent use of "okay" with the function of confirming as in "you know"	3 PP
9. Use of ellipsis and expressions of informal talk	4 PP
10. Use of affective forms of address	4 PP
11. Reaffirmation of C's opinion in SP's words	2 PP
12. Agreement with C's favorable opinions	2, 7 PP
13. Offer to make special arrangements or achieve best possible "deal"	11, 10, 15 NP
14. Maintenance of friendly tone	8 PP
15. Offer of new products and request in a non-imposing manner	1, 2, 3, 4 NP
16. Engagement in talk not related to sale	5 PP

PP = positive politeness   NP = negative politeness

events expressed their satisfaction with the business transactions that had occurred. They stressed the importance of the salespersons' willingness to attend to them, their knowledge of the merchandise, excellent service, constant attention and politeness. According to them, those factors worked together to achieve an atmosphere which made them feel that a sales transaction had been made in a non-imposing manner.

Yet the language analysis of the three events revealed a heavy load of rhetorical strategies on the part of the salespersons to persuade the customers to buy. This occurred in spite of two things: feeling expressed by both sides of the transaction that they disliked persuasiveness intensely and the failure of the customers in the events to notice the strategies.

A look at these strategies will reveal that they match the strategies of politeness described above very closely. Table 4 illustrates this observation.

Thus successful management of interaction was achieved through the subtle blending of persuasiveness and politeness, a difficult combination to achieve, but nevertheless possible because of individuals' desire to achieve their own goals in life in a context characterized by impressive cultural variability. Nine-Curt (personal communication) believes thus that politeness can also be conceived as the manipulation of interaction.

Conclusions and Recommendations

This study attempted to identify what Puerto Rican English language learners needed to know about sales encounters in St. Croix in order to interact successfully in the work situation.

Ethnographic and interactional approaches to language study were brought together as complementary tools for data analysis. Quantification of linguistic occurrences was supplied as an additional source of information for the language teaching program. This combination of approaches and data analyzing techniques made it possible for the researcher to offer a wide variety of linguistic and cultural information.

On the basis of the findings presented above the author suggests two types of recommendations for the bilingual program in St. Croix: one concerns the pure linguistic content to be included in the language materials and the second concerns the sociocultural ingredient for the program. First, the language materials must reflect the differences between the written and the spoken language and these differences have to be made clear to the learner. These materials must also be true to the linguistic reality of natural language data. That is to say, language materials which are to serve as models must include the elements characteristic of real Crucian conversation mentioned above.

Second, the sociocultural ingredient is perhaps the most dramatic of the bilingual program for it entails "learning a new shorthand for cultural knowledge" (Loveday 1982:57). Yet although difficult to attain, awareness and understanding of other ways of doing things is not insurmountable. There must be, of course, a "readiness to respect and accept, and a capacity to participate" (Hanvey, in Loveday 1982:56).

In terms of the Puerto Rican population, what does the cultural arm of second language teaching entail? First of all, it entails making students aware of the need to substitute the nonverbal code with the verbal one. Puerto Rican communicative style abounds in nonverbal communication (Nine-Curt 1984) and students of English must be able to see the need to utilize the verbal channel more frequently, in openings (greetings, approaches, and acknowledgements), closings (leave-takings), and changes in the flow of interaction (physical moves).

Second, students should be made aware of the social importance of language routines and forms of address in the Crucian speech community and the constraints which guide their use.

Third, strategies of politeness, that is, what is sociolinguistically appropriate for the successful management of interaction should be included in the language materials and formally studied and practised in the second language classroom. Their importance in interaction cannot be ignored.

Finally, because of the importance that tourism-related jobs have on the island and its present employment situations, the bilingual program at the secondary school level should offer its students a preparatory course for service-oriented working positions like the one analyzed in the present study. This course of study would have the following components:

1. A linguistic component embedded in the work situation.
2. An attitudinal component which would deal with students' attitudes towards the job situation, the job responsibilities, personnel hierarchy and service-rendering positions.
3. A job-related skill component geared towards the attainment of knowledge of job routine strategies attuned to the nature of the job.
4. A sociocultural component which would deal with students' cultural

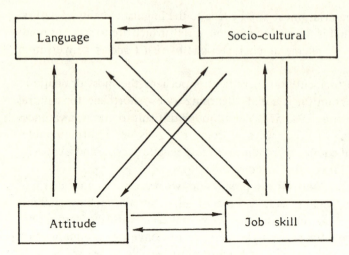

Figure 4: Components of suggested course of study

background as the starting point and whose goal would entail
crosscultural awareness in terms of the culture of the first language
and that of the second. This component would be rooted in the
multicultural nature of the Crucian context.

Figure 4 illustrates graphically this course of study.

This writer would like to add two other recommendations related to
the findings of the study but which were not part of the initial goal of this
study. Because of the misinterpretations that take place in Crucian daily
interaction, the U.S. Virgin Islands Department of Education and the College of the Virgin Islands should foster the creation of a series of workshops
in the development of crosscultural awareness for teachers and members of
the general community. These workships would be open to the public free of
charge and could be sponsored by the endowment offices for the humanities.

The second recommendation is related to a problem which was not the
object of this study, but was briefly mentioned in the introduction. The reference is to the educational problems faced by the black Curcian population who also seem to be facing a state of alienation in the educational process. While the language problems of these Crucian English speakers are
not as dramatic as those of the creole speakers in other Caribbean islands
(Craig 1979) where the language variation spoken stands at a greater dis-

tance from the standard language in the creole language continuum, the divergence between school reality and the Crucian's own reality is quite pointed. Ethnographic studies of this group in particular are needed and therefore suggested for the purpose of identifying the various elements which come together to constitute Crucian life.

From the perspective of an applied linguist, St. Croix is virgin territory and the list of possible studies is, therefore, endless. Yet, more important than this academic goal is the human goal of attaining crosscultural understanding and cultural awareness. With respect to this Hall stated (1976):

> Self-awareness and cultural awareness are inseparable, which means that transcending unconscious culture cannot be accomplished without some degree of self-awareness. Used properly, intercultural experiences can be a tremendous eye opener, providing a view of one's self seldom seen under normal conditions at home. Like all opportunities for growth and self-knowledge, the mere thought can be somewhat frightening. (1976:212)

> Possibly the most important psychological aspect of culture — the bridge between culture and personality — is the identification process. This process, which works admirably when change is slow but wreaks havoc in times of rapid change such as we are currently experiencing, is most certainly a major impediment to cross-cultural understanding and effective relations among the peoples of the world. Man must now embark on the difficult journey beyond culture, because the greatest separation feat of all is when one manages to gradually free oneself from the grip of unconscious culture. (1976:240)

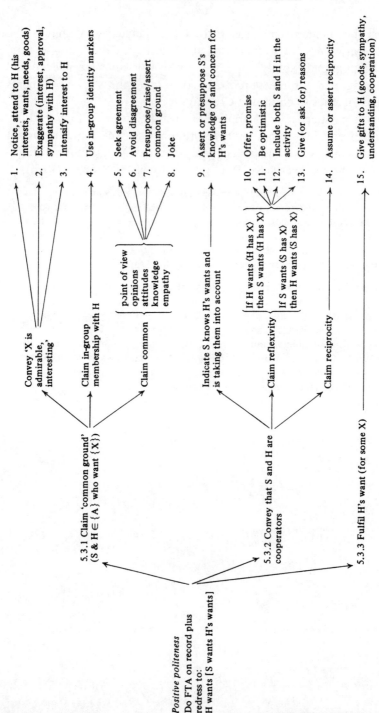

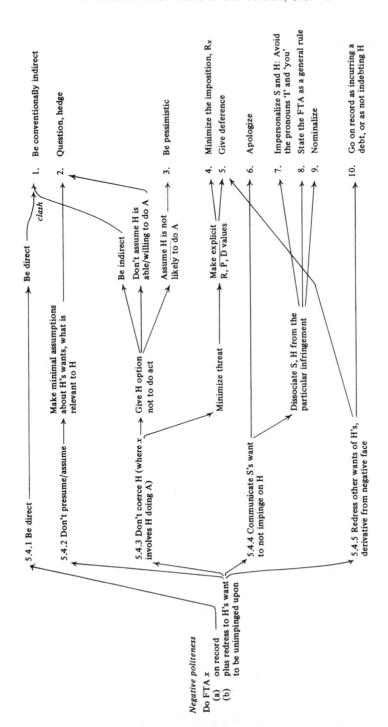

References

Boyer, W.W. 1983. *America's Virgin Islands: A history of human rights and wrongs.* Durham: Carolina Academic Press.

Brown, P. & S. Levinson. 1978. "Universals in Language Usage: Politeness Phenomena". *Questions and Politeness* ed. by E.N. Goody, 56-310. London: Cambridge.

Brown, G. & G. Yule. 1983. *Discourse Analysis.* Cambridge: Cambridge University Press.

Cohen, C. 1977. *Bilingual Education.* Rowley: Newbury House.

Corder, S.P. 1973. *Introducing Applied Linguistics.* Harmondsworth: Penguin Educational.

Craig, D.R. 1979. "Bidialectal Education: Creole and Standard in the West Indies". *Sociolinguistic Aspects of Language Learning and Teaching* ed. by J.B. Pride, 164-184. Oxford: Oxford University Press.

Di Meo, S. 1986. "Tourism Generated $531.5M for Territory: Commerce predicts continued growth". *The Business Journal* 1. 16.

Dookhan, I. 1974. *A History of the Virgin Islands of the United States.* St. Thomas: Caribbean University Press.

Firth, R. 1972. "Verbal and Bodily Rituals of Greeting and Parting". *The Interpretation of Ritual: Essays in honour of A.I. Richards* ed. by J.L. La Fontaine, 1-38. London: Tavistock.

Fishman, J.A. & J. Lovas. 1970. "Bilingual Education in Sociolinguistic Perspective". *TESOL Quarterly* 4. 215-222.

Frake, C.O. 1972. "Struck by Speech: The Yakan concept of litigation". *Directions in Sociolinguistics: The ethnography of communication* ed. by J.J. Gumperz & D. Hymes, 106-129. New York: Holt, Rinehart & Winston.

Goffman, E. 1967. *Interaction Ritual.* Garden City, N.Y.: Doubleday.

Hall, E.T. 1976. *Beyond Culture.* Garden City, N.Y.: Anchor Press.

Hatch, E. & M.H. Long. 1980. "Discourse Analysis, What's That?" *Discourse Analysis in Second Language Research* ed. by D. Larsen-Freeman, 1-40. Rowley: Newbury House.

House, J. & G. Kasper. 1981. "Politeness Markers in English and German". *Conversational Routine: Explorations in standardized communication situations and prepatterned speech* ed. by F. Coulmas, 157-185. The Hague: Mouton.

Hymes, D. 1974. *Foundations in Sociolinguistics.* Philadelphia: University of Pennsylvania Press.

Lauria, A. 1964. "'Respeto,' 'relajo' and Interpersonal Relations in Puerto Rico". *Anthropological Quarterly* 37. 53-67.

Laver, J. 1981. "Linguistic Routines and Politeness in Greeting and Parting". *Conversational Routine: Explorations in standardized communication situations and prepatterned speech* ed. by F. Coulmas, 289-304. The Hague: Mouton.

Lewis, G.K. 1972. *The Virgin Islands: A Caribbean Lilliput.* Evanston: Northwestern University Press.

Loveday, L. 1982. *The Sociolinguistics of Learning and Using a Non-native Language.*

Oxford: Pergamon Press.

Nine-Curt, C.J. 1984. *Non-verbal Communication* (2nd ed.). Cambridge, Mass.: Evaluation, Dissemination and Assessment Center.

Owen, M. 1981. "Conversational Units and the Use of 'Well ...'". *Conversation and Discourse: Structure and interpretation* ed. by P. Werth, 99-116. London: Croom Helm.

Sacks, H., E. Schegloff & G. Jefferson. 1980. "A Simplest Systematics for the Organization of Turn Taking for Conversation". *Studies in the Organization of Conversational Interaction* ed. by J. Schenkein, 7-55. New York: Academic Press.

Saville-Troike, M. 1982. *The Ethnography of Communication*. Baltimore: University Park Press.

Schegloff, E. & H. Sacks. 1973. "Opening up Closings". *Semiotica* 8. 289-324.

Schenkein, J. ed. 1980. *Studies in the Organization of Conversational Interaction*. New York: Academic Press.

Simounet de Géigel, A. 1986. "Strategies of Politeness: An intercultural approach". Paper presented at the annual meeting of the Speech Communication Association in Chicago.

Tsuda, A. 1980. *Sales Talk in Japan and the United States: An ethnographic analysis of contrastive speech events*. Washington, D.C.: Georgetown University Press.

University of Puerto Rico. 1970. The Social Science Research Center. *The Educational Setting in the Virgin Islands with Particular Reference to the Education of Spanish-Speaking Children*. Rio Piedras: University of Puerto Rico.

U.S. Virgin Islands Department of Education, Office of Planning, Research, and Evaluation. 1982. *A Study of Public and Private School Drop-outs in the United States Virgin Islands*. St. Thomas: Caribbean Research Institute of the College of Virgin Islands.

Wolfson, N. 1976. "Speech Events and Natural Speech: Some implications for sociolinguistic methodology". *Language in Society* 5. 189-209.

Linguistic Difficulties in Institutional Discourse

Eija Ventola

1. Introduction

This paper will concern itself with one type of institutional discourse, namely service encounters, and with the difficulties that language learners experience in this context. The general orientation of the paper is towards the learner and the language teaching materials. Specifically, the ways in which social interaction in service encounters is represented and taught in textbooks will be contrasted with the learners' actual experiences in encounters of this kind.

Let us begin with an analogy. If you come to a strange city, you may come well prepared and orientated to your new environment. You may have bought a map beforehand and have already in advance studied the route you need to take in order to get where you want to go in the city. Your goal or purpose has been worked out and you simply follow the route on the map to reach your destination.

When a non-native speaker enters a foreign society, whether for a short time or a lengthy period, ideally he comes prepared and has already worked out the routes he needs to take. Language teaching materials should function as his map of orientation. They should prepare learners to achieve different social goals by linguistic means in various situations they are encountering in a foreign society. But do we really know what information such a "discourse map" should give to the learners, and what information is presently offered in textbooks?

Keeping faithful to the analogy of travel, we will first illustrate how a textbook dialogue orientates Finnish learners of English towards one type of institutional discourse, namely service encounters in travel agencies. Then evidence will be presented from three areas of orientation which

cause problems to participants and which they have to sort out while
engaged in authentic discourse in travel agencies. The problems to be discussed will be concerned with institutions, with participants, and with communication channels. Finally, at the same time as pointing out the problems, we shall discuss how they are handled in language teaching.

2. Orientation to Institutions

Language teaching seems to orientate learners best to the institutional
organization of the situational contexts of discourse. Mostly the orientation
to institutions takes place by teaching learners those lexical items which
realize institutionally relevant objects and activities.

Let us see how such an orientation takes place in an example of
textbook dialogue. The dialogue is from a textbook written for 15/16-year-
old Finnish learners of English who are completing their last year of comprehensive schooling; that is, in the following year they will proceed to
either high schools or vocational schools.

(1)   14. *Before the Trip*
       Part A — At a Travel Agency
       Travel Agent Good morning. Can I help you?
       Mr. Linton   Yes, I'd like to book a trip to Copenhagen, please.
       Travel Agent How do you want to go?
       Mr. Linton   By ferry.
       Travel Agent How many are you?
       Mr. Linton   Four. My wife, myself and our two children. And the car.
       Travel Agent How old are the children?
       Mr. Linton   16 and 10.
       Travel Agent That's three adults and one child. Single or return?
       Mr. Linton   Return, please.
       Travel Agent When would you like to travel?
       Mr. Linton   On July 15th. And we would like to return on July 23rd.
       Travel Agent Hm. I'm afraid the ferry is fully booked on the 15th. How
                     about July 14th?
       Mr. Linton   No, I'm afraid that's impossible.
       Travel Agent What about the 16th?
       Mr. Linton   Yes, that's all right.
       Travel Agent Would you like a cabin for four?
       Mr. Linton   Yes, please. The cheapest you have.
       Travel Agent Let's see. That's a cabin on Deck C. And what make is your
                     car?

Mr. Linton   A Ford Fiesta.

Travel Agent   Right.

Mr. Linton   Can I book a hotel through you?

Travel Agent   Yes, you can. What kind of hotel do you want? And how many rooms?

Mr. Linton   Something not too expensive. Two double rooms, one with a bath or shower.

Travel Agent   For how many nights?

Mr. Linton   Four.

Travel Agent   Let's see ... There's a nice little hotel in a quiet side street which should suit you. The price includes continental breakfast.

Mr. Linton   That sounds fine.

Travel Agent   Right. Could you call back the day after tomorrow? I'll try to have everything ready.

Mr. Linton   Thank you very much. You've been very helpful.

Travel Agent   Not at all.

(Webster et al. 1982:108-109)

Part A of the unit involves a dialogue taking place between Mr. Linton and a travel agent. Both interactants are English. In the next opening in the book there are two supplementary parts to the unit (Webster *et al.* 1982:110-111). Part B — An Invitation — explains why Mr. Linton is in a travel agency. His daughter's Danish pen friend has invited the Lintons to come to visit Denmark and it is this trip that Mr. Linton is now organizing. Part C — Advice for Travellers — gives learners further useful information concerning travelling in general.

The learners' orientation to the institution of travel agency takes place in the lesson through lexical items. Mostly they are expressions of objects, e.g. *a travel agency, an agent, a single, a return, a cabin, a deck, continental breakfast*; but also some activities are given, e.g. *to book, to suit, to include*. The learners learn the meanings of these lexical items through the translation equivalents in Finnish (e.g. *a travel agency = matkatoimisto*).

Orientating learners to objects and activities in foreign institutions by teaching them relevant lexis through the translation method has a long and established tradition in language teaching. We all know that whenever one is entering a new area or field of expertise, it is very important to acquire the appropriate lexis. This also applies to learning professional jargon in one's native language. In linguistics there is a long tradition of study of language variation of this kind. Situationally relevant *fields* (e.g. Halliday 1978:143; Gregory and Carroll 1978:7) or *object-* and *activity-orientations* (Ventola 1987:60) are seen to be realized in texts as certain types of lexical, grammatical and discourse patterns, which in turn help us to recognize certain varieties of language — certain *registers*. A common distinction made on the basis of differences in institutional object- and activity-orientations is the one between technical and non-technical registers (for examples and a discussion, see e.g. Gregory and Carroll 1978:7-8; Barnickel 1982:35-83). Although grammatical and discourse realizations are no less interesting and important, we will limit the present discussion of the "field" to its realization in lexical terms.

Many restricted, technical fields are at least partly shared internationally. Thus it can be very easily forgotten that foreign societies may organize their institutions differently and that these differences will always cause linguistic difficulties for foreign language learners.

It seems that textbook writers are not paying enough attention to this fact. Too often the institution, and the lexis used to represent it, is presented as "known". It is trusted that a translation equivalent will explain the institutional orientation to the learner. In many cases this is so. The learner knows the institutional objects and activities and the ways they are organized into systems. In our dialogue example, for instance, the learner may be well-travelled and be aware of the construction of ferries, the room arrangements and the menus in hotels. Consequently, he has no difficulties in understanding and learning what *a deck*, *a double room*, or *continental breakfast* means. But for a less-travelled, Finnish comprehensive school learner the translation of *continental breakfast* as *kahviaamiainen* may suggest perhaps *coffee*, *porridge or yoghurt*, *rye bread*, *butter*, *cheese*, *sausage* rather than *coffee*, *toast* and *marmalade*.

Initially it may seem that we are here dealing with only a fairly superficial matter. But perhaps a comparison between Examples 2 and 3 will illustrate how not knowing the institutional systems of the society will cause serious difficulties in social interaction, and show that neither learners nor native speakers always know how to handle the situation when such difficulties occur. (In the examples, '*' plus italics signify simultaneous speech; 'C' stands for 'customer' and 'S' for 'server.')

(2)   C: uh if- are there visa requirements for Bali
       S1: you're on 'n Australian passport [rising tone]
       C: no
            an Irish passport
       S1: well you'd need a visa anyway
            Irish passport would need a visa Dave [rising tone]

```
S2:  where to
C:   *Bali
S1:  *Bali
S2:  yeah
C:   yeah
     *and do I handle that or do you [rising tone]
S1:  *and do you have a re-entry-
     oh no
     we can handle that for you
     do you have a-
C:   I do ... *re-entry
S1:  *re-entry yeah
     well as long as you've got that all you have to do is to get an Indonesian
     visa
C:   fine okay
```

In Example 2 the speaker is a native speaker of English, but not a native to Australian society. Yet she has lived in Australia long enough to know what the institutional system is. The concept of *re-entry* does not cause any problems in the interaction.

In Example 3 we can see how the same travel agents and a Finnish speaker of English run into discourse difficulties because the Finn does not know the institutional organization.

```
(3)   S2:  you don't need that (= visa to Fiji)
           just *a-
      C:   *don't need that [rising tone]
      S2:  just a re-entry permit into Australia
      C:   oh fine, that's good
           and ... *then-
      S1:  *yeah
      C:   I can-
      S1:  decide *where you want to stay in
      C:   *and-
           good
      S2:  have you been out of Australia in the last ... three years [rising tone]
      C:   yes I have been here for five months
      S2:  you haven't been out of Australia
      C:   no
      S2:  no ...
           so you won't have a re-entry permit anyway
      C:   pardon [rising tone]
      S2:  you won't have a re-entry permit
#     C:   I can't understand what that means
      S1:  no
```

\#   you just have to get a re-entry permit in your pasport
C: oh yeah
S1: okay [rising tone]
S2: okay

The interaction runs into problems because the learner in Example 3 does not know what *a re-entry* is. The institutional organization of people having to have a special permission to enter the country again, if they have left it, is new to her and she quite explicitly expresses that she does not comprehend what is involved: *I can't understand what that means* (the first \#). But in the same way as the learner is never really told what is involved in *continental breakfast* in Example 1, the customer is not really told what is involved in *a re-entry: you just have to get a re-entry permit in your passport* (the second \#).

The given examples appear to be relevant to language teaching in the following way. The textbook writers of Example 1 and the travel agents in Example 3 seem to take "the native view" of the institutional organization of discourse. They know the systems of the native society. But if they want to *give help* to the learner, they have to know the institutional organizations of the learner society as well as the target language society. In other words, people who teach foreign learners or have to interact with foreigners in their work must be "practising contrastive discourse analysts". Ideally they should know both systems, or at least be aware of the possible differences in the systems, and be able to predict the linguistic difficulties resulting from the differences. Secondly, they also have to be "practising applied linguists". They not only need to know how they can help the foreigner, by clarifying the differences in the systems. They also need to be able to instruct the learner to help him/herself. Example dialogues in textbooks very seldom teach learners how to deal with trouble in discourse, how to manage institutional organizations, and how to ask for help when discourse does not proceed. Such requests for help as in Example 3, *I can't understand what that means*, are simply not included in textbook dialogues.

The given examples may perhaps have exaggerated the question of field in institutional discourse and its role in language teaching. But the highlighting has been done for the following reasons. The teaching of field plays an important role in all kinds of language teaching, not just in teaching Language for Special Purposes (LSP). In whatever kind of situational interaction we are engaged, we constantly have to practise predicting the linguistic realisations of the field — or rather fields, since they can also keep changing during interaction. This places heavy demands upon linguists, applied linguists and textbook writers — upon linguists because they have to work out the different institutional object and activity orientations and their linguistic realizations, and upon applied linguists and textbook writers, because they have to be able to present the systems so that they will be useful to foreign learners.

3. Orientation to Role Relationships

Another aspect to which foreign language textbooks have recently started paying attention is the ways different *tenor* or *role relationships* are realized linguistically (for definitions of tenor, see e.g. Halliday 1978:144; Gregory and Carroll 1978:48-63; Barnickel 1982:152-156); that is, how such matters as social distance, age, frequency of contact, power and solidarity, influence the realization of registers (Poynton 1985) and what problems the learner has to face in these areas. The linguistic realizations of role relationships are seen as various choices of mood and modality, politeness markers, expressions of formality or informality, address terms and, more recently, in terms of who initiates, responds and challenges in exchanges (see e.g. Sinclair and Coulthard 1975; Burton 1980; Berry 1987; Ventola 1987).

If we consider the realizations of tenor from the point of view of foreign language teaching textbooks, it seems that such realizations as choices of mood and modality, politeness markers and formality have at least to some degree been included in textbook dialogues. For instance in Example 1, we have the appropriate choices of mood, modality and politeness markers in such expressions as *I'd like to book a trip to Copenhagen, please*; *Return, please*; *When would you like to travel*; *I'm afraid the ferry is fully booked on the 15th*; *would you like a cabin for four — yes, please*, and so on.

However, recordings of authentic discourse in travel agencies show that foreign language teaching is still rather off the mark, and that more research in this area is still needed. In the following examples, Examples 4-6, a service request by a Finn to a travel agent is contrasted with a service request by an Australian:

(4)   a Finn: we want to go to Finland
        an Australian: I was wondering how much it would cost to go to England,
                just the general price

(5)   a Finn: I I going to Perth
       an Australian: I'd like some information please on the Barrier Reef

(6)   a Finn: I want to go .. uh ... Queensland ... uh ... one week holiday
       an Australian: I was wondering er ... I's thinking about ... January Feb-
                      ruary ... I have some holidays and I's thinking about ...
                      some friends of mine are going on a trip to Alice Springs ...
                      and I was just wondering about the cost and so on.

The differences in the given examples reflect systematically contrasting features, which should be brought out explicitly in textbooks. In Finnish, requests are commonly realized by declarative mood, and politeness is expressed in the verbal group rather than by such politeness markers as *please*. Showing the learners authentic contrastive examples of this kind may help them to understand the differences in the language systems and in the realizations.

Those aspects of tenor which are connected with holding the floor in turn-taking and organizing discourse into exchanges have received less attention in language textbooks. Whether or not a discourse is organized in the form of exchanges is of course a matter of the communication channel. But role relationships play an important part in determining the rights and obligations for initiating an exchange (see Berry 1987). How does Example 1 represent the participant relationships? It is solely the travel agent who is in charge of the initiation of exchanges. She structures and directs the con-versations: *How do you want to go?*, *How many are you?*, *How old are the children?*, *Single or return?*, *When would you like to travel?*, *How about July 14th?*, etc. Example 1 has the appearance of an interrogation — the customer is questioned by the travel agent. The customer volunteers very little information.

In natural travel talk, the interaction seems to be structured into exchanges in a much more balanced way than in Example 1. The general principle between native speakers when interacting in service encounters is that of "co-operation". In travel agencies the co-operation concerns exchanging commodities: pieces of information or goods are both requested and given. Participants have their established roles to play in the procedure of exchanging goods and information. Usually discourse will begin with the customer requesting some information that the server knows, e.g. what kind of trips there are available, what kind of accommodation is offered, etc. But at the same time the customer is the "knower" and the "giver" of certain kinds of information, i.e. he knows where he would like to travel to, when, etc. Usually the customer gives this information when he lets the server know what service he wants, e.g. *I was ... wondering about a ... uh ... trip to ... Queensland.* Then it is the server's turn to be co-operative and give the information requested. But since the server does not know enough about the customer's exact plans, he is entitled to make further inquiries. This leads us to an interaction similar to the dialogue in Example 1.

(7)	C:	I was ... wondering about a ... uh ... trip to ... Queensland
#	S:	Queensland
	C:	yeah
#	S:	when'd you want to go ... *any any-*
	C:	*uhm*
	S:	roughly
	C:	September
	S:	September
#	C:	and I'd like to go somewhere that's not ... very popular, you know ... somewhere nice and quiet

Example 7 is in some ways similar to Example 1, in others not. In both, the interactants are saying more or less what their social roles in that particular interactive situation require them to say. The customer expresses his destination and the server, since she has not received enough information, requires a specification: *when'd you want to go*, as indicated by the second #. But whereas Example 1 represents interaction as an "interrogatory procedure", Example 7 represents interaction as a "co-operative negotiation procedure", where the ruling principle seems to be the following: turn-taking is primarily organized by the social roles, but when the discourse procedure cannot go on, because there is not enough information, the participants may request specifications or they may simply offer specifications. The third # indicates the point where the customer is offering a specification in Example 7: *and I'd like to go somewhere that's not ... very popular ... you know ... somewhere nice and quiet.* Furthermore, interactants confirm their understanding of each other's messages by dynamic moves such as the one indicated by the first #: *Queensland — yeah.*

In Example 8, it is the customer who requests a specification in the turn marked by the second #: *how long would that be for*, and the server who volunteers specifications, as indicated by the first and third #s.

(8)	S:	there's quite a few there which you can pick from
	C:	uhum
#	S:	you can see ... you know what- from a 171 dollars sort of thing
	C:	yeah

```
        S:   uhm
  #     C:   how long would that be for
        S:   that's for a week
        C:   yes
        S:   uhm
  #          and that's ... just the ... the flat sort of thing
```

Examples 7 and 8 suggest that the construction of exchanges in service encounters proceeds in a balanced, co-operative way in native-to-native service interaction. No one interactant is in sole charge of advancing the discourse to a new stage. If not enough information has been given, the interactants may be prompted or may volunteer to provide further information. If the purpose of the dialogue in a foreign language textbook is to show the native patterns of interaction, discourse analysis can and must provide help to foreign language teaching in how to present the exchange structuring of interaction in different types of discourse.

One final aspect of role relationships in discourse to which attention will be drawn here is the establishment of rapport or sociability. This aspect seems to be mostly ignored in textbooks. For instance in Example 1, the social distance between the participants appears to be at its maximum during the whole encounter. However, in authentic discourse we often find purely "phatic communion" stages in the unfolding of the discourse process (Malinowski 1966/23). Such stages, which can be called "approaches" (Ventola 1979), seem to decrease the social distance between the participants, and this change in the tenor relationships will obviously have consequences for the discourse which follows. Examples 9 and 10 illustrate the two types of approaches which can be recognized. Example 9 demonstrates a contextual approach, whereas Example 10 is a personal approach.

```
  (9)    C:   it's lovely and warm in here
         S:   hm isn't it [rising tone]
         C:   actually it's not actually cold
              it's just that it-
         S:   the wind gets into you
         C:   yeah
         S:   yeah it's always the way
         C:   uhm

  (10)   C:   I thought they'd be all be sort of booked out because we're always late
              you know
         S:   yeah
              *I'm like-
         C:   *never organized
```

S: no
     I'm a bit like that myself
C: (laughs) oh good
     you'll be understanding

These kinds of approaches appear in textbooks only rarely. Yet, when they are included in the unfolding of dialogue, they seem to increase the comfort of participants greatly by decreasing social distance. But it seems that when facing these approaches in travel talk, learners do not exactly know what to do — how to respond to and elaborate on the approach that has been initiated.

(11)   S: your country's nice too
              I've been to Finland a couple of times
       C: yeah
       S: fortunately ... in the ... summertime not in the wintertime
              [2 secs — pause]
       S: Finland's a little too cold in the *in the-
       C: *yes it is
       S: but in the summer I've been-
              no it's very beautiful
              I liked I liked Finland very much
              [4 secs — pause]
       C: okay ...

In Example 11 the native speaker again and again tries to create rapport, but the learner's short confirmations *yeah*, *yes it is* and the silence are not very encouraging. The discourse falls flat. Of course there are also occasions where the learner tries to create rapport, but without any success.

(12)   [6 secs — pause: S is seeking information in a travel book]
       C: too cold to be here
              it's better to go somewhere
              [14 secs — pause: S continues reading the travel book]

4.   Orientation to Channels of Communication

In different situations interactants have also different *channels* or *modes* available for discourse. The choice of mode influences also the register realizations. The crudest and most fundamental difference which has traditionally been recognized in linguistics as a mode choice is the difference between the spoken and the written mode (see e.g. Halliday 1978:222; Halliday 1985; Gregory and Carroll 1978:37-47; Barnickel 1982:84-151).

Very often in foreign language teaching mode is treated as if it was a matter of a single choice — once made, it is maintained throughout the situation. This of course is not valid in most discourse situations. More appropriately one should, in fact, say that social interaction involves "an interplay of various channels", verbal and non-verbal. This fact has largely been neglected in textbooks.

Textbooks do not seem to pay much attention to the variety of channels used in discourse. For instance in Example 1, no linguistic recognition is given to the fact that most likely when the server is making all the requests for further specification, she is also simultaneously feeding the information into a computer. Otherwise she could not be receiving the information that *the ferry is fully booked on the 15th* so quickly. Frequently agents also have to call other agents to find out further details about the tours they are selling. All the shifts of mode have their linguistic realizations, of which the learner should be aware.

When discourse proceeds and different channels are selected for the transmission of messages the co-participants have to pay attention to the changes of mode. In Example 13, for instance, the customer very quickly has to adapt herself to the written mode, when the travel agent quotes the text in a travel brochure:

(13)   S: they don't seem to say anything about insurance
            oh here we are
            "in your own interest we strongly recommend taking out insurance that
            covers cancellation and curtailment, baggage insurance, expenses due
            to sickness, accidents or delays caused by matters beyond Maori Trek's
            control" ...
            so they don't have a special one
            so I'll get you our brochure

When Example 13 is compared with Example 14 we can appreciate the differences in the linguistic realizations of written and spoken modes. In Example 14 the server explains to the customer what she has to do when taking out insurance.

(14)   S: just read the policy through
       C: hm
       S: you have to take ... one section of that
            and then you take the rest of it
            you can't take like segments of it
            you've got to take the whole thing [rising intonation]
       C: so I take uh ... A completely
            etc.

Lastly, from the language teaching point of view, it is interesting to note that interactants may have different preferences for which channels to use in discourse. Learners often prefer to rely on written information. Consequently, their first concern in a travel agency is usually to get brochures to take home to look at, as Example 15 shows.

(15)   C: you have no brochures from ... or ... so cheap than possible
             *that's why we thought that-
        S: *the cheapest way

Also the travel agents recognize the linguistic difficulties of the learners and do not elaborate their explanations as they do with the native customers. Native customers usually have the content of the brochures explained to them, whereas the servers feel that the best way to transmit information to non-native customers is in the written mode. This is apparent in Example 16 (both #s).

(16)   C: is it good or ... good ho- hotels
        S: yes they're reasonable in Alice Springs
             the Territory or the uhm El ... El Kiara *motel
        C: *oh yes
             can I uhm get uhm some ... *papers and-
  #   S: *now I'll write it down for you
             [16 secs — pause: S writing the information down]
        C: how er how much earlier I must *pay this and-
  #   S: *I'm writing it on here
             [1 min 3 secs — pause: S continues writing]
        S: there we are [hands the piece of paper to C]

Many different mode realizations can be found in authentic discourse data, and for the learner it should be interesting to see what channels play a role in the discourse type in question and what effects the channel choice has on the linguistic realizations. Textbooks tend not to represent social interactions as multichannel situations in the way they really are. Thus, when faced with the complexity of the reality, the learner may initially feel somewhat stupefied and perplexed.

5.   Conclusion

This paper has concentrated on discussing different patterns of orientation to social situations. The focus has been on how such orientation is realized in authentic service interactions and how it is represented in language-learning textbook dialogues. Three areas of orientation to the communicative situation have been emphasized: firstly, *field*, the various institutional objects and activities involved; secondly, *tenor*, the participants' role relations; lastly, *mode*, the various communication channels available. One important aspect of social interaction has not been dealt with, however — namely *genre*, and how knowledge of various genre typologies and generic structures can be valuable to learners of foreign languages (see Ventola 1987).

One particular type of encounter, that of a travel agency, was chosen as an example, and the linguistic realizations in a textbook and in authentic discourses were compared. It was shown that foreign language textbooks do take some account of orientation to institutions, participant relations, and channels of communication. Yet numerous matters were revealed by discourse analysis which seem to need immediate attention in foreign language teaching. It was suggested that those engaged in language teaching and in discourse analysis should co-operate more effectively, so that language learning could benefit maximally from recent discourse research.

This paper began with an analogy, that of foreign language learning functioning as a map for orientation to a strange city. Maps can be inaccurate or get outdated. The visitor is then left on his own. In the same way foreign language learners have to learn some day to be on their own. Teachers and textbooks can orientate the learner to meet the demands of communicative situations, but they cannot accompany the learner into these situations. We do not want to turn our learners into linguists; but, in my view, applied linguistics and foreign language teaching can and should turn them into "linguistically well-informed speakers" of a foreign language. The learner has to learn to analyse his own linguistic behaviour, and to learn from his own behaviour as much as from the behaviour of other learners and of native speakers. It is with this that my final point is concerned.

Example 1, from the textbook, has represented social interaction as something which is very controlled, very complete and very correct. But learners should not only experience the well-formed patterns of native behaviour in social interactions. Their first attempts in social interactions will be anything but well-formed. Very likely they are going to be involved in texts similar to the one in Example 17.

(17)   C: I I going ... erm to Perth
        S: yeah

[3 secs — pause]
C: Is it ... er ... very cheap ... er journey ... to Perth
S: yeah
C: if I go by ... hm by bus or ...
S: train
C: train or
S: fly
C: fly *(laughs)
S: *(laughs)
C: yeah ... good
S: what — you wanna know how much it costs do you?
   or what you want to know
   [2 secs — pause]
C: I ... I ... go to now
S: you wanna go tonight ... no sorry
   go on
   tell me again [2 secs — pause]
   what you want to know from me
   what you want me to tell you
   [1 sec — pause]
C: hm (laugh)
S: go on ... it's alright
C: if ... if if you ... give me a brochure *a brochure
S: *oh I see
   on Perth?
C: yeah
S: yeah
C: yeah
S: you want some brochures to look at
C: yeah *I can ... look at ... later
S: *yeah ... okay ... yeah

Why shouldn't the learners also be given examples of this kind in their textbooks? They could compare such learner dialogues with native speaker dialogues, make suggestions on repairs, and so on. Such activities would train learners to analyse the kind of discourse mistakes which they are also likely to make in their social interactions. Yet at the same time, from such examples as Example 17, they get positive reinforcement of language as a tool for realizing social interaction. They see how interactional purposes can be achieved and how interactants manage to establish a certain degree of rapport with one another in spite of the linguistic difficulties. Even without a map the strange city does not appear so frightening.

References

Barnickel, K.-D. 1982. *Register and Stile* (*Hueber Hochschulreihe 45*). München: Max Hueber.

Berry, M. 1987. "Is Teacher an Unanalysed Concept?" *New Developments in Systemic Theory: Vol. 1, Theory and Application* ed. by M.A.K. Halliday & R.P. Fawcett, 41-63. London: Frances Pinter.

Burton, D. 1980. *Dialogue and Discourse*. London: Routledge & Kegan Paul.

Gregory, M.J. & S. Carroll. 1978. *Language and Situation: Language varieties and their social contexts*. London, Henley & Boston: Routledge & Kegan Paul.

Halliday, M.A.K. 1978. *Language as Social Semiotic*. London: Edward Arnold.

———. 1985. *Spoken and Written Language*. Geelong: Deakin University Press.

Malinowski, B. 1923/66. "The Problem of Meaning in Primitive Languages". *The Meaning of Meaning*, Supplement 1, Tenth edition ed by. C.K. Ogden & I.A. Richards, 296-336. London: Routledge & Kegan Paul.

Poynton, C. 1985. *Language and Gender: Making the difference*. Geelong: Deakin University Press.

Sinclair, J.McH. & R.M. Coulthard. 1975. *Towards an Analysis of Discourse*. London: Oxford University Press.

Ventola, E. 1979. "The Structure of Casual Conversations in English". *Journal of Pragmatics* 3. 267-298.

———. 1987. *The Structure of Social Interaction. A systemic approach to the semiotics of service encounters*. London: Frances Pinter.

Webster, D., L. Elonen, L. Kirveskari, D. Robinson, S. Tella & T. Wiik. 1982. *Jet Set 9*. Helsinki: Otava.